CW01597229

The Hammer of Greatness
BLADE HONER
Book One

The Hammer of Greatness

BLADE HONER

Book One

by

Maria Kvilhaug

Copyright © 2014 by Maria Kvilhaug
All rights reserved. No part of this book may be reproduced, scanned, or distributed in any printed or electronic form without permission.
Second Edition: 2014
ISBN 10: 149919076X
ISBN 13: 9781499190762

Contents

Introduction

ᛚᛁᛐᛁᛚᚢᛁᛌᛙ

Runic inscription from the Oseberg ship burial. It can be interpreted as "Man knows little" or as "I who am small am the sanctuary" – or both.

In 834 AD, two ageing, high-ranking women were given a splendid ship funeral at Oseberg in the kingdom of Vestfold, Norway. The women were likely connected to a religious cult. DNA-studies have shown that one or both of these women may possibly have had partial origins in eastern Europe and that the youngest woman may have been aged between forty and sixty when she died. As a child, she must have seen the very start of a new era, where the ancient, Heathen and "barbarian" Norse customs of Scandinavia were first challenged by the surrounding world.

We are back at the very dawn of the Viking Age; The age of Charlemagne, Empress Irene and Harun al-Rashid, Ragnar Lóðbrok, King Sígurð Ring and Queen Ása. Most of Scandinavia is Heathen, tribal land, divided into several kingdoms and tribal confederations. The Viking (pirate) Rus have only recently settled in Aldeigjuborg (Staraya Ladoga) by the river Volkhov, and have begun harrying the neighboring lands for slaves and other trading goods to sell to the Khazars and the Arabs.

Thorbjörn, the last living member of the Thunder Priest clan, persecuted by the Svear kings, has found sanctuary in the Baltic river lands and begotten a daughter, Thordís, who is to carry on the legacy of their secret knowledge about Thunder.

And then the Vikings arrive... Orphaned, Thordís, the last Thunder priestess, embarks on a quest to save her half-sister Zivah from rape and slavery, befriending the most rogue and ruthless pirates in the known world.

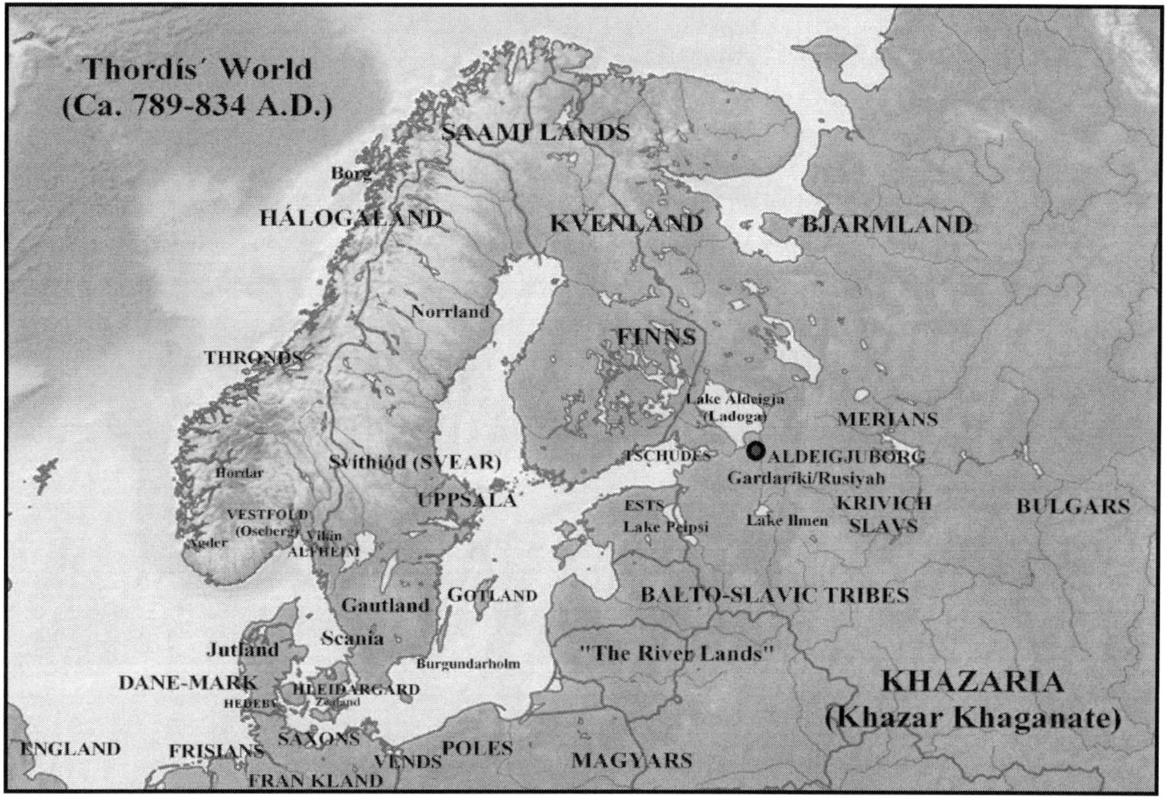
Thordís´ World
(Ca. 789-834 A.D.)
SAAMI LANDS
Borg
HÁLOGALAND
KVENLAND
BJARMLAND
Norrland
FINNS
THRONDS
Lake Aldeigja
(Ladoga)
MERIANS
Svíthiód (SVEAR)
TSCHUDES
ALDEIGJUBORG
Gardariki/Rusiyah
Hordar
UPPSALA
ESTS
Lake Peipsi
Lake Ilmen
KRIVICH
SLAVS
BULGARS
VESTFOLD
(Oseberg)
Vikin
Agder
ALFHEIM
GOTLAND
BALTO-SLAVIC TRIBES
Gautland
Scania
Jutland
"The River Lands"
Burgundarholm
DANE-MARK
HLEIDARGARD
HEDEBY
Zealand
KHAZARIA
(Khazar Khaganate)
SAXONS
ENGLAND
FRISIANS
VENDS
POLES
MAGYARS
FRAN KLAND

Readers´ Reviews on «BLADE HONER Book One: The Hammer of Greatness"

A beautifully written story.
Maria Kvilhaug weaves Norse mythology and historical fiction into a gripping and heart opening tale that is fresh and new, rebirthing the stories of our foremothers. Maria's confident, powerful, and compassionate female characters lead the way in book one of the Blade Honer trilogy.

April 7, 2014 By Erick

Can't wait for book 2!
Really enjoyed this book. The characters draw you in and you find yourself concerned for them. The plot pulls you along as it becomes a real page turner.

April 8 2014 By Andy

It takes courage to let a woman hone you...,
Immediately it is apparent the author is a great storyteller with the ability to construct such vividly consumable imagry. It is also evident that this comes from a depth of understanding of both the subject matter and the truth of what complex creatures humans are (especially when stripped down to our barest moments). Thouroughly enjoyable read. Captivated. Devoured every delicious detail.

April 9, 2014 By Jason DeHaven

Maria has enchanted me with this must read. Thank you!
In common with fellow dyslexics I share a passion with books and have an extensive library that is either unread or only partly read.
In fact, as do many, I have only ever read two books completely; Swallows and Amazons by Arthur Ransome and The Da Vinci Code by Dan Brown. Now there are three!

16 April 2014 By Dom Kiddell

Gripping and transportive glimpse into end of Viking age mystery cult,
Maria does an excellent job in writing a captivating novel that convincingly brings alive the early tumultuous Viking era. It stands on its own as a novel with complex characters and a rich narrative told by the heroine Thordis.
The richness though of the novel IMO is that it is historically inspired and if you are familiar with Maria's formal scholarly background on the subject, and her individual research on the old norse periods freya.theladyofthelabyrinth.com its obvious that this is much more than a historical based fantasy, but instead is a deeply inspired and informed story that frames well the larger forces of the age thrust upon the norse people

The ruthless Rus vikings are brought vividly to life through the perceptive lens of the heroine Thordis who with her sister is taken captive by a group of Rus viking pirates. Nothing is left out from the narrative, the plundering, the violence, and the rape, but what is revealed are many new layers to the motives to the lives and ways of these men. The complex power dynamics of the deeply male hierarchical ordering of these viking men are vividly and convincingly described, right down to the intense and primal way eye contact was used in communicating rank and submission. So too though are the forces which spurred the organization of such rogue men. It is an age of violent expansion in many forms, violent kings, totalitarian monotheisms, slavery and I think that Maria's Rus viking characters do a great job of capturing the deeper dilemma many of these men found themselves in and given the forces at work its is more understandable how such hardened rogues came into being.
Of course the central feature of the novel is the narrator and heroine, Thordis. Its really a fascinating story that is being painted, and we learn a little of the thunder god lineage through the character of her father Thorbjorn. Her role, along with the role of her sister Zivah really start to come to life at the end of the novel and certainly leaves you hungry to read the next novel.
Overall if you are into old norse culture and religion or even just that time period in general this book is a very worthwhile read. I enjoyed it and was very captivated by it from start to finish..

March 31, 2014 By Nick

"...our 13yr old daughter is devouring your book. Just today she came to me and said: "mom, have you ever read something before, and felt as if you've actually read it before...as in, reading it and feeling as if you already knew what you were reading as you were actually reading it." She then motioned to her head and her heart and tried to further explain that it's "spooky" to her, yet very "neat" that she should feel that she "KNOWS" these characters, knows this book.

Brigitte von Stetina

Never did I want to put it down and stop the magic of the story."
Maria Kvilhaug's book The Hammer of Greatness was thrilling, invoking, and insightful. Never did I want to put it down and stop the magic of the story, even for a moment. The characters feelings and views were portrayed so well that sometimes I would believe I was the character; and I couldn't sleep at night because I was thinking about it. This book made me wonder about how my ancestors must have lived, and where I come from. I believe we're lucky that Maria Kvilhaug is here on this earth, that she has done so much research, and was able to create this book. If she hadn't, I wouldn't be in so much anticipation for the next one!

June 12, 2014 By Via Willow

An amazing voyage into an enchanting age,
Maria is an amazing story teller. The author has a special gift to captivate her readers and transport them to another time and place. The imagery of the novel is rich and the words are poetic and captivating. The reader can not stop, and would like to know what happens next. The doors of imagination are opened to an age of the old gods and their enchanting invokers/godars. It seems as if this is her own story from another age. She must have lived it herself. Great Novel!

May 6, 2014 By Alex Farahmand –

A good read!
This book can definitely give one a glimpse into what it may have been like back in those days. Maria Kvilhaug has done an excellent job weaving her studies of Scandinavian and European Histories into a historical fiction I don't want to put down.

June 4, 2014 By Aaron Olson

One of the best book I ever read!
A friend recommend me this book, and this is definitely one the best books I ever read, it has something what make me understand not just myself, it feels like I was living in this times long time ago. I don't know if I really was or if it is just because this book is perfectly written. I never read a book where you are able to feel all spectrum of emotions in the same time, and that make's you realize how relative everything is. This book is to me also a treasure chest of deep wisdom. Freyia (Maria) thank you for your wonderful work! I am looking forward for the next book.

July 22, 2014 By Ivana

GO FOR IT !!
Awesome book !!!. I am a amateur viking age locally self appointed expert with 48 years under my belt in the field . I have found the "HAMMER OF GREATNESS" has expanded my knowledge of the time period , kept my attention thought the real to life people populating the pages. The Author can tell a story and knows her subject . this book is on par with Ken Follet´s "the pillars of earth" GO for IT!!!

July 31, 2014 By: Robert P

Relevant Primary Source Quotes

"I saw the Rūsiyyah when they had arrived on their trading expedition and had disembarked at the River Ātil. I have never seen more perfect physiques than theirs—they are tall like palm trees, are fair and reddish, and do not wear the qurṭaq or the caftan. The man wears a cloak with which he covers one half of his body, leaving one of his arms uncovered. Every one of them carries an axe, a sword and a dagger and is never without all of that which we have mentioned. Their swords are of the Frankish variety, with broad, ridged blades. Each man, from the tip of his toes to his neck, is covered in dark-green lines, pictures and such like."

(...)

"They are accompanied by beautiful slave girls for trading. One man will have intercourse with his slave-girl while his companion looks on. Sometimes a group of them comes together to do this, each in front of the other. Sometimes indeed the merchant will come in to buy a slave-girl from one of them and he will chance upon him having intercourse with her, but the Rūs will not leave her alone until he has satisfied his urge (...)"

(Ibn Fadlan of Baghdad on the Rus Vikings A.D. 921)

*

"As for the Rus, they live on an island ... that takes three days to walk round and is covered with thick undergrowth and forests; it is most unhealthy.... They harry the Slavs, using ships to reach them; they carry them off as slaves and... sell them. They have no fields but simply live on what they get from the Slav's lands... They carry clean clothes and the men adorn themselves with bracelets and gold. They treat their slaves well and also they carry exquisite clothes, because they put great effort in trade. They have many towns. They have a most friendly attitude towards foreigners and strangers who seek refuge"

(Ahmad Ibn Rustah on 10th century A.D. Rus Vikings)

*

"King Adils and his men ran up to the king´s farm and raided there, some took the cattle and chased it down for the beach-cut, and there had been unfree folks, men and women, for the herding of cattle, and they took all of them. Among the slaves there was a girl who was so marvelously lovely, and she called herself Yrsa. Then Adils sailed home with the goods. Yrsa was not placed among the slave girls, for it was soon observed that she was intelligent, spoke

well, and in all respects was well behaved. All people thought well of her, and particularly the king; and at last it came to so far that the king celebrated his wedding with her, and Yrsa became queen of Svithiod, and was considered an excellent woman."

(SNORRI STURLUSON, YNGLINGA SAGA 28, ON A LEGENDARY 5TH CENTURY A.D. EVENT)

*

"Now, one day as Hoskuld went out to disport himself with some other men, he saw a stately tent far away from the other booths. Hoskuld went thither, and into the tent, and there sat a man before him in costly raiment, and a Russian hat on his head (...) "I am called Gilli the Russian." Gilli asked what he and his companions wished to buy. Hoskuld said he should like to buy some bonds-woman, "if you have one to sell." (...) Hoskuld then saw that right across the booth there was drawn a curtain; and Gilli then lifted the curtain, and Hoskuld saw that there were twelve women seated behind the curtain. So Gilli said that Hoskuld should come on and have a look, if he would care to buy any of these women. Hoskuld did so. They sat all together across the booth. Hoskuld looks carefully at these women. He saw a woman sitting out by the skirt of the tent, and she was very ill-clad. Hoskuld thought, as far as he could see, this woman was fair to look upon. Then said Hoskuld, "What is the price of that woman if I should wish to buy her?" Gilli replied, "Three silver pieces is what you must weigh me out for her." [Hoskuld buys the slave woman even though she turns out to be mute, and very expensive](...)

Hoskuld then went home to his booth. That same night Hoskuld went into bed with her. The next morning when men got dressed, spake Hoskuld, "The clothes Gilli the Rich gave you do not appear to be very grand, though it is true that to him it is more of a task to dress twelve women than it is to me to dress only one." After that Hoskuld opened a chest, and took out some fine women's clothes and gave them to her; and it was the saying of every one that she looked very well when she was dressed." (...)Every one clearly saw that there was something betokening high birth in the way she bore herself, and that she was no fool."

(LAXDÆLA SAGA CHAPTER 12 ON THE PURCHASE OF A PLEASURE SLAVE A.D. 948)

Old Norse (ON) Terms, Titles, Places and some Historical Names

- **Age of the Stone Temples:** The Megalithic Age in Scandinavia (dolmens, passage graves, stonehenges and mazes)
- ***Aldeigja*** (ON): Lake Ladoga close to modern day St. Petersburg
- ***Aldeigjuborg*** (ON): A Viking settlement established ca 750 A.D. or earlier by the river Volkhov south of the Aldeigja
- **Al-Mahdi:** Abbasid Caliph who introduced the first large-scale persecution of Moslem Heretics in the eastern Caliphate (lived ca. 745-785 A.D.)
- ***-arr*** (ON): Warrior or Spear. A word often used to make masculine names.♂
- **Ása Haraldsdóttir**: Queen Ása of Agder, mother to Halfdan the Black (ca.795-840 AD?)
- **Ása the Bad Ruler:** The psychopathic daughter of the equally psychopathic Ingjald the Bad Ruler, mentioned in *Ynglinga saga*, lived possibly during the 5th or 6th century AD
- **Atonement** (ON: *Són*): Old Norse term for Sacrifice
- **Auð the Deep-Minded** (ON: *Auðr hina Djúpugda*) Three different "Deep-Minded" women called Auð are mentioned in the saga literature, always being pioneers (like the first female settler of Iceland) or the beginning and end of a lineage (like the 8th century Auð mentioned in this book, who established a new Danish royal dynasty with her son Sígurð Ring (begotten by a Russian Viking lord) and a new Swedish royal dynasty with her first son, Harald Wartooth.
- **Berserker** (ON: *Bérserkr*): "Bear Clothed" – Battle rage, seizure of fury/ man with the ability to go berserk.
- **Big Tunic Land** (ON: *Stóra Serkland*): The Abbasid Caliphate with base in Baghdad. A Viking *serk* was a wide undergarment akin to a tunic reaching below the hips or down to the knees. The Vikings observed that such clothing, only bigger (longer), was used as a common garment in Arab countries and named them after that. They called their lands either *Serkland* (Tunic Land) or *Stóra Serkland* (Big Tunic Land).
- **Big Tunic men** (ON: *Serkmennir*): Arabs
- **Blue Land** (ON: *Bláland*): Africa.
- **Blue Man**: (ON: *Blámaðr*): African, black-skinned, dark-skinned man
- **Danu**: The goddess Danu is of ancient, Proto-Indo-European origin, and seems to have denoted a water goddess in origin. A goddess Dānu is attested in the Rigveda, and also the river names Danube (Latin: Danuvius), Dniestr, Dniepr and Don derive from the name. The Rigvedic Danu was the mother of a race of Asuras called the Danavas. A shortened form of the name appears to have been Dā. The Greek goddess Demeter (Da-mater), is also associated with water several times. Julius

Pokorny reconstructs the name from the PIE root da:-: "flow, river", da:-nu: "any moving liquid, drops", da: navo "people living by the river, Skyth. nomadic people (in Rigveda water-demons), fem. Da:nu primordial goddess , in Greek Danaoi (Danaans, Greek tribe, Egypt: Danuna). In Irish mythology, Danu (modern Irish Dana) is the mother goddess of the Tuatha Dé Danann (Old Irish: "The peoples of the goddess Danu") primarily seen as an ancestral figure. As the mother of the gods, Danu has strong parallels with the Welsh literary figure (or goddess) Dôn, who is the mother figure of the medieval tales in the Mabinogion.

- **-dís** (ON): "Goddess" – much used in women´s names, like Thordís
- ***Elja*** (sg.)/***Eljur*** (pl.) (ON): Co-wife/co-wives, co-concubines. The term described the relationship between women who shared the same husband or master.
- **Ests:** A Finnish tribe giving name to Estland in the Baltic
- **Follower** (ON: *Fylgja*): A female guardian spirit, often an ancestral mother, or a goddess, norn or valkyria, or an animal representing the personality of her owner. People were thought to have one, nine or many woman-followers, as well as one animal-follower each, always female. It was also common for clans and tribes to have a **Clan-Fylgja** (ON: *Ættarfylgja*), the divine soul of the clan´s or tribe´s ancestral mother.
- ***Freyia*** (ON): Lady, female ruler, Sovereign (a title or honorific used for high-ranking females and name of most important goddess in Old Norse Heathen pantheon.)
- **Freyia´s Hall** *(ON: Höll Freyiu:)* "Lady´s Hall" - The womb
- ***Freyr*** (ON): An old word for Lord, male ruler, Sovereign, King. By the time of the Viking Age the word was only used for the god of the same name, replaced by *Heri* and other words for lord and master, such as *Rig, Dan* etc. A Viking Age god of sex, virility, fertility, rain, sunshine, kingship, law, order, cultivated nature. Brother to Freyia. ♂
- **Freystone** (ON: *Freysteinn, Frösteinn*): Lord Stone = the penis
- **Full Troth** (ON: *Fulltrú*): A person´s patron god or goddess
- **Gabija** (SLAVIC: "The Protector"): Goddess of Fire
- **Gaut** (ON: *Gautr*): Geat, from Gautland (Götaland)
- ***Gautland*** (ON): Götaland - The Land of the Geats, divided into East and Western kingdoms, the southernmost part of Sweden.
- ***Góði*** (ON): Priest, Law Man, God (A title) ♂
- ***Gotland*** (ON): An island to the east of the southern coast of Sweden
- ***Gyðja/Gyða*** (ON): Priestess, Goddess (A title) ♀

- **Halfdan the Black** (ON: *Halfdánr Svarti*): Son of Guðröðr, the Ynglinga king of Vestfold, and Ása, the princess of Agder. Conquered many Norwegian kingdoms and became the father of Haraldr Hárfagri, the king who united all Norway under one kingdom. Historical person, mentioned in *Ynglinga saga* and in Halfdan the Black´s saga etc. Contemporary with the Oseberg burial in 834 AD (He was perhaps born around 810 AD).
- ***Hálógaland*** (ON): "Land of High Flames" – the northernmost kingdom of Viking Age Norway, corresponding to the contemporary counties of Nordland, Lofoten, southern Troms and Nord-Trøndelag.
- **Harald Wartooth** (ON: *Haraldr Hilditann*): Legendary Swedish/Danish King (died ca. 750 A.D.)
- **Harun Al-Rashid:** (Lived 763-809 A.D.): Caliph in Baghdad, known from many stories in "*1001 Arabian Nights*"
- ***Hel*** (ON): The goddess of the dead/ The world of the dead, also known as *Níflhel* or *Níflheimr* – the Misty World. A place where souls go through ordeals (see: Judgment of the Norns) and souls are recycled in a mill/cauldron from which new streams of life emerge. NB: Not to be confused with Christian Hell.
- **Hel-Maiden** (ON: *Helju mey*): referred to in Edda and Skaldic poetry (ex. *Sólarlióð*)
- **Hel Rune** (ON: *Heljurún*): Death Rune, Death Fate, (title of a priestess of human sacrifice based on the title *haliurunnae* from Jordanes´ *Getica*. Description of the Hel Rune is partly based on Ibn Fadlan´s description of such priestesses among the Rus in the early 10th century and on the account of such priestesses among the Cimbri in the 1st century BC)
- ***Heri*** (ON): Lord, Master (a title or honorific) ♂
- ***Hleiðargard*** (ON): Lejre in Zealand, Denmark, an important royal site since the 5th century AD, mentioned in Beowulf as the seat of King Hrotgard.
- **House-Bond** (ON: *Húsbondr*): Lord/Patriarch/land-owner – "God of the Household"♂
- **House-Freyia** (ON: *Húsfreyia, Húsfrú, Húsfrya*): Lady of the Household ♀
- **Ingjald the Bad Ruler** (ON: *Ingjaldr hinn illráði* – 5th -6th century AD Ynglinga king mentioned in the *Ynglinga saga*)
- **Ivarr Rules Widely** (ON: *Ivarr Víðfamni*): 7th-8th century AD king of Scania (southwest-Sweden) who took the seat of Uppsala from the Ynglinga lineage under Ingjald the Bad Ruler, according to *Ynglinga Saga*
- **Judgment of the Norns** (ON: *Nórna dómr*): Referred to directly under said term in the Edda poems *Sólarljód* and the *Fafnismál* as a place of judgment for nine days after death in the seat of the norns.

- **Latgáli** (BALTIC): An ancient Baltic tribe resident in present-day Latvia
- ***Magni*** (ON): Greatness, Might (name of Thor´s son)
- **Maiden** (ON: *Mey/Mær*): A title/honorific for girl or young, unmarried woman
- ***Miklagarðr:*** Byzants/Constantinople (Istanbul)
- ***Miöllnir*** (ON: "The Grinder" – "Thunderbolt" – "Lightning"): Thor´s hammer, a very ancient symbol
- **Norns** (ON: *Nórnir*): Goddesses of Fate in life and death (fates, ladies of the loom, kindly ones)
- **North Way** (ON: *Nordvégr*): Norway – consisted of some 30 kingdoms, earldoms and republics.
- ***Óðinn*** (ON) Odin: Spirit/Inspiration/Poetry - a god of poetry, ecstasy, inspiration, witchcraft, shamanism, death, war and the afterlife. Aligned with Mercury. Had become the "All-Father" in Viking Age sources.
- **Ólaf the Tree-Feller** (ON: *Ólafr Tretelgja*): Son of Ingjald the Bad Ruler, became king of Vermland
- **Ólaf Geirstað-elf of Vestfold** = (ON: *Ólafr Geirstadalfr*): Brother to Halfdan the Black, king of Vestfold
- **Oseberg (**ON: *Ásabergr* – "The Mound of the Gods") – Viking Age burial site in Vestfold, Norway, the most splendid ship bural from the Viking Age, two high-standing women buried with many cultic items in 834 A.D.)
- **Peace of Wisdom** (ON: *Fróðafriðr*): An Old Norse legendary Golden Age
- **Pērkons** (BALTIC)/**Peron** (SLAVIC): The Thunder God
- **Ráðbarðr** (ON): An eight century Rus "king" (Sea King – Viking) who assisted Harald Wartooth and married his mother.
- **Rus** (SLAVIC/FINNIC term for the Scandinavian slavers 8th-10th century, originally "rowers" or "blondes". After the Rus lord called Ruric (born ca. 830 A.D.) created a multi-ethnic (Norse, Balto-Slavic and Finnic) society, his tribal identity gave name to the Russian nation.
- ***Saga*** (ON): History, Story – a name for the mother goddess Frigg
- **Sea-King** (ON: *Sækonungr*): A Viking lord who owns a fleet of ships and many men beneath him. Appear on the legendary/historical scene in the Baltic/Finnish seas from about the 5th century onwards.
- **Seið** (ON: *Seiðr*): Magic, witchcraft, divination, shamanism, secret mysteries
- **Shadow-walker** (ANGLO-SAXON: *Sceadugenga*): Sorcerer master of darkness, invisibility, out of body travel

- ***Síf*** (ON): Female Relative, a word for female relatives generally ("Name" of Thor´s golden-haired wife)
- ***Svearíki*** (ON): The Empire of the Swedes = Sweden, particularly Svíthióð, but expanded.
- ***Svíthióð*** (ON): The Svear Tribe / Great Svear – "Sweden" north of Gautland, south of Norrland, Uppsala area
- **Thor** (ON: *Þórr*): Thunder. A Norse thunder god responsible for protection of Earth, gods and people, and of oaths ♂
- **Thorsgóði** (ON: *Þórsgóði*): Thunder Priest (A title, Thor´s priest) ♂
- **Thorsgyðja** (ON: *Þórsgyðja*): Thunder Priestess (A title, Thor´s priestess) ♀
- **Thrúð** (ON: *Þrúðr*): Power (the name of Thor´s daughter)♀
- **Thunder Warrior** (ON: *Þórarr*) fictional title, but there was a popular Old Norse masculine name derived from the term; Thorarin (ON: *Þórarinn* – "The Thunder Warrior") ♂
- **Tschude (or Chud)**: A warlike Finnish Tribe known as slave hunters in Sámi lore
- ***Týr*** (ON): Beast, God (A god of victory)♂
- **Valhalla** (ON: *Valhǫll*): The Hall of the Slain/Chosen (An afterlife paradise for worthy warriors)
- ***Valkyria*** (ON): Chooser of the Slain/Chosen - a fate goddess choosing victory and death in battle and who takes the chosen slain to Valhalla among many other things. A kind of norn.
- **Viking** (ON: *Víkingr* – "Those who stay in the bays" / "People from Víkin (=East-Akershus, Norway): Pirates
- ***Væringjar*** (ON): "Those who stay put" – "Varangians" (The Rus)
- **Yrsa** (ON: She-Bear): The mother of Hrolfr Kráki in *Ynglinga Saga, Hrolfs saga Kráki* etc.
- **Wand-Witch**: Based on the ON title *Vǫlva* from *vǫl* – "wand" used for a woman who was a professional practitioner of seiðr
- **Žemyna:** (BALTO-SLAVIC: The Earth Goddess)

Some Personal Names in this Book and their Meanings (ON=Old Norse)

Agnarr (ON): Respect Warrior ♂
Arnsteinn (ON): Eagle Stone♂
Arnulf (ON: *Arnulfr*): Eagle Wolf♂
Ása (ON): Belongs to the Gods ♀
Auðr (ON): Abundance ♀
Aziza (ARAB): Beloved ♀
Bera (ON): She Bear♀
Grim (ON: *Grímr*): Masked One (also name of Odin) ♂
Gunnarr (ON): Battle Warrior♂
Halldís (ON): Hall Goddess ♀
Hallgrim (ON: *Hallgrímr*): Hall Mask, Mask of the Hall ♂
Haraldr (ON): High Lineage ♂
Hialti (ON): Hilt ♂
Ivarr (ON): Linden Bow Warrior ♂
Laimi (FINNISH): "Luck" ♀
Njál: ON version of Irish Niall, English Neil, uncertain meaning.♂
Oláf (ON: *Ólafr*): Ancestor-Descendant ♂
Rannveig (ON: *Rannveigr*): Shield Power Drink ♀
Ráðbarðr (ON): Council Beard ♂
Runarr (ON): Rune Warrior ♂
Shumayl (ARAB): Complete ♂
Skeggi (ON): Hairy, Bearded ♂
Sígurðr (ON): Victory Origin ♂
Sígtrygg (ON *Sígtryggr*): Victory Certainty ♂
Suri (PERSIAN): Princess ♀
Thióðolf (ON: *Þióðolfr*): Great Wolf, Tribeswolf♂
Thora (ON: *Þóra*): Feminine form of Thor ♀
Thorbjörn (ON: *Þorbjǫrnr*): Thunder Bear ♂
Thordís (ON: *Þórdís*): Thunder Goddess ♀
Thorgrim (ON: *Þórgrímr*): Thunder Mask ♂
Thorolf (ON: *Þórolfr*): Thunder Wolf ♂
Zivah (SLAVIC): Beautiful ♀

Oseberg

(Vestfold, Norway, 834 A.D.)

The Christian priest that Vestfold-Ólaf bought from the Agder Vikings last year believes I am the Whore of Babylon. I know because one of my people was present when the fuzzy slave priest held a rather heated little talk about that issue before some of the other slaves who are curious about his faith, and so I went to see the little man myself. He still refuses to wash himself and Ólaf is too kind to force him, so I met the priest out in the open and held my breath most of the time. I asked him why he thought I was from Babylon when I have clearly never been there, and the little man went red and then pale from fear, and said it was a cover word. I asked him to explain the cover word, but his stuttering and stammering explanation seemed to me like running porridge.

He fears most things, that one. He even fears his god, he says.

Seeing as there was no sense to be had from the priest, I asked him how many years had passed since the Madonna gave birth to his god, and he told me quite proudly that it was now 834 years since that happened. I asked if the Madonna was still a virgin after so many centuries, and the priest assured me that she still was, the poor woman. But she was a human goddess too, and through her womb a god could enter this world of songs, so I asked the priest what the difference between her and me really was. He said that we were absolute opposites. I said that opposites are mirrors onto each other and that there is nothing more powerful and divine than the union between absolute opposites, what *I* ought to know better than most, but the ignorant and fearful little man seemed to disagree, going all red and white. I shrugged and walked away; whereupon he began talking about becoming a martyr if I had him punished, and when I kept walking away he screamed after me that his lord had sacrificed his life for us. Then Halfdan the Black boxed his ears a little just to teach him some manners. They are terribly bad at those, the Christians. They have no manners at all.

Man knows little. I who am small am the Sanctuary.

I am going to sacrifice my own life for my people tomorrow night, beneath the light of the whole Moon lord. I will die the threefold way. I fear it not. I have known it for a long time and always been prepared. Geirstað-Ólaf, Agder-Ása and Halfdan the Black, they who built this mound for us, they have all tried to persuade me to let a slave go in my place, but I told them that I had to fulfill my fate. I have lived out my score of years and I have lived them well. The men that I made keep coming from all parts to speak their fare wells. I have held them all, and let them know that they will all come together in me on this great voyage to the Star Ocean, and to the lands of the immortals. The fifteen richest of them left a horse each, for us to ride across divine fields.

Tomorrow night, I shall go into the grave with my mentor, Sígrún Wand-Witch, and together we shall set sail at the river of Hel, and journey once more on the Serpent Ship.

I am the Sheath of the Hall of the gods. I am the Vessel that unites the tribes. And I am the Atonement. But when I still belonged to the world of men, I was a great blade honer and a most insufferable spear enticer. My life turned out to be a great story, like a spectacle for the gods.

I am looking forward to death. I think I shall sit at the prow and ride the dragon, just like I did when I began to move through the verses of this most colorful song that was my life; when I came to live as a child among the Viking Rus, and learned of their contrary ways.

Do you want to hear more, or what?

The Village in the River Lands

(The Baltic, A.D.775-790)

*

Thunder Bear

On the seventh night before the red-haired stranger came to the village, people had observed Thunder lights flaring high in the night sky. These heavenly flames were rare in the river lands, and the entire village had been standing outside that night and watched the nine colorful flames dancing, whirling across the heavens, while the Thunder priest sang of the ancient and distant adventures of the Oak Man, Pērkons, as they called the Thunder lord in those lands. They believed that these lights are the sparks that rise when the Thunder lord is making love to the Sun maiden's nine daughters.

On the third night before the stranger came, the heavenly lord had returned to his wife Žemyna only to find that our precious Earth mother was in danger; for that night there was a tremendous thunder storm which lasted for three days and nights on end. And the Thunder priest sang the old songs of lord Pērkons who was pursuing our giant enemies from the outer heavens. Driving his iron chariot pulled by the red and the white ram, the great lord forcefully hurled his battle-axe after the attacking rock-giants again and again, each blow followed by a massive roar of thunder. The lightning seemed to be striking everywhere, but in his mercy, the Oak Man had mind to let flow the rain ceaselessly for as long as the battle lasted. The villagers shuddered in their huts and sheds, families gathered together for comfort.

It was a mighty battle, and such divine ferocity brought about an increasing worry about what would happen if lord Pērkons *lost* the battle for our Earth. To strengthen him, the people prayed throughout the days and throughout the nights, placing their offerings of bread, salt and honeycombs on Gabija the Fire-goddess's altar, pouring their offerings of beer directly into the Earth mother. The two ladies would bring their offerings of nourishment to the lord, through fire and through soil. And the Thunder lord grew in power, and the people cowered within their shelters, hoping that the intensification of the heavenly rumble meant that he was about to win once more.

The Healer and her two year old daughter, Zivah, had no further family with whom to seek comfort. They would have been welcome in any hut, but the Healer had long since learned to stay aloof, and to never show fear. Her mother had told her, as her mother before her, and her mother before that, and this was a truth told from healing mother to healing daughter since time immemorial; that a Healer must keep her fears to herself before her people, just like a mother must before her children. For if the mother is frightened, the children lose all hope. And so it would be if a Healer showed her fear before the people who depended upon her skills. It was the third night that she lay with her daughter in her arms, listening to the roaring thunder, all alert and ready to escape the house should it be the target of a misplaced thunderbolt. The Healer pulled her daughter close and hummed a song that made the little one fall asleep. She continued humming herself into sleep, and only a little later she dreamt.

She dreamt of walking aimlessly through the forest, soaked by the rain, in pain, and so tired, so very tired, and yet kept awake by the perpetual thunder and strikes of lightning and the wetness of it all. There was a sense of bottomless despair and intense pain, and yet a determination to move forward nevertheless. The Healer was accustomed to sensing the feelings of other people and knew in her dream that she was looking through another person's mind. Somebody – a man by the feel of him - was lost in the forests. The Healer forced herself not to wake from the realization. She needed to know more if she was to help this one. She strained her eyes and tried to see through the eyes of the stranger. Then she felt how the stranger almost fell back in shock as a huge, male bear suddenly stood before him. She gasped as she saw the bear rise on his hind paws, roaring, accompanied by a frenzy of thunder. Suddenly the Thunder Bear looked through the eyes of the lost stranger and straight at *her*, his eyes red like glowing coal.

"*Help*," he said to her, "*I need a healer*."

The Healer had sworn an oath to always help if she was asked. She shook away the fear she felt in the presence of such a ferocious beast and reached out her hand to touch him. She felt her hand against the thick fur, but then the Thunder Bear seemed to become less solid and her hand went through the fur and right into his heart. She felt an ache of soul's pain there that was beyond anything she had ever felt. Tears ran from her eyes as she stood there and felt the heart wound of the Thunder Bear, but even as she felt his pain in all parts of her being she stood her ground and did not let go of her firm yet gentle grasp around his heart. It happened as it always did when she held a living being with her listening hands. Unheard cries from within faded when they reached the great Listening. And slowly, slowly, little by little, the pain also faded. The Thunder Bear met her eyes. His eyes were not red anymore, they were a light blue, and there was a little Sun sparkling within each of them. Then there was another rumbling roar of thunder, and the Healer woke up in her hut.

Little Zivah was sleeping soundly, and the Healer could sense that the storm was abating. She could no longer sleep and got up to make herself an infusion. As she drank it, sipping slowly, she thought about the dream. Upon finishing the cup, she went into the sauna and distributed the heating stones, just enough to make the room warm. Then she prepared a very large bed in there.

At dawn on the third day the storm had abated completely and the sky had begun to clear. The people gathered in the center court to check up on each other and make sure everyone was well, and to survey the damages done to the village. Soon they were pleased to learn that nobody had been injured and that there had been no fires and no serious damage. The realization was so uplifting that the village cheered as one and decided to go to the Oak Grove and give thanks at the Shrine of Pērkons for his great victory and his most successful protection. The procession was led by the Thunder priest, an old, skinny little man so feeble of body that people gleefully marveled at how he could still be chosen by mighty Pērkons to embody the power of Thunder. But the little Thunder priest was well-liked and his people were kind-hearted too. Nobody wanted to replace him before he himself chose it. He had been a Thunder priest all his life, and the protection of their village this night only served to prove that Pērkons still favored him as their priest. The old priest was followed by the Fire women, three women who carried the holy flames that were to light the altar of Gabija the Protector, goddess of fire. The Fire women would prepare the altar before the Shrine of Pērkons, then the Thunder priest would sanctify it and invoke the lord, and then the villagers would offer their gifts and their thanks. As the villagers, carrying their gifts, reached the Oak Grove, they all stopped and waited reverently while the Fire women and the Thunder priest entered the sacred grove.

Just a little while after the three women and the old priest returned, still carrying their torches. The women had not lit the altar. They all looked shocked. The priest was pale and he was trembling violently. His eyes were round with surprise. He opened his mouth to speak a few times, but not a sound came out. The Healer stepped forth and touched his arm gently, while carefully relieving one of the Fire women off her torch before she dropped it, her hands shaking so much she hardly knew she was still holding it. The little man calmed down at her touch and finally stuttered; "Pērkons…"

"What are you saying, Old Brother?" the Healer said.

"Pērkons… the Thunder lord is… he is in… he is *here*…!" The Fire women, still speechless, nodded affirmatively when the Healer looked quizzically at them. A murmur went through the crowd.

"Where is he, Old Brother?" the Healer asked softly, appearing calm as the alarm begun to rise among the villagers. "He is…he is in the grove," the priest whispered, and began trembling again, pointing uncertainly at the entry to the grove. The Fire women nodded again, still shaken.

"It is true, Old Sister," one of them said to her, "the priest speaks the truth. We all saw him!"

"Pērkons is in the Grove, before the Mother Oak, before his altar," the priest continued, his voice a little stronger now. Then he gasped and whispered to the Healer; "I think he is *injured*!"

The Healer helped support the old man as he, still stiff with terror, painstakingly led the procession into the Oak Grove. The villagers were too stunned to even whisper among themselves. Utterly quiet, the old man and the young woman walked to the Mother Oak, followed by their people. The Healer came first, supporting the priest, and saw the man that was lying on the ground, utterly unconscious. Her heart trembled. It was the man from her dream.

She had not seen him then, she had only seen him as the Thunder Bear. Now she understood why the priest had talked of Pērkons. The man was huge, like a bear indeed, taller and much broader in frame than any of the village men. His hair, although greying at the temples, was massive and long, and even when soaked with mud and what she still thought must be wet soil, she could see that his hair was an unusual flaming red. So was his long and thick beard. He was dressed in leather and fur just like her own people, but he was wearing something she had never seen before, a shirt made out of iron threads that seemed to be woven into each other.

She gasped when she discovered all the weapons. In his belt there were not only one small and two rather large knives, but also a proper sword, of a kind that her people never used – they hardly owned swords at all. His right hand was still clutching firmly a battle axe worthy of the Thunder lord. His left hand still held a long spear.

Among his many weapons, only a quiver half full with arrows had been slung carelessly away, but the bow was still fastened to his back, what must have caused some bodily discomfort where he was lying unconscious on the ground. A cloth had been wrapped firmly around his left thigh and was red-brown with blood. The mud had disguised it somewhat, but as she looked at him, she realized that his entire frame, clothes and skin and hair, was smeared with crusting blood. And on the ground around him were the tracks of a very large bear having passed this way.

A little breeze blew through the grove and caused the hem of his cloak, which had covered half his chest, to move a little to the side, revealing a hammer pendant. It looked very foreign to her, but still even a small child would recognize it as the ultimate symbol of the Thunder lord. It seemed ancient and was beautifully wrought in four different metals. And it felt immensely powerful even from a distance. All the villagers glanced briefly at the pendant before they respectfully averted their eyes, never to look directly at it again. An excited murmur began to spread through the crowd. She heard the whispers, the talk of how the lord Pērkons had been injured in battle and had entered their village through the eye of the Shrine. He must have chosen this exact shrine for a reason, the story soon went, because he knew that they had the best Healer, and, the villagers agreed after only moments of doubt, the best Thunder priest.

Stories spun in a crowd will soon turn into truths that can never die, so the Healer broke its spell before it was too late. "This is not Pērkons," she said in a loud and deep voice. The villagers hushed and went quiet. The Healer sat down by the body of the giant man and touched his neck. "This is a man, not a god," she said, in the same imposing tone. She felt her little daughter Zivah sitting down next to her, her little hand reaching out to gently touch the unconscious man. The crowd gasped, but the little girl paid them no heed.

"Man," Zivah said testily. The Healer nodded.

"Man!" Zivah confirmed.

"See," her mother said, looking up and around at the crowd, "even a child will know that this is a man if she only takes a closer look." The Thunder priest approached cautiously and squatted down next to Zivah. Tentatively, he reached out and touched the giant. Then he looked shamed, as did the Fire women, and the Healer regretted her comment about the child.

"It is a man," the priest admitted, "You must forgive an old fool."

"You are no fool, Old Brother," the Healer said, "We all had time to look closer at him now, while before you saw only what we *all* saw when we first came to the Shrine. He is a man, but as men go, he is certainly a remarkable sight, and his likeness to the Oak Man is not to be overlooked. This must mean something… something…" The Healer paused, sending the thought to the old priest.

"He must have been sent here… It must be a sign from Pērkons!" the priest exclaimed, and the whole village let out their breaths in unison, relieved. Their little priest had saved his face, and even as the story had to turn in their minds somewhat, it still retained some of its foreign thrill.

"Yes, it is a sign," she agreed, still supporting the old man, "and I will tell all of you about the dream I had this night. I think it is significant. But you must quickly make a… a very big and strong stretcher and carry him to my hut. I have already prepared a bed for him." While the villagers stared at her in awe, the Healer studied the body of the stranger and added, more to herself than to anyone else; "I think I made it just about big enough."

Wresting the weapons out of the giant stranger's powerful hands had been a difficult task even though he was unconscious – lifting him up and placing his enormous body onto the stretcher had been challenging as well. He was a heavy man. When he had been carefully deposited on the large, newly made bed in the Healer's sauna, she asked them all to leave except the Thunder priest, Zivah and the three Fire women. The little man was wise enough to be humbled by his earlier blunder and grateful to the Healer for saving his pride. He sat down cross-legged by the wall and minded the heating stones, so as to keep it just warm enough to heat up the body of the stranger, who had been dangerously cold. When the Healer thought he was warm enough she removed the blankets, and with the support of the women she began pulling off the chainmail. She looked curiously at it before she folded it carefully and put it to the side. Then she took a pair of scissors and began cutting off his leather clothes. Beneath the leather there was textile, but it was so dirty and smeared with blood that she cut that too. The only thing she left alone was the hammer pendant. The women helped remove the pieces while Zivah just watched and learned in silence, like any two-year-old would.

They discovered the wound that had made him sick when they removed the wrapping and the pieces of cloth that covered his left thigh. There was a deep, long stab-wound there. He had obviously known how to wrap a wound, for he had managed to stop the blood flow. There had even been an attempt to prevent illness by placing some herbs there, showing that the man or whoever had treated him knew a little medicine. But if he had been outside in this weather for some days it would have been impossible to keep the wound clean, and now it was clearly infected. It would have to be washed, first. His entire body had to be clean before she could treat an infected wound. The women brought her warm water and sponges to wash him with. As the blood and the muddy soil vanished, they stared at the paintings that were revealed. The Healer forced their attention towards the wound and began cleaning it with boiled water infused with herbs and honey before she sewed up the wound and used a clean cloth to wrap it. Only then did she allow herself and her attendants to look at the skin paintings.

They were tattoos, of course, blue-green spirally lines and patches making up a whole tapestry of symbols that covered his broad chest and his strong arms and shoulders, as well as his back. Beneath the tattoos was a skin so covered in old scars that they gasped when they realized what all those pale lines were: old cuts and stab wounds of varying ages. The priest ignored the fuzz that the women made at first, thinking that the women were, naturally, simply fascinated by that powerful body. Even he had to admit it fascinated him – how could anybody grow this big and this strong? The women's failure to giggle ceaselessly eventually caused the old priest to realize that there was something more universally interesting going on. He craned his neck and when he began to make out the lines, he got up from the floor and approached. He gazed thoughtfully at the symbols and at the pendant, and met the eyes of the Healer, who had begun cleaning up her medicine gear.

"I will tell you of my dream now," she said, and told the dream about the stranger and the Thunder Bear. She knew that she only had to tell it once. The three Fire women listened attentively and would spread the story as surely as wind spreads dust. When she had finished her story, she began tracing some of the images with the brush of a fingertip. She had made out several symbols of thunder and lightning, as well as beast-like symbols that she could only think of as bears. She gestured to these images and said; "I think he is the Thunder Bear. I do not know what that means. But he is the Thunder Bear. And now I must speak to you in private, Old Brother." She looked at the Fire women, who did not seem particularly eager to leave just yet, but when her gaze did not waver, the women took Zivah and left the sauna, proceeding to let the village know all about the dream of the Thunder Bear. The Healer smiled after them as the room went quiet.

“What is it that our people may not know,” the Thunder priest asked.

“I do not know if I should tell them or not – yet. Of course they must know eventually. But I want to talk to you about it first. This man…” she glanced at the sleeping man, now covered in blankets again, “This man is *Rus*, Old Brother. He is a *Rus-man*.”

“Are you certain?” The priest said, incredulously, “How do you know, Younger Sister?”

“I have… I have seen one before,” the Healer admitted.

The priest raised his eyebrows, surprised. The Healer suddenly looked vulnerable, and for the first time in quite a while he remembered how young she still was. She had been only thirteen years old and orphaned when she gave up her birth name and became the Healer. That was ten years before, and her path of healing had been blessed all the way. Nobody had even had time to think of her as a maiden, not even herself. But she was a beautiful woman, possessing the sort of graceful charm that often led the gazes of men and women both to dwell upon her with an expression of awe in their eyes, rather than the sort of allure that encourage men to desire and women to envy. That did not mean she was not a woman like any other, the priest realized. And surely there would be men who saw beyond the inaccessible grace of a holy woman.

“I shall not judge or tell,” he said mildly.

“Three years ago there came some traders here,” she began, “you know how it is.” He nodded and smiled a little. Everybody knew how that was. Foreign traders and the travelers who went with these represented most of the contact that the village had with the world at large. For the village maidens, their visits provided a steady flow of fresh, handsome young men. Not only was there the odd exotic foreigner - most of the travelers were tribal members from distant villages out to look for prospective brides and a little thrill and fun to go with the search. The village maidens always went to the shores to “fish for husbands”, as they said. It was how they had always done, and how the village had grown. Young men must leave their homes and find wives in other places. Young women must make sure they capture the young men in their sweet nets before they slip back into the river and flow into other women’s eager hands.

“Well I went down to the river like the other young women,” she said, “to look for medicines from foreign lands,” she added innocently, and the priest nodded patiently, smirking only a little. “But there among the traders and the young travelers there was a very tall man. Quite handsome. Very pale skin. Dark blue eyes and chestnut hair and a nicely trimmed little beard. Our eyes met at once and it was as if I could not see anyone else then, and so it seemed that he saw me also. Without speaking, he just came up to me, his eyes meeting mine all the time, and there was a question in them, and I nodded. Then he took me by the hand and started to walk away from the shore. I had never... nobody has ever done that with me before. I don't know if anybody ever does that at all. He just led me away, just like that. And I just followed. It was as if I had been hypnotized. He seemed to know where he was going even though I am certain he had never been here before, but even so we suddenly found ourselves by the small lake where my Medicine Hut is. Nobody else comes there but me. I was so surprised that he just found it, just like that. But then there are people who just know how to follow their feet. He looked at me, questioningly, and I nodded again, and we walked into the hut. And then..." She smiled at the memory. "He had magic, Old Brother. His magic strengthened my own. There was something that happened then that is beyond anything I learned before. I cannot say what it was. It belongs to me only, and to him that I shared it with."

"I see," the priest said uncertainly, and only a little disappointed.

"That day and night I discovered all his body paintings. I had never seen the like before. And he also had those scars – so many scars gathered over a long time – even though he was not as old as this one here – on the contrary he was not much older than me. But he must have been exposed to violence for a long time, and a lot of that time too. Some of his scars he must have received even as a little boy. He was not as broad of frame as this one here but he was unusually strong and tall, and compared to his slim frame there were those massive shoulders as if he had been...climbing a *lot* or, or perhaps swimming or rowing - all his life by the looks of them. He had been carrying a spear and a bow and arrows, but that is common enough for a hunter and quite wise for anyone to take into the forest. But I also discovered that he had a lot of knives and a battle axe hidden away beneath his cloak, and two swords. I had never seen anyone so well armed or so... almost reverent about his weapons. And I understood that these were not hunting or wood-cutting or even tanning blades. I had never seen anything like them before but I was and still am certain that he must have been a warrior, like those we hear about in our legends and from the traders who bring tidings from the larger world."

"He kept his weapons away from me, but close enough for him to grab swiftly, laying them out in the hut as if he was preparing for hostile entry. But he was all calm about it and when I looked worried he had a way of making me feel comfortable and safe despite all the...

precautions. I realized that he wanted me to know that there was no threat in this for me but rather a way of showing that he could protect me. I had no idea what he thought I needed protection from – I have walked these forests alone since I was a toddler. I understood his intentions were good and I thought it must just be his custom. But I had never known anything like that. I thought he must come from a place where there are lots of bandits and wars, like we hear of. I wondered if he may perhaps be a Tschude or an Est or a Veps – how would I know; I have only *heard* of those warlike people of the north. I had no idea what any of them would look like. All I knew was that they are known for their blue eyes and the cloudlike paleness of their skins. I was very curious. Just before he left the Medicine Hut the day after I asked him where he was from. He could not speak our language, as I could not speak his, but with gestures he understood what I meant. He pointed to the northeast and said; *Rus*. Then he pointed at himself and said *Rus* again, and then he… he…" She paused, looking befuddled. The priest leaned eagerly towards her. It was the first time he had first-hand information about this strange breed of people.

"He *beat his chest*, Old Brother. He *beat his chest* while he said *Rus*."

"What did he do that for?" They both looked puzzled, but since he asked, she replied; "I think he was … *proud*, Old Brother. He was smiling very broadly. And beating his chest. I think he was proud to announce that he was Rus."

They both paused while contemplating the shocking sight of a man beating his chest and showing off his pride – and at that even a pride in being one of the least welcome people in the known world.

"Did anyone else see that?" the Thunder priest asked.

"No, Old Brother. He had disguised his tattoos and spoke not at all when he was in the village. It was only when we were alone that he showed himself. I was so astonished that… I did not tell anyone, Old Brother. I was afraid they would… I was worried. You know what they say about Rus. But now it has come to this, Old Brother, and… I recognize the sort of tattoos and other features among his belongings. I am not in doubt. The Thunder Bear is a Rus-man."

The old priest gazed anxiously at the sleeping man. He had never seen a Rus before, and he was old. He did not think anyone in the village had ever seen a Rus. But they had heard about them. The rumors that came with the river traders had grown slowly, over the last decades, and intensified over the last few years. Nobody seemed to be certain about whether they were men, or beasts, or demons. Like the other peoples of the north, their skin was milky white and their eyes often blue, but adding to all that northern paleness which must surely be a result of living with all that snow, they also seemed to possess flaming red hair or else hair so bright-colored it was almost white, and they grew very thick beards the likes of which nobody else had seen. It was said that they came from the north on flying dragons, while other said they were ships that seemed to glide above water, which might explain how they could navigate them into rivers that even skilled rafters would be careful about entering.

The stories were many and most probably not all were true, but what seemed to be agreed upon was their cruelty: how they would abduct all the young women and children of an entire village, and often kill anyone who opposed them, or even just kill for the fun of it. They never seemed to want to abduct grown men – these they would kill at sight, and they would hang men who had tried to fight back – hang them from trees and stab them while still alive. And they raped the women before the eyes of their brothers and sons.

Stories of such tribes of demonic men had been passed on across the network of rivers that was their world since time immemorial. Just as some demon tribes had dissolved over time, others had appeared. The Thunder priest knew the stories of old. The once feared Goths had been replaced by the Huns, then these had been replaced by the Poles and the Magyars and the Bulgars, and the Avars and the Khazars, and then the fear of the Khazars in the south had faded before the northern Tschudes, and now even the Tschudes seemed kindly compared to the Rus. He had always suspected that they were all the same sort, really, and that their shared cruelty simply seemed to replace one another on the altar of time. Their neighbors in the south and east and north had long since been forced to learn how to defend themselves, even if they often stood weak before the demon tribes. But his people had found their place in the secret heart of the river lands a long, long time ago.

What did such tidings matter to them, who lived deep within the forest marshlands and crooked river weavings? For all those decades and centuries that had passed, with all the stories of demonic hordes, one terror replacing the next - *they* had lived sheltered for hundreds and hundreds of years - sheltered from all but the rumors.

But he remembered the ancient songs; songs of terror and battle and loss; songs of how just a few people survived the massacres or escaped the slavers. The survivors had fled north and west from the great sea and sought shelter then, deep in the forested river lands. This had happened a long, long time ago. The villagers of the river lands had been safe here for so long that the old songs of war no longer felt real to them. They were no warriors anymore. They were just hunters and beekeepers and amber gatherers, peaceful people who kept to themselves and only heard stories about the greater world from passing traders. Why would they ever want to seek out of their peaceful river lands? For even with all the stories they heard about foreign splendor and excitement, these were always overshadowed by the stories they heard about demon tribes, about warrior people from the south and the north and the east, people who seemed to be little more than rabid beasts; but surely were human; greed-ridden slavers and killers and rapists. Now that he looked at the man on the bed, knowing that he was one of *those* people, he shuddered.

"Too close," he whispered to himself, "They have come too close."

The Wounded Rus

When the Thunder priest left the sauna, Zivah entered and walked tippy toe over to the sleeping giant. She studied him carefully and finally looked up at her mother.

"Father?" she asked. The Healer drew her breath.

"Yes, Zivah, he is… he is akin to your father. But we shall keep that a secret for now." Zivah brightened.

"Secret!" the toddler said happily. The Healer pulled her close and hugged her. There was no saying what could happen to a demon's daughter. She hoped that the Thunder priest heeded her words. By midday, Thunder Bear entered a fever that signaled the start of his internal battle. The Healer poured infusions and fresh water down his throat while heating the sauna further and covering him with blankets. Still he was shivering from cold, and as the fever continued into the night, she worried about him. Zivah, drowsy now, suddenly went up to the Rus-man and snuggled up to his great arm beneath the blankets and promptly fell asleep. The Healer raised an eyebrow and considered it a little before she decided to snuggle next to her daughter and the man everybody already called Thunder Bear. And there they all slept through the night. The Rus-man was still unconscious in the morning, but the fever had abated a little. The Healer heated more stones, changed the sheets on the bed and cleaned him again while Zivah watched.

The village elders and the Thunder priest gathered in her hut, other villagers standing by on the outside, wanting to hear reports. She told them of his condition but said nothing about his identity, and was relieved to discover that the Thunder priest had not said anything either. She suggested that they leave him alone until he was better and said that it could take several days before he regained consciousness. The villagers obeyed, and right enough the days passed with Thunder Bear going through his fevers, every night warmed by the bodies of the Healer and her daughter.

The Healer kept a breed of long-haired cats that had been passed down from mother to daughter since time immemorial. The cats are sacred, her mother had told her, and they have medicinal properties of their own. And these cats always *see*. So in the day when some of the cats liked to stay indoors to rest, she opened the door of the sauna partly to see how her cats reacted. One of them, the one that the Healer called White Paws, entered the sauna and examined the patient for a while before he settled on top of his chest and started to purr. The Healer was puzzled. Her cats usually settled right where the sickness was and she had expected White Paws to settle on the Rus-man's left thigh, where the wound was. But there the cat was, purring away on top of Thunder Bear's muscular chest. Cats are always right. She remembered the dream and realized that the wound on his thigh would not heal unless his heart was healed too.

She sat down next to the sleeping man and shoved her hand gently in beneath the blankets and the purring cat until it settled softly on his chest, the weight of White Paws on top of her hand, feeling the vibration of the purring going through her hand and into the Rus-man's heart. She silenced her mind and concentrated on the sensation of his skin beneath her hand and the waves of purring. Her hand felt the breath and the flow of blood that moved within him. She felt the tensions of his chest and knew how they had hardened over time, hardened with grief and bitterness and rage. What could have befallen him, what has he gone through, to make him feel this way, she wondered. She recognized the grief and the sense of loss, even the shame of having done shameful things, but she had never before felt such depths of despair. He was like a thunderous raging bull ramming his head into insurmountable obstacles. They were making him crazy.

Her lips started to tremble violently as she felt the pain of his heart ever deeper. He had done bad things, she knew that now. He had committed terrible crimes and his soul was torn by them. There was such a confusion of feelings now that she had a hard time maintaining her grasp around his heart. She felt as if she was being sucked into a vortex of rage drawing her ever deeper into his bog of hidden terrors. But she maintained her grasp, and White Paws continued purring. It was a battle, and it was a battle that only required that she stayed there and saw him, stayed there and heard him, stayed there and felt him, to the very end.

She had almost given up the battle when she felt his body take a deep breath. Then the pattern of his breath changed, became deeper and calmer. His chest seemed to expand just as the tensions gave way. Tears were running down the sides of his closed eyes. White Paws rose and stretched, yawning. The Healer gently withdrew her hand. The fever was gone, but Thunder Bear still slept.

"Rest now, Rus-man. Rest for as long as you can," she whispered and went to feed the cat.

It was nine days before he opened his eyes.

She did not even know. She was busy preparing her medicines when she noticed that White Paws was sitting on top of the Rus-man's chest again, staring into his face. The Rus-man was staring back. He had blue eyes, she saw, quite like in the dream of the Thunder Bear. As she watched, the sky blue of his irises seemed to pale in the center and intensify around the frames. They reminded her of the eyes of some wolves, the wolves that had almost white eyes framed by a dark blue rind. There were people to the east and south who were said to be able to take on the hides of wolves, and they could be recognized by such eyes, she recalled. But then she had heard that such abilities and such eyes were also said to be common among the northern Finns, especially among the Tschudes. Perhaps they were common among the Rus as well. Now his wolf's eyes met the cat's eyes in a silent game of wills. The cat and the man watched each other calmly.

The Healer stayed silent and watched as White Paws got tired of the staring game, yawned and walked nonchalantly away as if he had actually won the contest. The man's eyes lit up at that, showing a sense of humor, and his fond gaze followed White Paws, his face turning slowly to see the cat walking out of the sauna. Then he slowly turned his face back again and met her gaze. Just as he had with the cat, he just looked at her. But now that he was meeting her eyes, the paleness of his dark framed eyes slowly gave way to the previous sky blue, and another light seemed to be lit within them.

"*Sól*," he whispered, maintaining eye contact.

"*Sool*?" she replied uncertainly.

"*Sól*," he nodded, and smiled a little. It was obvious that every movement was tiresome. But she saw the friendliness in his eyes, a surprising trait. *He is a kind man*, she thought. It was not that surprising, because her cats and her child all seemed comfortable around him, but then it would have been hard even for a large and violent man to be hostile or threatening while utterly unconscious. The things that she had felt when she held his heart made it difficult to understand how he could carry this light within at the same time. But the eyes never lie. He lifted his index finger slowly and pointed to the fire place, and then to the sky. He made a small circular movement and pointed to the sky again, and repeated the word *Sól*. Then he pointed at her and said the word again. She frowned. Then she pointed to the sky and made a similar movement that she thought better would serve to symbolize the Sun goddess. He nodded eagerly.

"*Sól*."

"Saulé," she corrected him, speaking the name of the holy Sun mother as she knew it.

"*Saah-uh-leh*," he attempted.

"Yes. Saulé," she said, nodding affirmatively and made a gesture to symbolize the Sun again. The Rus-man smiled broadly now and gestured towards her.

"*Saulé*," he said to her and fell asleep again.

The next time he woke, the entire village council had gathered. The council consisted of all the men and women of the village who were old enough to have grandchildren or else had showed themselves worthy of particular reverence due to some skill or renowned wisdom, such as the Healer. After the Rus-man had woken and spoken once, she invited the Elders into the sauna, where they quietly sat down on the floor in a circle around the giant stranger. The Healer sat by him, waiting with a thin meat soup that she hoped she could make him drink. He had not taken any other nourishment than water and herbal infusions since he came to her hut, and nine days and nights had passed already. When he finally opened his eyes, he seemed calm. He seemed to be alert and aware of their presence, but made no movement as to betray any emotion whatsoever. But his eyes lit up when the Healer hovered above him.

"Saulé," he smiled at her. She blushed a little. It seemed blasphemous, to have someone call you by the name of a divinity in the presence of others. He noticed her embarrassment and corrected himself.

"*Sól*," he said. She smiled. Only the two of them knew that Sól and Saulé meant the same. She smiled but shook her head mildly and pointed to herself.

"Healer," she said. He repeated the word and looked quizzical. The Healer pointed to her medicine pouch and to the small table where several other plants and ready medicines had been placed, and said the word “medicine”. He nodded to signal that he understood. “Healer,” she concluded and pointed at herself. The bear-like stranger nodded solemnly, signaling understanding, and repeated the title while he pointed at her, and then looked curious. She knew that he understood that she had given him a title, not a name, but he did not seem to realize that the title meant that she had no name. Maybe it was different where he was from. Maybe even a Healer could have a name where he was from. He pointed at her again, saying, “Healer….?”

She shook her head and shrugged. “Healer,” she asserted.

“Sól”, he said, and there was that little light in his eyes again which made her blush. She kept her face lowered and concentrated on the food while she began forcing soup into his mouth. He looked a little embarrassed about being fed like a baby in the presence of others, but did not object and quickly enough finished the whole bowl. He still looked hungry then, but she saw in his eyes that he was ready to be introduced to the circle of elders that surrounded them. She helped him sit up a little so that he could watch them more easily, and they him. The Thunder priest came forth and greeted him. The red-headed stranger looked at him and mimicked his greeting signal. He was a swift learner, they noticed, his mind was all set on understanding. The two men looked curiously at each other. Then the priest pointed at himself, at the Healer, and at all the people in the sauna. “*Latgáli*,” the priest said. He pointed at himself and all the people again and repeated the name of the people; “Latgáli.” Thunder Bear looked around and made a gesture towards all the people in the room.

“*La-aht-gaah-leeh*?” he said.

“Yes, that is the name of our tribe,” the priest said, although the stranger could not understand him. But he seemed to have understood what he meant anyway. The Healer drew her breath. She was expecting him to say “Rus” next, and braced herself for the reaction. But Thunder Bear pointed at himself and said; “*Gaut*.”

“*Gaah-oot*?” the priest tried. The man who was a Gaut nodded eagerly and realized that nobody had ever heard of any Gauts before. “Norseman,” he said in his language.

“*No-ohrd-maahd-ur*..?” the priest repeated, upon which the Gaah-oot nodded hopefully.

“Yes, I am a Gaut and a Norseman,” he said in his language, and the entire council repeated the now recognizable words slowly: “*Gaah-oot Noohrd-madur?*”

He nodded amiably at them while pointing at himself and making signs that seemed to refer to more people than himself. They understood that this was not his name but the name for his people, but they had never heard of these folks, and the villagers exchanged uncertain glances. The Norseman frowned and looked around the room. The Healer knew that he was trying to figure out the four directions. She pointed to the east and said; "Saulé". Then she moved her pointed fingers from the east and followed the room, raising her arm a little as she swept across the southern part of the rounded room and began descending her arm in the west, repeating their name for the Sun mother, knowing that he understood the meaning of that divine name. The Gaut then pointed directly towards the northwest and said; "*Gautland*."

The Elders spoke mutedly among themselves. One of the elder women said; "I think perhaps the *Gaah-oot Noohrd-madur* is speaking of the Goths. I did not know they still existed."

"They might, but I think they moved down southwest, not northwest," an elder man suggested.

"There is only ocean in the northwest."

"I do not wish to shame you Old Sister, but I am certain there are some islands up there. A big one too. I think it is actually called Goh...*Gothland*."

"Gotland?" said Thunder Bear the Gaah-oot, and they all looked curiously at him and nodded. But the Gaut shook his head determinedly and said; "*Ekki Gotland: Gautaland*!" The council looked confusedly at each other, hardly understanding the difference between the two words.

"Obviously," one of the elder men said, "he is in fact from that large island in the northwest that someone call *Gothland* but he calls it...*Guh-ooh-tah-land*...and he calls himself a...a *Gaah-oot*." The Gah-oot nodded enthusiastically. He pointed at himself and repeated the word Gaut, then he showed with his hands a signal that could only mean "many", said the word "*Gautar*", then pointed at the ground and said: "*Land*".

"I think he means that Guh-uh-tah-land means the Soil of the Gah-oots. Or the Guh-ooh-tar, as they are many," the Thunder priest suggested, and everybody nodded thoughtfully. The Thunder priest drew his breath and cast a glance at the Healer. He just had to ask. He did not have to say where he had it from. The priest cleared his throat and looked at the Gah-oot. "*Rus*?" he asked.

The Gah-oot went pale. His gaze moved swiftly to the Healer, who shook her head discreetly at him. He swiftly looked away from her so that nobody would notice their silent exchange and shook his own head slowly. "*Ekki Rus*," he said, shaking his head in denial, but he looked doubtful and bitter all of a sudden. It was as if all the power he had mustered to stay up suddenly waned. The Thunder priest decided that it was better to ask more later. He wanted to know the most important part. He took out his amulet, shaped like a thunderbolt, and pointed at it, saying; "Pērkons". Then he pointed up and made a sound that could resemble a thunder, and repeated the name "Pērkons" – the name of the Thunder lord. The Gah-oot nodded and tried to say the word: "*Peehr-koo-ns*?" The whole council nodded in unison. "*Perun*?" He asked, and they all exchanged glances.

"That is what they call Pērkons down southeast of the river Nemunas," the Thunder priest said quietly. "The Sloveni, they call him that. Perun."

"He does not look like a Slav", one of the elders objected, and the others nodded. They had all seen Slavic people many times, and they did not look so very different from themselves. The stranger seemed to grasp their confusion and shook his head. He pointed to his own hammer pendant and said; "*Peehr-kohns. Perun. Thór.*" He pointed at his hammer again, then at the sky, and then made a sound so perfectly in the likeness of a thunder roar that the entire council gasped. Many of them still had their jaws dropped when he proceeded, repeating the word: "Thór." He pointed upwards and said; "Thór." When everybody agreed that "*Thór*" seemed to be his word for thunder and also his name for the Thunder lord, and was indeed the same as Perun and Pērkons, the stranger who knew how to make thunder from his throat pointed at himself and beat his chest, saying; "*Thórbjörn.*" He had to repeat the word a few times until they got it as right as could ever be expected: "*Thór-be-yurn.*"

"*Thór-be-yurn…*" the Healer said, "I think that is his name."

"His name has thunder in it. What does…*bee-yurn*... mean?" one of the elders asked. They all looked at him. "Bee-yurn?" she asked.

"*Björn,*" he repeated and beat his own chest affirmatively, "Thorbjörn." He pointed to his hammer again and repeated the word *Thór*. She nodded. Then he pointed at one of the tattoos that depicted what she had thought may be a bear. He made some sounds that were so terrifyingly similar to the sounds which bears produce that there was no doubt in anybody's minds. Her dream had been true. His name may sound different in his language, but it meant the same as they had called him ever since she had told them about her dream. He *was* Thunder Bear.

A Norseman in the River Lands

His full name and title was Thorbjörn Thorgrimsson Thorsgóði of West-Gautland, but after the initial fuss they made about trying to understand the meaning of his first name and where he was from, not to say trying to pronounce his name right, he decided to just let them call him Thór-be-yurn the Gaah-oot, because that was as close as they got. Often enough they called him something else, what sounded to him like *Peehr-kohns-lah-kees*, and he understood that it meant the same as his name did, Thunder Bear. It also seemed to mean something to them – there was something about an omen dream and the thunder storm that had brought him here.

He knew that the round hut that he was lying in was a sauna, but it was never heated beyond a temperature that he could live with and stay warm in. Besides he knew that women of these lands often used the sauna during summer for other purposes than a sauna, and that it was also a room dedicated to the Earth mother. They called her Žemyna here, he had learned, and they thought she was the Thunderer's wife rather than his mother. Apart from that it seemed that they knew the same gods that he knew by other names. But they seemed to know the Sun maiden by almost the same name.

When they had gathered around him that day he woke up, he had soon become certain that his people and theirs must have stemmed from the same stock a long time back. It had not been so easy to see that at first, because they looked different from his own folks. These people were somewhat darker all in all, their hairs varied between a deep honey blonde to chestnut brown and almost black. There was not a light yellow or red head among them. And there were few blue eyes. Their eyes were mostly brown or green or even somewhat yellow – but only the Healer and her daughter had eyes the color of amber and gold. Their skins were tanned by the Sun in a way he hardly ever tanned, although he knew people at home who could go quite brown on a hot summer. The men here shaved their beards like slaves and shamed folks do, but he knew that this unmanly habit was customary among many tribes and not all of them had been that puny regardless. The beardless men of that village with that girl in that he tried not to think about - they had been fierce fighters.

When he got accustomed to their looks he began to see how similar they were to his own after all, and he began to hear words that might just be of a recognizable kind. Surely they shared a common ancestry - even if this branch of the tribal tree seemed to belong to the puny sort. Even by just looking at the old men seated there he knew that they had never been warriors. Both men and women were short and wiry, agile and strong in their own way, slender in shape, graceful in the way of forest-dwellers. They were the perfect hunters and trackers, but there was surely not a warrior among them. And they had taken his weapons and hid them from his sight. It was an odd thing for a man like him to find himself completely in the power of beardless strangers who could not even fight. But he had no weapons and even if he could have fought well enough without any there was a weakness in him after the infection that his wound had caused, and he had to lie still for another nine days and nights before he was allowed to carefully hump around with the support of a large stick that the Healer had given him. By that time he had long since decided that there was no point in trying to escape the village. Firstly they did not seem hostile towards him, only curious. Secondly, the Healer was intriguing beyond words. Thirdly he knew of nowhere else that he could go. If the Ladies of the Loom had seen fit to place him here, then he would stay and wait for further signals. Meanwhile he put his mind to learning the ways of his hosts as swiftly as possible.

He had been taught how to travel since childhood, all the advice of those older than him, always the wise words of old. He remembered his father Thorgrim's words: *"When we come to another shore, whether it be another shore of our own lands or one of a different land, then we will always be met with a wall made by men, just as we always set out our warriors to encounter and question the stranger and the visitor. In order to break through that wall the visitor must show himself trustworthy. The newcomer is the one who must prove himself worthy of hospitality. The newcomer is the one who must adapt. For even if he does no wrong the newcomer is the one most likely to attract negative attention. And so when you enter a settlement you must always keep watch. If you find yourself among strange people, and you still know not how much you may come to depend on them, then you must watch and listen, you must look and learn. You must listen to the speech of people and learn their ways and how to please them. If you know how to please them they will welcome you, for there is nothing a human being enjoys more than when an outsider works hard to become part of your fold. Because such efforts are ways of showing that their fold is attractive and then they can feel proud. And there is hardly anything people like better, Thorbjörn my son, than when they find a reason to feel proud about themselves and their own kind. Can you think of anything people may like better than that?"*

"No," he had said.

"I can," Thorgrim had said. Thorbjörn his son had been young and was still taught in the way of questions and answers, which had always been his people's way of teaching youngsters. Knowing how to ask questions was the first step towards wisdom; and besides the one who asks is also bound to listen.

"What is that, then, father?"

"What people will like even better than a reason to feel proud of themselves is the person who gave them reason to feel that way. A warrior and a traveler must always think strategically. On the one side you must know how to either flee or even better how to cut down your enemy, and you must know where to do it, and when to do it, and most importantly you must learn how to know who your enemies really are. On the other hand you must make sure to have as few enemies as possible, and as many friends."

"Is this the same for a Heri, father?" He had asked, eagerly. Like his father, he would one day be a Heri, a lord of his clan, which in his case consequently meant that he would be the high lord of several related clans. They had once been a tribe of their own. To many people the Heri of the Thunder priest clan, the great Thorsgóði, was almost like a king. Thorbjörn had become quite conscious about that fact lately and had already begun to feel the burden of responsibility. There were whispers in the fields and in the harbors and the markets, and whispers in the night. The whispers spoke of the return of the Thunder Warriors to the throne of West-Gautland. He did not dare ask further, but had begun to study seriously the ways of lords and masters.

"It is the same for a Heri as it is for any ordinary warrior and for any traveler. A lord must pay particular heed to this, for you will have many people in your power and many to protect. And you will need your underlings to love you and respect you and rally to you without a moment's hesitation. A Heri's most important task is to keep his people and his land united and to be the point where they unite. You must be a House-Bond to the land and to the people of that land. The people are the land, wherever they are. You must love and please the land like a House-Bond must love and please his Freyia, and in the same way as a man must do with his wives you must also know how to rule your people honorably and wisely without ever showing weakness, and in a way that must induce deep respect as well as deep love. To run a Household, the Hold needs a Bond to bind them, and the House-Bond is that knot by which the Hold may unite and become a house, a family, a clan, a tribe, even a kingdom... And the Heri of a land will be that House-Bond where the land's people unite and to whom they will rally.

But people will never unite nor rally if they do not feel strongly for the Bond that binds them. Dissatisfied underlings become like dissatisfied women, they will strike at you and betray you when you least expect it. You may punish them all you like but it will ultimately be your own fault. Neither your underlings nor your women can help what they are. ***You*** *are the one in power and all* ***they*** *can do is respond to how you rule them, each according to their nature. It is your responsibility to keep them happy and eager to strengthen you and please you. So whether it is as a lord or as a House-Bond or as a warrior and a stranger and a visitor among foreign folks, you must make people like you."*

"How do I make people like me?"

"You must cater to the dreams of men and women and give them cause to think of you and then of how good they are feeling today. Then they will be your friends and stand up for you if poison arrows are directed in your way. It does not matter if you are traveling or at home, when it comes down to it. Making friends is the best shield a warrior can ever wish for wherever he finds himself in the world. Encourage all good things you see in the people around you. Place yourself in the listening position, the one who is eager to know what they know. That will make them feel proud too. You may even learn a great deal. But more importantly it will give you friends and brothers. This way of dealing with people will make your women happy too, and having happy women at home is a better thing than you can yet imagine, son."

"What is there about happy women that I cannot imagine," Thorbjörn had mused, *"I like it when they are happy."*

"Because they give you sweets and smile so sweetly to you, that's why you like it when they are happy. But happy women are the key to a man's fortune."

"How is that so?" he had asked, quite alerted. Everybody always spoke so well of his father, and there was always something intriguing about the way women nodded approvingly whenever Thorgrim Thorsgóði was spoken of. Thorbjörn had pricked his ears, savoring the key to his good renown.

"There is nothing like the praise and admiration of women," Thorgrim had said, *" And you must always remember that women spread rumors like the Sun spreads light and will exchange stories about men as surely as the she-wolf will howl her tidings across the mountains and the fjords. The other she-wolves listen and the more entertaining the song the more they join the chorus. It is in their nature, and there is no stopping it. You should not even attempt to stop*

that sort of chatter, unless you want them to spread lowly rumors about you, of course. The worst fate always befalls a man who leaves a trail of angry women. A man's fame and respectability depends on the verdicts of women. And a man's fame and good reputation can often be the only thing he owns when things really matter. There is no point in trying to silence a woman's words, for they are powerful and magical and will surface in hidden places if you are not man enough to face them directly. A woman's verdict is holy, Thorbjörn. A woman's verdict can change the course of his fate."

For those nine days and nights when he lay awake in the round hut of the Healer, Thorbjörn the Gaah-oot watched and listened. Apart from the Healer and her little daughter, three women of different ages often came by to assist in attending him, especially in the beginning when he needed help moving at all. They seemed to pay special attention to the hearth and torches – all things that had to do with fire. They kept addressing flames and fire as "*Gah-bee-yah*" and after a while he understood that it was a name and that the fire was a goddess to them. He understood that they were a sort of holy women, just as the Healer surely must be one, and so he calmly accepted their care even if it felt somewhat humiliating to be washed and touched all over by strange women who did not act particularly respectful around him. But it was better to be clean than not clean, and he could not do it himself. As soon as he could, though, he made them understand that he preferred doing it by himself and went a deep red when the youngest woman set up a very disappointed expression that made the two others break out in laughter followed by hysterical giggles, naughty glances and suggestive movements.

There were several old people, men and women both, who kept looking into him, always staring at him and touching him as if he was a strange sort of beast, while chattering among themselves. They did not seem to think there was anything rude about staring or touching a stranger. At least, that was what he hoped, for if they stared at him despite knowing how rude it was it meant that they were hostile towards him. It mattered what these old folks felt, he sensed, having guessed that these people belonged to the sort of folks that were still ruled by a council of elders.

Sometimes a group of people from the village would drop by and gather in the room. In the beginning they just came in and stood around by the walls or squatted down, and then they would just stare. He had to force himself not to grab something to hurl at them. It was probably a way of testing him, he thought, and he did not mind because he knew well the testing games due to an unknown stranger who suddenly turns up among strange people. He would just have to pass the tests. But it was hard to be tested by men such as these. They were all so puny, so very obviously beneath him - and yet they stared at him like he was nobody, and allowed their women and children to do the same. It was like a daily humiliation, and he had to remind himself over and over that this sort of staring was not a sign of hostility among these people. He had learned that when he came to Aldeigjuborg. The new slaves, those people from the river lands and the great forests, they always had a hard time understanding the silent language of the eyes. They always had to learn the hard way how not to stare at their superiors.

His shame tugged from within.

You are humbling me, gentle Ladies of the great Loom, he thought to himself, *you are humbling me and honing me and I shall accept your verdict. I deserve this humiliation.* And with those thoughts he calmed himself and employed his self-control like a true warrior and bore the humiliation as gracefully as he could muster, while concentrating on making out the words they spoke and figuring out what the words might mean. In the beginning he tried to recognize any Finnish words since he had always thought that the people of East Land spoke a brand of Finnish. He knew some of the Finnish languages that were spoken in these lands, and had thought it would be easy to learn the dialects of a people who only lived a little further to the south. But as he strained his ears and listened to the speech of this forest people, he realized that there were few words of the Finnish sort. In fact, as he kept listening to their speech, he realized that their language reminded him more and more of the language of the Krivich Slavs by the lake Ilmen, a language that he knew passably well by now. As soon as he recognized the similarities he had an easier time making out separate words and word forms, and sometimes he even thought that he understood a little of what they were talking about.

It was good, he thought after a few days, that he had prepared himself for humiliation, because as soon as the rest of the villagers felt certain that he was not going to assault them like a rabid bear they began touching him too, so rudely thrilled by the braids in his beard that he had taken so much care to make after washing his beard and hair that very morning, hoping that they would see him as a human being if he paid attention to his appearance like decent folks do. They were absolutely stunned by the long facial braids and one of the young maidens actually came over and, giggling, pulled testily at the left braid. He snorted disapprovingly and glared at her sideways, the way an inferior would show his discontent to a superior, but not even this admission of inferior foreign status, despite being so very obviously a man of noble birth, seemed to encourage the young village girl to pay heed to his irritation. Instead of respecting him in return, she pulled again and giggled loudly before scurrying back to her giggling friends. He had to really force himself to remember his uncustomary place as the inferior newcomer. She said something and they all broke out in chuckles and even loud laughter and *pointed* at him. And then the whole village laughed. It was almost unbearable, but he put up a broad smile and laughed with them, thanking the Gentle Ladies for their faith in him.

If the edge of a man's soul needs some honing, then the honing will come, by death or by challenge. The fates could have cut his life short, but instead they were taking care to sharpen the blunt edge. The gods must be dearly entertained by his life song. All he could do was to prove his worthiness by accepting the verdicts of Fate with as much grace as he could muster.

The Healer saved him as she came inside, looked at the giggling girls and then at his face. She hushed them all out and sat down next to him, smiling mildly. She said something and gestured a little, and he understood that she said they did not mean any harm.

There was only one person apart from the Healer whose company he enjoyed. It was the feeble old man who was carrying a Thunderbolt hammer pendant and a staff of office. The man was very interested in his tattoos and his pendant, and kept talking of the Pērkons, the Thunder lord. He was the only villager apart from the Healer who treated him respectfully, and who often just sat there with him all quiet, humming to himself, giving him an encouraging pat on the shoulder before he would take his leave. The old man was a Thunder priest like himself. He wondered if the old one knew.

When there were no villagers around, there were the cats. Thorbjörn spent much of his time watching the large, thick-furred cats that kept walking around and sometimes settling on top of his chest or belly, purring away as if they had every right to use him as their mattress. He had never seen such tame cats before, and yet at the same time they seemed wilder than other cats he had seen. Wild animals that were somehow accustomed to humans, and felt completely safe around them. They actually seemed accustomed to being treated reverently. The Healer let them do whatever they pleased and always treated them with respectful care, so he did what she did – let them do whatever they wanted. They seemed like magical beings, and when he got used to them he also realized that it was easier to relax and sleep soundly when one of them snuggled on top of him. They created those strange rumbling sounds that caused vibrating waves of calm that seemed to work themselves into his body and mend things in there that seemed broken. He most probably had several broken ribs, and as he lay there he could sense how they were mending little by little. It was better to just stay put until they were whole once more.

The little girl came around often. She was so very sweet, and looked so very much like her beautiful mother. Her eyes seemed to have been made out of gold, he thought, they were golden, like honey or amber, a color he had never seen in eyes before, apart from the eyes of her mother. Both mother and daughter had the same golden, amber-colored hair and lightly tanned skin, and they both seemed to glow with a bright light that made him think they must be incarnations of the Sun maiden come to live in this world of stories. The little one – her name seemed to be *Zeeh-vah* - kept calling him "*teeh-evs*". It took him several days to realize the word meant "father". Thorbjörn's eyes suddenly flooded with the waters of grief. He remembered his children, all dead.

He looked at the toddler greeting her mother, saying "*Maah-teh*". Mother. The Healer had entered the hut to look for her daughter and met his eyes. She saw everything. He knew that she had seen the terror and the pain that he carried, and he knew that she saw his sadness now. Zivah pointed at him and said something about "teeh-evs". The Healer blushed a little and nodded, hushing the girl out of the hut. She turned to look at him for a moment and smiled before she also left the hut. She understood his need to be alone and closed the door before another curious villager got a chance to just drop by to stare at him.

Thorbjörn wondered what her real name was. The people called her *Mah-sah-veh-seneh* to her face, but he had noticed that they called some of the other women the same thing, especially the elder ones, and he guessed it was a title they used when addressing her directly, a title used for special women. When they spoke about her they called her that word which sounded like "*poos-loo-tah-yeh*". It was the same term that she had presented herself as, another title which obviously meant Healer. She was so beautiful. The way she moved, so gracefully, so gently, and yet so powerfully. She was very slender, much less curvy than the women he had used to like before. But even if she was thin and sinewy rather than soft and curvy, the soft elegance of her features, the light that she emanated and the grace of every movement she made, always knowing what she was doing, always calm – he thought she must be a goddess.

It had been a long time since he saw a woman of such rare beauty. He remembered Thora his sister and Halldís his wife, Rannveig and his kinswomen – fair women all, and all long dead. He could still hear their screams when they burnt to death. He could still hear the screams of their children. After that he had seen many women. Many sad women, many frightened women, many women who seemed to have lost their souls. And that one. The one who had looked at him and kept his eyes locked with hers while she let him see what he was doing to her. While her soul died right in front of him. He felt the shame dig deeper into his heart than ever before.

After nine days the Healer gave him a stick that she had been working on for a few evenings. She used to keep the door to the sauna open so that he could watch her doing her evening chores while seated in front of the fire, humming her songs and telling stories to the little girl. Sometimes she was singing in a different language, one that made his spine shiver because he recognized it. It was a forgotten language, one he had thought nobody else in the whole world knew. He was looking forward to learn her people's language now, eager to be able to talk to the Healer properly. Now she helped him get up and made sure that he was able to walk around before she allowed him to go out into the village. As she ushered him out of the door he stopped and looked around for his weapons.

"Do you not want to go outside, Thór-be-yurn?" she asked.

"My… things?"

"What things?"

He had tried to ask her about his weapons before, but she had acted as if she did not know what he was talking about. But later he had seen her examine his weapons one night before she placed them carefully inside a large chest. He looked pleadingly at the chest.

"No, Thór-be-yurn. You do not want to frighten people," she said determinedly. He took a deep breath and felt as if he was walking outdoors for the first time all naked. On the other hand he knew how to make a weapon out of any reachable object within the blink of an eye, and with that thought in mind he stepped outside and thought this must have been how the lord Thór felt when he had to walk into the land of the Devourers without carrying a single piece of steel. He had been given a staff by a wise woman from those heavenly East Lands and used that staff as his weapon. Needless to say he had returned victorious. He looked thoughtfully at the staff and at the Healer and smiled.

“I am sure you can whack people in the head with that staff if that is what you want,” she teased.

“I not understand, Healer,” he said, and she giggled a little and shook her head, letting him know that it was not important. He started walking, and she followed behind with Zivah, observing him carefully. He towered above everyone else and seemed to be as broad as the two broadest-shouldered men in the whole village. And he seemed to be seeing and hearing absolutely everything, like an expert hunter. Even when supported by a stick there was something about his stature and his stances that made her think that he must have been a very powerful man once, someone used to ruling others. She had never really seen the sort but could well imagine it from all the stories she had heard of kings and queens and rulers. If she had not known better she could sometimes have thought he was like a god in the flesh. The villagers did not fail to be impressed by it either, and hid their awe and their unease and their befuddlement behind jokes and laughter. And when Thunder Bear looked alternately confused and alternately amused, he seemed a little less imposing and safer to be around.

A New Life

Thorbjörn enjoyed that day, a sunny and beautiful and pleasantly warm summer day in a beautiful little village lying very close to a river, surrounded by fertile forests and marshlands. He had no idea where he was, but believed that he had been running for seven days and seven nights in a southern direction before that bear showed up in the night and roared at him. He had just fallen then and remembered only a few dreams he had had until he woke up in the Healer’s sauna. She had conveyed to him that he had been sleeping for nine days and nights on end. Two by nine and then seven days had passed since he had remembered his sacred vow and paid heed to it even though he knew that it would cost him all and his life too. But here he was, like a man reborn. He did not deserve it, but if the Kindly Ladies had decided to give him another life then he could only accept and see what they had in store for him.

The village was surrounded by groves and yards of fruit trees and berry bushes as well as countless beehives, but as far as agriculture went they seemed to mostly content themselves with small vegetable plots close to their little wooden huts. Until that moment Thorbjörn had just thought that the villagers were a little short on bread and porridge grains this year, or that the Healer had placed him on a diet during his recovery. What grains they did seem to possess, and from which they made a sort of thin bread that his kind would only have made during famine or poverty, they must have bought from the outside world. He went down to shore and saw that the villagers used the river for fishing and gathering shells, eggs and precious amber. All over the village there was a sense of ceaseless yet relaxed activity where work and social interaction was more or less the same thing. People sat in groups and worked together, seemingly choosing their work randomly or where they thought something needed doing, and perhaps more according to who they wanted to sit with than what they wanted to do. It seemed that things would get done eventually, no matter who happened to do it.

While they worked, they were chattering ceaselessly or else singing songs that gave rhythm to their work. He had a hard time making out if there was any important difference between the work of men and the work of women. At first it had seemed common enough, because all the work groups seemed to consist of mostly either men or women, with the exception of the river gathering and fishing work which was done by everybody together. But then he realized that even if they worked in all male or all female groups, the work that they actually did had little to do with gender. There seemed to be no man's work and no woman's work, just work that needed doing. In the beginning he thought there was no system to that at all. As to hunting, he had thought they were all men, having noticed that the men certainly hunted, but soon he had also seen two young women slip out into the forest carrying bows and arrows, and another returning from the forest carrying some small game caught with a trap, and he had noticed that the Healer owned a bow too.

After a while, the only sort of work that seemed specific to one sex was the work with fire and hearths and stoves. That work was always done by women. The women, obviously, cooked and tended the fire, but they did not spin or weave like most women do in most other places. They dressed in hides and furs and textiles that they had bought in from abroad. He had never before thought about how much women's lives at home was caught up in the preparation of textiles, from fiber to finished cloth and then into the latest fashions, and everything else between shoes and tapestries, sails and blankets, towels, sheets and even tents and fishing lines. Here, where women had time to do everything else, they did. Only later did he find that wood-cutting, timber and the construction of houses and boats was indeed considered men's work just like it was at home, what took some time to discover because women often assisted in some way or other, if nothing else so by shouting orders. It turned out that the women owned the houses and decided how they wanted them built even if their menfolk built them.

Apart from the small distinction of women being in charge of the hearth and the fire, that first day outside in the village he saw people of both sexes and all ages working all sorts of chores, some with the fishing and the river gathering, others with the tanning of hides and preparing of fur, some with the drying, smoking or salting of fish and meat, and others with the butchering of game, and then some with the polishing of amber, and others working with beeswax and honey. There were bees everywhere. On the third day, the Healer noticed his fascination with the bees and looked curiously at him.

"In Gautland no… no *bzzzzzz*," he said with the few words he knew.

"Are there no bees where you come from?" she asked, incredulous.

"No, no… *bees*. Thank you for the word, Healer," he said. She smiled. All the villagers seemed flattered when he thanked them for teaching him a word, and he thanked them for each one, making them happier and happier, warming up to the newcomer a little more with each time he made them feel knowledgeable and skillful. "And cats… he pointed at one of her long haired cats, "not many cats."

"No cats and no bees? How is that possible?"

"Too cold," he said, "They freeze." He looked doubtfully at the furry cats. They allowed him to touch and examine their fur, and he had noticed that as opposed to the cats he had seen before they seemed to have at least two layers of fur, one thick woolen layer and another layer that was, as he had seen after some came indoors during a heavy rain, actually quite waterproof. They had big paws and looked ferocious.

"In winter, these cats, they no freeze?" he asked.

"No, they grow more fur. The colder it is the more fur they grow."

"In winter; great white?"

"We get lots of snow in winter. Snow. For some three turns of the Moon."

"*Snow*. Thank you for the word, Healer. Cats no like snow?"

"They do not mind snow, Thór-be-yurn."

"Maybe they can live in Gautland," he pondered, more to himself than to her. He knew that people kept cats because they were great at hunting rodents, and he had seen ships that brought cats with them for that purpose, and the cats had saved all the grain and foodstuff on that ship.

"Do you grow grains in Guh-tah-land, Thór-be-yurn?"

"Yes."

"How do you deal with rodents?"

"We kill, or dogs kill. But cat may be better."

"Much better," she agreed.

"You no grain here?"

"We do not grow grain here, no. We gather some wild grain but mostly we buy it."

"You buy?"

"Yes, from the river. River traders. We give them amber, timber, furs, leathers, hides, beeswax and honey and river pearls too. They give us grains and wool and other textiles." She pointed at the things that she was mentioning, and he thanked her for all the words and stored them in his memory. He had a keen mind. "Why cats if no grain?" he asked.

"Why, we still have to *store* grain," she said, "but our cats have a different history that I may tell you one day. Our cats came with my lineage." He was still trying to confirm to himself what he thought she had said when the old Thunder priest approached him and asked if he wanted to see the place where they had found him.

After three days of humping around in the village, steadily followed by a train of laughing children, repeatedly met by smiling faces and giggling women, Thorbjörn began to suspect that the heavenly ladies could not be overly offended with him, and he also began to hope that the great lord might not have dismissed his servant just yet. A Thunder storm had protected him during his flight and led him to this place where time seemed to have stopped and where peace and kindness seemed to be the order of the day. There were no slaves here and no lords either, and hardly any other weapons than those meant for hunting. He had known people of a similar kind, but all their gentleness had not helped them, and they had been weary and frightened of those who were stronger than them and did not wish them well. In this river land village there seemed to be no awareness of the cruel world of axe and shield at all. It was as if he had returned to the Era of the Peace of Wisdom.

He had not thought such worlds existed anymore.

When the old Thunder priest of the village led him to the place where they had found him and the place turned out to be a temple dedicated to Thór, or Pērkons as they called him, he knew that he had been given another chance to make things right. He would be a Thunder warrior again, even if it meant that he had to be one without carrying any arms, and by treating puny men as if they were his equals.

Humility can be the greatest blade-honer a man must face in order to become truly great.

Thorbjörn Proposes Marriage

On the fourth day he was allowed to walk around on his own, and Thorbjörn stood reverently to attention as the Healer handed him his stick before she went outside of the hut. He stood by the door and looked after her as she walked into the forest on her own carrying a bow and arrows, a large bag and a digging stick. Thorbjörn walked back into the hut and stood before the chest. He began opening the chest carefully.

"That is my mother's chest," Zivah said behind him. He turned around and saw the little toddler, all on her own.

"Mother says only she can open that chest," the girl said snottily.

"Mother is right," he said.

"She is not your mother," the girl said.

"Thank the gods for that," he said in Norse.

"What?"

"I speak in… in Gah-oot."

"Oh," Zivah said, "Mother says I look after you today." He raised his eyebrows as the little one went over to him and reached out for his free hand. He had to lean forward and bow down to reach her hand, so little that she was, and after walking bent for a little while he swept the toddler up and placed her astride his shoulders behind his massive neck. Zivah gleefully grabbed his braids like they were reigns and Thorbjörn walked on, supporting himself with the stick in his left hand while maintaining a light grasp around Zivah's right leg. The girl was whining with joy and he felt his heart warming.

He remembered his little girls and the last time they were gathered when the gathering had a happy ending. The Summer Solstice celebration they had enjoyed some months before the fire. All his daughters and their different mothers had gathered around him. The oldest daughter, the little Thunder priestess, his sister's child, had been carrying his first wife's firstborn son in her arms. The boy was but a baby then and all Thorbjörn's children before him had been girls. Seven little maidens with flowers in their hair, aged between two and six all of them, red golden hair flowing beneath their flower wreaths as they were running around the Frey-pole like little goddesses, laughing and chattering as sweetly as birds. It was as if they all came back in this one who seemed to know that she could trust him and who always called him father.

As he moved through the village and listened to the speech of people and talked to anyone who approached him in some way or other, he overheard a conversation between two elderly men and realized that he understood their speech much better than he understood the other villagers. He walked over to them and talked to them. It turned out that the two men were of the tribe of Krivich Slavs who lived by lake Ilmen. Fortunately it seemed to be a long time since they had any contact with their home tribe, for they did not seem to realize that he was a Rus. And so Thorbjörn made two new friends by asking them questions about the place that he had come to. The two elder men told him that they had come to live in the village over three decades before, after they had travelled with the river traders for a few years. It was the custom, they said, that young men travel until they find a suitable bride and a place where they could live happily. They had met many girls on that journey, but eventually they had each fallen in love with a village maiden in this place and married here.

"How did you get to marry them?" Thorbjörn asked. For all that time when he had known the Slavs, he had mostly thought of them as either slaves or slavers, and never thought to ask them about their customs. He had just learned what he needed to communicate. Now he wished he had learned more, for just as their language was similar, so they seemed more similar to this people he had come among than any other.

"The girls liked us, and then we had to show ourselves worthy to the village," one of the men said.

"How did you do that?"

"We helped out. Showed our skills. Brought in game. Showed that we could contribute. That is how a man wins a wife around here. When we knew that we wanted our girls for wives we told them that we would hunt for them. That is how we say we want to be their husbands, to promise that we will bring in the game. The girls agreed by saying that they would cook for us. Then we were married, and afterwards there was a celebration where our hands were tied and we were adopted into the tribe."

"What if the man wants to take his bride home to his people?" The two men looked curiously at him. He looked back at them, equally curious.

"The women here, they stay," one of the men said, and the other nodded. "Women stay," he confirmed, "men travel. Men move into their wives' house. The women are the land. The women own the land. A woman needs her mothers and aunts and sisters and cousins around her. A property passes down from mother to daughter. Men are freer to be alone and to travel and make new brothers. Sons move away and find brides elsewhere when they have shown to her people that they are men worth having around. That's how men are made."

Well that makes sense, Thorbjörn thought, understanding the concepts behind the tradition. A young man must prove his worth before he can marry, that was clear. A woman did not have to do that; having children and tending her chores well and behaving appropriately - those were enough proof of her worth as always. A man was something else. But he had a hard time figuring out how something like that could have worked where he was from. Men needed their brothers more than women needed their sisters where he was from. He frowned a little.

"What happens with the menfolk if families are at war with each other?" he asked.

"What do you mean, Thór-be-yurn?"

"I mean, what if two clans or tribes are at war and the two sides both have men who come from the same clan? How can they fight their own kinsmen?"

"The Latgáli do not fight, Thór-be-yurn," one of the men said. The other nodded affirmatively.

"They never fight?"

"Never. Not in many hundreds of years anyway," the other man said. "They have a legend about a war that happened a long, long time ago. When they still lived further to the south," the first man said, "they had large towns then and rode horses and had warriors like other folks. And then they were crushed. Almost everybody died. Most of those who did not die, the women and the children, they were taken away as slaves. The survivors fled and fled until they came to the River Lands and created a new life for themselves. They found here a people who claimed to have escaped in the same way an even longer time before that. These natives were the ones who held the rule that land must pass from mother to daughter. It was their condition when the southerners came, that they follow the same custom, and so they did. They mated with them and became many tribes, among them the Latgáli."

"Who were the native people?" Thorbjörn asked, curious.

"Nobody knows, Thor-be-yurn. But they said that they were the oldest people of these lands, the first-comers. We just call them the Old River People. The Old River People did not till the soil. They did not make metals. They lived by hunting and fishing and gathering wild plants. The Latgáli do till the soil, but not here, not so deeply within the River lands. The Old People showed the newcomers how to live from the River lands without tilling the soil. But the newcomers remembered how they made bread and porridge, and began trading with villagers who lived in places where the soil could more easily be worked with. We buy our grains and vegetables from the outside. We exchange them with our furs and our beeswax and our honey and amber." The three men nodded thoughtfully.

"But the Healer descends from those people, Thór-be-yurn," one of the men continued; "She is a direct descendant through the mother line from the Old River People. She is a better hunter than many of the men here. You should see how well she aims her bow! But she never brags about it. She is such a great tracker too; she often just tells the young hunters where to go. When they have luck they give her a part of the game. And she still knows songs that were passed down in that language, magical songs that she sings when she heals. It is a language nobody else knows. Her knowledge too, it is an ancient Healer lore, a lore that reaches back to the first people who settled in the River Lands, the Old River People."

"What is her real name?"

"She has no name. She gave up her name when she became the Healer."

"She is very young."

"She has some three and twenty winters, Thór-be-yurn. She looks younger. And she looks older too, sometimes. Much older. She carries the souls of her foremothers within." Thorbjörn felt a tingle move down his spine. He knew what that meant. He knew it better than most people. He knew it better than the two men who were explaining it to him.

"Still she is young to be the only Healer in the village?" he asked.

"Her mother and her grandmother, the women who taught her, they died in a plague that happened ten years ago."

"Ten years ago," Thorbjörn repeated slowly. It had been ten years ago since his family was murdered, his lineage wiped out. "What happened?"

"There was a plague brought by a trading raft. Half the village passed away – mostly the very old and the very young. But the two older Healers tended everybody and finally they caught the plague too and died. Only their apprentice, our Healer, remained. She was but a girl of thirteen but she went to the task without hesitation and has proved her worth and her skill and her wisdom many times. We all revere her." The man pointed at the little girl who had gone tired of listening to a language that she did not understand and had begun digging thoughtfully in the ground, looking so much like her mother at her work that all the three men just watched her for a while.

"The Healer passes her knowledge onto a daughter. Little Zivah will be the next Healer," one of the Slavs said. Thorbjörn nodded again.

"Can the Healer marry?" he asked innocently.

"Of course she can. It would be a great honor to marry the Healer. She has to have daughters to pass on the knowledge. Better with more daughters than just the one; as even Healers can die. We have all thought about it but nobody has dared to ask her if she would like to take a man. She is a very highly respected woman."

"Has anyone proposed to her?"

"Do you wish to propose to her?"

"I do not know," he smiled. The two men smiled back knowingly.

"She is very lofty," the first one said, "few men would dare approach her with such intentions. She has never been with a villager. Only with visitors. Traders. Her daughter is the child of one traveler, nobody knows his name. Maybe she prefers foreigners. Good for you, Thór-be-yurn!" The three men laughed, and laughed even more when Zivah turned to look suspiciously at them, frowning.

That evening, the Healer returned not only with a bag full of plants and roots for her medicine collection, but also with a deer. It had been killed clean with an arrow to the throat.

"Your kill, Healer?" He asked. She nodded. She looked thoughtful as she studied the carcass and the bag of medicines.

"You look after plants, Healer. I will prepare the… the animal."

"Deer, Thór-be-yurn," she said, smiling, "this animal is called a deer."

"*Deer*. Thank you for the word, Healer. I will prepare the deer."

"It is woman's work," she said, which surprised him.

"I see men do," he objected.

"Sometimes men do women's work," she said, as if so much ought to be obvious, which it was. Even where he came from everybody needed to know everything about how to survive because there could always be times when those you depended upon fell off your life's ship.

"Is it a woman's work to hunt?" he asked. The Healer smiled.

"No, but sometimes women do men's work," she replied.

"You like hunt?"

"I have no man to hunt for me," she said, "All women must know how to hunt. We learned a long time ago that we could not depend on anyone else to hunt for us or our children. We have stories about that, of women who waited in vain for the return of their hunters while their children starved. The men had been killed. Then all the women swore they would learn how to hunt. It was a long time ago. I know that story in a language that everybody else has forgotten. That is how old it is."

He watched her when she told him and realized that she was the most beautiful woman he had ever met. There was a tug in his heart.

"Some men tell me they promise to hunt for wife," he said.

"Yes," she said and met his eyes, looking very serious, "that is the greatest promise a man can give. A woman can afford getting pregnant and look after the little ones if she knows that someone will hunt for them."

"You alone when Zivah born?"

"Yes. And I hunted with her in my belly and her at my breast."

"The villagers - they not hunt for you? You are their Healer."

"They hunt for me but I never ask them to," she said and went to open her medicine bag, "and sometimes they forget that I have extra mouths to feed. You eat a lot, Thór-be-yurn."

He said no more and went to prepare the carcass. And then, to her surprise, he cooked for her. She looked dubiously at the hearth and how he tended the fire and had to admit that he knew his way around.

"Do men work the hearths in Guh-ootah-land?" she asked when she had tasted the meat and smacked loudly in approval of its perfection.

"Gaut often man, no woman, long travel, no woman. Man cooks. Tends fire. Makes clothes. Plant medicine. Man does everything, so man sometimes do woman's work, as you say." The Healer nodded, but frowned when Thunder Bear spoke in his own language; "We Norsemen tend to work our way around just about anything if it can make a good woman happy." Thunder Bear grinned at his own speech. The Healer did not understand the Norse words he had uttered, but settled happily for the way they made her feel.

At first he mostly listened and watched. He struggled a little with understanding how the ranking system of the village worked. Thorbjörn was used to treating people according to their rank, but it was very hard to make out rank here, or to know exactly what rank he had among them at this stage. But it was difficult. He had noticed that everybody averted their eyes before his sacred Mjöllnir pendant, but they seemed to have little consciousness of doing so. Just as he had suspected when he lay in his sickbed and the people came in to stare at him and touch him, they simply did not seem to be that aware of the language of the eyes, and they were far less sensitive about another person's bodily self. It took him a long time to stop being confused when people would sometimes just stare at him without being hostile and challenging. They were not even aware of how rude and threatening that was to him. The men kept, as he would have expected, a respectful distance to him. But he was not certain whether that distance was how they usually behaved or if it was just because they were a bit stunned by him. They seemed a lot more easygoing between themselves. Whenever they looked at him he saw they struggled to conceal their awe. He was a lot taller and bigger and stronger than any of them. Even if they did not know the rules that he had been brought up with, they seemed to instinctively know how to avert and sometimes even lower their eyes to him, although he no longer expected it and always averted his eyes respectfully in return, so as not to imply that he was above them either.

The women were something else entirely. Women, even children, constantly failed to avert their eyes to him as if they did not think he was worthy of respect. But he hid his internal reaction wisely, knowing that their ways were different and that they did not think themselves disrespectful at all when they looked at him as if they were his equals. He had understood that women did not rank beneath men in this place – sometimes he wondered if it was the other way around, even, but he dared not ask in case he offended any of the men, and he could not make up his mind about how this worked. Clearly, the women here were not that shy before strangers as he was used to. Even now that he was walking around in his full height without a stick, the village women failed to be impressed by his powerful stance, at least in the way he was used to. He felt like a boy again, fair game for any woman or girl who wanted to hone him and remind him that he was no warrior yet. It had been so long since the torture games of maidens had been a crucial and all-significant obstacle on his steep path towards manhood. It had been so long since he became a Thunder warrior, so long since he became the head of his clan and an oath-bound Thunder priest.

He was used to being revered. Even when he was reduced to a simple rogue Viking of no standing in the world of laws and men he had been imposing enough to generate respect from other men and submissive politeness from all the women and children he had encountered anywhere, whether they were slaves or free. The women here, they were impressed by him for sure, but they were impressed in the same way they would have been impressed by an exotic beast or a beautiful fabric. Girls would run up to him and touch his back, his arms or his chest just to see what he felt like, and then they would giggle among themselves, right in front of him, as if he was not even there. They did not ask permission to touch him before they just did. Children touched him too, and stared openly at him with gaping mouths. As flattering as it was, their fascination for his largeness, he was not used to women and children treating him like that, and he had to force himself not to snarl and glare at them in return. He was perceptive enough to realize that it was not because they failed to respect him, but because they did not see how touching a man's arm or chest or back like that could be disrespectful. Not to say how they never tired of trying to pull at the braids in his hair and his beard.

While they were *giggling*.

He would just have to accept how they were. He was the outsider and could not make demands of them. Eventually he concluded that the best thing would be to treat almost everybody as equals whether they were men or women or children - although elders and people of special office were indeed treated with a little extra formal politeness. He spoke to everybody all the time. He asked questions and learned their language. He helped out everywhere he saw that he could help, and soon enough got a reputation for general skillfulness. As his former health returned to him, he also proved immensely useful whenever great strength was required. He seemed to possess the strength of many men. A resourceful man, people began to remark. One who could contribute. One they could easily welcome into the village and into the tribe. Like a young man, an outsider must prove his worth.

He had learned a long time ago that when traveling it would always do a man good to ask people about things that he knew they were good at. *Make a stranger talk about something he knows well, and you will soon find that the stranger is your friend*, his father had told him a long time ago. He had always employed this strategy when abroad – until he came among the Rus. When he realized that he was among real Vikings he had shut down and kept to himself. With them he had not cared to make any friends. He had not cared for his well-being or his safety. But even as rogue as they were the Rus *were* his own people after all, and they were all in so many ways outsiders - together. He had minded the ranks, followed his Heri's orders and minded his own business. Nobody really expected more. Unlike in most other lands, where he had found that people constantly chattered and fussed about each other, it was an acceptable trait to be withdrawn among his people. Even if his reserve did not make him many friends, apart from the odd silent company of another man just as withdrawn as himself, such reserve in a man was respected and often considered a sign of both wisdom and trustworthiness. They said Óðinn walked among people that way, silent and listening, like a shadow in the halls. A man who spoke little was less likely to spread gossip and more likely to keep secrets.

As long as he did what he was supposed to do the other Vikings had left him alone – until that day when he remembered his sacred vows and was a Viking no more. He shook off the memories of that fateful day. He could not afford to be withdrawn here. Not when he had been given another chance at life with a people that fascinated him. With a woman that dazzled him. He knew that it meant something, that she was a woman of such an ancient and noble lineage. She carried the wisdom of her foremothers as surely as he carried that of his forefathers, an ancestral lore that reached back thousands of years. They were meant to meet. He was meant to stay here. He had to adapt.

Whenever he got tired he withdrew to the sauna under the pretext of still being tired after his sickness. As soon as he had gathered strength he made it his mission to fit in and be liked. He remembered his father Thorgrim's words: "*People like to feel that they are good at something and they like people who appreciate their skill and want to learn from them because they feel recognized. And pay attention to their language and the way they speak and think and act. The more you speak and think and act like them, the better will they like you and respect you. This is very important when you travel, son, when you find yourself among people whose customs are different from what you know. Then you must grasp the reigns of your own ways and open your eyes and ears. Then it is more important than ever to make friends. You will have no brothers and sisters out there, no people to call for help. You must* **make** *kinsmen when you are traveling.*"

And Thorbjörn smiled and laughed despite himself when women casually touched him, made funny antics when people stared at him, played with the children, respected the cats and talked amiably with everyone, and minded his manners around the elders. He showed an interest in everything they did and learned their language swiftly and with obvious eagerness. He left everybody feeling so very… *capable* at something or other.

He never revealed to the Thunder priest that he knew far more about Thunder than the old man could ever have suspected. He let him keep his respected position and treated him reverently and kindly just like everybody else did. Thorbjörn even had him sing the songs of Pērkons to him, and never told him of the songs that *he* knew. The old priest was so flattered by Thunder Bear's interest in the lore of Pērkons and the rites he conducted in honor of the Oak Man that he started to think of Thunder Bear as his apprentice, the one who would take his place eventually. And Thunder Bear humbly listened to the river people's lore about the god that he had been born to serve, accepted the old priest's teachings and said nothing of his own powers or of the knowledge carried by his lineage.

Thorbjörn proved his skills and contributed. He hunted and fished and made all sorts of tools, prepared the hides and the furs and learned the arts of beekeeping and amber gathering and oil making. He showed his skills at making boats and rafts and all sorts of construction. He cut wood more effectively than any other man in the village. He paid particular attention to everything that needed mending or improving in the house of the Healer where he still lived. And he let Zivah call him "father" and treated her as if she was his daughter in return. It was not difficult to love her. She was so very much like the seven daughters that he had lost.

It did not take him long to be generally well liked. And somehow, the Healer never asked him to move out of her sauna to make a home elsewhere. One night they could not sleep. He was sitting upright in his bed within the sauna and heard the soft sound of her steps in the room next door. She looked in through the gap of the door and mimicked the sound for "infusion". He smiled and nodded. She came over to him and squatted down with two mugs of warm drink. They sipped their cups thoughtfully and watched each other.

"You are my Sun, Healer. You make Thunder Bear rise like Dawn must rise in the presence of the Sun mother's glorious rays."

She smirked at his words.

"I can see that," she said approvingly, "it is practically Midday already."

"I want you. I will hunt for you," he said quietly when he put the cup down. She just nodded and fell into his arms.

A long time after, she was snuggling in that bear-like embrace. She met his eyes.

"You are so small and tender," he said fondly.

"It is just because you are bear-sized," she said contentedly.

"You have eyes like a doe, my Saulé. How can a doe rule a bear like you do?"

“I am a doe and a she-wolf too, Thunder Bear. I am fierce.”

“I know that now, Doe-Eyes,” he teased, “A doe she is when she walks among people, a she-wolf she has for her secret face.”

“You make poetry in our language now, Gah-oot?”

“I make poetry in any language accessible to me, Doe-Eyes. And I want to hunt for you.”

“I can hunt as well as you can, Gah-oot! Or does your people not approve of women hunting?”

“I like a woman who can hunt as well as any other man,” he said, “it is just that they told me the words. I have to promise that I will hunt for you if you are to be my wife. You said it was the greatest promise a man could make to a woman. I want to make you the greatest promise. I swear that I will hunt for you, even if you want to hunt right there with me.”

“Then I will cook for you,” she said drowsily, because they were the proper words.

She never asked him about the Rus.

Thunder Goddess

I was born eight years after Thorbjörn my father came to the river land village. Before I was born, Thunder Bear and the Healer, my parents, had a daughter born one year after he came to the village, conceived of that first night they spent together as man and wife. Two years after that there was a boy. But not long after he was born, an illness swept through the village, and for all her skills the Healer, my mother, could not save her two youngest children. Fifteen people died that year. My parents and little Zivah grieved heavily, but after two more years the Healer gave birth to Thorolf my brother. The villagers thought his foreign name was as difficult to pronounce as the name of his father, and just like they called the father Thunder Bear in their language, so they called the son Thunder Wolf, because that was what his name meant in their language.

Two years after Thunder Wolf, I was born, seven days before the Summer Solstice. The night when my mother went into labor to give me the light of day there was a terrible thunderstorm. My father, who had always heeded the village customs before, suddenly declared that he did not care about the rules that said no men could be present at a birthing. Where he was from, he said, knowing how to perform all the basic acts of survival was something both men and women had to learn, and surely a man could suddenly find himself alone with a laboring woman and then what good would he be if he knew nothing of childbirth? The women raised their eyebrows and looked at each other, wondering what kind of world he had lived in where men could so frequently find themselves utterly alone with a laboring woman that all men learned the art of midwifery. But it was true what my father told them. What he did not say was his real reason for declaring his midwifing skills just at this point. His wife had told him that she thought it was a girl in her womb this time. She had guessed right about the child's gender for each of her three previous births and had told him that she knew that Zivah was a girl from the moment she was conceived. Thorbjörn knew that he was going to have another daughter.

He had considered all his known female children, the ones that he had named. There had been the two daughters he had had with Halldís his wife and the one he had begotten from the Sacred Night as well as the daughter he had begot with that Finnish woman and the daughter he had by his concubine Rannveig. Then he counted in the twin daughters born later by his sister Thora, whom he counted as his daughters even if they were not of his seed. It was no longer the custom at large but the Thunder priests had always minded the tradition, and as the two girls were born by his father's as well as his mother's daughter, he rightly counted them as parts of his direct lineage. When Thora had the twins outside of wedlock he had knee-set them and named them like a father would, and they carried his name as did the daughters of his own seed. And then there was the one girl that the Healer had born him who died along with the newborn son. All his six-and-two daughters had died, but there had been eight of them all together, just as surely as Thorolf had been the third son.

It was his ninth daughter who was about to be born, and she was to be born seven days before the Summer Solstice, and she was to be born during a Thunder storm. She would be the last daughter of the Thunder priest line. He knew what this meant. He *had to* be there to look for the signs.

*

Just as the night's thunder storm abated and dawn rose again, on the seventh day before the Summer Solstice, I was born into the presence of my sister Zivah, my father Thorbjörn and the three Fire women, and of course my mother the Healer. My sister was just about to receive me when our father's hands brushed her away and took me into his great hands. He looked at me and met my eyes, eyes too alert for a newborn babe, the dark blue frame around the rinds of my irises and the pale blue that almost seemed white. He saw that I had the eyes and then he examined the mark that the great lord had left above my heart. It was in the shape of a Thunderbolt hammer.

"Mjöllnir," he whispered in his own language, "my daughter has Mjöllnir on her heart." He kissed me. "You are welcome, Thordís, you are so very welcome back into this world of songs." The tears were running down his cheeks as he smiled. "Her name is Thunder Goddess," he declared, not even bothering to ask my mother. He held me high and spoke out thunderously in our Norse language; "Hear me oh lord of Thunder, hear your Thunder priest. Hear me all gods and all goddesses and the mighty mother Earth. Hear me now for I am of your lineage: My name is Thorbjörn Thorgrimsson Thorsgóði. I am descended from Thordís the Thunder priestess and the great Smith of Heaven. I am descended from the lineage of the Thunder priests that once ruled the land they now call Gautland. I was the last of my line, but I have survived, and I have prospered, and I have had a son. And now I have a daughter as well. She is the ninth daughter and he is the third son. I have begotten two children to carry on the Red Gold of the Thunder priests."

He raised his voice further as he set me on his knee; "I declare to the norns and the gods and everyone present that this child is my daughter and that I am Thorbjörn her father. Her mother is a holy woman among the East-landers and carries the blood and spirit of an ancient and most noble lineage. This child is our daughter. I declare that her name is Thordís and that she is a Thorsgyðja like she was the first time that she was born. Behold the Thunder goddess. Behold this little Thunder priestess. She is my most ancient mother and she has returned into my hands as my daughter. I am honored. The Thunder priestess has returned and she has my protection and my guidance for as long as I remain alive, and then beyond."

When he finally gave me over to the attending women, Thorbjörn looked at his wife and his stepdaughter and was surprised to see that Zivah was weeping. The child saw his surprise and broke out in another fit of tears, turned around and fled the room. Father looked at the Healer with eyebrows raised.

"You took her charge from her," she said gently, "She is ten, and this was her first time to be a midwife. I had promised it to her. She had so looked forward to receiving her sister."

"I am sorry, my love."

"Tell that to Zivah."

"My love, Zivah is a child. I cannot apologize to her when I was doing something I had to do."

"Why not?"

"It is just how I was raised. I will try to explain it to her though, if that helps."

"It might," my mother said quietly and looked thoughtfully at her husband, who had already turned his attention back to his new and special new daughter Thordís. Me. Then he remembered his charge and turned to leave the room. Before he parted he turned to speak another command; "Her name is Thordís, wife. It means Thunder Goddess in your language. I will tell you more later."

The women gaped after him as he left. Nobody had ever heard of such impertinence from a husband. To think that he would just name the child without even consulting the mother! And more importantly, come to think of it, without consulting *them*, the women who brought forth the prayers of people to the gods and received their approving or disapproving signs. Not even they had been asked. But the Healer looked to them and said; "You heard him. This is her name; *Thór-dees*. It means Thunder Goddess in his language."

"Maybe we shall just call her Pērkoné," the oldest Fire woman said snappily, "like a female Pērkons." The other women nodded grudgingly. "*Pērkoné Dieviete*," another Fire woman tried and almost shuddered. "It seems blasphemous, to call a girl "goddess," the third volunteered, and they all looked challengingly at my mother.

"Then call her Thór-dees," my mother said, feeling tired.

"What eyes the little one has!" the youngest Fire woman suddenly exclaimed.

"She has the Thunderbolt on her chest," the oldest Fire woman said quietly. All three of them went quiet. Hushed and serious they watched the sacred shape that had been marked on my chest, right above my heart. There was no misunderstanding an omen like that, even if they did not know exactly what it meant. It was a mark of divine possession.

"I think your husband knows things, Younger Sister," the oldest finally spoke, gazing searchingly at my mother.

"My husband knows things, Old Sister," the Healer said calmly and slept.

My mother's people called me Thunder Goddess in their language, because that is what my name means. But my father always called me the same in our own language. My name was Thordís Thorbjörnsdaughter Thorsgyðja. I was the first and the last Thunder priestess.

The Legend of the Thunder Warriors

Thorbjörn found Zivah down by the river. “Daughter,” he said, and drew his breath. He had not even considered apologizing until he saw that vulnerable back of his stepdaughter as she was kneeling on the shore and looking into the water.

“I am so sorry I took your charge, Zivah. I did not mean to offend you,” he said.

“Why did you do it?” she whispered, still looking away into the running river.

“It was a ritual, my daughter. I had to do it. I was so excited I forgot that it was your first birthing. I should have told you beforehand, so you would have understood.”

“You did not do it with the others. You stayed out with the men and sang and drummed like men are… are *supposed to do*.”

“Where I am from little girls do not tell men what they are supposed to do. But never mind that. I acted differently because this is a different matter. All men think their own children are special, but this child, this girl – she actually *is* special. She deserved the welcome that I have always been oath-bound to give her.”

“Why?”

“It is a long story, Zivah. I will tell it to you, but I want to tell it to your mother and Thorolf at the same time. Will you come home? If your mother has the strength for it I shall tell the story tonight.”

*

That first evening of my life, while my mother nursed me at her breast and Thorolf my brother snuggled into her arms and Zivah tended the fire, Thorbjörn told them the Song of the Thunder Goddess. “I come from an enormous island on the other side of the ocean northwest of these river lands,” my father began. He was standing, like all Norsemen do when they tell stories, standing so that he could gesture and move and give life to the song. His family stared at him with big wondrous eyes, even I who could not yet understand any human speech, even Thorolf who was surely too little to understand. But we could all behold in wonder the dancing figure of our father the Thunder Bear and let our souls be carried away by the deep rumbling voice he used to create the beat of his stories. He could tell his stories as well in his wife’s language now as he could in his own, and could pay heed to both rhythm and rhyme.

"We call your lands Estland; that means East Land, because you live to the east of us. Our island has been called by many names; by many tribal names and by poetical calling names. We think of her as a goddess, our land, and as the path to the northernmost end of the broad-faced Earth. In the southernmost tip of the main island lies my tribal country, Gautland."

"A long time ago now, my tribe, the Gautar, was being attacked from the north by a tribe called the Svear. The Svear won through deceit and trickery, having our entire royal line wiped out. Zivah, that royal lineage what vanished was descended from the great Bee Wolf."

"I love the story of the Bee Wolf," Zivah said, temporarily softening up to that mindless stepfather who taken her charge.

"I know, but this is not the story of Bee Wolf the Gaut and the monster-slayer. This is the story of my lineage, a lineage known as the Thunder Warriors, or else as the Thunder priests. Our lineage has lived in those lands of the southeastern fold of North Path Island for a long time before the Gautar came. I come from a lineage that trace their ancestry back to these people who lived in our lands long before the Gautar came. Wife, I know that you know songs in a forgotten language, in a language that only you and our lineage still remember." The Healer nodded.

"I have been told that your ancestors, through your mother line, count their lineage from the people who spoke that language, the people who lived in these lands before anybody else did."

"My people began living here after the Great Winter of old," mother said.

"And so did my ancestors live in North Path Island countless of ages past. They too spoke of a Great Winter." Their eyes met.

"I have often thought that many of the words that we use and many of the gods and powers that we know of, as well as their sacred songs, they are so similar among your people and among mine that I think we must descend from a common stock, far, far back in time," Thorbjörn said, "and I think that the ancient language of the Healers that you still know songs in, wife, is akin to a language of ancient days that I also know songs in."

"When a tribe of our ancestral people first came to the North Path Island, they found there Finnish people who lived in tents and who hunted the great herds of animals across the plains, the mountains and the forests. But there was plenty of space on North Path Island and my ancestors settled on the empty shores and built there ships and boats with which they explored the rivers and islands and fjords while their families tilled their crops in the valleys. They brought with them an ancient lore of knowledge that has often been referred to as the Red Gold. And the song-carriers of their time used that lore to construct great stone temples, remains of which stand to this very day all over Gautland my country and in many other parts of the North Path Island."

"The stone temple builders who carried the lore of the Red Gold knew countless things that are now forgotten; secrets about the nature of our mother Earth and the nature of the oceans and the stars and the celestial siblings. And they knew the secrets of Thunder. From this knowledge they could work marvels. It is said that they came from an ancient tribe of people that has moved all over the face of holy Earth. They pursued wisdom and knowledge rather than riches and pleasure. They considered themselves gardeners of the holy mother of all natures. They took care of the land and the people."

"The era of the stone temple builders of the North Path Island lasted for more than twenty man's ages, a thousand turns of the Sun goddess and perhaps even much more than that. But then the world started to change. There were great waves that flooded large parts of the North Path Island and created new oceans that had not been there before. Many wise people died then, and many others turned to savagery. In other lands there were great changes too, and tribe after tribe of folks from the eastern steppes and mountain plateaus moved westwards and northwards in search of a place to settle, for their homelands had become inhabitable, or famine had led them to move."

"Then a tribe from the east came to settle in many of the northern lands. From the languages that I have heard spoken, wife, and from the way they share so many similarities and so many sacred stories in common - I think that this tribe passed through these river lands before they came to the Northern shores. And on their way they blended with the people who lived there, whether it was by force or by friendship. Then they came to North Path Island and found the last surviving priests and priestesses of the Red Gold there, the leaders of the people who had survived the floods; my ancestral people. The eastern newcomers were impressed by our knowledge and when they found that they were better off as our friends than as our enemies they made truce with us. The tribes married into each other and became one people. They and we together became what we call ourselves today, Norsemen. It means Northern Men, because we think of ourselves as the northernmost people in the known world."

"We have similar songs of the olden times," Mother said.

"I know, wife. Our ancestors of many roots have crossed paths before as surely as their branches have crossed paths in our time."

"Please continue your tale, husband. Are you listening, Zivah? This is the same story I told you, told to us by a man from the other side of the great ocean. Can you now see how the songs are true?"

Zivah nodded meekly, and Father continued his tale.

"It was during this era when the new and the old peoples of North Path Island were still getting used to each other that my ancestral mother was born. She was born to an ancient family of Stone Temple Priests, to a mother and a father who both knew parts of the lore of the Red Gold. Nobody knew the entire body of the lore any longer, but even that which had been forgotten was carried on in sacred songs encoded with all the knowledge that was needed, secret riddle songs that were easy to remember even by children, yet carved with invisible runes, symbols waiting to be decoded. The ancestors had created those hidden runes in songs because they saw too many people seek great power, people who possessed not the wisdom or the responsibility to carry such power. They saw that those who are greed-ridden will never be able to muster enough dedication to try and solve the riddles, and so they made riddles that only the most dedicated students would ever be able to grasp, if they had fortune with them."

"The girl who was born then was the ninth daughter of her father, who was a priest of the Wind. She was the third daughter of her mother, who was a priestess of the Sun. Her mother went into labor on a night ridden by thunder and storm, and gave birth at dawn when the storm abated, seven days before the Summer Solstice. They said she had the eyes of a she-wolf and that she was aware like an adult, and that she carried the mark of the Thunder lord above her heart. They called her Thunder Goddess. That was her name. In the Norse language she has been remembered as Thordís." He paused and turned his attention to the newborn babe. They all looked at me with wonder. But before they could ask any questions, Thorbjörn continued: "On the day of the Summer Solstice, when Thordís was seven days old, a very tall man with a hooded cloak approached her and said that it was the will of the weaving ladies that he passed on his songs to the Thunder Goddess at that very moment. Her parents said that she was much too young to receive the sacred songs. Then the Oracle who had come with him, a famous Wand Witch, interfered and said that this child was not an ordinary child but a goddess, an ancient and powerful goddess that had risen out of Death. The Wand Witch said that this goddess had a sacred destiny to fulfil before she could return to her divinity, and that she would born and reborn until she had fulfilled her fate. When her fate was fulfilled, then the age of war that had already begun to bear bitter fruits would be over."

"And then her parents stepped back and let the tall man sing the ancient songs to their daughter in the ancient language, and then he sang them in the new language. And the babe listened and watched the man with her icy blue wolf eyes and did not make a sound and did not fall asleep before he had finished the song. They said it took him three days and nights, and yet the babe listened."

"It is said that one afternoon, as the little Thunder Goddess was walking through a field, the Thunder lord chose her, and struck his hammer at her. She was only seven years old, but our lord claimed her. She was penetrated by lightning, striking right down through the crown of her head, its Power running through her entire body and into holy Earth. When she fell over, her family thought she would surely die. But Thordís did not die. Her spirit soared through the skies for nine days and nights, while her body lay sleeping in the cot where her people tended her. Her soul was carried by the lord Thunderer and taken through all the realms and met all the gods face to face, and she was allowed to see behind their masks. Then the great lord returned her to her body, and when she woke up, she knew all the secrets of Thunder."

"She was a child then, and could not add words to her knowledge, but as she grew she explored the things that her lord had shown her when she was in the power of his Lightening, and then the songs that she had been given on her seventh day of life began to sing themselves within her mind, and she began to decode that which had long been forgotten. Little by little she knew all the secrets of Thunder that had come through that ancient lineage of Red Gold carriers."

"When she became a young woman, and her family wanted her to marry, she told them that no man could marry her, for she belonged to the lord of Thunder. They pressed her of course, pleaded with her, tried to persuade her. She must carry on the family lineage, they said, for she was their only daughter, and the lineages moved through the mother line among us in those days, just as it does among you still. But Thordís kept refusing each suitor who sought a place at her hearth until her family began to chide her for her selfishness."

"Then Thordís went to the ancient stone temple that her parents tended to, and prayed. She prayed for day and nights on end, until a great thunderstorm broke out and made the temple and the whole Earth tremble. As the dark and thunderous clouds parted during night, she saw a great man emerge from them, his eyes like lightening, and his hair reaching out in all directions with rays of red light. The lord of Thunder was taking the shape of a man before her eyes, and asked if she would offer herself to him. Thordís accepted the charge and placed herself on the great stone altar, laying down on it, offering up herself as a sacrifice. They say the lord came to her then, on the altar, and entered her. Then his power and his knowledge was hers, and she became his Síf, that is, a woman under his protection, like a sister, or a wife, or a daughter. Ever since, every Thunder priestess in our lineage has been a Síf to Thor, a woman under the protection of the Thunder lord."

They all looked at me again.

"Is… is that word, *Seef*, is it how you say Žemyna?" Mother asked.

"After a fashion," he said, "but Žemyna is what you mostly call holy Earth, while we call Sífs all our kinswomen and all the women and girls that we swear to protect. And yet we can also refer to the Earth as our Síf, for she is our most ancient kinswoman."

"What happened to that, to that Thunder *Seef*," Zivah asked. Thorbjörn proceeded: "Thordís Thorsgyðja – the latter means Thunder priestess and was her given title – she birthed two children who became the mother and the father of a great lineage. Her children carried on the ancient Red Gold that their mother had revived in her lifetime, carried that lore and the wisdoms and power of that lore, down through her descendants. We believe, for many good reasons, that Thordís has guided us all ever since, whether it was as a bodily incarnation of herself or as a following spirit. That knowledge, the Red Gold, it is of a kind that can take a man or a woman to the sphere of the gods and beyond, but it could also be employed in the world for protection. The Thunder Goddess showed her descendants how to invoke and how to bear and how to wield the Power of Thunder within themselves. Her son Magni wielded that power and one of his grandsons was Thorarinn, the first Thunder Warrior. He knew the Power of Thunder as his ancestors had taught him, and when his enemies descended upon his people he learned ever so swiftly and with devastating results how to channel that thunderous Power in battle."

"Devastating?" Mother said, frowning. She thought her husband had sounded remarkably proud when he spoke of devastating results.

"Devastating to their enemies, of course," her husband said, and she was surprised to see how content he looked when he said that. For a moment she even thought that he would beat his chest. He did that sometimes, when he was alone or only with her. She remembered the first time they hunted together and he roared and beat his chest when he brought down the bear that had been harassing their beehives for quite a while. She had hushed at him and told him that he must never act like that before any other villagers.

"Why not?" He had asked her then.

"Because you seem… proud," she had replied.

"I *am* proud," he objected, "I just killed a bear, woman. Should I not be proud?"

"Well you may be happy about it but you cannot show off like that. It is rude, and disrespectful to Medeinė the Forest mother. She loves all her wild children and it is by her grace that she sends game in our ways. There is nothing to be proud of."

"I just took down a *bear*!" he had exclaimed, exasperated.

"You ended the life of another living being," the Healer had stated, as a matter of fact, "if there is any appropriate feeling to go with that it would be to be grateful for the gift and for the fact that the game was not you."

"Your people are a bunch of puny softies," he had replied grudgingly, "and now I can see why it is so."

Despite himself, he had never beaten his chest in anybody else's presence after that first blunder. He had learned to pretend that the game he brought down was something of an afterthought that had happened during that nice day in the forest and for which he would give thanks to the Lady of the Forest. But one day she had come over him while he stood inside the Oak Grove and thought himself undetected. He had just finished making his offerings when he suddenly threw back his head and roared like thunder, beating his chest repeatedly. His eyes had shone afterwards and she had seen the wildness that he used to conceal in the presence of her and all her people. He seemed closer to himself. And then she had walked up to her husband, touched his arm and said, "Thunder Bear. You must observe the village customs, but I want you to know that I embrace the whole of you."

Now she wondered what the whole of him really was. Thorbjörn met her gaze.

"We did not live in these peaceful river lands, wife," he said darkly. "At the time of the first Thunder Warrior the first Age of War had begun. Then like now there seemed to be but three options for the people of our northern island: To win, to die, or to become slaves, serfs, hunted game in our own ancestral lands. We saw it happen back then just as we have continued to see it happen over and over, for thousands of turns of the Sun. Those who cannot defend themselves must flee or else be killed or captured. Those who flee become hunted, fair game. Those who are captured are taken as slaves. Those who are defeated become a lesser class of people. Only those who know how to fight and win can survive and live well. We had to harden the shields of our heartstones in order to protect our Sífs and our children. We had to learn how to take pride in killing an enemy, learn to take pride in receiving scars. We had to learn that because we saw that without that pride we would perish, because without that pride we would be weakened by the horror of carnage and death. We had to make friends with the game of blood and death if we were to be able to channel the power. And so we made Death into our most beloved goddess, and adored her in all her shapes, and even if she came as an old and terrifying hag not one among us would hesitate to kiss her passionately."

"You see, wife, we *had* to become warriors. Even then we were among the last people who remembered the lore of the Red Gold. Our foremother knew that we had to learn how to channel divine power in battle if we were to survive as a clan, and more importantly if we were to protect the sacred lore. Her son was the first warrior to use that power, and he taught it to his sons, as it has been taught from father to son ever after."

"Do you… do *you* know how to channel that power?" Zivah asked, and her mother tried to hide her smile by turning her attention down at my newborn face and pale blue gaze, humming. The Healer was not entirely surprised at the revelation and he did not have to reply. Wife and husband smiled conspiratorially at each other and Zivah looked a little confused.

"Yes, Zivah, I have seen Thunder Bear channel that power. I have seen it when he took down the bear and when… Well, he can control that power and he channels it when he has use for it in any… in any way he wants," our mother said vaguely, and Zivah nodded uncertainly. Thorbjörn, grinning only a little, returned to his tale.

"Thordís' lineage grew and prospered and became a tribe, known for their red hairs and their ice blue eyes and the mighty stance and large frame of their menfolk, as well as for the wisdom and magical powers of their womenfolk. We were called the Thunder Warriors then, while we were still a tribe. Then our worldly powers faded before the might of the Gaut clan, a clan that also grew and became a tribe of its own. Eventually, the Gautar ruled the lands and named it Gautland.

But the Thunder Warriors survived as a powerful clan within Gautland and continued to carry on the sacred lore of the Red Gold of the Thunderer. We became known as the clan of the Thunder priests. When I grew up, I and my sister were the two descendants of our generation that were to become clan leaders. I have told you of the customs of my land and I have told you that the rule at large is to count all lineages through the father line. But within the clan of the Thunder Priests we followed both lines. We followed the mother line that descends directly from the daughter born to Thordís by the great Thunder Smith, a woman called Thrúð. Her name means Power in your language. And we followed the father line that descends directly from her son Magni as well. His name means Greatness in your language."

"This happened because the ancient people of the stone temples had followed the mother line where the newcomers followed the father line, and nobody could agree on which was best, so they made an array of compromises. Within our lineage, Thordís decreed that we should follow both lines simultaneously and make sure that the father line and the mother line sometimes came together and recreated the strength of our direct line. This was because we carry the blood of the Thunderer in our veins and must strengthen that blood as often as we thought responsible. In each given generation, a daughter of the mother line and a son of the father line would unite in a ritual we call the Sacred Nights, and if those nights bore fruit the child would belong to the whole clan and be destined to be the next Thunder priest or Thunder priestess. In each generation there would be a girl and a boy chosen for this purpose and they would both lead the clan, each leading the clan from within their own spheres, as appropriate to man and woman respectively. My sister and I were born together as twins from the Sacred Nights. It was unusual that the two chosen ones were siblings, usually they would be distant cousins. But we were both chosen, Thora and I."

"When we came of age, our father Thorgrim died and we took our places in the High Seat of the Hall of the Thunder priests. There had been a daughter from the Sacred Night, and I had knee-set her and named her as my daughter. That is how fathers acknowledge our children where I come from. When I became the head of the clan, I married a woman called Halldís. She bore me two daughters and a son, and I knee-set them all. I also had a… a… you do not have a word for it. An extra wife."

"An extra wife?"

"Yes. A woman of lower standing than the man, one who will be content with being a second wife. We call them concubines. Her name was Rannveig. I gave her a house over by a harbor town where I used to go to conduct business and swore to her that she would have my protection and that I would care for her and her children."

"Did you not love your wife, the one called *Haahl-dees*?" Mother asked.

"I loved Halldís my wife very much. She was beautiful and wise and a marvelous wife. We were great friends and quite passionate about each other, although perhaps not quite as passionate as you and I."

"Then why did you take another woman?"

"Why, I traveled a lot. It was nice to have a woman there too. And I loved Rannveig well."

Mother had looked a little astonished, my sister told me many years later. "But did they not *mind* each other?" she finally asked.

"They were quite good friends, actually. They used to visit each other too. They were childhood friends and now that they had become, ah, another word you do not have, but when our women share a man they call each other *Elja*. It is a bit like saying sister or cousin, in the sense of admitting that they are related."

"*Related*?"

"Well their wombs receive the same seed. That is a way of being related," Thorbjörn explained patiently, oblivious of the expression of disbelief that sometimes passed across his wife's face. "In any case, my wife was of a very high and noble family and Rannveig was just another peasant's daughter, but they had played together all their childhood and when I asked Rannveig if she wanted to be my concubine, both my wife and she were thrilled because as Eljur they got an excuse to dally together as friends and equals. Almost equals, in any case. Equal enough to openly maintain a friendship. They were also good friends with my sister Thora and did not mind that her daughter was also mine, and when Thora had twin daughters by another man and refused to say who he was, I knee-set my sister's children and called them my own, like any full brother would. My wives even accepted the girl that was presented to us by a Finnish woman that I had, uh, visited. She was just going to guide me across some mountain plateaus one winter, and then we had to take shelter from a storm that lasted more than three days, so who could blame us anyway?"

He did not pause to hear what my mother thought of that before he continued; "Nine months later the Finnish woman showed up with a babe on her arm. My women had been buying charms from that woman for years so they liked her well and saw that her daughter was red-haired like me. When they came together and demanded that I take responsibility, I knee-set the girl and called her my daughter too, and all of my women were happy. I was now the father of seven daughters and bound to protect four women, who in turn were bound to provide for me, and everybody was content. My head sometimes hurt from all the birdlike chatter in my halls, but a wise man makes sure to choose for himself women who like each other, who can meet and enjoy each other's company."

"Is that so," Mother murmured, almost speechless, "well, I hope you will choose wisely then, husband, because I have a hard time imagining that I could ever accept such relations."

Thorbjörn broke out into a broad smile; "My Saulé, I have known so many women! It is with you that my soul sings. And I know your customs, my love. I would not offend you with another. It is just that our customs are different in North Path Island. It is common for a powerful man to have more than one woman. And our women are not brought up in a way that allows for much jealousy. I can assure you that my wife and my concubines were very happy about the arrangements."

"Do not forget your sister!" the Healer snapped, and added drily; "Maybe they were just happy to get some peace and quiet every odd night."

"Can we hear the rest of the story?" said Zivah impatiently, and Thorbjörn, somewhat red of color all of a sudden, continued his tale;

"I will tell you this, wife, that there was laughter in our hall. Often enough all the three mothers of my children gathered together in my hall with all our children. I still remember their laughter when they played around there all day. I had one son and seven daughters altogether, but because they came from different mothers not one of my eight children was above the age of six when they were killed."

"Your children were *killed*?" Zivah asked, horrified.

"The kings of the Svear who ruled our country had spent generations trying to wipe out every remnant of the royal Gaut clan – the clan that had descended from Bee-Wolf Dragon slayer. But even when there was not one single descendant of that royal clan left, the warlike Gautar refused to accept foreign rule. Many insurgents operated in secret, looking around for other candidates. They looked for a suitable clan to place in the High Seat of all Gautland. And soon enough their eyes turned towards the Thunder priest lineage, and the stories of our former greatness and the tribe of the Thunder Warriors began to flourish where they had before only been whispered. Hooded men approached me in the night, suggesting that I, the Thunder priest and the leader of our clan, should accept the High Seat and establish a royal Gaut dynasty that was both new and ancient."

"They wanted you to become their… their *King*?" Zivah gasped.

"Yes, that was what they wanted. But I did not wish to be anybody's king." He sighed; "It did not matter to the King of the Svear that I had refused to lead the new Gaut insurgence. All that mattered to him was that I and my lineage had been singled out as the most likely royal candidate to the High Seat of the Gautar. Our lineage had, by all ancient laws, precedence before any Svear king. This Svear king was not even a real Svear, a usurper of that ancient Svear High Seat, but what did it matter? He sent his people out for us. We did not know. We were not given any warning, and there was no way we could have been prepared for anything like what happened, at that time." Thorbjörn's face seemed to have gone grey like ashes. His family sat quietly and waited until he was ready to continue.

"It was during the Sacrifice to the Elves, when the nights grow long, where we honor the spirits of our ancestors before the winter comes just like you also do, in the hope that they will stay benevolent towards us during the time of cold and darkness when their powers are great. The spirits want to be remembered, and may get angry if we fail to honor them. It is a time when all the families gather, and no outsiders are welcome into the houses, lest they offend the sacred peace and the communion with the ancestors. We had all gathered in the great hall, my wife and my concubine and our children, my sister, our cousins, parents, grandparents, uncles and aunts, nieces and nephews. All of us had gathered as we had always done at this celebration. It was a gathering of the entire Thunder priest clan by the Hall that had been built close to the burial mound of our ancestral mother and the ancient stone temple where she had received the Thunderer. It was a wonderful celebration, as it always is in a family where the members love and cherish each other."

"We had eaten and drunk together, and I was lying in bed next to my wife that night, when the image of our clan Follower, the first Thordís, appeared before my inner eye and spoke from within my secret ear. She told me to go outside into the night and sit on the mound where they say she had been buried. For there were great events about to happen, she said, and she needed me there, at her mound, to show me something of importance."

"And so I got up from the bed, I dressed and armed myself, and went outside in the night. There was a full Moon that night, so I did not light any fires, and I went in the light of the great Moon god to the burial mound of our clan's mother. I sat down there, and prayed, and waited to be shown what she had said she would show me. Little did I know of how the Svear spies held it in them even to disregard that most sacred of nights."

"Suddenly I heard the sounds of men and horses moving through the darkness. They did not see me, as I sat quietly upon the mound, hidden by the shadows of the great oak trees that surrounded the sacred burial mound, and I did not move to do anything, because I understood that they were too many. I wanted to get up and run towards the hall, I wanted to warn them, shout, make them come out of the hall, but something kept me seated there, as if a power greater than me had paralyzed me, and I saw only how the hall was set ablaze with fire. I watched and listened then as my women, our children, my sister and our daughter, and all my family and lineage died, screaming, within the burning hall of our ancestors."

Silence followed while Zivah and our mother struggled to even conceive of such loss and such cruelty. Father was pale now, his face wet with tears, and his eyes appeared to be burning, as if the fire he had seen had imprinted itself in his eyes. But he drew his breath and finished his story.

"I knew then that our clan Follower had chosen me, and only me, to survive for reasons I could not yet fathom. I was the only living member of the family, apart from very distant relatives no longer attached to the legacy. Our clan had perished after thousands of years of glory. I stayed hidden in the grove come dawn, watching as the murderers inspected the charred remains of the hall and the people who had died within. They tried to find me among the dead, but could not. What happened later is a long and sad story, and it is not to be told this night. The only thing I will tell you is that while I lived in exile, before I came here, I met a very old and very wise woman. She knew many things and possessed tremendous powers. They called her the Hel Rune. It is an ancient title that means several things at once. But essentially, it means Death Goddess in your language. As I told you before, my people learned to embrace that goddess a long time ago, and her love for us in return has made us into powerful warriors. One day as I was walking by the burial mounds of that place this old and very holy woman came before me and asked me whether I was seeking her cold embrace already. I looked at her and said that I saw no reason not to. Then she grinned at me and invited me to sit down before her as she cast her lots for me. I sat down before the old one and listened to her prophecy. She looked at me with her ancient eyes and said that I would find a far softer embrace if I kept on living. But before I could find that embrace I would have to see the truth about myself and remember my vows of old. If I could do that, she said, then there would come a time in my life when I would give seed to the birth of a… a very special sort of woman. Then she told me that on the seventh day before the Summer Solstice, my ninth but only daughter would be born at dawn after a terrible thunder storm, and she would possess the eyes of the she-wolf and the mark of the Thunder lord. The child would be Thordís my clan mother, reborn to fulfil her fate, reborn just as her entire lineage had perished to secure the continuance of the Red Gold."

Father looked at me, passionate now; "This is her, my wife. My children; this is Thunder Goddess who has rejoined our mortal ranks. She is my ninth yet only daughter and she came with all the signs. Can you now see what this little girl means to me? Can you forgive me for greeting her in my own way, Zivah?"

There was a long silence. Then Zivah spoke with strained and trembling voice, a sharp pitched tune: "Why, if your, if your *only daughter* is a, is a, a *goddess*… then there is no wonder why you did not think that *I* was worthy of receiving her."

And with those words Zivah went brusquely to her sleeping cot, where Thorolf had already been placed, and rolled over on her side with her back to her parents. Our parents calmly ignored her, never suspecting that her reaction came from any deeper pain than a child's temporary fit of jealousy until it was too late to dig it out with the root.

Fatherless

The Healer had always been blessed with quite easy births and swift recovery after. By the last day before the Summer Solstice she was up and ready to go into the forest searching for plants, having wrapped me up at her back. She called for Zivah to join her, but my sister shook her head and said she had other plans.

"*Other plans*?" Mother asked, incredulous.

"The other girls are going to work with the cutting out of clothes today. They are going to work down by the river. I have thought to join them."

"You have more than enough clothes, daughter. We need to take these roots today before the Sun turns. I have never showed you how it is done. They are very fragile and we need them. Let us go."

"No, mother, I do not want to go. I have no intention of becoming the next Healer."

The Healer stared at her daughter with her wide doe eyes, not quite believing that the words of her daughter had really been spoken. "Zivah," she whispered, "how can you say this? You have always followed me. You are the next Healer. You know that."

"There is no law that says I have to. Why can I not just be like any other girl? When am I ever going to enjoy myself with other girls my own age? Why can I not just be a *maiden*?"

The Healer sighed. "Zivah, I understand your longing. But when I was but thirteen years of age I was the only surviving Healer in the village. I had to rise to the task even though I was hardly more than a child. We are Healers, daughter, we have been Healers for countless generations. We cannot dally like other people. Our kind cannot afford the childhood and levity that others enjoy. We have responsibilities. It is important that you know all the most important things before you reach womanhood. The calling can come when you least expect it."

"Mother, I am saying that I no longer wish to follow that path. I want to be an ordinary girl and an ordinary woman. You have another daughter now. She is a lot more important than I am."

"How can you say that?" Mother whispered, "You are my first born, Zivah. You will always be precious to me."

"Yes, but that one," Zivah said and nodded sulkily towards the bundle on our mother's back, "that one is a lot more precious, because she is important in a way that I am not. And she is your husband's *only daughter*. She can surely take up the burden better than I ever could. Look, she is already on your back, ready to learn the holy arts."

“I cannot leave her behind, Zivah. She is a newborn babe.”

“Of course not. Just go, mother. I have no interest in this. I will do any chore you set me to as diligently as I owe you, but I am finished with the Healer’s path. There is nothing more to discuss.”

The Healer was speechless. She met her young daughter’s eyes and let her see the hurt and disappointment in them, but Zivah, unmoved, stared back at her with eyes as hard as steel. Our mother turned around and walked away into the forest on her own. And so I was the one who accompanied the Healer as she spoke to the plants and carefully dug up the special roots. And this was how it was for as long as our mother lived.

From that time on, Zivah sought the company of other village girls and spent her days doing her chores in their company. She only came home when evening fell or if there was a special task that had to be done in the house. She made sure that Thorbjörn and the Healer could not rebuke her for anything, for she performed all her chores and more to perfection, and they always treated her kindly and praised her for both skill and diligence, yet she felt their secret eyes on her, their worry and their concern and their disappointment with her unexpected choice. Those eyes only caused her to stay away from the house even more.

*

For the first seven years of my life, I followed my mother almost every day as she went about her business both as a village woman, as a hunter and as a Healer. By the time I learned to walk they say people had to force themselves not to scream with laughter because I walked more like a tracker than any baby they had ever seen. I was copying my mother’s catlike stalking through the woods where she frequently went on her own and that with a small babe. It was she who taught me how to stalk and not to be stalked, how to track and not be tracked, and how to follow my own feet. Mother had a way of stunning a beast by the way she looked at it, and with that look even the grumpiest of wolverines would grudgingly move aside and leave us alone. I could not tell how it happened but I seemed to learn the same arts just by being there with her. I watched while she did her digging work, how she spoke to the plants, how she sang to them, how she touched and how she cut them. And she let me see through her eyes, and then I knew how she could have their attention and how they could have hers. The forest was alive, she said, it is the body of Medeiné the forest goddess, and that goddess has always been a friend to the women of our line, for she was our most ancient mother, and we of that lineage must search the forest as often as possible. I knew the ways of the forest and all her plants and animal children as well as their tracks and traces before I could even speak words to my knowledge.

In the village I watched while my mother prepared her medicine plants and remedies, always singing the same songs to the same sort of blends and the same sort of plants. Even before I could speak and understand all the words I knew countless songs, and with each verse I could recall what my mother did with the plants, the work of her hands, and also what the remedy was for and how it should be applied. Some of the songs were sung in an ancient language that nobody knows anymore, and yet I can remember the verses and the words and somehow I know what they mean, even if I do not know that language. When she was not doing her medicine or healing and mending people, activities I also watched from day to day and year to year, she would be working on all sorts of things, and liked particularly to work with leather and fur and bone. And with that work came other songs, songs that she sang with the other women as they worked together, and I was there always, watching, listening, and remembering everything I saw them do and say.

But there was a time every day just before sunset, and of course also other times when there was room for leisure, when Father took over my charge. He had been taking Thorolf almost everywhere since the boy was two years old, that year when I was born, because he knew the importance of the Healer's daughter and understood how early the roots of such knowledge had to be planted. Thorbjörn told his wife that it was common among his people that a father took care of his sons from a very early age also and that he thought it only proper that his son should begin to learn more manly ways as soon as he could walk and be without the mother's milk. Just as I followed Mother, Father soon had the little boy following in his trail all day, obeying his orders like an adoring puppy, copying his every movement and expression. He spoke to us his children mostly in the Norse tongue. Now that I had arrived Thorbjörn had realized that the language had to be transmitted. And every day he gathered Thorolf and the little baby that was me, and took us somewhere down by the river bank or up by the Oak Grove where he would tell us the ancient stories of his people and the lore of his land. He taught us the stories in verses that rhymed and made for a merry beat, and that way we learned the words even before we knew what they meant, and remembered the lore even before we understood any of it.

*

There were only a few times that Zivah volunteered to look after us, and only grudgingly did she accept to look after me. Even when she was told to look after my brother Thorolf and me she usually took us out into the village, where we trailed her doggedly as she entertained her friends with her charming presence and her sweet and sometimes bitter jokes. Where she felt rejected within her own family, she had discovered that the other girls looked up to her and admired her for her graceful beauty and charm. It was part admiration and part envy, she knew, and she learned fast how to play on her friends' eagerness to please her and their wish to be like her. Her friends learned to fear her sharp tongue when she rebuked them and almost fight for her attention and her praise. The way she could make them dance to her tune without even knowing that they were doing so was intoxicating to her.

The girls loved to tell and retell stories of the olden times, stories from when their people had lived closer to the outside world and known the wonders and the terrors and the adventures of heroes and princesses. Zivah loved those stories, so much more entertaining than the dreary stories that her mother and stepfather kept retelling. She enjoyed especially the stories of foreign princes who came to a distant shore and found a poor girl who was in fact a princess, and how he rescued her and whisked her away from that dreary place. Zivah often dreamt of such tales, dreamt of being a beautiful princess held captive in the most boring river marshlands in the whole wide world. One day a foreign prince would come and whisk her away, she told her friends, and he would fall violently in love with her and give her the most beautiful dresses made out of the finest fabrics and she no longer had to wear fur parkas and leather trousers or low-quality river pearl necklaces. He would give her jewelry made out of precious stones and let her live in a castle.

The more she retold that story, the more real it became to her, and the more real it became to her friends. The girls loved to listen wide-eyed to her fantasy as she elaborated all the parties and the dresses and the adventures that she would have once the foreign prince came to find her. She would tell of how he would discover her, and then she would show how she would be standing, looking beautiful and vulnerable, and then he would take her as if he had always owned her, and she would breathlessly swoon into his arms as he whisked her away on the most amazing ship that had ever entered the river lands, and all the heroic warriors who had accompanied him to find his lost bride would cheer. The girls would at that point be jumping excitedly on their feet and beg her to tell them about the heroic warriors, upon which Zivah would reassure them that there would be an exotic foreign man for each one of them, ready to whisk them away to the exciting world of colorful fabrics and jewelry and parties. By the time I was five years old I had heard the story so many times I had tired of it like I tired of no other story, and although I kept my thoughts to myself and tried hard not to even think it out loud within my own mind, I had begun to suspect that my beautiful sister and her chattering friends formed a council of adorable yet very silly girls.

When Zivah was twelve, she had her first Moon blood. If she had followed the Healer's path there would have been rites that my mother would have performed for her, but as it was Zivah was sent to the Women's Hut with other girls and women who were bleeding. I was too young when I left the village to ever learn what the women of the river people did in the Women's Hut. But I know that Zivah and the other young women were taught and told many things from the older women, and that whereas there were secret rites that only women knew, and we could hear their songs and drums and laughter all through the long nights, most of what they talked of had to do with the secrets of their bodies, with birthing and nursing children, with pregnancies and with the whisperings of men and women in the nights.

In many ways the river people observed far fewer rules and laws in these regards than Norsemen do, but they were a lot shyer also. While we Norsemen are not shy at all for as long as we feel entitled to our partner, it was the custom of the River People to ignore the very issue of entitlement, yet always be discreet and seek away from others if they wished to play the games of pleasure. Zivah had thus grown up with far less sight of these things than I was to experience, and all the new knowledge about the thrilling dealings in the shadows made her thoughtful and quiet for a long time. She often spent her days secretly pondering about the mysteries of pleasure, sometimes casting careful looks at men and boys when they ran naked into the river or when they returned to land. One evening she caught herself staring at her own stepfather when he undressed before bed in the evening. Father looked up, met her eyes, understood and averted his own gaze immediately, turning away from her. He pretended that nothing had happened but Zivah had seen him as if for the first time, and for the first time since they had explained the details of lovemaking to her she suddenly realized exactly what that entailed. The women had reassured her that the mating of men and women was not at all like the mating of beasts, but she was no longer so sure about that. And when she saw the sight of her mother's husband before her inner eyes over and over she thought she would die from terror.

He had always been so safe for her. Ever since he came to them she had loved him. She had snuggled into his embrace from the first night he was there and had followed him around everywhere when she did not follow her mother. He had taught her those marvelous winter arts, made her bone skates that allowed her to feel as if she was flying across the frozen river. He had made those long sticks that he called skis and taught her how to slide through the forests and down the hills faster than a deer in winter. He had made her first hunting bow for her and told her countless stories.

And then I had been born.

In Zivah's mind, all he seemed to see was me, her sister; his real daughter; the one that mattered. Oh he saw his son Thorolf just as well, but Zivah did not mind Thorolf. She loved her little brother. It was the little girl that had stolen her stepfather's love from her. Thorbjörn spent hours every day teaching us the songs and stories in his language, in our Norse language. Zivah sometimes listened in but mostly kept away, and with the years she felt more and more left out as Thorbjörn, Thorolf and I could speak to each other in a language nobody else in the village knew. The betrayal was so terribly deep and so heartbreakingly painful that she began to detest him. She thought he had lied to her all those years, let her call him father, even called her daughter and treated her as such, but now he had shown what he really felt about her. His people followed the father line only, he had said several times, with some internal clan exceptions. As far as she had understood his detestable origins, this meant that she was *nobody* in his world. She was just a stranger to him, a girl of little consequence, born from his wife's womb years before *he* put his precious seed in her. She was certain that all he had ever wanted was her mother and the children that she bore by him. Zivah was just there, after a fashion, little more than an unnecessary appendix to her mother. The hurtful hatred she felt for him blended into the terror she felt when she recalled the sight of his nakedness and realized what it could do. It was the first time she was able to imagine that act vividly and even as much as it terrorized her she could not stop thinking about it.

One night when her parents thought that all their children were sleeping, she stayed awake to notice how the huge man and the tiny, wiry body of her mother, both naked, slipped into the sauna together. They shut the door after themselves, and she had known that they used the sauna for many years and never minded it. For the first time in her life, when she was certain that they would be oblivious, Zivah got up and tiptoed quietly over to the sauna entrance and peered through the little holes in the wooden door. After watching them for a while she started to move backwards away from the sauna, eyes wide with fresh terror and heart over-pouring with a fresh flow of hatred towards the man she had once considered her father.

She had been wrong, she knew. It was nothing at all like she had imagined. It was far worse. She thought she had never seen such violence. The women had told her about violent men and how girls and women had to be careful around strangers and foreigners. Clearly he was one of them, and yet he lived right there in their midst with her mother's blessings, a mother who called herself Healer. Zivah studied her mother that morning, wondering how she could be so cheerfully calm and graceful after what she had been through in the night. *She must be putting up a mask*, she thought.

After considering the matter for a whole day she sought up her mother while she was tanning a hide, and offered to help her. The Healer smiled happily at her daughter. It was the first time in three years that Zivah had sat down with her of her own accord, the first time she volunteered for her mother's company since I had been born. My father had taken me and Thorolf to the river for a bath.

"Mother," she said, "you must forgive me, but last night I peered into the sauna and I saw you there with… with Thór-be-yurn."

"Did you now," Mother remarked and continued her tanning. Zivah detected a light red color forming at her temples though. She had learned to recognize secret signs of agitation and how to play on them. For the time being, however, she was too agitated herself to grasp the opportunity.

"How can you let him treat you like that?" she asked bluntly.

"I do not understand what you mean, daughter," the Healer said uncomfortably.

"Why, Mother! He was… he was being…" she began, but her mother stopped her with a glare that almost frightened her.

"You should refrain from passing judgment on that which you do not understand, Zivah," the Healer said coldly, "all things are not what they seem."

"I know what I saw! He is a brute, and you… you… you just…" She spat out the last words; "you just surrendered and let him… he *hurt* you!"

"Is that what you think, Zivah, that your father hurts me in the nights and that I let him?"

"He is not my father; he has said as much himself. And I saw what I saw! How could *that* not have been painful? What am I supposed to think?"

"Maybe you should stop thinking so much," Mother said, "and trust me when I say that your father – for he is in all practical ways your father, Zivah, your father has never ever hurt me and never ever will. The love that we share is limitless and our friendship is deep – and likewise our passion for each other is beyond most passions felt by men and women. There was no violence in our play last night. The games of pleasure can simply look a little disturbing sometimes, even though it is neither terror nor pain that is being felt."

Zivah looked disdainfully at the Healer, the mother who in Zivah's eyes had lost all her grace, honor and dignity that very night, and who knows for how many nights before that when she thought about it. She knew that her mother sensed what she felt and made no secret of her feelings either. Let the Healer know how my regard for her is lost, she thought to herself. Zivah glared challengingly at her mother, angrily daring her direct gaze.

"I would never surrender to a man like that," she snorted.

"Then you will be missing out on something very sacred," the Healer said softly and met her eyes with unbearable calm, "for there is no greater power than that which comes with surrender. Not even the power that comes with conquest is greater than that."

Zivah stared at her mother for a moment before she got up and left. Clearly her mother was deluded, perhaps spell-bound by the devious spells that the foreign intruder had bound her with. Maybe she could not even recollect what really happened with her during nights. It could only be that, she thought, it could only be sorcery. For she had never thought she would live to hear the most respected woman in the village speak such utter nonsense.

Thunder Wolf's Death

That fateful day Zivah stomped away from her mother, her feet took her down to the river where I and Thorolf my brother were bathing with our father. She glared distastefully at Thorbjörn when he came out of the water and failed to cover himself immediately. He had always been remarkably indiscreet about his body and seemed never to notice the nakedness of others. But he noticed that she was staring at him, and he could see her expression.

"If you do not like what you see you do not have to stare," her stepfather growled, glaring back at her while he got into his breeches. He had always used those glares to keep his children in line, she realized, a glare that would freeze you to the spot and reconsider your behavior within the blink of an eye. He only used it if someone behaved really badly, and she knew that he thought she was being rude now. In fact, he looked like he was struggling to control his anger. She had provoked him daily for years, and as much as he had tried to be patient and kind with her, she could see that he was beginning to lose his control. She stared at his powerful frame and became painfully aware that they were alone on the shore together, us children still playing obliviously in the river, and she realized that she would never be able to fight him if he were ever to attack. She took a step back while still staring at him. To her surprise, his eyes suddenly went from angry to sad.

"Why do you fear me, daughter?" he asked quietly.

"Because I know what kind of man you are," she snarled.

"Do you, now. Well, Zivah, I do not know what I have done to deserve your hostility and even less do I know how I have earned your fear of me. The only thing I can say is that I would never hurt you, ever, and that I will always be your father no matter what you think of me."

"If you say so," she said coldly. There was a part of her that wanted to reach out to him and be his little girl again, the one he played with and taught and told stories to, but it was too late. Where he was concerned the only joy she felt was when she could see how hurt he was by her words. She wanted to make him feel how much he had hurt her. She wanted him to be hurt just the same. It hardly mattered that she no longer quite remembered why she wanted to hurt him in the first place – there was always a new reason presenting itself, such as the sight she had beheld that night.

There were some voices from the village calling his name. Then a couple of young men came bursting through the bushes and lit up at the sight of Thunder Bear. *They should only know what he does to my mother when nobody else is around*, she thought while making sure to maintain that aloof and tender stance which she had discovered always impressed the men.

"We need you up at the beehives, Thór-be-yurn," one of the men said, "there is this large stone that has fallen down that needs moving and only you are strong enough to do it." The others nodded enthusiastically at her stepfather while sending nervous glances in her direction. She had to smile to herself. Even as her father rejected her, every other male in the village seemed to be utterly dazzled by her, more and more with each day, and she enjoyed the power of her influence. Thorbjörn noticed her glee in her little pastime and frowned, but said nothing about it. "Zivah, look after your siblings, will you? They are still enjoying themselves out there," he said instead, and

Zivah nodded sulkily before he left. We children swam like fishes so it was not very hard work to just guard us.

*

How it happened always remained a mystery to us. She had sat down by the river to watch Thorolf playing with me in the water and sometimes she smiled a little at the sight of him, although the smile was always wiped out whenever I entered the range of her vision. I was very little still but I had begun to realize that the beautiful sister I had always adored really did not like me and that there was very little I could do to please her at all. I did not know why, and like the small child I was I kept trying to make her happy, hoping that she would grant me one of those rare smiles and perhaps even a hug. It had happened sometimes, I think, even if it was hard to remember whether she had given that affection freely or just for the sake of appearances. The more I tried, however, the less kindly she felt towards me. At the time I had not yet understood just how deeply she despised me, and when I discovered her sitting on the shore looking sad I got out of the water and ran up to her, crying her name in greeting.

"There, there," she said impatiently when I hugged her and quickly pushed me away from her. I smiled brightly at her; "Come and play with us, Zivah, we are playing in the river!"

"Sure you are," she said, "but I am not going to stride around naked out in the open like some people do."

"Everybody bathe naked, Zivah," I giggled, trying to imagine my sister going into the water with all her clothes on. I burst out in giggles at the image that formed itself and stopped myself quickly when I saw her angry face.

"You are just a little child," Zivah said importantly, "you do not understand the ways of women." I shook my head amiably to agree with what seemed to be an obvious fact. A far as I was concerned, thirteen year old Zivah was a woman grown, at least if she said so.

"I fail to see how you can be special when you are such a stupid little girl," Zivah said icily to me. I was but three years old that summer and knew no response to such a statement. But I was stunned at the naked hostility that now had surfaced in my sister. I blinked uncertainly at her and suddenly caught sight of the most beautiful butterfly I had ever seen. The butterfly seemed so much easier to deal with right then and like any child would in such a situation I gladly let myself be distracted. The butterfly was about to vanish into the fruit yards that surrounded the village, and I ran after it to see where it lived. I was already quite a distance into the fruit yards when I heard Zivah shouting my name. I did not know why she had been so angry but I knew for certain that I did not want to be close to that anger, so I kept running after the butterfly and paid no heed to my sister's calls until she caught up with me and grabbed my arm so hard it hurt.

"What are you doing, you little fool?" she shouted at me, "You scared me half to death! What do you think that father of yours is going to do with *me* if *you* got lost in the woods and eaten by a bear?" I deemed it unwise to respond and followed her meekly as Zivah pulled me by the hand, oblivious of my efforts to force back the tears produced by her anger and by the pain of her hard grip. When we returned to the shore we looked for Thorolf and saw nobody. Not until we saw a small body floating face down in the water, caught up in river weed.

Zivah's screams alerted the village. I stood at the shore and watched my father wade out into the river and seize my brother's five year old body in his great embrace. I stood there and watched when he shook the small body and tried all sorts of life saving maneuvers. I stood by the river banks and watched when he threw his head back and screamed so hard it seemed like the world was breaking into shattering pieces. I stood there and saw my father the Thunder Warrior seized by an indescribable rage that made his eyes turn into red glowing stones of burning coal. The villagers stepped back, their jaws dropping. For the first time since he had come among them they actually feared my father.

He stood up on his knees where he had squatted above his son's lifeless body and looked directly at Zivah. For a while he just glared at her with those red glowing eyes, unable to form a word with his mouth. He seemed to be sputtering and wheezing, as if trying to speak but not being able to. I looked at Zivah's face, white with terror, body paralyzed to the spot, waiting for the dreaded words of blame to form, waiting for the blow. Even I feared my father just then, and we all startled when he got up to his feet, hovering above us all, still with his eyes glued at my terrified sister.

The words that he finally spoke were not words of anger. His voice seemed hollow and lost. His eyes were paling, from red glows to those dark framed white irises that people referred to as wolf eyes. The thunderous rage that seemed to have seized him before abated and he suddenly looked like a very tired old man.

"Must all my children die?" was all that he said to her eventually. He asked her, sounding almost curious, as if she would know the answer. As if she was somehow behind the deaths of his other children. Then his gaze withdrew into himself and stayed like that for the rest of that year. Our mother came to the shore then, walking unsteadily until she reached the little boy. Then she fell over him, hugged and rocked him in her arms and cried, it seemed, for an eternity.

All I remember after that was the embrace of the feeble old Thunder priest when he lifted me up and carried me to the Oak Grove for purification, followed by the other villagers. It was decided that nobody was to blame. Danu the river goddess had taken Thunder Wolf into her arms because she loved beautiful and brave youths and wanted him for keep. Now he would live happily with other children who dwelled in the loving embrace of the flowing lady.

The Yearning River Woman

After Thorolf's death, both my parents as well as my sister withdrew into their own separate and very internal worlds for many months following that fateful day. I grieved in my own way. Thunder Wolf was dead, the brother who had been brought to this world to protect me, or so my father had told me. I had a vague feeling that my lack of obedience to my elders had affected this loss of my born protector and created such grief in the people that I loved. And like children are wont to do I made some decisions then that I forgot ever making later, although I was long a living proof of their effects. After what had happened, I stopped crying, I stopped smiling, laughing or playing carelessly like other children do, and I always obeyed my elders.

The intensity of their grief gradually gave way to everyday village life and my father and mother lifted their gazes from within their secret hearts and saw each other again, and even better; they began to see *me* again. It was almost mid-winter when they began to remark on the fact that I no longer laughed or cried or played like other children. I just followed grown folks around and watched what they were doing and tried to learn what I could, and did whatever I was told. I seemed to be at loss if people failed to tell me or show me what to do, which was why other children became too difficult for me to deal with. I never understood what the other children expected of me, and learning what people expected me to do had by then become my most pressing concern. I hardly even spoke unless it was to oblige people by replying earnestly to whatever they asked me or talked to me about.

After trying to work with me, my parents had me speaking to them at last, and I kept asking questions and commenting on things I heard, but I always seemed to carry the same serious expression. Sometimes people told me not to stare so at them, because my gaze unnerved them. Mother said it was because I had wolf eyes like my father sometimes had when he concentrated hard on something, only I tended to have them all the time where his would go a calm sky blue when his mind relaxed. When she said that, I replied that my eyes were thus set in their wolf spirit all the time simply because I was concentrating hard all the time.

"How is that possible?" Mother asked, "Everybody must relax their minds sometimes."

"I do not know how to except in sleep," I said somberly.

"What are you concentrating on?" she asked.

"Everything that transpires around me at all times," I said, "And sometimes that is a lot of things."

"Do you remember everything you perceive then?" she asked.

"Yes," I said, and added that it could be tiring at times.

By the time our parents saw Zivah she had moved so far beyond their reach that they never really knew her again. Winter was giving way to spring, the weather was warm and Zivah was entering her fourteenth year. Zivah had long since begun to grow into that astonishing beauty that was, admittedly, at times her most redeeming trait. Nobody was surprised that she was turning into a rare beauty. Even from she was a toddler it had been clear to all who saw them that my sister had inherited our mother's slender gracefulness, her soft and handsome features, her large golden doe eyes framed with thick dark lashes, her soft and kissable mouth and a full head of cascading, darkly honey-colored hair.

Now that she was becoming a fully grown woman she surprised everyone by growing the most alluring curves known in the river lands. The women of the river lands tended to be more slender and more sinewy than the Norsewomen, their breasts were moderate and their hips were narrow. But Zivah had the body of that old goddess of beauty that she had been named after but that they now called Laimé, which made the older name acceptable as a personal name. Her slender waist was framed beneath with shapely and generously rounded hips, and crowned above with full breasts that could hardly be disguised even if they were covered by fur. With these new appendixes to her willow-like body, Zivah learned to move in a new way that emphasized both her curves and her agile grace. Even village boys and men who had seen her grow since childhood suddenly found themselves staring after her with half open mouths at times.

The way men and boys gaped at her and admired her so openly made Zivah feel even better than when the girls sat dotingly at her feet and tried to copy all her movements. She discovered that she could employ an array of mimicking expressions and sounds that could produce the most entertaining effects in the men and boys who inevitably fell victim to her little traps. Mother began to receive complaints from the mothers of young men and boys who had returned in tears after believing that Zivah cared for them and found that she did not. But Zivah said that it was hardly her fault if a young man got it into his head that she would want him when all she had done was being friendly to him, just like she would be to anyone. And nobody could really tell her differently. In fact, the girls and women of the village defended her because they liked her and agreed that it was not her fault that men were dazzled and their judgment blinded in the presence of such beauty. But the village was small and soon enough the boys and men who lived there knew exactly how she could fool them with that charm of hers and gave up trying to approach her, since humiliation was the only outcome that had ever resulted from a dalliance with the Healer's daughter.

Zivah turned her attentions towards fresher supplies.

As a girl she had imagined foreign men coming to find the captive beauty that they had heard so many praising words about and whose beauty was famed so far and wide. She had dreamt that dream about herself so many times that she began to play the part. Whenever boats and rafts and small ships reached the village shores for trading, Zivah would parade around the shore, looking inaccessible yet mysteriously alluring, as if she possessed a secret of sorts. As she had predicted, the rumor about the unusually beautiful, mysterious young woman who seemed to be looking for her lost love at the river shore did surely spread, and before the summer was through, Zivah indeed became famed in the river land. Curious young men came to look for her from other places. Zivah, always flattered by their attentions and sometimes even going as far as taking them into a secret place, was always disappointed to find that they were all men of the river lands, men who sought nothing but a wife with a hut and a piece of land of her own with whom he could settle and live the sort of life that his kind had lived for centuries on end. She thought they were all impossibly boring after a few hours, when she left them stranded and feeling like the fools she thought they were.

Just like the village men had figured out that it was better to leave her alone, the rumors of how she treated her suitors and would-be-lovers also spread. But for as long as they were rumors of a distant shore maiden the allure kept working as well as ever, and Zivah never seemed to run out of hopeful admirers coming in from all over the river lands. She kept going to the shore with her giggling trail of friends and loved learning about all the splendors and excitements of foreign lands. And she kept dreaming of her prince. The one who would whisk her away from that dreary little village in the middle of nowhere, whisk her away forever, and in their trail there would be the heroes, whisking off her friends, and then they would all go away and live happily ever after.

I once heard my father comment upon the girls' shared day-dream, a much retold fantasy that was now common village knowledge.

"All whisked away by foreign princes to live happily ever after?" He laughed bitterly, "Those girls would probably have to contend themselves with staying alive for some time after. Or maybe death is a better option." Mother looked at him with her mouth open.

"Why do you speak so, husband?" she asked, "they are only foolish dreams that young girls nourish." Thorbjörn snorted dismissively; "Where I am from we do not *let* our maidens nourish foolish dreams."

"Why not?" his wife asked.

"Because foolish dreams will blind a maiden and cause foolish acts."

"It is a harsh world you come from, husband, that cannot allow a young girl her dreams."

"Tell me then wife, what good do those dreams do her? How will they help her when she must make her way through this world of harshness and pain and wilful men? I envy you, wife, and I envy your people. Every day I look at you all and wonder if I am living in a dream. You are so blessedly sheltered from all the horrors of the world. Oh, wife, Zivah and her friends have no idea how fortunate they are to live here. I can see why they complain about the men, they are a puny lot when the truth is to be told, but if they had been out there in the world and seen what kind of men really rule the world, what kind of men those princes and heroes really are, ah, then they might start to appreciate the gentle ways of the river land men. None of you people can possibly begin to imagine what kind of life most pretty young women of their age must lead in that exciting great world that they keep chattering about. These dreams are not innocent, wife, they are terribly dangerous. Those foolish dreams she nourishes can blind a maiden and cause her to make fateful choices that will never turn out to her benefit."

"I suppose I can see what you mean. In any case you know a great deal more about the world out there than I do," my mother said, "but how is it even possible to take a girl's dreams from her?"

"We just do not accept such nonsense," Thorbjörn said and frowned as he did, trying to remember how that had ever worked. He just remembered that a father's failure to accept a notion was usually enough to make a young maiden immediately regain her senses and recognize foolishness for what it was. When his wife asked him how it was done, he had no way of explaining it without offending her, so he kept quiet about the respect issue.

Where he was from women honored their men in ways that the river land women could never imagine. It had been hard for him to adapt to a world where women would sometimes even give him direct orders. His wife had learned how to respect him after trying out several strategies. When she realized that a direct request only made him look gloomy and constantly fail to remember what it was that she had asked of him, she tried to talk to him about it, which made him shut off completely. Eventually she had learned how to just casually remark that something or other needed doing and that she might see to it later. She would not stop to wait for confirmation, only pretend not to register the sulky grunt that meant "yes" while walking away and not paying him any further attention. To her astonishment, the things she wanted doing after her requests had been put forward in that very indirect manner would be done as soon as she turned her back, and done well also. That way, she had learned that her foreign husband did not mind doing what she wanted him to do. He just did not want to feel that she ordered him.

Thorbjörn knew that his wife felt that she had made a great effort to adjust to his pride out of love for him, and he rewarded her in every way he could. But she who had only known the village of her birth could not possibly imagine all the adjustments that he had had to make to be able to live among her people. If she thought that he was unusually sensitive about his manliness and authority she had no idea how much he had been holding back for the sake of pleasing her and her folks. The only habit he had not been able to change was the habit of always doing the exact opposite of what a woman told him to if she tried to order him about, a habit countered and balanced by the fact that he would always do exactly what she wanted if she knew how to ask respectfully.

After more than a decade of living in the village, it was only to be expected that all the women and children knew exactly how to get Thunder Bear to work for them. But that was just as it should be. They even made jokes about it in the village square, he had discovered, smiling at the memory. There had been one impertinent wench who was standing around looking lofty while another equally impertinent old woman spoke about that roof which needed mending, while facing the opposite direction of the lofty wench. When she had finished talking about the roof, the old woman, still without even looking at the lofty wench who was supposed to be Thunder Bear, whistled and pretended that nothing had happened. The entire village had been rolling over in laughter when there issued a grudging snort from the lofty one before she hurried over to the "roof that needed mending" while looking over her shoulder to be certain that nobody saw her. The villagers had been laughing their heads off. There was nothing a man could do to save face but to laugh with them at his own expense. And Thorbjörn had found that he had lived so long in the river lands now that their gentle and casual customs had formed him. He no longer regarded them as impertinent, chattering weaklings. He thought they were wise in many ways, albeit heartbreakingly innocent. It was easy to be lulled into the timeless peacefulness of their quiet and friendly life. Thorbjörn no longer remembered many of the ways of his own people. And he had no idea how to educate Zivah without them. He wished to the gods that she would never have to learn the hard way. But when had that sort of prayer ever worked?

*

My father's attention faded and he got that distant look about him, that well-known painful shade which descended upon his features to remain there for a while. My mother and I minded our own business until he looked like our Thunder Bear again. Then I sat with him for a long time and neither of us spoke at all. We just liked to sit together sometimes and feel what it felt like to share that steady roar of power flowing within our bodies. Nobody shared that flow except us two. Mother would smile at us and say that we looked like a huge bear with a very small cub where we sat together. But she knew of the bond that tied us together in an understanding too deep for words.

Thunder and lightning flowed in our veins. My father and I were the last of our kind.

At the Market

At fifteen, Zivah was more beautiful than ever. She was also fully aware of that fact, and milked the attention that her beauty caused for all it was worth. Her discontent with the eventless village life grew with every day and when we heard of a market to be held in a nearby village she complained so pitifully about how she never got to see anything of interest that Father suddenly declared that he would take us all there if his wife would grant him the steel she had once wrested from his fists. Zivah and I gaped at Mother as we tried to imagine how she could ever have managed to wrestle anything at all from those fists. Mother laughed and opened the chest.

"Your father come from a very different sort of people than us," she explained, "they are warriors and never walk outside their door without them. When I found him lying unconscious in the Oak Grove that day he was still clutching his weapons and I had a hard time wresting them off him. But I took his weapons and kept them away so that he could learn how to live in the world without being armed at all times."

"Without being armed at all," Thorbjörn grunted, trying hard to disguise his excitement when he peered cautiously into the forbidden chest of the Healer.

"You have had your bow and your knife and your hunting spear, my love."

"And I have never objected. But if I am to take our daughters and you out of this village I shall have my steel or we shall never go."

"Why, what are you afraid of?" Zivah asked mockingly. He looked thoughtfully at her.

"Afraid I am not, girl, but I am wary of everything, like the wild wolf of the forest is always alert. And so should you be wary of danger, Zivah. If I am to take you out of this place I have one more condition. Apart from the weapons I demand that you all obey me without question at all times for as long as we are out there, and all the way home. I am sure you can save your sour words to me for later, daughter, seeing as I am actually doing this to please you."

"*Obey me at all times*," Zivah began to mimic him, but stopped when she noticed the glares of both her parents.

"If I am to protect you I need to know that I can trust you to follow my orders. That is all, Zivah," he said quietly.

"Yes, Thór-be-yurn," Zivah said, "If you take me to the market I promise to do what you say. I just do not understand why it is necessary to point it out. I always do what you two tell me." Our parents exchanged glances. As far as I was concerned, being five, I knew that Zivah always did her chores and obeyed them both, but being the one who followed her around like a shadow I also knew that she did whatever she felt like when they were not around.

Apart from hunting expeditions in the forest and a few fishing trips downriver, Thorbjörn had not left the village since he came to them. It had been thirteen years. He had not ever wished to leave, carrying in him a fear that if he ever left this place everything would change. Life in the village seemed to him like a dream, the dream of a place where no evil existed and where the people grew up without knowledge of carnage or slavery or war. It was a place where people lived as equals and shared everything with each other and treated each other with kindness and trust. None of the villagers seemed to be aware of how unique and precious that was, but he knew it well and held on to the dream, refusing to expose himself to anything that could rupture that wondrous world.

But Zivah needed a strong husband, that much he knew, and she was not going to find him if she stayed here. He had often been around without her knowing it, making sure that she did not get fooled by some trader with less than honest intentions. Nightmares about his stepdaughter being whisked away by a foreign prince who turned out to be a slaver had haunted him ever since he learned about her foolish fantasies. Better if he could go with her and look at the young men himself, directing the girl towards a man who could protect her. Because Zivah, he knew, needed protection, and often enough she needed protection against her own recklessness. *A warrior is what she needs*, he had often thought, *a man that she can respect*. But he was a warrior and she had no respect for him at all. He caressed the steel of his blades and spoke endearing and encouraging words to his weapons. *She has never seen me as a warrior though*, he pondered; *she has just seen me as the big foreign man who failed to be her father*.

"Father, are you going to fight bad men?" I asked, watching in fascination how my father treated those weapons as if they were living friends.

"If I have to, Thunder Goddess," he said mildly, "but pray it will not be necessary." I nodded solemnly. Father looked at me and smiled reassuringly; "It is just a small trip upriver, child, but where I am from a man is always prepared. It is better that way. You will know that you are safe with me." I nodded again, and Father sighed. "I wonder if you are ever going to laugh and smile again, child. Or weep, for that matter." I shrugged, because I did not know when I would do any of that. It was as if I did not remember how. All I knew was that I loved my father, so I went over to him and leaned against him, which was my way of hugging him. He knew that and pulled me close.

The whole family got onto the raft and said farewell to the villagers. We brought many furs, jars of honey and basketfuls of herbs and remedies, and bundles of beeswax and a litter of kittens to sell at the market. Mother carried her bow and arrows just as did Zivah, while my father was fully armed in the way of a Norseman. He disguised all his weapons beneath a large woolen cloak though, so as not to appear conspicuous so deep in the river lands where men hardly ever wore anything but hunting weapons. I sat in the front and watched the water stream by while the three adults, Zivah included, paddled away to move us upriver.

So far I had never seen any other place than the village, the river shore and the nearby forest. It was awesome to see more of the world for the first time, and I watched eagerly for any change in landscape. As soon as we reached a river junction and began moving downriver, the adults relaxed their oars and sat there just as I did, enjoying the sights of variation. The raft moved so silently that we spied countless wild animals on the way, moose and deer, bear and big cats, otters and beavers and salmon and many other animals who sought the river for water or food, hardly even aware of our presence. Mother and Zivah were fishing while Father kept an eye on absolutely everything, looking like a rock where he sat, so very quiet. I imitated him and discovered the art of seeing just like that. The more quietly I sat, watching and listening to the world, the more I seemed to see and hear, smell and feel. After a whole day like that I thought something in me had changed. It was as if all my senses had improved considerably and the world that I thought I had known had become a place vibrant with life that I had not even suspected was there at all. It was as if my whole self was expanding, and suddenly I realized that I could know everything that was going on within a very large radius around me even if I could not see or hear it. When I became conscious of my new talent, Father turned to me and winked. He said nothing, but he knew.

We did not make camp that night because we had brought food enough to eat and wanted to get to the market as quickly as possible. Father remained seated, watching out, while Mother and Zivah and I slept. But I woke many times that night and looked up at the starlit sky and began to realize what a big world it really was. In the morning we made camp and fried all the fish that we had caught, eating hungrily. Father slept for a few hours while Mother, Zivah and I walked quietly around looking for plants and herbs, roots and barks, nuts and seeds that could be used for all sorts of medicinal and edible purposes. It was the first time in my life that Zivah joined us in that pursuit, and at some point she sat down on a rock and stared out into the air with empty eyes.

"Why is Zivah doing that?" I whispered, tugging at my mother's parkas when we were outside of hearing range.

"She is feeling her loss," Mother said.

"What loss?"

"She was going to follow in my path and become the new Healer. She chose not to. But the blood of the Healer runs in her veins as surely as it does in you and me. She may be regretting it."

"Why did she choose not to?"

"Have you ever wanted to be someone else than who and what you are?"

"No."

"Have you ever wanted to have something that someone else own?

"No."

"Have you ever wanted to have the affection that is given to someone else?"

"No."

"Then you are blessed, daughter, to not be plagued by the demon of jealousy. For that demon causes injuries to the soul that only serves to feed it further. Pray that you will never know what jealousy feels like. It is the worst illness a human being can suffer."

Mother said no more. I glanced over at Zivah and suddenly understood a great deal more about my sister. She was suffering greatly. I felt sorry for her but did not know what to do about it. Obedient as always, I followed my mother's suggestion and prayed to the gods of below and above that I would never know what jealousy felt like.

When we returned to camp, Father was awake and ready. So we moved downriver and upriver for a whole day and another night, and it was almost midday on the third day before we reached a river junction where we found a village much larger than our own, with a great market. Along the shore there were many rafts and boats, and there were people there who looked different from those we were used to, traders who came from faraway places. We introduced ourselves to the villagers and were allowed to set up our tents and our stall. Father and mother sold their goods that day, talked to many people and heard tidings from near and far, and enjoyed themselves thoroughly.

Zivah and I were ordered to stay within seeing distance, but the market was big and we walked around looking at everything, and Zivah was able to make a few bargains regarding textiles and jewelry that she hardly ever got in the village. I followed her like a shadow, she ignoring me as much as she could while still looking after me, but this was how it always used to be.

I saw how the men looked at my sister. Mostly they just looked at her with an expression of appreciation, even awe. But I did notice a group of men who looked at her as if she was some sort of tasty dish that they could devour. I had never in my life seen anyone look at another human being in that sort of way, and wondered if they were the cannibals I had heard of in some of the scary legends that young people liked to tell to even younger people. I regarded the men who were possibly cannibals and became more and more certain that they wanted to eat my sister. I wanted to run back and tell Father, but then I would have to leave Zivah alone and what if the cannibals came and ate her as soon as I turned my back to them? We were on the far end of the market from our parents and could barely see them. They were busy haggling with a customer over some of the precious furs and enjoying themselves thoroughly.

And just as I was pondering how to get Zivah away from the attention of the cannibals, one of them got up and walked straight towards us! I went up to Zivah and clutched her hand. I could feel how she wanted to wriggle out of my grip but restrained herself so as not to look like a bad sister in front of everyone else. She punished me by gripping my hand right back, hard. I yelped a little and forced back my tears, but refused to let go of her. She gave up and relaxed her grip a little as the man came up to her and spoke to her.

I could hardly believe it, but Zivah reacted to the cannibal exactly the same way she reacted when someone she thought was passably handsome approached her. She smiled shyly and acted somewhat aloof, but interested. She allowed herself to blush just a little while fluttering her lashes, what always used to make young men fall into a stutter when they tried to speak. The cannibal surprised her by maintaining eye contact and smiling to her. I thought his smile was a vicious grin, but Zivah's interest was only intensified by the novelty of a man who failed to lose his wits around her. The cannibal spoke our language but with an accent, and was obviously from some distant tribe. They spoke and joked and the cannibal was making my sister giggle and blush for real. And to my horror, the cannibal suddenly seemed to notice me, smiled overbearingly at me and leaned over to tussle my hair.

"What a head of flames the little one has," he said to my sister while I felt his claws on my head. I just stared at him as I had been doing ever since he came over, and he frowned a little.

"Not much of a talker, is she?" he commented while grinning to Zivah. My sister giggled again. "The girl does not have the wits appropriate to her age," she said, "she never laughs or smiles or cries like children do, and she only speaks when she thinks she has to. She is very serious. But I am looking after her, she is my half-sister, you see." She set up a sad face and the cannibal suddenly looked like he felt really, really sorry for her.

"You are a good woman, Zee-vah!" he exclaimed, and there were tears in his eyes, "It must be such a heavy charge on your fragile shoulders, looking after a half-wit sister." Zivah blushed again and suddenly looked terribly vulnerable, her lips trembling slightly while a few teardrops formed in her eyes. I never ceased to be amazed at how good she was at the masking game. It always stunned me when she did that.

"It is nothing," she whispered and flashed those doe eyes at him, "it is what a sister must."

"Of course it is. But if you were my woman I would make sure you had people to do that sort of chores for you."

"People who do my chores *for* me?" Zivah looked genuinely surprised at the very notion. I was amazed too, having never before been exposed to such a concept.

"Of course," the man said, "where I and my friends are from we have other and lesser people who can do the lesser chores. A woman like you should not have to work at all. She should just walk around looking beautiful and wear beautiful dresses. I can imagine how beautiful you will look if you were dressed in fine silk." I wondered how Zivah could fail to notice how rude or how lacking this man was in eloquence, repeating the same word for "beautiful" three times in a row. A word said three times in a row becomes a spell, everybody knew that, but Zivah was already spell-bound.

"What is silk?" she asked, almost forgetting to maintain her lofty act.

"Silk, ah, Zee-vah, silk is the most precious fabric you could ever get. So soft, so fine, and so splendid to the eyes. Just like you. It is a fabric made by magic, by countless little sprites that live far to the east of these lands. We trade with it, but it is terribly expensive, you understand. But if I had a woman such as you I would dress her in silk all the time."

Zivah regarded the cannibal as if he was the best thing that had ever happened to her, and I could not help myself but tugged at her hand again.

"Wait," she wheezed at me while continuing to speak to the cannibal some more. When they finally parted, he took her other hand for a moment and squeezed it while he looked into her eyes, smiling that horrible cannibal grin. When we moved back towards our parents I asked her why she had been so friendly with the cannibal.

"*Cannibal*?" she spurted, incredulous.

"He wants to eat you, Zivah," I said honestly.

"Eat me? You foolish girl. He wants me. He wants me to be his woman! He wants to dress me in silk you little idiot."

"No, Zivah," I said patiently, "he wants to eat you and his friends want to eat you as well." Zivah cast a glance towards the men who were seated together. They looked at us and smiled amiably. I still thought they were grinning as if they were hungry wolves and Zivah was a really fat doe.

"What notions you get in that little red head of yours," Zivah laughed, "they are nice men, Thunder Goddess, and I do not want you to ruin my chances by speaking of cannibals. I forbid you to speak of this to Father and Mother, do you hear me? Your cannibals are just children's fantasies anyway, but I don't want our parents to start worrying about this, seeing as they think you are some sort of ancient goddess they are probably going to believe you also. But if you ruin my chances here I am going to hate you and make your life miserable!" I nodded to that and said nothing.

But when Zivah continued their dalliance the next day and the day after that, I began to feel a little distressed. I had begun to suspect that Zivah could not see what I saw so clearly, and it was a worrying and confusing notion.

"Father," I said eventually, "Am I really a half-wit?"

"A half-wit? Who told you that?" I bit my lower lip and resolved to further questioning. "Well am I?" I asked, sincerely wanting to know the truth.

"No. You are not a half-wit. You just have a difficult fate to handle. You are a very ancient soul in a very young mind and a very young body. I am sure it must be a little overwhelming for you. And then there will be those who cannot see properly with their eyes who may think that you have a weak mind, but they will not know that they are underestimating you. If people underestimate you, then you can use that for your weapon. You see, there is hardly anything more dangerous than underestimating your enemy. That is the key to all falls."

"Oh," I said, a little befuddled, "Do I have enemies?"

"Everybody have enemies even if they do not know all of them. Better to be alert and see what you see than trust that others will do it for you."

"Are there people who cannot see properly with their eyes?"

"Yes, too many."

"But you think that I can see properly?"

"Definitely."

"Because I think that some cannibals want to eat Zivah but she does not see that they want that and she thinks they are nice and want to have her wear silk and never work."

"Is that so," said Father, not at all surprised. I knew then that he had already noticed.

"I commend you, daughter, for seeing with open eyes. You have the sight of the warrior, while Zivah…she is Zivah. But she is your Síf and mine, and we must protect her. And now I have something to ask of you."

When Zivah secretly sneaked out from the tent in the night, unseen I followed, and not long after Father followed also. He caught up with me and placed his enormous hand upon my tiny shoulder, saying nothing. He shoved me quietly behind him and continued to follow Zivah with me in his trail. When we reached a little beach on the river bank we saw Zivah standing there in the moonlight, so beautiful, while the cannibal moved up to her, smiling that hungry smile of his. Father tensed. The couple giggled and talked a little, and suddenly leaned towards each other for a kiss. Swifter than anyone could have expected, Thunder Bear stood between them, glaring down at the man, who grew a look of terror in his face before he backed away and disappeared into the darkness. Thunder Bear turned to his stepdaughter.

"Walk," he commanded, and the look in his face was of a kind that Zivah decided not to argue just yet. But she looked at me with a glare of pure hatred that froze me to the spot.

"The child said nothing," Father said, "I saw everything that transpired today and I knew what you were planning without anyone needing to tell me. But you should heed your little sister, Zivah, for she has the eyes of a she-wolf and she knows what she sees where you are blind." Zivah clearly did not believe him and kept casting angry glances at me while we walked back to our tent.

Thunder Bear's Shame

Once inside the tent, Zivah sat down and stared into the fire until everybody had settled around. She was the one who broke the awkward silence. "I had thought myself a woman grown for the last few years," she said, "I had not expected to be told whether or not I could meet a man in the night." Mother mused a little. She was not quite certain what to say to her daughter's statement. True enough, it was not the river people's custom to supervise the love lives of young folks.

"You still live at our hearth," Father said, "and we must protect you. That man you were dallying with, and his friends, are not trustworthy, Zivah. They are very dangerous men."

"They are cannibals," I contributed. They all looked strangely at me, so I added: "They want to eat Zivah. I have seen it in their eyes."

"You little fool!" Zivah wheezed, "Can you not see that the little one is a half-wit, Mother? Father? Are you so attached to your dream of the Thunder Goddess that you cannot see what she is? She never plays or runs about like other children! She just follows somebody around and stares! That is all she does! She never smiles or laughs or cries or even reacts to *anything*!"

"It seems she reacts very soundly to danger, however," Father remarked drily, "maybe you should start watching the world a little more the way your little sister does instead of just watching those childish images inside your head what leave you blind to the actual world."

"You just want to control me, Thór-be-yurn," Zivah said, "Just like you really think it is your privilege to control all the women around you. That is just the way of your people, is it not? You Norsemen get to tell your womenfolk what to do or not."

"That is because we know that we have to protect our womenfolk, Zivah," Thorbjörn said calmly, but his voice was deepening and he looked somewhat angry, "and our women know that we are the masters of defense and protection. They would not ever question our judgment in cases of security. They know that we will give our lives to protect them and unlike you they know how to respect that!"

"Give your lives..." Zivah laughed mockingly, "I have heard you speak of honorable conduct among your folks, Thór-be-yurn, but I have been gathering some more intelligence these last few days. Do you know what they are saying about Norsemen around here?" My parents went quiet. "If you do not want to say it then I will. They say that Norsemen have come from the north and west and entered these lands with the sole purpose of killing people and stealing everything they own. And they even steal people! They steal women and children away from their homes and treat them terribly and sell them like goats to foreign folks!"

"Are those stolen folks the people who do the chores for other people who can walk in silk dresses?" I asked innocently, and they all looked at me for a moment, stunned. Zivah looked angry, but Father chuckled a little. "Yes, Thordís, the people who do the chores for other people are the people who are taken and sold like goats to those who wish to spend their lives walking about in silk dresses," he said and looked meaningfully at Zivah, "And when a man tells you that he is going to make you into one of those silk dress people who has other people to do her chores for her, it means that he is the sort of man who buys people who have been stolen from their homes."

Zivah looked so angry I thought she would burst.

"He is *not*! Those serving people have lived there a long time, he said so himself, they have been born to do those things and they never complain and besides I know well that your people both steal and own other folks like we own our goats!"

"The important thing, Zivah, is that nobody gets to steal *you* and sell *you* like a goat," Father said; "And believe me when I say that those men will do that without a moment's hesitation. They may not be cannibals in the sense that Thunder Goddess says but rest assured that they will devour your soul and your heart for the fun of it and sell you to other men later."

I heard Mother gasp, while Zivah went deep red, then white and then red again. She seemed to be spurting with anger. "I know why you are thinking like that, Thór-be-yurn," Zivah said, "it is yourself that you are speaking of, is it not? You think that everybody else must be the sort of man that you really are." Her glare was so challenging and her words so piercing that Thunder Bear was rendered speechless for a moment. He searched for words and looked back into her anger-ridden eyes trying to understand what his stepdaughter was aiming for.

"Why do you not tell us about the time that passed between the moment they killed all your family and the moment you showed up among us?" Zivah said icily, "Ten years, were they not? Ten years between leaving your land and ending up among us? What did you do in all those years, Thór-be-yurn? Who did you live with? And what *are* your people the Norsemen doing, entering our lands in ever increasing numbers?"

We all looked at him. Taken a little aback, Father looked from one to the other and sighed. "I will tell you their story, then," he said finally, "and I will tell you of my place among them. You all have the right to know." We settled in, knowing his stories would always take time.

"There have always been many tribes on our North Path Island," Father began, "and we all have different histories and different customs. Most of the tribes that live by the coastlands and fjords and down in the fruitful valleys, as well as on the islands along our shores, are Norsemen. It does not matter what tribe we belong to; we are all Norsemen. We Gautar are also Norsemen. We call ourselves that because, even though we come from different tribes we all share an ancient origin and we all speak a language that we call the Norse language. We call ourselves Norsemen and we call our language Norse because we think we live in the northernmost place in the whole world. We are the Northern people."

"There are some people who live in the deep inland forests and wide mountain plateaus of our great mother island, people who speak a language that is akin to those of the Finns, and they are smaller and gentler than we Norsemen are. But Norsemen have spread into many other lands than our mother island. We have spread into the land west of here that now belongs to the Danes and the Saxons – Norsemen all, and a Norse tribe of Anglos settled in England even further to the west. My own tribal ancestors, the Gautar, separated into two tribes first. One part went to live on an island called Gotland, and because dialects always evolve differently in different places, they began to sound different from their ancestors and they became known as the Gutes. But then there was another tribal schism, and a whole tribe of the Gutes as well as some Gautar from the mainland went south into Poland and on from there in many directions, but even if they have parted into several tribes they were all known as Goths, but most of them are gone now, assimilated into other peoples in the southern parts of the world. We who descend from those who remained in the homelands still call ourselves Gautar." Thorbjörn paused and looked carefully at my mother before he proceeded.

"But some few hundred years ago began an era of famine and pestilence and wars. There were landless men, then, men without a clan, men without wives and children who had few other options than to offer their services as ship crew and as warriors. Many men ended up living on the ships of other landless men who had been able to afford a ship. And these men lived lives of endless seafaring and trading and…and other things. They were uprooted and lost in the world. These seafaring men who lived on their ships are called Vikings in our language. I do not know if you have a word for that in your language. They lived in the seas and the fjords and sometimes their trading expeditions failed them, and sometimes they were poor. And they had no clan and no people among the land dwellers, and when there was famine nobody would help them. That was when they became Vikings. They were so called because they hid in the inlets of seas and fjords. We call those inlets *víkir*, and those who dwell in them are called *víkingur*. That is why we call them Vikings. But it really means that they were robbers, because from those inlets of the seas and the fjords they attacked people – innocent people, helpless people – and they took everything they needed and much more than they needed eventually, for they hardened their hearts and nourished their greed and their bitterness against the land-working folks. And they robbed the hard working people of their wealth and their food and sometimes they took their women to please themselves with."

Zivah and Mother looked pale.

"I think those are called *pirates*," Mother said meekly, looking wide-eyed at her husband, who nodded. He braced himself and continued his tale.

"There have been Vikings in the oceans for hundreds of years already. They have forced the tribes of Norsemen to become fierce and warlike. It was not the first time there was a call for warriors, it had happened before, but there had been peaceful times as well. For the last hundreds of years the people of Gautland have had to defend themselves against both Vikings and the aggression of a neighboring tribe to the north of us, the Svear. I come from a lineage where all men were fierce warriors since time immemorial, and for a few hundred years the Gautar our people have flocked to our halls and courts for the sake of learning the secrets behind our battle arts. The people of North Path Island learned how to fight and how to defend their own and stand their ground, and the Vikings had to turn their attentions elsewhere. They started to explore the eastern lands.

They started to raid the shores of Finland and… and they discovered a new and lucrative business. The Tschudes of East Land, to the north of these lands – the Tschudes told some of those Vikings that they could earn well if they were willing to sell women and children to them. The Vikings wondered why the Tschudes wanted more women and children to feed, and the Tschudes told them that the dark-skinned peoples who live to the south of the world are very rich and would pay very handsomely for light skinned women and children. So the Vikings captured women and children from the villages of Finland and East Land and sold them to the Tschudes, who sold them to the Khazars, who sold them to the rich people down south who wanted light-skinned servants to use for their pleasure and for the doing of chores while they walked about in silk."

Zivah snorted contemptuously at the last remark, still not quite willing to see the connection between her wish to walk about in silk while other people did her chores and the fact that other people would be stolen from their homes by heartless men.

"But what if the women and children did not want to go there?" I asked.

"That did not matter at all to any of the men who abducted them, or to the men who sold them, or to the men who bought them."

"Why did it not matter?" I had never heard of such things.

"Because they had no heart, Thunder Goddess," Father said, and his voice sounded strained as if he were in great pain.

"Let me continue my tale, will you?"

"Yes, father," I said obediently.

"To begin with, the Vikings raided the coastlines of Finland and East Land, and abducted women and children there before they sold them to the Tschudes. There were also a couple of raids back in the homelands, on the mother island, but there was a woman called Bera, and very fittingly her name meant She-Bear. She was abducted along with other women onto the ship of a sea-king named Arn."

"That name means Eagle," I said, always intrigued by what names meant in both my parents' languages."

"What is a sea-king?" Mother asked.

"A sea-king is what the Vikings call a man who owns several ships and has men under him as crew on all these ships. These men were of the worst sort you could imagine – although I doubt that you two or any of your people could ever imagine anything like them - and yet somehow this Bera won a great influence over these Vikings and made them vow to not take women from the homelands anymore, appealing to a wish to be taken seriously by powerful tribes that may serve better as trading partners than as enemies. She pointed out that there had been at least one Sea-King who had ended up as a properly respected land-king after he aided a king in battle and helped protect their shores against enemies. He was married to the king's daughter, an only child, and became the founder of a new royal lineage. As much as they liked roaming and raiding, would they not really wish to be able to stay the winters in a good home full of loving wives and children, and feel the pleasure of respect and praise from their neighbors rather than their perpetual terror? And then she spoke of the greatness of her sister Norsewomen and how they deserved better from their own kind. The Vikings understood the wisdom in her words. But she could not make them stop abducting women elsewhere."

"Years passed by and then the Tschudes rejected the Vikings' captives one late summer, and told them that they could no longer sell their cargo in the south because they had been barred from traveling down the river on account of hostilities with the people who live by lake Ilmen. The Vikings, now led by Bera's son, Arnsteinn the Sea King's Son, stood there north in East Land with a whole herd of frightened and wailing women and children that they could not get rid of and could not afford to feed. They fought the Tschudes then and moved through their territory and came to an enormous lake that they called Aldeigja. But your people call it Ladoga." Mother nodded in recognition. She was beginning to understand where this was going.

"From the great lake they sailed south but upriver into the Volkhov and found a small settlement there which they…Well, they decided to settle there. That woman, Bera, was good at dealing with people, both foreigners and Vikings. She made her son Arnsteinn promise her that they would stay put there. They began to build a small town, a place where they could gather their strengths during winter and set out from into the world during summer. The raided women and children of that fateful year became their permanent servants then, where they had kept none before, and the prettiest ones were taken as concubines who were almost as wives apart from not being free folks. But while the men of North Path Island only take free women as concubines, they set a law that said that concubines had to be… you do not have a word for it, but they were not allowed to be free. But they did marry some women from the neighboring tribes and took them as proper wives. With servants taking care of all the work that needed to be done if they were to have food and clothing and shelter, the Vikings began exploring the surrounding countryside, hoping to find their way down to the Land of the Big Tunics where they paid so well for light-skinned slaves."

"They explored the main rivers first, and finally they met the Khazars of the south and established a trade with them there, although I have heard of Vikings who have had permission from the king of the Khazars to move through their land – and they have gone all the way down to the great Caliphate and traded directly with the folks there. But the Khazars control the trade route so mostly all trade goes through them now. The Vikings named their new town right south of the lake Aldeigja and called it Aldeigjuborg, and they have come to terms with several other tribes of that area and live in peace with their neighbors there. At least they have lived in peace ever since they showed that they could not be beaten and their surviving neighbors decided that it was better to marry off their daughters to these Norsemen than trying to fight them. Now there live in Aldeigjuborg mostly Norsemen but also some Tschudes and northern East-landers and other Finnish folk. Most of their women are from around these eastern lands. They have become a tribe of their own and they call themselves *Væringjar…*"

"*Varang-eeh-ar*?" Mother tried.

"Yes, that is about it. It means "The Ones Who Stay Put" in the Norse language. It was because they were the first Vikings in hundreds of years to establish a town and a place to… to stay put. But the natives around here call them the Rus, which means "rowers", because we do row a lot. And it has become more and more common for the Norsemen of Aldeigjuborg to refer to themselves as Rus." He paused again. His wife was pale but said nothing. He knew that she had known, deep down.

"I thought the Rus were a sort of demons," I said, "or cannibals."

"They are," Thorbjörn said. We stared at him, all quiet, although Zivah volunteered with another disdainful and triumphant snort. "They are not demons as such," Father explained, "They are men just like me. But I will tell you something about demons, my daughters, something that I think your mother knows well, being a Healer. A demon can be born out of the pain that a human being carries. If there is a pain too deep to be cured, a pain of the soul and heart, it becomes a festering ground for little sprites that grow into hungry demons…"

Zivah and I looked uncertainly at our mother, who nodded patiently. She knew this well. "These demons feed on the pain that birthed them. Children; they will do everything they can to recreate the same pain in the most dubious manners, in a way that makes the host - that would be the person who experienced the pain in the first place - in a way that makes the host incapable of even recognizing that it is in truth the same pain showing up in a new guise. The pain blinds the host and makes him crazy. The demon of pain takes over his mind. And sometimes such deep pains happen to so many people at the same place and in the same area that whole tribes are affected by it."

Father sighed and looked at me, "My little Thunder Goddess. I have told the story of how our lineage was destroyed by the Svear to your mother and sister before, and I will tell that story to you soon enough. Suffice it to say for now that there was a bad, bad king of the Svear who lived to the north of us Gautar, who killed our king and his entire lineage. We who were of the clan of the Thunder priests were the sole contenders then to the High Seat of Gautland, and in his fear of us the king of the Svear came in the night and burned down our hall where we had all gathered for the Elfin sacrifices. The spirit of our ancestral mother, the spirit that has been reborn and lies hidden within you, Thunder Goddess, she woke me up that night and made me leave the hall and thus she saved my life. But I had to watch while all the people I loved, my women and my children and all my kinsmen and all my *Sífs*, all of them got killed in that fire."

"You all know the Thunderbolt hammer pendant that I carry. It is very, very ancient. They say it was forged by the Smith of Heaven and given to Thunder Goddess as a morning gift. There were two hammers, one for each of their children. I told you before that Thordís of old had a boy called Magni and a woman called Thrúð, after the children of Thunder. Their names mean Greatness and Power. The one that was given to Magni was passed down from man to man, and it was called the men's hammer, or the Hammer of Greatness. The hammer that was given to Thrúð has ever after passed from woman to woman of the Thunder priest lineage, and it was called the women's hammer, or the Hammer of Power. "

"In our generation, I was the one to carry the men's hammer while my sister Thora carried the women's hammer. After the fire that burned down the Hall of the Thunder priests, the Svear looked around for proof to take to their king, proof that I was dead. These men knew that I carried a very special sort of pendant, and so they looked for my hammer. I was still hiding, watching them that horrible morning as they scavenged through the charred remains of my ancestral home. Then one of them exclaimed something and held up an object that was too small for me to make out, but I knew that it was the hammer pendant that my sister Thora had worn, the Hammer of Power. It had not melted in the fire, for the metal that made it is divine."

"The men, in their ignorance, did not know about the women's hammer, and so they believed that the hammer was mine and thus proof of my death, and so they took it and brought it to their King as evidence. Now that it was too late to save my kin, I decided that I should not let the Svear know that I was still alive, lest they stop me from taking my vengeance."

"Did you, Father?" I asked eagerly, "Did you avenge them?"

"No, my daughter, the Ladies of the Loom wanted me elsewhere, and brought me onto unknown paths. I had to steal a horse in order to get away from Svear warriors, and as I rode away from my homestead, somebody spotted me, and this was reported. Soon, all the King's men were searching for me everywhere and anybody who hid me were in great danger. Many people were still willing to hide me, but I was not willing to put them at risk. Winter was coming, and I rode northwards until I found a Finnish camp. They are the Finns who live to the north of Svíthióð. Now, they call themselves Sámi, and in my youth I had made some friendships there." He smiled sadly.

"I stayed with the Finns all winter, and their Spirit Caller, they called him the Noaidi, he healed my soul and allowed me to say goodbye to all my family at the shores of the river of Hel. They told me to go to the east, as there would be a new life for me there, and I would father more children to inherit the knowledge that only I now carried, the knowledge about thunder. I thought that more important than destroying our entire lineage by dying in an attempt of vengeance."

"And so, come spring, I ventured to the eastern coast and found a ship that took me down to Gotland. Nobody recognized me there, and thought me to be just another rogue warrior without a Heri…" he looked at us while we all formed the pronunciation *Heh-reeh* with our mouths,

"A Heri means a lord, a man who rules someone. Most people have a Heri above them, a lord, and if you do not have a Heri you better either be one yourself or try to get one. It is the Heri who offers protection and unity in our world. And when I roamed about on my own, people pitied me because they thought that I was a warrior without a lord, seeking his fortune. I called myself Grim then, of no family, and by that single name I lived for many years, and kept my hammer pendant tucked beneath my shirt so as to not draw attention to it."

It was well-known that I never laughed or smiled, but I did clap my hands together then at the humor of the name that he had chosen, because I knew that the name Grim meant the Masked One. Father had told me that the lord Óðinn often went by that name when he moved in disguise among people. Now I pictured my father roaming around in a hooded coat like a god among unsuspecting folks. He met my eyes and smiled sadly before he continued his tale.

"I found a ship that was going to sail to the east, and I noticed that the crew largely consisted of warriors, and since I was a great warrior myself, I asked if they needed another sword hand. They said they could never have too many, since the seas were dangerous and crammed with Vikings, soldiers of the Sea Kings. I was tired and desperate and suspected that there were Svear spies who were onto my trail still, and so I joined the crew without realizing that they were also Vikings. Once aboard, I was made to swear an oath of allegiance to the captain."

"Oaths are sacred, as you well know, and among my people an oath of allegiance is more sacred than anything. I swore myself to the captain for seven years, to serve him and obey him for as long as he honored me as his warrior. I thought that was a safe oath, because when I had been a Heri of men I had never asked a man to do a chore that was dishonorable to him. That was what it meant, to swear to serve a man as long as he honored you as a warrior. In the ancient customs of our people, a warrior is bound to honorable conduct. But in the eyes of the Vikings, a warrior is purely about having and employing the might to take whatever you want, or more importantly, to take whatever your Heri wants you to take." He went silent.

"So you became a pirate," Zivah said, clearly eyeing a triumph.

"Yes," said Father.

"You killed people and stole all their things and sold women and children away," she stated.

"Yes," said Father. We were speechless.

"Father," I said, feeling uncertain, "were you a cannibal?"

Father suddenly looked so very old.

"No, daughter, we did not eat people. But what you think of as cannibalism is not always about eating people's flesh. Sometimes there are things folks do what devours the souls of others. In that sense I am sure I did things that… I was no better than a cannibal, Thunder Goddess."

"I hear the Rus rape women also," Zivah said, locking her eyes with Thunder Bear's.

"Zivah…" Mother whispered, but said no more. Thorbjörn did not avert his eyes but looked back at Zivah, yet for a moment I thought he actually feared her then.

"What is rape," I asked.

"Rape is when a man takes a woman and forces her to play the pleasure games with him even if she cries and begs him not to," Zivah said, "is it not so, Thór-be-yurn?"

"Yes," he said hoarsely.

“Why would anyone want to play with someone who does not want to play with them?” I asked, not quite grasping the issue altogether.

“Yes, why would anyone want that, Thór-be-yurn?” Zivah mimicked me, mocking us both. For the first time in my life I saw my father speechless, and my mother too.

“You say you were sworn for seven years,” Zivah continued, not at all intending to lose this chance at finally crushing the man who had failed her as father, “and from what I have gathered seven years must be about the time you stayed with the Rus, am I correct?”

Father nodded and suddenly lowered his eyes. He was looking shamed.

“So how many people did you raid and kill and steal, Thór-be-yurn, in all those seven years?”

“More than I can count,” he said meekly and met her eyes again, allowing her to see the painful sadness and the shame he felt. But even at that openness she did not mellow.

“And how many women did you rape along the way, Thór-be-yurn? Too many to count also?”

“No,” he said quietly, “I can count that.”

“Really,” Zivah grinned, “let us hear the number, Thór-be-yurn.”

“One,” he said, “I raped one woman.” Zivah leaned back a little and looked triumphantly from one to the other. Both mother and I looked helplessly at our Thunder Bear. It was as if our whole world was about to break into shivering pieces of uncertainty. Only Zivah was ahead of us, looking like she had known something that we did not, and now she had turned out to be right after all these years, right about the detestable nature of the man we loved.

“Did she cry, Thór-be-yurn?” Zivah asked after a little while, her tone of voice like poison acid, “Did she beg you to stop? Did you hurt her? Did you like it, taking her against her will?”

“No,” Father said, as simply as that.

“*No*,” Zivah repeated, “*No*? Why do I have a hard time believing that?”

“I can tell the whole story if it matters to you all,” he said.

“Please do,” Zivah said, “let us hear all about it. You are so good at telling stories, I am sure you can make even your little rapist’s adventure into something entertaining.”

Thorbjörn lowered his eyes to her again and drew his breath.

“It was my seventh summer with the Rus,” he began, “and even if I had been on raids each one of those seven summers I had never taken a woman for myself. I had a… a companion in Aldeigjuborg, a woman I shared with some other men, but she was not, well she was not free but I do not think she felt like we were raping her. We treated her quite well and she acted like she was affectionate with us, so I did not count it as rape. There were always some men who liked to take frightened women during raids. But even if you think that Rus are all rapists, Zivah, there are plenty among them who do not find attractive the wailing of women. I did not partake in such games."

"But you did not mind when others did," Zivah wheezed.

"I tried not to see or think of it," Father said.

"How very noble of you," Zivah mocked him.

"You are mocking me, daughter," he said, "and I am not proud of this. But a man's heart hardens when he sees no other option than to accept the misery around him lest he wants to get killed. Let me continue my tale. I have told you that we went on raids. We attacked people, killed anyone who opposed us and took captive all those who could not escape us. For the most part it was very easy for us, because there are hardly any people in the world today who can compete with us Norsemen in direct combat. It was almost like walking in and picking up anything we wanted. We killed those who tried to oppose us not because we really had to, seeing as they were useless as warriors, but because we wanted to create the rumor that it was better to just submit to us if people wanted to spare their lives. And that worked quite well too. We sometimes joked about how people would just surrender at the sight of us. And women, the women were too frightened to resist the men who took them."

"But that summer we came to a tribe that turned out more ferocious than we had anticipated. They fought back and they fought well, even the women. The raid became like a real battle. And that was when I was seized by…" He paused, searching his mind.

"I do not know a word for this in your language, but it is a sort of rage. A battle-rage. Our people have cultivated the art of such a battle-rage for countless ages. The Thunder Warriors were the first to discover its power, allowing our bodies and minds and souls to be seized by the power of thunder, so that we can wield that power and be invincible in battle and oblivious to pain and fear. When the raid turned into a veritable battle, I was seized by the battle-rage. I had learned how to invoke and wield and be in control of that power since I was a boy. It ran in our veins. There is not a Thunder warrior or Thunder priest in our lineage who has not been able to wield the rage. But I had been so far removed from my ancient roots that I no longer knew how to control the rage. When it seized me, I was in its power, and all I knew was a wish to hurt and maim… and when I had killed my last enemy and heard the cheering break out among the men, my comrades, I knew that we had won and I was still thirsting for blood. And I ran into the village and found a hut and entered it."

"There was a woman inside, a very young woman, hardly much older than you, Zivah. She was holding some sort of weapon that she tried to use against me and I brushed it away. That was when I knew what the other men had talked of, that the women were always too frightened by our very appearance to be able to resist at all. I saw the terror in her face as she looked at me and I saw how she just gave up. Just like that. It was so easy, almost as if I was not forcing her at all, because she just surrendered to terror and just let me. There was no resistance on her part and nobody to stop me and I could just take her if I wanted to. That power dazzled me all of a sudden. I clasped her by the throat and threw her back on a bed that was there and then I fell over her and took her."

Thorbjörn suddenly seemed to gasp for his breath. His eyes had gone all red. His body seemed to experience a great trembling. Even Zivah was too agitated to say anything. He looked up at us again and met all our eyes.

"As I was taking her, she just looked at me. She locked her eyes with mine. And then the lights of her eyes just died. I saw it. I was there above her and I saw how I killed her soul. Then the rage suddenly left me and I withdrew from her. She was all still, as if she was dead. But she was breathing. She had become like a breathing body without a soul to spark it. I had done that to her. I. I walked out of that hut and told everybody that there was nothing inside, nothing alive anyway. My comrades grinned and moved on to other spoils. That was the only thing I could do for her then, to prevent her becoming the prey of more men such as myself." His voice broke.

"That night I remembered older vows that I had made. The vows of the Thunder Warrior. They were vows that we had made in honor of Thor our lord, the great Thunderer who relentlessly protects his mother Earth and all her children. Our greatest oath was this; that we should follow in the Thunder lord's footsteps and protect the goddess and all who are like her. Women and children, those who are soft and in need of protection. I had sworn to protect the soft ones all my life, and I had turned against that sacred oath and become the very opposite. It was my seventh summer as a Viking and closing in on the time where I was no longer bound to my captain unless I renewed my oaths to him. After that raid we went directly to the south and sold our cargoes, and then we got the idea of trying to move up north through the river lands that we had not yet explored. We had heard that there was a river running north and into the lake Peipsi. That is a grand lake up north of here from where we could swiftly reach the northwestern ocean and from there the entry river into lake Aldeigja, that is, the Ladoga, and from there we could move upriver into the river Volkhov to Aldeigjuborg. And so we went into the river lands and when we had made sure we were on the right track we attacked a village there. My Captain was a vicious man. He took a captured girl, who was crying and shrieking because we had… we had killed all her family."

His voice broke again.

"The Captain could not bear the wails of the young girl, and so he pulled her out of the flock of captives by the hair, and by the hair he pulled her to the steer board. He tore off all her clothes so that she stood weeping in front of us all, naked and trembling, and then he raped her in front of all his men, and tormented her with words and deeds in many other ways. I watched the spectacle unfold before me, and could not bear the sight. I felt my hammer burn on my chest, and knew that I could not stand by and watch anymore. I had to act on my oath to the god, and be a warrior of Thunder once more. And so I interfered. I went up to the Captain and told him that only a lowly coward would torment a defenseless woman so, which is the truth. Only cowards pick fights with women. He was furious, of course, and told me to withdraw my accusation of cowardice. To accuse someone of cowardice is the worst thing you can do to a Viking, to any Norseman. I refused to withdraw the accusation, and then the only way for the Captain to maintain his honor was to challenge me to battle. I killed him with a blow of my axe, and then his two brothers descended upon me, and I killed them also. The other Vikings were now without a leader, and there was a great deal of confusion before they determined whether to recognize me as their new Captain, or whether to kill me. The Captain's young son was there, it was his very first raid, one young man named Gunnarr, hardly more than a boy. But even as young as he were he had shown himself as a warrior that summer and a cruel one too, one who liked the wailing and suffering of his victims, just like his father and uncles had done. Young Gunnarr rallied the men and shouted to them that they were sworn to him now just as they had been sworn to his father and they owed it to both him and his father and uncles to kill me. And the Vikings heard that and decided to kill me."

"There were thirty men descending upon me, and I had to fight my way out of their midst. I was wounded, but I fled into the forests and ran towards the south. The Vikings followed me until night descended and then for another four days and nights, and then there was a great thunderstorm that lasted for three whole nights. I think great Thor aided me in my escape, honoring my choice to restore my honor as a Thunder warrior. The rain and the thunder made it easy to escape, and the Vikings finally gave up the hunt. I had nowhere to go, and so I just kept moving south for several days. My wound was infected, and I began to have fever dreams, and I knew that I would die. The Vikings lost me, but I kept running as if I was trying to run away from my entire life. I stumbled into a bear on the last night, and thought she must be my Follower. Our people believe that when a man meets the Follower that walks before him, the one who has the shape and nature of a beast, then she is usually an omen of death. I had always known that my Follower who walks before me was a bear. So I accepted death, but the bear just moved away, and later I wondered if she had been a real bear, and that she thought me to be too strange to attack, since she was just standing there when I met her."

"The Thunder Bear!" I exclaimed, thinking of his name.

"Indeed," he smiled faintly and continued his story: "Then on the third morning when the thunder storm was abating, and I was moving, stumbling through the thick forest, more dead than alive now, and suddenly I thought I had reached a shrine of the Thunder lord. I fell down and do not remember any more before I woke up and saw the beautiful face of your mother. You all know the rest of my story."

A great silence descended upon our tent for a while. As far as I was concerned, Father had more than made up for his crimes when he was willing to fight thirty men in order to defend a woman he did not even know, and after a while Mother spoke softly; "Thunder Bear my husband. I have held your heart in my hands and seen all the terrors and all the shame that you have carried within. And I have seen what sort of man you really are, what you have proven to me every day for the last thirteen years of our life together. I forgive you and all your sins. I love you and I always will, because I know that you have a great heart and that you are a great man."

"Mother, are you spell-bound by this monster?" Zivah suddenly cried, looked like she felt betrayed, "He just told us all that he had killed and stolen and taken women and children away from their homes to be owned like goats and that he raped a woman!" She turned viciously against Thorbjörn.

"You are clever, aren't you, to tell that story and then disguise it behind another story of your own heroism. But it does not work with me, Thór-be-yurn, because I have seen what you are a long time ago. You must have some great sorcery about you to dazzle the mind of the Healer like you do, but you have not fooled me! You are a killer and a thief and a rapist, Thór-be-yurn, and there is nothing you can do to change that truth!" She glared at him and then at Mother. "It *sickens* me that my mother lets you into her bed every night."

Mother and I were too stunned to speak. Thorbjörn just sat there and looked empty-eyed and sore. Then he slowly got to his feet while he kept his eyes lowered. "I am shamed as I should be," he said quietly, placing his hands before his face for a moment to illustrate how shamed he was, "and my presence is offensive to a woman in this tent. I cannot blame her. I shall stay outside this night."

"Thunder Bear…" Mother began, but he turned and stopped her objections with a haunted look.

"The maiden's verdict is just and holy," Father said and left the tent.

Our Enemy's Head

At dawn the next morning we swiftly packed our things in silence and put on the new clothes that we had bought at the market. We said our goodbyes to the other families who had been there and set out upriver on our raft just as the Sun rose above the trees. Zivah sat facing the way we were leaving and did not even bother to offer help paddling, and my parents left her alone. She had run off early that morning, claiming to need to go, and returned just before we started looking for her. Father cast some glances at her and peered with wolf eyes down the river but said nothing.

Our parents paddled the whole day until we reached a junction where we began moving downriver and they could relax their oars. They were weary then and decided to camp for the night even if the Sun maiden still stood bright in the western sky. Zivah kept casting glances upriver as if she was expecting someone to follow. After eating, our parents lay down to relax a while, and Zivah said she wanted to go and look for eggs down at the river bank and that she wished to be alone. After she had left us, Father looked at me and nodded. I slipped out of camp and followed my sister's tracks. It was just a while further upriver that I saw Zivah standing in a clearing with the cannibal who had approached her at the market. They were whispering together and Zivah was giggling a little and blushing, looking thrilled and more beautiful than ever. The cannibal was grinning with that same vicious smile that Zivah seemed to be oblivious about. Then he took her gently by the hand and led her down a narrow trail. I sent a thought to my father and followed them.

The trail took us down to another clearing by the river bank, and there was a raft and five other men who sat on the shore, and as they turned to look at Zivah and their leader they grinned in that same vicious way. It was only then that Zivah seemed to look through the veil of the spell they had cast on her. I saw her turn and I saw her face as she realized that the men were soul-eaters and darted in my direction. I saw the shock in her face when the cannibal seized her and muffled her scream with his hand and she discovered that there was nothing she could do to get away because he was so very much stronger than her. I saw the men move up to assist their leader while they grinned and chuckled and whispered jokes among themselves. They began carrying my terrified sister towards the raft.

Then I felt Mother's presence right next to me, her finger to her lips to tell me to keep silent, and I saw how she began pulling at her bow. She had not even had time to pull when a huge shadow darted by past us and down towards the river bank and the soul-eaters. We watched as the shadow suddenly moved among the men with the speed of lightning, watched the flashing of blades and steel through the air, saw the showers of blood and heard the silent thuds of bodies and body parts falling, one by one, six bodies in all, and then some. It happened so fast that Mother never even had time to shoot.

And then there was a terrible silence.

I saw Zivah standing there with her widest eyes and her jaws dropped, covered in blood splatter and trembling, watching the six mutilated and very dead men lying on the river bank. I saw my father standing amidst the corpses covered in blood and gore, suddenly raising his bloodied sword and his bloodied axe up against the sky, roaring like a bear, roaring like thunder. He shove his sword into the ground and roared once more, shouting in the Norse language that only he and I understood; "Behold my victory, oh gods! Behold my victory, oh ladies of the great loom! Behold the blood by which I nourish you, oh Earth! To victory! Týr! *Týr! Týr*!"

Then he beat his blood-covered chest with his fists and roared a third time. His eyes were like glowing red coal when he looked at us again, and his gaze was wild like a beast's, and he screamed at Zivah while gesturing sweepingly towards the men. "*Did any of these men rape you, Zivah*?" he roared. Zivah shook her head in terror.

"*Did any of them hurt you*?"

"They… no… they… I think they were going to…" she whispered, sobbing, "He *tricked* me."

"*Which one was the man who tricked you*?" Father bellowed. Zivah pointed at the dead man with shaking hands. Father considered her composure for a moment and then looked at mother and I, who had somehow come out of our hiding place without even noticing that we had moved, and were now standing there and watching the gushing of blood from the dead men and our blood-covered kinsman, too stunned to do anything but gape at the sight. Then Thunder Bear spoke to all three of us in a voice so deep it felt like the Earth herself shook at the sound of it.

"Now you must be the she-wolves of your secret hearts," he growled.

The Thunder warrior's command worked like a spell. I saw the change in my mother's and sister's eyes, and I felt it in myself. All the shock, the concern and the confusion was gone in the blink of an eye. The horror of seeing that beastly and red-eyed man, covered in blood and gore, standing among men whom he had just chopped and sliced to death, and realize that this man was our Thunder Bear - that horror was gone. All we knew was that bad men had tried to steal our Zivah and eat her soul, but our hero had saved her and made sure those men could never harm anyone ever again.

Then all three of us looked at the roaring Thunder Bear smeared in reddish gore, darting murderous eyes, and we thought that he was *beautiful*.

Before we had time to react Father had taken his axe and chopped off the head of the man who had tricked Zivah. We stared as he took the head and lifted it by the hair, roaring again, slowly turning around himself in the opposite direction of the Sun's path so as to make a circle of blood on the ground. Carrying the head by its hair, he moved around the corpses seven times while he cried to the ladies of below that this man was a traitor and a soul-eater who ought to be doomed to wade upriver in the dark lands of Hel for an eternity and all his men with him. When the head had stopped leaking blood, he moved out of the circle and up to Zivah, holding the head up, its face towards her face. Zivah stared into the face of the man who had come so close to destroying her life forever.

"This man can never hurt you again!" Thunder Bear shouted, "This man is doomed and this man is bound. You have received his fate into your hands." He held the head out to her.

"Take it, daughter" he growled, "take the head of your enemy into your hands." Zivah, like in a daze, took the head in her hands.

"Say it," Thorbjörn growled, "say the words."

"I am holding my enemy's head in my hands," Zivah whispered, as if she had already been taught the words. Thorbjörn nodded.

"Louder, daughter. Say it out loud."

"I am holding my enemy's head in my hands," Zivah said, and her voice only broke once.

"Again."

"I AM HOLDING MY ENEMY'S HEAD IN MY HANDS!" Zivah cried powerfully, and tears began running down her face.

"Now spit on his face," he demanded. Zivah spat into her enemy's face.

"You honor me," Thorbjörn said and took the head back. He turned to Mother and gave her the head. She did not need further urging. The gentle Healer trembled only a little when she held the head, spat into the face and spoke the words: "I am holding my enemy's head in my hands!"

"You honor me," her husband said and took the head, turning to me. I actually reached out my hands, wanting to spit at my enemy's face too, but Father suddenly looked at me with unexpected mildness and spoke to me in Norse; "You will not lack for head-gifts, daughter. Let this day be about your sister." I nodded solemnly and watched when Father took the head and hurled it into the forest.

"Let his head be eaten by beasts and his body rot by the water," he said and turned to us again. "You can kick the bodies now," he said. I do not know why that suddenly seemed like such a good idea to us, but we started to kick at the dead bodies as well as the parts of dead bodies while we screamed and wailed until our throats were sore and our bodies ached with our efforts. It appeared that we were a lot angrier with those men than we had realized that we were until we began kicking their corpses. While we feasted on their deaths, Father just stood there and watched us doing that with an expression of pride in his face. He was proud of us, he said later, because we had become like she-wolves, proud of us and grateful to us because we had honored him that way in the manner of the women of his people.

We began walking back towards our camp while the Sun was setting, but Zivah suddenly had a hard time walking at all. Mother looked frightened but Thorbjörn said that it was only to be expected after such a shock. He picked up his stepdaughter and carried her into the camp where he gently put her down on the ground.

"I do not want to stay here this night," Mother said, and Father agreed. It was not good to stay close to the unburied bodies of dead enemies, even if he had done all sorts of rites to bind their souls. We all took off our clothes and placed them on the fire. The bloodied clothes burned while we washed thoroughly in the river and put on our old traveling clothes, looking like new again.

It was dark already when we set out on the raft, but the Moon lord graced us early with his pale blue light, bathing us in that purifying glitter while we let the river take us home. Mother, Zivah and I sat in the front of the raft with our feet in the water, because the Healer said that the running water would take away the shock. And that way we sat for a long time in silence as we watched the Moon and the stars and the running river. Then Zivah turned around to look at Thorbjörn, and her face was wet with tears.

"Father," she said, "I have been so foolish."

He had to force himself not to agree whole-heartedly with her. He concentrated on the fact that she had once more called him father. "You were just innocent of the ways of men, Zivah," he said gently, "and now you know more."

"You said the other night that my verdict was holy," Zivah said, weeping openly, "so hear my verdict upon you now, father. I think you have paid and been redeemed for your crimes, and I shall never disrespect you again. You have honored me more than I deserve. I beg your forgiveness." She turned around again and began sobbing into her own hands while Mother held her. Nobody needed to speak. I glanced at my father and saw that his tears were streaming too. Swiftly I averted my eyes in respect for his ways.

Zivah's Suitor

What I remember best from the time after the market was how my parents made me a little bow and tiny arrows and taught me how to shoot. Like my mother and sister, I had a talent for shooting and aiming right at my target, and this showed early. I started joining my family when hunting and learned the ways of tracking and stalking prey in a new way. As often as not our hunting trips were not all about shooting prey but about learning how to live in the forest and how to learn from other beasts. I was shown how to stalk a wolf pack once, just to observe their behavior as a group. Both my parents took care of these teachings, sometimes the one and sometimes the other, and often enough all three of us went. We were all three together when we stalked the wolves and my father told me to look out for how the wolves spoke together in the language of eyes and subtle movements. When I began to see how they always established rank between them even in the friendliest of encounters, he said that this was also the way of his people, and that they were very much like wolves.

Zivah had mellowed considerably towards my parents after the incident with the soul-eaters, but still seemed to prefer to be without me if she could choose. But when the winter snow fell thick that year she sometimes joined Father and me on our skis and often we went out just to practice with our bows. These times were precious to me because my sister often changed then, looking genuinely happy and sometimes even spoke amiably with me. She had become awfully quiet for a while. It was only to be expected, but we had agreed not to tell the villagers of what had happened, seeing as they had a somewhat more complicated system of laws regarding the killing of other people than those laws my father had followed when he swiftly and without hesitation cut down six men for attempting to abduct his stepdaughter. But he had tried to gather the council and speak to them of the general danger and suggest ways in which they could prepare themselves in case of attack. The council failed to take his suggestion very seriously and was more worried about the people getting frightened for no reason at all, but they agreed that my father could make out strategies for escape and warning and that if any of the young men in the village wanted to learn some of his battle arts, then they could, if they so wanted. It was generally assumed that nobody would want that, but even so, ten young men did show up at our hut one day and asked Father to teach them the battle arts. From that day on, he regularly took them away from the village to some secret spot in the forest where he taught them many things.

While these things transpired, Zivah had nurtured the notion that she ought to settle for a nice young man who would surely treat her with kindness. After that incident when she felt the soul-eater's iron grasp around her she was even more afraid of violence from men that she had been before when she had only imagined what that could be like. One of those young boys that she had grown up with and who had long since been left standing by was given another chance. It did not take more than one encouraging smile on her part before he was attending her doggedly and following her around wherever she went, hoping for good words from her. She thought him only slightly annoying and more importantly quite safe and used him to explore the arts of pleasure for the first time. To begin with she discovered that she enjoyed it and kept encouraging the relation. Then, little by little, she began to go terribly bored with him just as she had gone bored with all the others.

She was sixteen and I was six when that young man came to our hut with a following of his family, mother and aunt and sister first. He was carrying a young buck that he had killed himself, and his body was painted and the party merry. The whole village seemed to swell with anticipation, and my parents sat down in front of the Healers hut, completely uncertain where the rest of the village was utterly certain; that Zivah would accept the young hunter's proposal. Such proposals usually happened in private if the woman was already a mother or above a certain age. So it had been when my father proposed to my mother when they were alone. But for a young maiden there was supposed to be a public ritual, a ritual that usually only happened if the suitor was absolutely certain that the young woman liked him. Now the entire village was gathered before our hut, and my parents were seated by the outdoor hearth, and I had sat down next to Mother. There we all waited for Zivah. The young man was still standing there with the buck thrown casually across his shoulders, and the weight of the carcass was beginning to burden him. We all exchanged uncertain glances.

After a good while, Zivah finally came out of the hut.

"Zivah," the young man said, "I have hunted for you. I will always hunt for you and any children to come."

Zivah went pale as a sheet. She looked at the man whom she had been dallying with for almost a whole year now, and felt quite upset. She could not remember ever having made him any promises. The young woman knew well that he was passionately in love with her, but that was not her fault. She sat down with a thump and looked expressionlessly at him when he carefully placed the buck down on the ground in front of her, trying hard not to show how heavy he thought it had become. Zivah said nothing and kept staring emptily out in front of her. And there we sat, waiting for somebody to do something. While there had been chattering and laughing before an uncomfortable silence gradually descended upon the village. The young man's mother and aunt and sister began to look meaningfully at each other and then contemptuously at Zivah, and then contemptuously at our mother, who was beginning to look somewhat troubled.

"Zivah," Mother whispered pleadingly, "are you going to cook for this hunter?" Her daughter shook her head slowly and the young man almost dropped his jaws.

"It is such a beautiful buck you caught today," the Healer said gently to the devastated young man, "I am sure your mother and sister and all your friends will be happy to partake in the meal."

The young man stared in disbelief at Zivah before his face changed and turned bitter. "I hope your foreign prince comes for you soon, so I will not have to see your deceitful face around here every day," he wheezed.

Mother sat shame-faced and watched as the villagers dispersed and the young man took the buck and walked back with his following of relatives and friends. They were all looking coldly at Zivah when they left.

When they had left us we looked speechlessly at Zivah, who returned our gazes and assumed a look of surprise when she saw her stepfather grin approvingly at her. Thorbjörn even winked at her. Mother looked at him too, shocked, and asked what he was smiling about, seeing as they had just born witness to disaster. Zivah's reputation was in serious danger. At that, Zivah excused herself and left us, storming away into the forest to be alone in the Medicine Hut. Mother sighed, got up and followed. I looked at Father who was smiling and shaking his head, murmuring to himself in the Norse language. The only word I could make out was the term "blade honer." And then he chuckled again, as if there was something he was very fond of that amused him.

"What is a blade honer, Father?" I asked.

"Well you know that my blades and edges need to be honed every now and then to stay sharp?"

"Yes."

"And you know that we often call one thing by the names of completely different things?"

"Yes."

"And so we call blade honer those women whose ways are so challenging to men that they serve to hone sharp his soul's blade. And when a man sees a chance to have that soul honed and has the courage to grasp that challenge, why, then he has embarked on the path towards greatness."

"Oh. Is Zivah a blade honer?"

"I did not see it before now. I always just thought that she was just fickle and foolish. But now I have seen it with my own eyes and it explains a great deal. Zivah was never taught, but she is a natural. She is a blade honer born."

"Can you be taught to be that?"

"Yes, or let us rather say it is a natural trait in most women, one that some have a particular talent for, and that can be encouraged and polished into a great art. Many wise women use that art and become the creators of great men. Our foremother the Thunder Goddess was one of the greatest blade honers there ever was, and so it has been with all the women of our lineage."

I was too young and too eager to understand Zivah to grasp the relevance of this concept to my own self. "Is that why she rejected him?" I asked, "Because she is challenging in her ways?"

"She was honing him, Thordís. She was honing his soul's blade. Clearly she has liked him well enough, but found him somewhat lacking. He could have stood up to her challenge. He could have accepted her verdict and returned home, where he could have tried to figure out how to impress her. If he had been able to let her hone him, he would have tried to find out what was lacking and done something about it, and proved himself. Even if she would never have him regardless, he would have grown and become a better and greater man. But it takes courage to let a woman hone you, a sort of courage that is not cultivated among your mother's kind. The men here are too weak, and that is why Zivah can never settle with any of them. Zivah tried him and swiftly found proof that he would never be up to her challenges. Did you see how he responded? He was defeated already and admitted it, even throwing in accusations against her, like a coward would. Zivah probably suspected as much and now she knows what a coward he really is. He does not want challenges, and that means that he has no idea about who and what she is. He sees but the image of her that he has entertained in his little head. She wants one who can see into her secret heart. She wants a man who can grow ever greater. She cannot help wanting that. It is as I say, she is a blade honer born. She cannot accept less than greatness."

I do not know if my father did anything to attract Zivah's young suitor to his battle-trainings, but I do remember discovering after that the young man had begun to train with the other young men who had sought Thorbjörn's mentorship. It seems that the poor boy had risen to the challenge after all, and would have become that sort of man what could keep Zivah's interest alive if Fate had allowed his life to continue. Alas, she did not allow that, but she did see him die like a warrior, and it was soon clear that he no longer hated Zivah for spurring him on to that path. His soul was honed sharp.

The villagers, however, did not see the situation in quite the same way. After this incident they were whispering among themselves, often and openly letting the young woman know what they thought of her, having so clearly misled a nice young man of the village. She had always been fickle they said, and later there were other words, words about certain Healer's daughters up through the course of time who had refused their mother's legacy only to see their inherited talents turn against them and everyone who loved them. They were the women who became meddlers in the dark arts, it was said. And when that was being said a few times, they also began talking about me, that strange girl who never laughed and never cried and who never played like other children, that foreign-looking red-headed girl with those ice cold wolf eyes watching everything and saying nothing.

Was it not something about those two girls when their brother died, little Thunder Wolf? And what about *that man*? Word was passed that he was in fact a Rus, and everybody knew what was being said about the Rus. They were demons of the Underworld, come to wreak havoc and disaster on decent folks, wielding witchcraft and supernatural strength, riding dragons and abducting the young. Had someone else seen how he laughed when his stepdaughter humiliated that nice young man?

And the Healer worried, remembering tales of her own. Only Mother's respectability and the esteem that she always showed herself worthy of seemed to prevent more serious accusations against her daughters and against her husband.

Homeland

The old Thunder Priest died the following winter, and I recall my father taking me to his bedside when he lay dying. The thin old man turned his head to the side and regarded me fondly, and said; "This really is *her*, is she not?" Father nodded and said, "Yes, my old friend. This really is her."

"Thunder Bear," the old man whispered; "All this time you have let me pretend to be your mentor, your teacher in the lore of Thunder. I am grateful to you. I am grateful that you had the greatness within to let me live out my life with my title and standing intact. Let me tell you now that I was never deluded. I knew who you were. I know what you are. And you have taught me more and taken me further than I had ever imagined before. You have honored me."

“You have honored me, revered Old Brother,” Thorbjörn said, and the dying man smiled faintly and whispered, just as he let out his last breath; “It is you who are the old one, Thunder Bear.”

The death of the Thunder priest only intensified the village’s general suspicions against the Healer’s family. The old man had taken Thorbjörn under his wings for all this time, but now there was one less elder to speak his case. Zivah, Father and I were often subject to secret whispers behind our backs. I sensed the change of attitude in my home village that last year spent among them. I began dreaming of my father’s homelands. And as if he sensed my new direction, Father began speaking more and more about his homelands, making sure that I knew all the most important stories and all the most important verses, the verse-frames, the ritual responses and how to behave politely, and most importantly how to behave around powerful men. Thorbjörn taught me many things about our people; our customs, our lore, our history and our clan’s lore, many things that would help me when I could be a child no more. He said that there had been many things revealed to him in his secret heart after what happened on our way back from the market, and it had made him feel the urgency of teaching me these things.

One early spring day he drew a map for me. He explained that it was an image of the known lands of the world-circuit. Up to the north of ourselves was Eastland, and beyond a great ocean river outlet there was another land called Finland. In both lands lived many different tribes of Finns, some who lived as simply as animals and others who had towns and horses, and others who were more like us, living from the forests but trading with the world outside. But their languages were very different from ours, although Father knew a bit here and a bit there from many Finnish tongues.

Up by the northernmost end of Finland there was a great strait and a frosty ocean, and that land was called Bjarmland. The Bjarmian tribes were terribly warlike and wild, what together with the extremely cold conditions up there had long rendered open the question as to whether North Path Island really was an island or, as the legends told of, a peninsula, connected to Bjarmland by a narrow land-bridge. One great Finnish tribe also lived on North Path Island, and they tended to call themselves the Sámi, although there were many branches of that tribe also. Father pointed down the eastern shores of the island.

“A lot of this land is covered by thick and ancient forests, so wild that people prefer to travel the coastlines rather than try and venture through. Up here in the north there are several smaller tribal lands, but from about this point…" he pointed, "… lies the land of a very ancient and powerful tribe called the Svear. Their land is called Svíthióð, that is, the land of the Svear tribe. Their kings live and rule from the great sanctuary of Uppsala, here. For more than twenty generations, these kings were of the Ynglinga lineage, descended from divine Yngví Freyr, the lord of elves and of all growth. Freyr is an ancient word for lord. Today, we would have said Yngví Heri, but the old title stuck with the god and… uh, and with some other old words for lordly things…"

"Like with *Freystone*?" I asked curiously, remembering when I asked him what he called his man-wand in our language. We had several descriptive words but only one that was the actual word.

"Uh, yes, like with that. The lord stone, yes. Uhm. Let us proceed with your lesson, daughter. South of Svíthióð lies our ancestral Gautland, what covers most of the southeastern part of the island, although the southwestern side, here, is called Scania. All these are ancient tribal lands. This island to the south of Gautland is called Gotland and the people who live there are called Gutes. They are descended from the Gautar."

"That would be us, Father? We are Gautar?"

"Yes and no. As I told you before we descend from a people who lived there before the Gautar. But we have blended with that tribe for time immemorial, so we must rightly call ourselves Gautar by now. But the people of our ancient lineage are the ones who carried on the red hair and the very light skin that can still be seen on people all over North Path Island, child. Now, see here, a little further to the south of Scania we have Burgundarholm, where the tribes of Burgunds lived a long time, although mostly Danes live there now. The Danes came from a place north of Svíthióð many hundreds of years ago, but there was a great war and the tribe had to move through Gautland and Scania until they reached this cluster of islands here. The largest one is called Zealand and is said to have been carved out of Svíthióð by the great Gefion Freyia, the Provider. She gave that island over to the divine tribe of Aesir ages past, and the Danes claimed that they were directly descended from Óðinn and had a right to that place. They built a very important royal seat at Hleiðargard near Roskilde, the place where our kinsman Beowulf once came to fight as champion for the Danish king. Later, they moved into this peninsula you see here called Jutland, where they met other tribes that had left North Path Island much earlier, during the Age of Flooding. The peninsula was named after the first people who lived there, the Jutes, but when the Danes came, the Jutes had been divided into several tribes. To the north lived the Vanir, who made truce with the Danes and blended into their tribe, and further to the south were the Anglos, the Saxons and the Frisians. As the Danes pushed south, the Anglos left to move across the western sea and settled what became known as Anglo-land or England. With them came also many Saxons, although half the Saxon tribe settled in the forests south of Jutland, this is now known as Saxland or Sachsen. But now we have moved out of North Path Island. Let us return to the homelands."

He pointed to a narrow fjord going from south to north, just to the west of Svíthióð. "This area here to the east of the fjord is called Víkin, the "Inlet". There are several tribes living here, but they were all once called Vikings, on account of being from Víkin. They say the first Vikings, as in pirates, came out of there, but nobody is certain if that is true or just coincidental. Here live very wild folks of the forests, we have Alfheim and Ránaríki, Vingulmark and Raumaríki… the people of Ránaríki believe they are descended from the ocean goddess Rán, and they are besides pirates and robbers like her. The Rauma tribe believes they are descended from the river goddess Rauma – lots of the tribes there are descended from river women just like your mother's people believe they are descended from Danu. Alfheim, now that is thought to be the ancient realms of the light elves and the people who live there are fair and mysterious, a forest people. Their king is always called Gandalf, and he is as much of a Seið-man as he is a king. They also guard the forest land here right to the north of the fjord; Vingulmark, the Impenetrable Forest. That land is thick with ancient oaks and only elves are thought to live there. On the western side of the fjord do we find Vestfold where the exiled Ynglinga kings of Uppsala now have taken up their reign."

"As we move further north it can be noted that there is an enormous mountain ridge going from this area and all the way to the very north of the great island. That is why we call this mountainous land on the western part of our island "North Way". But in all of North Way there are at least thirty tribal lands and even more tribes, many are kingdoms while others are ruled by tribal council only, and they are too many to name right now. But I shall list them for you so you may remember. Suffice it to say that the peoples of North Way are those who now live truest to the oldest ways, still observing many of the ancient customs of Norsemen that once were held holy by all the tribes."

"Why is that not so in the other parts, then?"

"There have been many a turbulent age throughout the course of time, daughter. The last great upheaval began more than a hundred years ago, when the last Ynglinga king to occupy the High Seat of Uppsala attempted to become king of all the neighboring tribes. His name was Ingjald the Bad Ruler. He wanted to create a kingdom called Svearíki, the reign of the Svear. By deceit and treason he subdued five out of six tribes, including Gautland, but he could not take Scania. He sent his daughter Ása to marry Guðröð, the king of Scania. Ása was a very cunning and ruthless woman, exactly what her father liked, and he let her rule beside him. Like her father, she was called the Bad Ruler too. She managed to have both her House-Bond and his brother, Harald the Valiant, killed by traitorous means, hoping to take the High Seat of Scania for herself and her father."

"But they had not counted on Harald's son, Ivarr. Now Ivarr posed such a threat that queen Ása Ingjaldsdaughter had to flee back to her father in Uppsala. Ivarr took the High Seat of Scania, and from there he invaded Svíthióð by allying himself with the suppressed folks of Gautland and the other tribes who would not accept the rule of the Ynglinga king. But instead of offering freedom in return for support, he installed himself as king over what his predecessor, Ingjald the Bad Ruler, had called Svearíki. As such, Ivarr became king of Svíthióð, Gautland, Scania and Gotland. Not long after, he took most of Zealand and parts of Jutland as well. He became the greatest king anybody had ever seen in North Path Island and beyond, a king of Svearíki and Denmark together. His name was Ivarr Rules Widely. He was a descendant of the great Hróarr of Hleiðargard, the king who ruled when Beowulf our kinsman defeated the monstrous Grendel. As such, he was descended from the Skioldunga lineage what had ruled Denmark almost as long as the Ynglinga kings had ruled in Svíthióð."

"What happened to the Ynglingar, then? To Ingjald the Bad Ruler and his daughter Ása?"

"Father and daughter committed suicide when they realized that all was lost. But there was a son too, his name was Ólaf, and he was a very noble and peace-loving man. He had not been favored by his father at all; the vicious daughter was more to their father's liking. Perhaps he did not think that Ólaf was his actual son, I am not sure. But there were many Svear who now were discontent about being ruled by the Skioldunga king from Denmark. They considered the Ynglinga lineage sacred and divine. So they followed Ólaf Ingjaldsson as he made his way into North Way, and he was known as Ólaf the Tree-Feller, for he built land in the unpopulated forests of Värmland east of Víkin and Alfheim. This was before his descendants began conquering or else marrying the royal daughters of the North Way tribes. Some of the Ynglinga kings ruled many tribes there, but nowadays they rule only in the kingdom of Vestfold, a very rich land that lies here to the west of the Víkin fjord, and sometimes they have ruled other tribes by marrying their princess."

He pointed at the map.

"Last thing I know, Halfdan the Mild was king of Vestfold and Raumaríki in North Way. But if we move back to Ólaf the Tree-Feller, there was a great famine during his days. Now, this is about a hundred years past. The Svear believed that famine was caused by a king's inadequacy, so they had Ólaf sacrificed to Óðinn, who had become their most important god by then. Later they followed his son by a North Way princess, Halfdan. Many of the North Way tribes still followed the mother lines and the Ynglingar could gain power in these tribes by marrying the female heirs. They changed into following the father line as soon as the Ynglingar entered, though."

He paused a little. "Now, the famine was wide-spread and reached all the tribes of Svearíki, including Gautland. No matter how they sacrificed, the goddess of the land held back her providence. Pestilence abounded, and so did lawlessness and theft, murder and violence. Hordes of warriors without land or hope became Vikings and sailed to the east. This was how they eventually settled in Garðaríki. It was a time of rebellions and wars against the supremacy of Ivarr Rules Widely and his successor Rurik the Ring-Slinger."

"Rurik was married to Ivarr's daughter, Auð the Deep-Minded. She was Ivarr's only child and thus the end of the Skioldunga lineage, seeing as that lineage had passed down the father line. She gave birth to Harald Wartooth. When Harald was still a young man, less than twenty-five, it became clear to both of them that Rurik was planning to give the throne over to another son by another wife. Auð, who was his sole reason for being king in the first place, divorced him, but when he refused to give over his power to their son, she took Harald and many men with her and sailed to Garðaríki, where she met with one of the Sea Kings who ruled a large fleet of Viking ships. His name was Ráðbarð. She convinced him to follow her and Harald Wartooth in an attack on King Rurik the Ring-Slinger."

"With the aid of ferocious Rus Vikings, Harald Wartooth took the High Seat of all the lands in Denmark and Svearíki. But our people, the Gautar, kept rebelling against the foreign rule. Harald was too powerful for us Gautar to fight effectively, but the rebels never truly gave up. During his reign, Harald proved himself a great leader and warrior many times. After twenty years of ruling, he grew weary and was beginning to feel the aches of old age. He feared that he would never die in battle, but it so happened that his mother Auð had given birth to a son by Ráðbarð the Sea King, a young boy by the name of Sígurð Ring, and he was born the same year as I was born, Thordís, some five and fifty years ago."

"Did you know him?" I asked.

"Yes, indeed I did. We were friends of sorts when we were young lads. Now, his much older half-brother, Harald Wartooth, also had a son by the same age as us, called Rurik after his father. In honor of his mother's wishes and to give thanks to his stepfather who had helped him to the throne, Harald offered half his kingdom to his younger half-brother. Sígurð Ring should be king of Denmark, Scania and what was henceforth to be called West-Gautland, while Rurik should be king of East-Gautland, Gotland, Svíthióð and the lesser tribes north of there. To share his kingdom, Harald Wartooth had only one condition."

"What condition was that, Father?"

"That Sígurð let Harald die in battle. It was because Harald's Full Troth was Óðinn, and Harald believed that the god would only accept him if he died fighting. So they staged a massive battle to be attended by any warrior who wished to prove himself. It was called the Battle of Brávellir, and it happened thirty years past. There Harald Wartooth died as he wished, and many men with him, all to enter Valhalla for having shown the courage to die in a battle that was nothing but a spectacle to entertain the gods and give the old king a good end."

"Did you fight there?"

"No, only those men who sought that form of glory did participate. I was hardly seventeen and I did not worship Óðinn."

"Is Sígurð Ring still alive like you are?"

"Sígurð Ring still rules his lands, last time I heard, which is a while ago, I grant you. He is, or was, a great king. But Rurik Haraldsson, who ruled in Svíthióð and East-Gautland, was never popular among us Gautar, and neither was his successor, Thorolf Wavy Nose. Before I left the Rus more than fifteen years ago, I heard that his son Vemund was to succeed him, and I presume that he is no more esteemed than any of his predecessors. But it was Thorolf Wavy Nose what sent his men after us Thunder priests and had our clan wiped out. He was the king what kept searching for me, and who may still be searching for me if he is still alive. His son surely will, for whatever king now rules there, he keeps the women's hammer in the Uppsala treasury, daughter, and he will have heard of the Hammer of

Power and knows that if it is united with the Hammer of Greatness, a great fortune may be his and his only."

"Is that true, Father?" I looked curiously at the Hammer of Greatness which my father carried, the men's hammer. He had told me that it contained the memories of all the men who had been Thunder priests before him, ever since Thorarinn the Thunder Warrior and his father Magni, son of lord Thor.

"No, daughter. Their perception of the hammers is utterly erroneous. But they are based on the truth. I cannot reveal that truth to you yet, daughter, you will have to be initiated. Suffice it to say that only we who are descended from Thordís and the Thunder priests will know how to empower the two hammers once they are reunited. We have the Thunder in our veins, and only with that Thunder will we be able to invoke and wield that power."

"That should have been my hammer, should it not, Father?" I asked, "The women's hammer?"

"Yes, Thordís. The Hammer of Power is your rightful legacy. It holds the memories of your ancestral mothers, ever since Thordís the Thunder priestess. Sadly, it is kept stored away in the treasury of a king who knows nothing of how it truly works. It is like a joke of fate, Thordís, that the women's hammer should have been abducted and kept prisoner, while the men's hammer is lost in Viking lands, with no son existing to inherit such a great legacy."

"A joke? How so, Father?"

"You will understand what I mean when you are older," he said, and got that sad weight over him that sometimes burdened him.

"I will have to fetch it, then," I said thoughtfully. Father placed his enormous hand on my back.

"Perhaps you will, Thordís. Anything is possible. But as it now seems, you will have to carry the men's hammer after me and pass it on to your son. Perhaps he will be more capable of retrieving your legacy for you, child. It is a man's world out there."

"Father," I said after a while, "The villagers do not like us anymore."

"I know, child. I know. They like your mother, though. As long as she lives we should not be in any danger here."

"Even Zivah…"

"Yes. She carries her father's blood."

"What does that mean? Did you know her father?"

"Perhaps I did, a little. I am not sure. But I think Zivah has the journeyman's spirit alive in her. That is why she is thus restless. And perhaps she senses the changes to come. Perhaps she has sensed them a long time, and does not wish to attach herself too much to this her birth-place."

"What changes?"

"Better not speak of them until they present themselves, Thordís. We must always live right now."

We sat quietly for a while until a spectacle presented itself right there before us. Father pointed at one of the tiny kittens of my mother and told me to watch intently. The kitten was playing with the corpse of a recently departed fish almost its own size when three large dogs approached, clearly wanting the fish. The small feline immediately recognized the challenge and stood above its fish, shooting back and wheezing. I worried a little, seeing as the kitten was so tiny and the dogs so very big and strong. But the kitten stood its ground, and after a while of staring and a few feeble attempts to take the fish, the dogs withdrew and left the kitten to continue playing with the fish.

"The stance is everything, Thunder Goddess," Father said, "the stance and the attitude and the utter lack of fear. If you stand your ground and show yourself fearless, even those much mightier than you will respect you. And out there in the great wide world, the respect of great men is of utmost importance, especially for the likes of you. You must always stand your ground, my child, even when you are backing off, even when you are helpless."

And then he told me the story of Yrsa the she-bear, a girl who had been captured by Vikings yet whose bearing had been so impressively noble that it had turned the minds of the Vikings in her favor. She had been so well-spoken and dignified that she was not placed among the slaves, but walked freely on the ship and was eventually so well-liked that she became the Queen of Svíthióð, and a mother to the hero king Hrolf Kráki.

Zivah seemed oblivious about her reputation in the village and only snorted when she heard complaints, walking about more aloof than ever. Their disdain for her only served to prove that there was no future for her in the village. She knew that she had been a fool at the market, but now that she had learned the ways of the world, or so she thought, she would know better. She had just been unfortunate and made a poor judgment on her very first trip outside of her birth village. Next time would be different, of that much she was certain.

She had kept some of her doting friends and I had overheard them once, down by the river banks.

“I still wish that my prince would come,” Zivah had said, looking longingly down the river. “I still wish there was someone out there who could take me far, far away from here. I have dreamt about him all my life. I cannot think that such an old and long-lived dream is just fancy.”

And her friends had cooed at the thought and looked down the river just like she did. One day they would come, the foreign prince and all his men, bound to desire them and come to whisk them away into a world of adventure and daring and the wearing of splendid dresses.

They had no idea how true their vision was.

Vikings (790 AD)

*

River Dragons

I remember well that day when I first saw a Viking ship. In fact, I saw three, and I thought that they were dragons to begin with, having learned my father's songs about such creatures. Even though he had told me about his people and about the Vikings, I was still a child, and my life in the village had always been harmonious, stable, and protected. Nothing could have prepared me for the sight of Viking long ships, gliding silently down the river. It happened during my seventh summer. I had been with my father that day, helping him in the butchering of a stag that he had killed. While we worked with the carcass, our hands bloodied, I asked Father if he missed his homelands.

"Of course I do," he said, "but what I miss is no longer there. My family, my clan, our homestead – all of that is gone. It was one of the reasons why I became a Viking despite everything. I hoped that if I could gather enough wealth and fame, I might become a captain myself, with men of my own, and then I could return and avenge them all. But that would have been my only reason for returning."

"Do you still want to avenge them?" I asked. From his songs and tales, I had learned that vengeance was important to the Norsemen, the only way of settling matters such as these, and if one generation could not accomplish the task, the next generation inherited the duty. And from the songs I had heard, the next generation meant me, even though I was a girl, since I was his only living child.

"No," he said, "I changed, daughter, when I met your mother. In fact, I changed on the day when I saw that poor girl on the ship and remembered my vows to Thor. As I lay in the sick bed with my wound that your mother tended I recalled all the people I had killed, and all the people I had taken away from their homes and sold into slavery, and I knew that I had indeed avenged myself, only on the wrong people. I was no better than the men who killed my family. And so, when I could stand and walk about again, I made a ritual and a vow, where I asked to be released from my duty of vengeance and paid atonement for the people that I had destroyed."

I felt my shoulders relax. I did not have to inherit my father's duty.

"When I came among the River People," he said, "I learned a different way of life. And I found that it was a better way of life."

"How so, Father?" I asked.

"In many ways, coming here was like waking up in another time, long past. This village, this life that people lead here – it reminds me of the tales I had heard about our own past, when people lived in peace and prosperity. We have legends of peaceful times where people devoted themselves to wisdom and knowledge. To us, that state was a legend, something to dream about during the long winters. When I came here, I saw that it still existed. Your mother's people, as a whole, they are very wise, my child." He laughed a little and continued; "When I first came to know them I thought they were the puniest men I had ever met. Not a warrior among them. Even our women are stronger and better skilled for battle than these village men. But now, I think that the River People are wise and kind hearted. I am grateful and honored to live amongst them."

We finished the work and bathed in the river. It was late in the summer, but still hot. Father left me by the riverbank when he carried the fur and the butchered parts of the stag into the village. I stayed there at the bank, enjoying the heating rays of the Sun Maiden drying my bare skin. There was nobody else about right then, and I closed my eyes, enjoying the sensation of being alive, listening to the birdsong and the buzzing of bees, and the soft sound of water splashing against the shore.

Suddenly the birds went quiet, and I heard a strange rumble, as of distant thunder. I opened my eyes, but the light of the Sun Maiden blinded me, and so I squinted and saw the strangest sight. A dragon! I sat up and leaned forward, watching, as a great dragon glided by down the river, silently. Then I realized that it was a ship, the largest I had ever seen. Until then, most of the river steeds I had seen had been little more than rafts and even the largest boats of foreign traders had not been anything like this. At the prow and at the stern I saw the large heads of dragons, looking quite like Father had drawn them up for me in the sand before, when he told me about dragons. There was a great sail, red in color, and with a symbol in the middle that was unknown to me. At the sides, I saw a long row of shields, all painted with various images, and oars that were still, lifted, drawn back towards the oar ports. At first, the ship itself dazzled me with its exotic splendor.

Only when I had gazed at it for several seconds, what felt like hours, did I see the Vikings. They were quiet, terrifyingly quiet, as if they were statues of our gods, immovable, standing behind shields, staring solemnly towards the shore – towards me. I stared back, and could distinguish bearded faces and large heads of hair, although some were disguised behind masks and helmets.

The ship continued down river, but was followed by a second, and then a third, and each one of them was more glorious looking than the other – and each carried whole rows of what I almost thought were wooden statues, like the ones we kept in the village square and in the groves, the wooden statues of our gods. I was but seven years old, and even though some said that I was wise beyond my years about many things, I was still a child, and this sight was too alien for me to grasp. For a long time, as I sat there, I could not decide whether I was dreaming or not, and whether the men aboard the ships were really men or else dream symbols, silent pillars behind shields.

When the last ship had passed, I felt a sudden chill. I got up and got dressed, and then moved dreamily back into the village, where life seemed to go on as usual. I felt a strange and unusual sense of unease that seemed to paralyze me, and I just stood there for a while, village life passing before my eyes yet with my mind still partly inside a dream of dragons and wooden pillars, until my sister Zivah spotted me and rolled her eyes mockingly.

"What are you standing there for, sister? You are looking dumber than ever, standing like that, staring and gaping. Did the Sun strike you down?"

I gazed at her, my beautiful sister, still so young, but at seventeen, she was a woman fully grown. For the first time I consciously wondered why she hated me so. We were born of the same mother. I shook my head slowly and said, "I saw the dragons," and then I pointed down towards the river.

"You saw what?" she asked, still with that mocking tone in her voice.

"There was a dragon," I said, "a dragon on the river." I still felt confused, uncertain about the reality of what I had seen.

"You have had a vision? Of dragons?" She made a grimace that clearly signaled her disgust with me, and I decided that I could not tell her more about deeply personal matters such as visions, so I left her and went back to our house where my mother was preparing medicines. Still dizzy after what I had seen, I found comfort in doing something familiar with my mother. She was humming and singing small songs of praise to the plants that she was using, and I found myself chanting with her as we worked. And so hours passed by, and I told nobody else about what I had seen, since I thought they would just mock me like my sister had, and because I was uncertain if I had seen what I had thought I had seen. It was as if the vision of the dragon ships faded, and I began to believe that it had really been a dream.

At supper, Father had invited many people to eat outside our house. We still had many good friends in the village, all things considered, and Father had a way of endearing people to him. The pieces of stag were roasted on open fire, and there was a good ambience among us. There was eating, drinking and talking, laughing and singing and the telling of stories. Darkness fell, and we were still sitting there after the meal, and I sat quiet, soaking it all in – the scents, the sounds, the faces of my mother's people. I felt everything so strongly then, even more powerfully than usual, as if I wanted to draw the spirit of the entire village into myself, so that it would be with me forever. I did not know why I felt that way. Father eventually came up to me and patted my head. I liked the way he could just whisk me up in the air and place me on his shoulders or on his lap, and now he did both. First I was sitting on his shoulders, and I saw all those people smile at the sight of me, seated high up on my red-haired giant steed. It was an unusual thing, seeing them all look approvingly at me, and it is a sight I always kept in my heart since; the one time I felt that I belonged among them.

Then Father held me on his lap and brushed his large hands through my own thick, red locks. "Why are you so dreamy, little Thunder Goddess?" He asked, kissing my cheek.

"I saw the dragons," I said. He frowned.

"You saw *dragons*?" He looked very surprised. Now that I am grown and remember these things, I understand that his surprise at first was not about what I said I had seen, but because this was the first time I ever said something that could be remotely interpreted as a child's fantasy. He must have wondered how I had suddenly become so imaginative, and perhaps he recalled that time when I had spoken of cannibals. His surprise was soon replaced by worry.

"Ships with dragon's heads," I corrected myself, "and aboard there were wooden pillars only they looked like men. They looked like you. And some had masks on. I think they were Rus. I think perhaps they were Vikings also." Father stared at me. The idea that I had suddenly developed an imagination was swiftly cast away from his mind. He knew his daughter, and knew well that I never spoke a word of untruth.

I was simply trying to describe something that was too alien for me to explain properly, not even being sure that my sight had been real.

"How many were they?" he asked, his grip around me getting tighter.

"Three," I said, "and each had about thirty shields on the side and all the shields had pillars behind them, only they may have been men, but they were so still and so quiet I thought they might be pillars. Or statues. Like the gods." He asked me to describe the shields, the sails, and the men, and I dutifully informed him about every detail, until his growing worry made me realize that my vision may have been real, something very much of this world after all. He considered the time that had passed since I saw them and began to perspire heavily. His eyes were filled with water, as well as an eye-fire that I had only seen in him once before.

"Are they Vikings, Father?" I asked, quite calm and certain that Father would be able to deal with a few Vikings as swiftly as he had dealt with the soul-eaters. He took a deep breath.

"Yes, Thordís, they are Vikings," he said, "And we must make ourselves ready."

Preparations for Battle

Making ourselves ready proved a more difficult mission than it should have been. Breaking in to the party with people enjoying themselves and getting ready for bed: Just making everybody listen was quite a challenge for my father, but eventually he managed to get the people's attention, and had them alert the rest of the villagers until they all gathered in the village square. The second challenge was to get the villagers to realize the danger. Ours was a people that had not known battle or war for so many generations that we hardly knew what it was. Some women just started to cry, but more were simply incredulous, refusing to believe the confused tale of a child who had, it was pointed out, always been very strange. The men appeared generally more alert, mostly because of my father, whom they respected. Some of them had received training in the battle arts from my father for the last few years, and they knew that he would never have created such a commotion unless he had good reason. His students were the first to flock to him, but they were no more than fifteen young and rather inexperienced men apart from Father, and the Vikings were outnumbering us all. Realizing the impossible odds, some of the elders then demanded that we all leave the village and hide in the forest, but Father looked gravely at them and said that it was much too late.

"Why?" an old woman asked, "Why is it too late? Do they not attack from the river bank?"

"No, revered grandmother," Father said, "The Rus never attack from the river. They sail past, find a place to hide the ships, send out scouts, and then they return as soon as darkness falls, and…" He paused and looked around, knowing well that his next words could cause panic. "We are already surrounded," he said, "It is how they do it. They find a village and surround it as soon as darkness falls. Then they wait like wolves for their prey, yet they wait until dawn, just before people wake up. And then they attack. Anyone who ventures into the forest now will be seized by the Rus. So no matter what you all decide to do you must wait until morning and brace yourself for a vicious attack on our village."

He drew his breath and continued before the panic spread. "Now I am going to tell you that there are but three possible outcomes of this situation for each one of you. You will either escape, be killed, or be captured. Any man who tries to fight them directly will be cut down, so I do not recommend that you fight them unless you have chosen death before being captured. And before you chose captivity you must realize that if you are captured then you will become like a domestic animal to the people who will buy you, own you and treat you as something less than human. You will be like goats to these people, theirs to use as they please. Your lives will be in their hands. All women will be raped. You will be spread out into the world like dust in the wind never to see your homelands again. So I tell you this, people of my wife and daughters, if you choose to fight back, then you will die, but then you will also maintain your freedom. Escape or fight to the death; that is my counsel to all of you, for believe me when I say that death is the better option."

The villagers were now completely silent and were simply gaping at Thunder Bear. There was something about the way he had spoken that made them realize that his words were painfully true.

"I am asking all of you who know how to shoot a bow to find positions within the village from where you can ambush the Rus. Try to kill as many as possible, confusing and surprising them will give the rest of you a chance to get away from the village and away from the Rus. And to you brave shooters who decide to try and shield your friends with your arrows, make sure that when the Rus discover where you are, or preferably before, then run for your lives. None of you will be able to stand up to these men in direct combat. None, not even my students. So run for your lives. In daylight you know these forests better than they do and you can slip into unseen places. Get as far away as possible and then stay there for three days before you send scouts to check out the village. And then those who have survived and remained free may rebuild this place. But if you cannot escape the Rus, then remember my words. Your choice is simple then. It is die or be captured. And captivity can be worse than death."

The villagers were weeping quietly now.

The realization that we were already trapped and surrounded did indeed cause panic, but Father had somehow assumed an authority that ruled the whole village. He told them to hush down and pretend that they knew nothing, seeing as we were being watched. We still had time to prepare ourselves, he said, because if the Rus thought that we were sleeping in our beds by dawn, they would be surprised when we were all ready to flee or to fight. The Rus did not know our language, and so even if they had noticed that we were discussing serious matters by now, they had no way of knowing that we were discussing them. And so he made everybody pretend that the matter had been settled and that we were resuming the party. While people pretended to continue eating and talking, Father went his round and talked to everybody, men and women, who in any way could help defend our village. Fortunately, even if we had few fighting men, we did have a lot of shooters, also among the women, and now people discreetly went to get their bows and arrows, and make sure that they had enough of them. The rest of the village began to appear more and more like chicken do right after being beheaded, except that they were still clucking. Father was perspiring, his face a mask of despair, when he realized how poorly prepared most of the villagers were.

I was so tired at some point that I just fell asleep, and remember only how Mother took me and my sister back to the house and laid down on the bed with one daughter on each side. She held us close, and although I was half asleep, I heard her say to Zivah that she must always remember that I was her sister, and that sisters must stick together no matter what. Zivah did not object, and once that night, our eyes met as we were both resting our heads upon each of our mother's shoulders. She gave me a little smile, the first she had given me for as long as I remembered.

I woke up while it was still dark, from the sounds of my parents getting ready for battle. Mother had dressed in her hunting clothes, with breeches and a tunic that did not reach further down than below her hips. It was long since I had seen her dressed like that. Now she was fastening her dagger to her belt, and counting her arrows. The most important defense strategy that Father had devised was to place as many shooters in strategic places as possible. Most of the villagers, both men and women, knew how to shoot with a bow and arrows, and Mother was quite good at it. But she had never shot a man before.

"How do I shoot a man?" she whispered suddenly, staring up into my father's solemn face.

"It is like shooting a deer," Father said.

"Not, it is not," Mother replied, but my father shrugged. He nodded his head towards the bed, where my sister and I were still lying.

"Think about what they will do to our daughters. You know what will happen. Think about *that*, when you shoot. Be the she-bear I know you are. Protect your children. Kill or wound as many of them as you can manage. I know you can do it, woman."

Mother looked at us, and then nodded. "I can do it," she said.

"And stay *down*," he said to her, "Stay in hiding. If you are discovered, and you cannot shoot them, *run*. You do not have the strength to take on a man face to face. I could not bear it if they got you, Saulé."

"They will not take me. They would have to kill me first, or I would kill myself," Mother said. "Then we will meet in the next world," Father said, "glorious it would be to die in battle with you, my yellow amber Síf." They embraced, and kissed. Throughout all the years that they had been married, even with the loss of three children, they loved each other passionately, and I had never seen that passion fade.

Father came over to my sister and patted her hair. "I have always regarded you as my daughter, Zivah," he said, "I hope you know that. I love you. Now do stay hidden, for you are not a fighter, even if you can shoot a bow. When you have made sure that the path between our house and the forest is clear, you run as far as you can into the forest and you *stay* out there, you hear me? You *stay* out there for days before you dare to return, even if you find nobody else. They may still have men waiting for escapees in the forest, so you must be cautious as you run, and stay silent. They may linger, and they will be searching the nearby forest. So stay away. The forest is full of nourishment at this time of the year. You know the place where we have hidden equipment and provisions. Find that, and use it. Survive. If you can, you look after your sister and other escapees. But it is more important that *you* get away, for nothing worse could befall you than becoming the prey of a Viking. They *will* rape you, Zivah. And then they will sell you as a slave, and you will know no end to rapes. And if that happens, my daughter, if that befalls you, then make sure that you do *not* let them see you weep and wail. Maintain your dignity no matter what they do to you, no matter how humiliated you feel. Is that clear, Zivah?"

Zivah looked pale and confused.

"There is nothing these people respect, Zivah, except self-respect. If you can maintain your self-respect no matter what they do to you, then you will earn their esteem of you, and if you have their esteem then your life might improve for you. Remember that and be strong, child of my beloved," Father said.

"I will remember your words, Father. I will try to escape and if I cannot escape I will be strong. But why do you say… Should I *not* look after Thunder Goddess?" she whispered.

"Thunder Goddess will fare differently, Zivah. She speaks their language and knows some of their customs, and she is yet too little to be raped. Even Vikings have laws against that. She may stand a chance. In fact, she may stand a very good chance. You River People think she is strange, but her strangeness will be recognized in different manners by the Rus. She has those eyes of hers. She could make a grown man shit his pants if she wanted to. They will appreciate that. She belongs with those people as much as she belongs here. You think about saving your own skin, Zivah."

My sister nodded solemnly and shuddered as she cast a glance at me. Father looked at us, his womenfolk, his Sífs, and said: "If we are all still alive after this, we will find each other. If we die, we will find each other by the shores of Death." Zivah nodded, squeezed his hand and said, "Yes, Father."

His eyes suddenly filled with gentle love, and he squeezed her hand back. Then he came over to my side of the bed, while Mother went to hug Zivah.

"Thordís," he said, speaking to me in our own language, "I do not think I will survive this morning. You might. You will. The Thunder lord watches over you, and so does your soul within, the soul of the Thunder Goddess. And so I give this to you now, your heritage, our legacy."

He unclasped the silver chain that held the hammer pendant around his neck. Ceremoniously, he passed the heirloom over to me. I took the hammer reverently, and he helped me to fasten it around my neck. It was heavy to wear, and big for me then. Where the pendant had hung at the base of his throat, it hung closer to my belly. He smiled warmly at the sight, and then whisked me up for a last hug.

"Death is but a transition," he said, "and we will meet again on the other side. For as long as you live, I will watch over you, and when your time comes, we will be united. It is the same with your mother. Do not grieve us, for we will all be together again, and if you have the eyes to *see*, as I think you have, you will be able to know that we are with you."

He pointed at the hammer, "This sacred pendant contains the power of all the Thunder priests that have carried it for thousands of years. They are your forefathers. Perhaps one day you will have the women's hammer – the hammer of your foremothers - returned to you, but this will help you now. It is a world of men out there, and you need the experience and guidance of men to get by in that world. The fathers will watch over you for as long as you wear this, and they will guide you to proper speech and proper action. They will help you to make great men revere you. Remember what I have told you about Vikings, my child. Be strong. Do not show fear."

He paused to think before he remembered further important counsels. "Thordís, no matter what you see this day, you must stay calm. There really is no time for grief. You can grieve things later, when you are surrounded by friends in a safe place. For now, all you must do is survive and make sure you remain *free*. First of all, stay hidden, and do not ever cry or wail. If you are discovered, be a Thunder priestess. Remember your dignity. Remember your name, your lineage, and *invoke* it! Invoke our lord, invoke the power of Thunder, and call on your fathers. They are your protectors, always. You are the last of our line. We will be with you. We will be telling you what to do and when to do it. *Listen*. We *will* speak to you."

"Yes, Father," I whispered.

"Do you remember the song of Yrsa?" He asked.

"Yes, Father," I said, remembering the girl whose intelligence and noble manners had impressed the Vikings so much she became a queen among them.

"Be like Yrsa," Father said, "And be the noble born priestess you are. Be that kitten before the dogs that we saw, but mind the courtesies at the same time. They will recognize your bearing and they will respect that. And when you see that they respect you, then you must ask formally for protection. When a man has agreed to protect you, you will be safe. The forefathers will aid you in this also, and know to whom you must turn. They are protective of you, Thordís, you are their

Síf, and their spirits will affect other men into feeling protective of you also. They will feel as if you were *their* Síf."

I nodded gravely, each word he said etching themselves into my soul.

"Finally, my beloved daughter, you must be cunning. Things will transpire before your eyes that may upset you terribly, but you must shake that away from you just as you will shake away grief. You must *never, ever* interfere with *anything* they do. You must not press matters, or try to get things your way. I know you never do those things, but what you will see might cause you to change. Remember yourself. Your strangeness is your best asset now. Observe, be silent, let things pass the way you would if you were just listening to a story. You have not the power to change these things, and so you will let it pass, no matter what happens. All you can do is try and make sure that you remain free, and that you make men protect you by appealing to them with your rank and to their honor. You must not criticize or question *anything*."

"What about Zivah, Father?" I whispered, having heard his conversation with her. Father sighed; "If Zivah is taken, terrible things might happen to her. She might be raped, as I have told you about, and she will also be enslaved. You cannot stop it, and so you will not interfere."

"But…"

"You must obey me, child. She is your sister, but you will not help her by trying to interfere. All you can do is try and make those Vikings like you and revere you, and when you have gained their respect, you may carefully let it slip that you will appreciate it if she is treated kindly, and let them know that she is your sister, even if she has no Norseman for a father. The Rus acknowledge the father line only, Thordís, so even if she is your sister they will not regard her in the same manner as they will regard you, and she cannot pass for a Norseman's daughter anyway, since she speaks not our language and knows not our customs. But if they come to regard you highly, and they know she was born from the same womb as you, she may possibly be treated better than otherwise, and may even gain freedom. But that is all you can do for her, Thordís, you are but a little maiden, and you must not try to do anything more, since that may destroy you, and her with you."

I nodded sincerely, and asked, like the child I was; "Father, is it really true that I can make a grown man shit his pants if I wanted to?"

He smiled warmly and kissed my cheek.

"Yes, my heart's daughter, it is the truth," he said, "You have the gaze of a she-wolf risen out of Hel. Use it."

That was the last thing I ever heard him say to me.

The Last Battle of the River People

And then came dawn, and with it came the Vikings. I did not see the battle, hidden as I was inside our house. Zivah told me to get into Mother's chest, which was still large enough for me to sit in, that stood by the wall next to the bed. After I had gotten inside the chest, she placed a tablecloth and many objects on top of it to make it appear as if nobody could have hidden there. The chest had a peephole, a fact I had discovered years ago and often used for the purpose of spying on the adults. From it, I could see everything that transpired in the room. Zivah hid beneath the bed, not a very good place to hide, but it was close to a little back door through which she could flee if need be. I was not so sure if I was that safe within the chest as Zivah thought, for although I was less detectable, it would be harder for me to get away, and Vikings, I knew, were wont to loot for treasure, treasures often being hidden in chests. But I had never questioned the authority of my elders and was not about to begin now.

I sat quietly within the chest and clutched the hammer pendant. Being made of metal, it was cold to the touch, but seemed to radiate a heat that filled my entire body. I remembered the warmth of my father's body, how much he had felt like fire, and wondered if it had been the properties of the amulet that I was now carrying. I heard screams and shouts, and after a while I heard the clashing of arms. Then more screams, and more shouts, and more clashes.

It lasted for a while, and then the door suddenly opened and I saw my mother come running inside. Zivah began to get out from beneath the bed, but my mother hurriedly pushed her back under and hid herself by the wall, right behind the bed, her face a deadly white. I could not see her then, since she was hiding right next to the chest, but I heard her whisper that we could not flee yet, they were *everywhere*.

The door came up again, and this time, a man staggered inside. For a moment I thought it was my father, but then I saw that it was not. It was a Viking, and he was tall and broad and looked terrifying, with his face all painted or tattooed, a bleeding scar on his cheek, and blood splattered all over him. Whether it was his own or the blood of villagers I could not know, but he appeared somewhat wounded, or at least in pain. He looked around, and his eyes were the eyes of a rabid dog. I felt a cold run down my spine as I watched the man gazing towards the bed. Suddenly he bent down, grabbed something, and began to pull. He had gotten hold of Zivah's hair, and grinning, he was pulling her by her hair out from her hiding place. Zivah screamed in terror.

I had not been able to see my mother, but now I saw a shadow flying forward across the bed, like a big cat attacking. I saw her dagger flashing, and suddenly she was all over the Viking, screaming with a high-pitched, eerie sound as her dagger moved back and forth in rapid motion. The Viking waved his arms, having been caught by surprise, but suddenly he seemed to get a grip on his axe. I saw the axe move slowly through the air, as if time had paused, allowing me to see, moment by moment, the blow that killed my mother. Her beautiful face was cleaved through then, and she fell quietly to the floor. Zivah released a shriek of agony, and then she screamed again as the Viking suddenly fell also, with a loud thump. His face was directed towards me, and I saw the change in his eyes as he died. For some strange reason that sight made me feel hungry. I was of a mind to drink his blood.

I could not quite fathom that my mother was dead. Zivah fathomed it and then lost mind about everything. She wailed loudly, throwing herself at our mother's body, embracing it, cradling it in her arms and rocking it as if it was her baby. Her howls were loud, and I remember only thinking, perhaps whispering, *be quiet. Be quiet. You will attract them. Run. Run through the door and go to the forest like Father said. Run!* But Zivah was oblivious, rocking back and forth and crying violently, holding the bleeding corpse that had been our mother.

Surely enough, the door came open for the third time, and another warrior walked in. Unlike the other one, he was not staggering, nor was he wounded, and he took his time to check the room before he cautiously entered, arms in hand. He was the largest man I had ever seen, a giant, and even Father would have had to look up at him. He was also red-haired, and red-bearded, I saw, and carried a hammer pendant around his neck. I felt my interest rise, and clutched my own hammer. It felt as if voices were whispering to me now, voices like my father's, only they were many, and I knew that I was hearing my forefathers speak to me from the men's hammer. *This is the one,* the voices said, *this man is going to help you. Wait.*

I obeyed the whispers of the men's hammer, and waited, and watched. The red-haired Viking moved towards the girl and the two corpses on the floor. Zivah was watching him, yet she was still sitting there, holding the body, tears running down her face. She was silent now and somehow looked more beautiful than ever in her grief and her helplessness. The Viking looked at her with an appreciative expression in his face. He kicked the body of the warrior around to see his face, then looked towards the dead woman, and grunted disapprovingly. "To Hel with you, coward," he muttered softly, and I gathered that he had not liked the man who killed our mother very much. It gave me hope, and I held the hammer even tighter in my small hands, imagining that this terrifying giant was really somewhat like my father and would turn out to be nice to us even if he looked scary to start with. Then the red-haired Viking bent down and took my sister's arm, making her stand up. She was so terrified that she obliged him, and just stood there, staring at him, and I saw something in his eyes and thought about my father's explanation of that which was called battle lust. He shoved Zivah towards the bed and pushed her backwards upon it so that she lay on her back, and begun to open up his breeches in the front. Zivah began to sob again, but made no resistance, and I remembered my father speaking of women surrendering at the sight of them. I suddenly realized that what I was about to see was that thing they called rape, that which could kill the souls of women.

*

The death of her mother had simply wiped off all fear and all concerns. All Zivah knew then was her grief. She must have been maddened by it, for when the second and veritably gigantic Rus-man entered the hut sprouting a thick red beard and wearing a hammer pendant, she thought it was Thunder Bear who had come to rescue them, and she wanted to wail to him that Mother was dead and that it was too late, but she had no voice to speak with. Then he made her stand up, and she thought he was going to check on her if she was harmed, and she struggled to see what was wrong with the picture of him.

Slowly it dawned on her that he was not her father, but she had not quite grasped that yet when she felt the push of his large hand on her chest. It was such a gentle push, but it made her tip over and fall backwards nevertheless. If the sight of him had not been enough to paralyze her, then the light push of his hand convinced her that there was no way that she could ever resist this man and that all efforts to fight him would be humiliatingly futile. She felt something within her break and just give up.

There was no use fighting anyway, and nothing mattered anymore. She saw the man who had looked so much like her stepfather stare lustfully at her while beginning to open his breeches. He reminded her of the nightmares that had woken her sometimes when she was still barely more than a child, the monstrous and twisted, violent specter of her stepfather suddenly taking over that well-known and safe frame that would first appear in her dreams, telling her that he loved her like a daughter and that he was sorry for making her think otherwise. He would say that, in the dream, and then he would turn into a monster that wanted to eat her alive. And then she had seen what she saw and started to fear that her nightmares were true. He had won back her trust when he saved her from the soul-eaters, but now it was as if her fragile trust was being betrayed and he was finally going to hurt her after all, rape her and kill her soul like he had done with that other girl, and she felt as if her heart was breaking apart with grief. It did not matter that this was not really him. He was a man like him, and now she knew what he had tried to tell her sometimes, oh so cautiously, that this was the sort of man that ruled the world at large.

How foolish all her dreams had been, the foreign prince and the adventures and the silk dresses. It was all she had had to hold on to and now it was all being crushed. It did not matter what happened to her or what he did to her. It did not matter that she had promised not to weep or wail. She had no strength to wail but the tears ran freely and she began sobbing, crying over her disillusionment and her dream's betrayal while watching the red-haired monster and bracing herself for the rape, determined to look into his eyes when the lights of her soul went out.

*

Arnulf had almost been disappointed when he saw the young woman in the hut. He knew a rare beauty when he saw one, and this one was particularly so. He would much have preferred to buy her at a market, buy her as a broken girl who would only be too grateful when he brought her out of her misery and surprised her by offering her a life far better than she by then had dared to ever hope for anymore. To find this goddess of a woman on a raid was his misfortune and hers because she would always hate him for what he had done to her people, and she was already wailing at the mutilated corpse of what seemed to have been her mother. He looked her up and down and decided that she was certainly old enough and then he gave her the push. She fell back limply and without fighting like they always did, her face the very mask of terror.

He had made a point of always breaking in the women before they were taken aboard. Made them more docile, like, and the men would be more mellow after and treat the prisoners kindly. Arnulf preferred it that way. The youngest women and the girls were left alone, the official reason of which was because untouched women won a better price than those who had obviously been had already, seeing as the people down in big Tunic Land had a taste for that sort of thing. All his men knew that the unofficial reason was because their Heri had a soft heart, relatively speaking. But even if he did not like to hurt the girls, a woman grown needed to be broken and he was not about to let anybody else take care of this one. And then the beautiful girl started crying.

Arnulf studied her carefully. They had usually stopped crying at that point. Sometimes they screamed to start with, and tried to fight feebly, but eventually they all gave up and just let him, and she looked like she was beyond that already. There could be a whimper, perhaps, and a little sniveling, but by then they were always closing their eyes and opening their legs, or else looking at him with big eyes while they let him have his way. This one seemed to have forgotten that he was there altogether. She was weeping out of some deep emotion, her mother being dead, her life as she knew it being over, what did he know? What he *did* know, however, was that this woman showed no fear at all and simply grieved in her own way without seeming to care what he did to her at all. Arnulf frowned and tried to make up his mind about what he felt about that. He was really not used to being ignored, especially not by women. That was unusual.

In fact, there was this pleasant feeling of being *entertained*. He could appreciate that. In fact, such unusual conduct deserved some special treatment, and come to think of it he did not want her to remember him as the one who raped her next to her mother's corpse. It felt wrong, somehow, as if her opinions about him mattered. He closed up his breeches again.

*

I tried to open my mouth to speak when the big man looked as if he was going to attack my sister, but not a sound came out. Instead, I could almost hear my own thoughts. *No*, I thought, *you cannot do that. You are supposed to help us. You cannot rape my sister. Not with our mother lying dead on the floor. You cannot. You wear the hammer of Thor. You are supposed to protect her.* And those words kept running through my mind until it looked as if my message had reached the Viking, for he suddenly became still, watching the sobbing Zivah while he frowned. A strange expression suddenly crossed his face and

I recognized it as a vague resemblance of compassion. He tied up his breeches and made Zivah stand up again. She was sniveling, but remained silent as she stared at him with her huge doe eyes. His face softened considerably at the sight of her, and just then he reminded me somewhat of my father again.

But he was not my father. He was a Viking born and bred. Gently, but firmly, he turned her around and produced a rope with which he tied her wrists behind her back. Then he paraded her out of the house and disappeared.

I stayed in the chest for a long while, awaiting the guidance of my forefathers. I could still hear voices and shouts, but also a chorus of wailing from women and children which appeared to come from the same place, close to the river. I gathered that they had collected them in one place, and the voices I now heard around the house were of the Vikings looting our settlement. I remained seated for hours, until the place grew quieter, and the stranger male voices were getting less strained, happier. The Vikings had secured their victory and great spoils. The wailing of the women and children continued with steady intervals. And then I heard a big fire being lit, close to the riverbank.

Now, the voices said, and I got up and forced the lid of the chest open. The things that Zivah had placed there fell down and some got crushed on the floor. I climbed out, and looked around the house. I looked at the bodies on the floor, and contemplated that of Mother for a little while. It occurred to me that I should be rocking it and wail like my sister had done, but I could not feel my mother in that mutilated body on the floor. It was but a shell, and nothing of her was left. She had died courageously in battle, defending her children, and the ladies of the loom would judge her kindly. We would meet again on the other side. The only thing that mattered now was to follow my father's instructions and listen to the whispers that seemed to roll through my mind like mist, rising from the men's hammer.

I nodded solemnly to the voices inside my head and went to the closet where we kept our winter clothes. There was a fur there, the fur of a white wolf, with the upper head still intact. Mother had given it to me after she had made it into a winter cloak, and it was still too big for me. When I put it on, it covered my entire body, and the head of the wolf provided a formidable hood. If I rolled my eyes upwards, I could make out the shape of sharp teeth, fangs almost touching my forehead. My flaming, red locks hung loose, falling down in the front on each side down towards my hips. Appearance is crucial, I remembered my father say, appearance and bearing.

I let the hammer pendant hang outside of the cloak, visible, and for the first time in my life, I felt like a priestess. *You are the Thunder Goddess*, the voices whispered; *you are the priestess, the last of our line. You are our Sif, and we are with you*. It was as if I grew then, became taller, my back straightened, my chin lifted, and I felt something in my eyes, as if they were glowing with a fire that belonged to thousands of years of power. I knew that they had turned white then, the blue of them withdrawn from their centers, gathered in two sharp frames around the white, like the eyes of a hunting wolf. I had the wolf in my eyes and the wolf on my crown, and the thunder I carried within.

I heard a rumble then, and knew it for actual thunder. My lord was with me. *She can make a grown man shit his pants.* My father's voice reverberated through my soul. I had magically prevented the red-haired Viking from raping my sister, or so I was convinced. Now I would make him help me. I walked quietly, proudly, with all the dignity that came from the knowledge that my ancestors of countless generations were behind me, and that our lord Thor watched over me. And as soon as I felt that truth in my heart, I heard the roar of thunder again. I was only seven years old, but I was the last of my line, and I would be his priestess. The lord Thunderer would protect me. I knew it. I felt his power roar through my veins. Without a second glance at the bodies or at my home, I walked out of the door and left my first childhood behind.

Arnulf the Sea King's son

I saw the bodies of many men as I walked through the village. Most of the dead were male villagers of various ages, but no boys. The fallen who were Vikings were mostly covered in arrows, and I felt a surge of pride, thinking that my mother had taken them all down, which was probably rather exaggerated, but a thought I liked. I looked carefully at the corpses, searching for Father among them, and found his body as I came closer to the newly erected Viking camp. I stood for a little while before my father's body and noticed each one of his wounds. He had fought even after he had received the first blows, and he had died fighting. Thunder Bear had avenged himself. And then I felt about his body what I had felt about Mother's body, that he was not there anymore, his body empty like a piece of bloodied clothes thrown away. His soul was in my hammer now and would always be with me, and so I turned my head towards the future.

The Vikings had gathered at the riverbank and had made a huge pyre on which they were now placing their fallen brothers, one by one as they were collected from the ravished village. Nobody saw me at first. I saw five young men from the village hanging from trees, dead, wounds showing that they had also been stabbed. They had belonged to my father's little band of apprentices, and one of them was Zivah's suitor. I saw a large gathering of some forty surviving and captured villagers, mostly women and children and very young men, as well as some grown men who were quite obviously not able to fight anyone, tied in chains and ropes. From the forest came shouts, and I could see some Vikings return from there with more prisoners. I believe that half the village had been captured or killed. The rest were by now roaming the deep forests, waiting for the monsters to perish so that they might return and rebuild the village.

As I gazed upon the rest of my broken tribe, now in shackles, I felt as if they were also dead, and that their physical existence was hardly more than the shells of dead bodies, even if they still walked and wailed. I drew a deep breath and felt the presence of my fathers all around me, my Thunder warriors aiding me, reminding me of my father's words, to take care of myself, because that was the only thing a seven year old could muster on her own. I knew with my heart that the only thing that mattered now was not to become a shell like the captives already had. I would have to let all things pass before my eyes, and look towards my own survival, for there was nothing else that I could do. Thunder roared in the distance, as if to encourage me further.

Suddenly I was spotted. The villagers all went silent, staring at me, and the Vikings' heads were turned. Never had I seen so many faces, familiar and strange, stare at me like one. The whole place became deadly quiet, and before anyone had made a new sound, the roar of Thunder overwhelmed them all, and a ray of lightning suddenly struck down just before my feet. I could actually feel the jolt, so close was it, but I stayed put and as silent as I had seen the Vikings stand in their ships before, silent like a pillar. The skies were dark, and I heard the sounds of ravens and crows having gathered for the feast, as they flew up into the sky, shrieking. The sounds of wings were flapping through the air which suddenly seemed thick with the power of lightning. I could not have asked for a better performance, and thanked my god silently.

With the help of Thunder and the sacred birds, I had made an entrance, the way my father had told me about in many tales. *Making an impressive entrance can be a matter of life and death*, he had once said, *great entries have changed many fates*.

Both prisoners and Vikings appeared dumbstruck, awed, as I walked towards them, wearing my wolf-skin coat and my large Thunderbolt pendant, with my wolf's eyes and hair of fire, and I knew I walked like a queen. I think that in that moment, nobody gave a second thought to the fact that I was just a seven year old orphaned little girl. *You are the priestess*, my forefathers whispered, and I felt the glow of my hammer against my upper belly, burning through my skin.

As I approached, only one Viking dared to move towards me in response. It was the huge, red-haired Viking who had taken my sister. He walked slowly towards me, frowning, taking in the sight of me, as I did of him. We stopped, a few paces between us, and met each other's eyes. *He will help you*, the voices said. *Place your trust in him*. I could feel my voice rise from deep within my heart, carried by my ancestors, and when I heard myself speak, it was not a just little girl's voice anymore. My voice came out deeper than usual, deeper and powerful enough to be heard by all, even though I did not shout. "I am Thordís, the daughter of Thorbjörn Thorsgóði," I heard myself say, my voice intoned for ritual, the way I had been taught.

"He was the son of Thorgrim, also Thorsgóði, and he came from a long lineage of Thunder priests in the land of the Gauts, descending from the first Thunder priestess born in that land, in the time of the great stone temples. I am the last of my lineage, and I am the last Thorsgyðja. I am the Thunder priestess, and the lord Thor is my patron."

I heard my own voice rise, like thunder, and invoked my god; "Hail to you, warrior of the red hair, I can see you are an honorable man. I can see you are a friend of my lord. By the great Heat Rider! By the son of Earth! By the mighty lord Thor, who speaks to me! He has chosen *you* for my protection. I beseech your hospitality, and your protection, warrior."

Maybe my ancestors chose my words, but I had learned so many tales by my father that I knew how to make a formal speech, and so I do not know what powers caused me to act thus. But it worked. The giant, red-haired Viking stared back at me, clearly impressed, and for a moment, his jaws almost dropped. I could see his mind working, fast, recalling the thunder and the lightning that had struck right before me. It had left a charred mark on the ground.

"I am Arnulf, son of Arnsteinn, the Sea King's son by old Bera," he began, "and I am the Captain of those ships there. I am the Captain of eighty warriors, brave men all, although fifteen of them are now lying on the pyre."

The Viking called Arnulf spoke as ceremoniously as I had spoken, and having no further lineage to boast of, continued with the ritual answer to my charge; "Hail to you, priestess. It is true. The lord Thor is my patron, and the lord Thor has spoken to me, through you. You *are* the Thunder priestess. By his power, I accept your charge. I will be your warrior. I will be your protector. This I swear, by the name of Thor! In the sight of Thor! In the hearing of the great lord of Thunder! You are my Síf."

"Alu!" we both said simultaneously, sealing the deal with the sacred ale rune. The Vikings, who had stared at the spectacle with incredulous faces, suddenly appeared to wake up. They recognized that a sacred oath had been made, and suddenly they all began to bang their shields rhythmically, crying "Alu! Thor! Alu! Thor! Alu! Thor!"

It was important to continue my act, I realized, and so I walked on, as if I was part of a sacred procession. Arnulf followed reverently, taking his new role as my protector as a sacred trust. The flock of Vikings parted silently as I walked into their midst.

They were a menacing-looking lot. I had been used to Father towering above the villagers, but it was another thing to walk through a crowd of men all more or less his size and sometimes even bigger than him. Especially as they were all heavily armed and obviously dressed and made up with the purpose of inflicting terror in their victims. And there were those bloodstains all over and the knowledge of what they had just done. I thought about the kitten that had made its stand against three large and hungry dogs, and with that thought I looked challengingly at all the men, moving my gaze from face to face, noticing their very varied features.

To my surprise, each of the men averted his gaze as soon as I met his eyes. I knew a little about the language of the eyes then already, since my father had tried to explain it to me and made me observe the wolves. Averting the eyes is a sign of respect, he had said, and the one who considers himself of lesser rank is supposed to avert his eyes first. I felt a thrilling sensation run up my spine when I realized that these fierce warriors were all averting their eyes to me. I held on to the image of the brave kitten as I maintained my stance and made sure that each of the men in that crowd, those close enough to meet my eyes, had shown me the reverence they obviously thought was due to me. Then I moved slowly through the path they opened up for me, turned towards the great pyre and looked mutely up at Arnulf, who was observing me with an expression of curiosity, awe and amusement, all at the same time.

"Up there is my father's body," I said, "He is red of hair, and large. He was a Norseman, and a warrior, and he was a Thunder priest. I ask that he may join the pyre."

"Was that your father," Arnulf said, frowning. After having ordered some of the Vikings to collect the body of my father, he added appreciatively, "He killed six of my men before he died, avenging his own death that way. He was a great warrior, and very courageous. You must be proud."

"He did what he had to do," I said, "and he was a brave man. So was my mother. You saw her. She killed many of your men with her arrows, and she killed that man who came before you, just as he killed her. She also avenged herself."

"The dead woman in the house up there?" he pointed to our house.

"Yes, the very one," I replied, "I saw it all, and I saw how you treated my sister kindly."

"Your sister," Arnulf said, looking somewhat anxious. We both looked towards the flock of prisoners, all staring at us. I saw my sister among them, her face almost void of expression. I felt a certain resistance from my warrior then, and hesitated. *Do not press it too far*, the voices said, *do not interfere.*

"She is very beautiful," he said, momentarily looking like a child who was about to lose a piece of candy. "Is she also the daughter of the Thunder priest?"

It would not have served to lie, since Zivah did not speak the Norse language. "No," I said, "Zivah is my mother's child." I did not know how he would respond to this, but Arnulf, frowning, seemed to be pondering his options, obviously unwilling to let go of his price. Zivah was the most beautiful of all the young women in the village.

"I will honor your sister," he finally said, having come to a conclusion, "I will make her one of my concubines!" Relieved at this solution, he looked expectantly at me. I remembered that Father had spoken of a concubine and that she had been almost like a wife, which must surely be a better deal than becoming an ordinary slave. From the happy look on Arnulf's face, I gathered that he, at least, thought that he had made a very generous and noble offer, and I was in no position to argue, so I nodded gravely and said; "Then I thank you," and with those words I sealed Zivah's fate for her, hoping that it was a better option than she would otherwise have had. Arnulf, looking relieved, walked over to the chained captives and pointed at Zivah with his bloodied sword, causing her to cringe away in terror.

"This woman is mine," he declared in a loud and thunderous voice, "I claim her as my concubine. No other man may take her." The men voiced their agreement, and so that deal was sealed as well, but Zivah was left among the other slaves for the time being. Not understanding the Norse language, she knew not what had just happened, knowing only that it had to do with herself, with what I had said, and with the Viking who had pointed his sword at her. But she did seem to remember the Norse word for *concubine.* I saw the transformation in her face when she remembered what that meant and acknowledged what that meant for *her*. She did not seem to think that a better option at all. Zivah glared at me with pure hatred. I looked at the five young men they had hung before I came and saw the young man who had once wooed her. She must have seen it, seen how they hanged and stabbed her old sweetheart. The hanged men had all been apprentices to my father, and they must have fought.

On his own accord, Arnulf suggested that they also place our mother on the pyre, as a way of honoring me and because she had been a courageous woman who had died in battle, killing a man with her own dagger. I think he also hoped that Zivah would remember that as an act of kindness towards her, but she seemed oblivious of the honor done to our mother. All she saw was the death of her mother exposed to her once more and then all she felt was grief. As I watched the bodies of our parents burn, I heard Zivah's heartbreaking wails, and they seemed to go on for an eternity.

Fortunately, unlike the cruel men of my father's crew, these Vikings did not seem to be provoked by a woman's wails. Instead they seemed to respect it, for they averted their eyes and pretended not to notice the weeping of their captives at all. I remained as calm as before, as if I was just seeing a story unfold before me.

"The man who killed your mother was a coward," Arnulf said, and I figured that he was trying to comfort me, after a fashion.

"I know. I saw how you kicked his body," I replied.

"He deserved being killed by a woman," Arnulf declared. I wondered what he meant by that. He stood by for a while, curious about me, but too dignified to ask questions, and I remained silent.

Maintain your mystery, the voices said. It occurred to me that my father had foreseen this situation, or something like it, and prepared me for it. Everything that he had ever told me about his people, and about Vikings, now came back to me, guiding me through this trial. Eventually, Arnulf realized that he would get no more information from me unless he asked, and that would have been discourteous, so he left to do the things he had to do. I stood there and watched the fire burn as the Vikings began to prepare their ships. They filled them up with their prices – our meat, our vegetables, our furs, our amber, our pearls, our beeswax, our jars of oil and beer and honey – everything we had gathered and stored throughout the summer went into the ships, as did the chicken, other domestic animals, and many pieces of furniture and other things that the Vikings found as they looted our houses.

As I stood and watched the weave of fate unfold before me, I suddenly noticed that one of the Vikings was watching me closely, and recalled that he had watched me closely ever since I made my appearance. I had been too overwhelmed and focused on what to do to pay him any attention, but now I met his gaze and felt a strange stirring in my soul, as if in recognition.

The man was as big and broad-shouldered and terrifying as the rest of them, yet when I looked more closely, he had a special air about him, and a certain mildness to his face which the others lacked. His hair was very dark, almost black, thick and reaching down below his shoulders. Parts of his hair had been pulled back in two braids by the temples which met in the back to form a single braid. His dark beard was short and well-trimmed and allowed me to see a very handsome face with pure and regular features, a straight nose and two very intelligent, dark blue eyes which seemed to sparkle with alertness as well as amusement. He did not wear chainmail but instead a blue tunic, and a black wolf-skin cloak. He wore all the weapons of a warrior, but he was not bloodied and his clothes were not torn, and it occurred to me that he had not partaken in the slaughter. He had a dignity about him that seemed to stem from great authority, and it was clear from the way the others treated him that he held high regard among them. From the fineness of his clothes and the way his beard had been trimmed down short in a different fashion than the other men, who wore longer and often braided beards, I wondered if he was a kind of prince.

He was the only one among the men who did not cast sideways glances at me only to avert his eyes when I glared back at him. He just stood there and met my glare, looking amused, and after a while he gave me a little nod before he moved along to help with the embarking. I was not certain, but the nod seemed to be a nod of encouragement.

They were almost ready to embark when one of the men came down from the village, carrying what seemed to be a bundle of something small and precious. The man looked very beastly with his dark hair standing up from his head like spikes and a nasty looking scar after a blade that had once slashed across his whole face. Even with some blood smeared at his chin he still had a sort of handsomeness about him and surprisingly enough a very endearing expression of happiness. In fact he looked as excited as a small child, and the other men began to smile at the sight of him.

"What you got there, Njál?" one of the men asked when he approached, one whose hair was shaved on the sides and collected in a braid-tail at the top of his head and with just two thin braids on either side of his mouth and one from his chin instead of a proper beard.

"Well, Runarr," Njál replied, "I think it is one of them furry cats."

"Let me see," Runarr demanded, and took a good look at the bundle. "Why, is that not sweet?" Runarr cooed at the bundle, and more men gathered around, eager to see and to cooingly agree that the little furry cat was sweet indeed. The captives had gone silent and were staring at their captors as if they could not believe what they were seeing. Then Njál carefully lifted up the little beast and I recognized one of my mother's kittens born this spring. All the men looked at the small cat in fascination and smiled. And Njál cooed and smiled at the kitten that he was holding up to his face. The kitten seemed utterly docile, but the Rus warrior's smile caused a collective gasp among the captives. All his front teeth, both above and below, had been filed sharp so as to look like fangs. And then Zivah screamed.

"He is going to eat my mother's kitten!" she screamed and began sobbing again. The Vikings turned to stare at her and then at me.

"What is she saying then, priestess?" Njál said, looking directly at me. I looked back at him, and he averted his eyes quickly.

"She thinks you want to eat our mother's kitten," I explained. The Vikings began to laugh, and Zivah stopped sobbing, looking dubiously at us all.

"I was thinking more in terms of keeping it," Njál said, looking just like Arnulf had looked when he had worried about having to give up Zivah. I sighed.

"That is fine, warrior. Just do not eat it," I said to the Viking, as if I was a mother giving her child a leave along with a condition. The Vikings giggled again, and Njál flashed his fangs amiably at me.

"He is not going to eat the cat," I said reassuringly to Zivah, who had already gathered as much and now just glared resentfully back at me, remembering how I had very recently made her into the scary Rus giant's concubine.

"Of course I will not eat it," Njál of the sharp fangs said and suddenly looked sincere, "on the contrary I am going to be very nice to it. I hear they are some mean killers and very useful against them rodents, and besides, these little ones are holy to the Ladies, is it not?"

"Very holy," I agreed, even though I had no idea what he meant by that, but all the Vikings nodded meaningfully in agreement, and I heard someone mention that there was no better gift to give a girl than one of them kittens, especially the furry sort, while another pointed out that these long-haired beasts fetched a handsome price with them Tunic men, and then the men flocked to Njál and the kitten, awed and fascinated, handling the little one with gentleness and ceaseless cooing, commenting on how cute it was. I shook my head a little, all to myself. My father had done a good job teaching me so much about his folk already, but he had not prepared me for just how weird and contrary these Norsemen were. In the midst of all this misery I had a strange sense of being *entertained*.

Finally the captured villagers were herded aboard. It was evening already, but the Vikings did not want to stay the night in a village that they had ravished, and whose ancestral spirits and gods might descend upon them come darkness. I was the last to board the ship, making sure that I made another regal entry, walking proudly, shutting out the sight of my fellow villagers huddling in their slaves' chains. It was the ship that belonged to Arnulf. Several of the captives were gathered in the middle of that ship, below deck, and with them my sister. As all eyes were focused on myself, I went to sit by the prow as if I had a divinely given right to do so, and nobody objected. People, both captives and Vikings, kept glancing sideways at me and dared not meet my eyes if I glanced back.

You can make a grown man shit his pants, the voices said, and I wore that knowledge like my armor, even though I did not know how to actually make a man defecate. Deep down I knew well that I was just a puny little girl, but I was not going to let anybody else feel that way about me. I had to be the Thunder priestess, and could afford being a child no longer. When the three ships were ready, the Vikings got to their oars, and slowly we began to move upriver.

Terror and Beauty

The Sun was setting by the time we set out from the village. The Vikings vigorously rowed upriver for the rest of the evening and all through the night, taking turns at the oar seats. Seeing the way they seemed entirely accustomed to row hard for hours on end without a break, I began to understand why they were all so immensely broad-shouldered. We moved in silence, as if the Vikings had had enough of play, allowing their prisoners to grieve in peace. I remembered my father's tales about the Viking crew he had been a part of, and wondered if this lot was somewhat less cruel. At least there was no crying girl tormented before the eyes of everybody, and so far I had not seen a rape happen, at least not with my own eyes. Having seen Arnulf almost taking my sister on the bed the moment he had found her, I suspected that he was not the only one and that my sister had been unusually fortunate.

But after the slaves had been herded aboard, they were left in peace, given food and water, and I noticed that the Vikings acted kindly to the small children who sometimes got loose from their mothers, since they had not been chained. The children, of course, were terrified of the Rus, not just because they had seen them kill, but because their very appearance was designed to terrorize others. From the moment I came among them I had watched these men and kept finding them spectacular. Even the captives often forgot their own predicament and just sat back, gazing with open mouths at their captors.

They liked to keep their hairs long, sometimes hanging loose and well-combed, or perhaps with a few braids in it, like my father had done his hair, but just as often they had done their hair in ways I had never seen before. Some had shaved their head at the sides and done things to make the remaining hair stand up like spikes, others had dreadlocks that made their hair look enormous, often tied at the top of the head so that it looked like a fountain, and there were many other interesting haircuts. It was obvious that they wanted to look fearsome, and that they were skilled at it. Their beards were often braided, and I understood that they, like my father had, spent a great deal of time combing and braiding their hair and their beards, making sure they looked the way they wished to. I remembered how my mother had sometimes chided her husband because he was too vain about his hair and his beard, acting like a young girl about it, but secretly she liked that he cared about his appearance. There was no doubt that the Vikings did.

Most of them had tattoos with various symbols covering their arms, their chests, even their faces. I remembered my father's tattoos, and that he had explained to me that he had received most of them after his initiation, that is, after the Sacred Night where he had learned the mysteries of Thunder. Other tattoos had been placed there when he had learned how to invoke his animal Follower, so that there were many symbols appropriate for a man whose Follower is the bear. And some tattoos were placed there after victories in battle. The more tattoos a man had, the more victories, visions or sacred revelations he had had. I did not know if this pertained to women also, for father had not said, and I had as yet to meet another Norsewoman.

Apart from the hair, the beards, and the tattoos, all of them had at least one or two necklaces, some wore simple pendants symbolizing their patron deity, but often they appeared purely decorative or, as I was to learn, they could be symbols of status, of how many men they had killed, and how many victories they had enjoyed. Some of them had very large necklaces forged in iron or bronze, and sometimes added to with gold or silver. They also wore jewelry on their arms and wrists.

All this vanity, I learned, was primarily intended to make them look handsome, for like all Norsemen, the Rus Vikings were extremely concerned about their appearance. Their sense of esthetics, however, was obviously very different from what I was used to, and they seemed to appreciate as beautiful what most others would find terrifying. Most of the men were also quite covered in battle-scars, what often made them look even more fearsome. I saw at least four men aboard the ship who only had one eye, and one whose nose was gone. Adding to their fearsome appearances was their size, for they were perhaps the largest breed of people in the known world, and additionally, they often dressed to emphasize width or height.

Fate, the voices whispered, *this is fate, so let each one to follow the path of their life's thread.* I should have hated these men, hated them for what they had done to my tribe, to my family, but I could not. I could not even feel guilt about not feeling the appropriate outrage, although I was old enough to understand that I ought to. I just didn't. On the contrary I had the most inappropriate feeling of sad and yet still almost joyful anticipation, a sensation that I was on my way to meet my fate. We all were, even the captives. I glanced down at the huddling crowd of my fellow villagers, they who were now slaves, and remembered my father's words.

"Fate is the most powerful of all the divine powers that rule our world. She will take us where she wills, my father had often said, and the judgment she and her sisters pass on us when we die is not on the direction of our lives, but on how we dealt with it," he had told me once. And so I cast a glance at the slaves, who had been my people, most of whom had passed out with exhaustion by now, and knew that my fate would be different from theirs. The great lady who rules the tapestry of life had decreed it so, perhaps because my lord Thor had intervened on my behalf and protected me, his little priestess, and with him my forefathers whose memories lived on in my hammer pendant.

I was seated high at the prow board, and as I looked out behind the dragon's neck I felt as if I was riding a horse that flew above the water. A dragon's neck I rode, and felt the warm breeze of late summer caress my face and make flow my long hair. All the way that fateful day, dark clouds rolled through the sky, playing hide and seek with the Sun's evening rays. Thunder would roll through the sky, now closer, now further away, and in the distance we could see lightning strike down at the forest hills.

As the night fell, it became clear that we were not going to stop at all that night, the men taking turns to row the ship while others slept. I could not sleep, but kept watching the dark river and the night sky. The clouds had perished, and instead of thunder, there were great northern lights flashing and dancing through the starlit heaven. I had only seen them once in my short life, and such lights were not only unusual in this part of the world but particularly unusual at this time of year, but it happened, and nobody doubted that it had to do with me, the mysterious little Thunder priestess who had appeared out of nothing in an unknown village in the river lands.

I heard the oars splashing rhythmically through the water, softly, dreamily, the sounds of the forest at night, and that inaudible Thunder that must needs accompany the dancing blue, green, yellow and red lights up there, where my god was fighting his battles. As I sat there, riding the dragon, surrounded above and below with great dancing lights moving through the night sky, reflected in the dark water, I suddenly felt something stir within me, something I had never felt before. It made my whole body feel like tiny explosions, as if I was full of falling stars. Pleasant chills moved up and down my spine, and tears flowed freely down my cheeks although I was not feeling sad.

Arnulf approached me in the night, standing by the broadside to my right, and with him came the dark-haired man with the handsome face and the short, well-trimmed beard, the one I had thought may be a prince. They both stood there for a while, watching the northern lights and secretly casting small glances at me. I kept my face towards the front, but I had long practice in noticing everything that happened around me even when I did not watch directly, and so I sensed their presence, their awe at the great lights, and their curiosity about me. I pretended not to notice until Arnulf finally cleared his throat.

"What do you make of the lights, priestess?" he said, "Do they portend great tidings, perhaps?" I kept looking in the same direction while praying to my ancestors that they guide my response, for I had no idea what the lights portended. Finally the answer came to me; "They are the lights of my lord Thunder, who approves of this voyage. But the decrees of the rune-carving ladies are as yet unknown."

"What is he doing up there, then, your lord Thunder?" the dark-haired Viking asked. He had a different accent from the other men, I noticed, just as their accents were a little different from that of my father. It made me think he might be from a different land than the other men. I also thought I detected a disturbing tone in his voice, a tone I could not decipher but which made me feel that he might be testing me, or worse, perhaps be mocking me. I turned around and gazed at them. To my relief, I saw the eyes of both men widened, and I recognized awe in their gazes, before they both averted their eyes. Then I knew that my eyes were still in their wolf spirit. I looked at them and remained serious, calm. *I can make a grown man shit his pants*, I thought, and felt a surge of strength run through me.

"Who are you, who ask?" I asked.

"Apologies, young priestess," the dark-haired man replied, "My name is Thióðolf Skald, and my purpose here is to compose a fitting poem about this sighting, at the bequest of my friend and lord, Arnulf Heri." *Heri* was what the men called Arnulf, still the most common word used for lord or master when I was young. Thióðolf Skald continued; "I was wondering, seeing as these lights came with your presence aboard, if you were familiar with their origin."

I drew my breath. Father had told me about this custom. They were already testing me for wit, knowledge and eloquence.

"Thióðolf Skald," I said, "I have been told that the lights appear when mighty Thor is making love to the daughters of the Sun. Each light is the ray of a Sun Maiden, beaming in ecstasy as he holds her in his embrace. But this is the explanation of the River People." The men smiled, and Arnulf exclaimed, "The Sun's *daughters*? I never heard about them!"

Thióðolf said, "I have," and Arnulf shrugged, acknowledging that he was less informed than the priestess and the poet about such matters. But Thióðolf objected; "How could the Sun's daughters be about at this time, little priestess? The lady, the Sun, resides in the wolf's belly now, it is nighttime. Is it not more plausible that the beaming ladies are the daughters of the great Ocean of stars up there?"

He looked intently at me. I recognized that he was challenging me, with a glimpse of irony in his eyes. I recognized irony, since it had long been a favorite attitude of my sister towards me, and it had always made me feel uncomfortable, since I was not yet capable of returning it or defend myself against it. I gazed at the man, sensing a possible opponent. He was not as reverent towards me as Arnulf or the others, and I felt a surge of fear.

Everything depended upon these ferocious men seeing me as chosen, as wise. A holy woman, one of those my father had told me about, women who commanded respect even among the most rogue of men. The fear that my spell might fall apart seized me and made me panic, and suddenly I thought I needed to try a different way. I decided to try sweetness, and tilted my head a little. I may not be as beautiful as my sister and was still just a little girl, but I had heard that I was sweet to the eyes. I remembered how Zivah used to speak when she wanted to appeal to some man or other, and applied, for the first time in my life, a little coquetry as I spoke humbly; "You are my elder, Skald, and so you may be wiser than me in these matters. But I think the Sun is but hidden at nights, or so my father taught me. He said she was called then the Sun of the Giantess, she who shines darkly in Hel. When the great mother Night descends upon the world, the dark Sun shines, a twin to the bright Sun, her mirror image. These lights are the beams that emerge from the dark Sun, risen from death, dancing with Thunder."

Both men appeared impressed at my words, even the skald, and I was quite satisfied with my own eloquence, and happy that I had been taught to recite so many sacred words. The two warriors looked as if they were *tasting* my words in their mouths.

"Ah! Now that is poetry!" Arnulf finally exclaimed, clearly pleased, and patted Thióðolf 's back, "You had better transcend that piece lest I exchange you with my little priestess!" At that, he marched away, and Thióðolf turned to me, and smiled; "I ask for your guidance, Thunder priestess, for I fear that I may be thrown overboard if I cannot compete with you, and I doubt that I can. Let us be friends, what do you say?"

Friends. I never had friends. I was a seven year old girl who had never had friends, and here stood a grown man, a ferocious looking Viking, and offered up his friendship. I was uncertain if I could trust him, for there was something about this Thióðolf that made me feel uncomfortable, a feeling that nothing and nobody could fool him, and that he had seen through all my masks and into the reality of what I really was: a frightened little girl all alone among Vikings. I had learned a great deal about the Norsemen from my father, but had no experience with them in real life, and it was hard to make out what they expected of me. They were overwhelmingly different from anyone I had ever known, even from my father. I sensed my own disability keenly now, and felt deaf and blind among them.

"No man has extended his hand in friendship to me before," I said formally, "and I prefer to *know* the ones I have as friends. But I am not your enemy, and I thank you for the offer."

"Wisely spoken, eloquent maiden," the poet said, and then went silent. I could feel his mind working as he stood there next to me, watching me, the sky, the lights and the river. After a good while, he turned around to face the rest of the ship, and I also turned. The Vikings seemed to be alerted at once, looking expectantly at Thióðolf. There was something magical about the way he proceeded. I had heard about poets, I had learned to recite a lot of poetry, the songs sung by my father's lineage, but I had never seen how an actual skald worked, and how he performed his compositions. He appeared to grow, become more powerful, attracting everybody's attention. Even the cries of wild animals from the surrounding forests seemed to hush down. For a moment, he was the center of the universe.

And then his voice came, deep, strong, reverberating, as if the whole world was filled with his words. The sound of his voice made full the night, reaching not only the ship we were on, but also the two others that followed:

"Fire-Hooded Dragon Rider
Flying beneath Thunder's Passion
Daughters of the Sun of Darkness
Gleaming in the Earth-son's Embrace

Maiden Priestess touched by fire
Lightning struck before her feet
Through the terror and the beauty

She walked to the Viking fleet

River wolves upon the banks
Thunder Goddess moved the army
Spirit-mirror bathes in wing's streams
of the eagle, gaze of Hel."

The entire crew went quiet on all the ships, and I had to stop myself from gaping. I had never heard poetry like that before. My father had taught me to recite many old poems, and I knew that they were full of riddles, hidden meanings that my father called metaphors, but they had always been quite understandable, telling the story of gods, and of people who had lived before. Never had I heard a poem that described a current event. This poem was almost incomprehensible to me, but Father had taught me the basics of how to solve poetical riddles. My mind began to work at deciphering the lines, but I was distracted by the reactions of the audience. The total silence that had followed the recitation, I realized, came from the fact that all the Vikings were busy deciphering the poem they had heard as well.

Then cheers broke out from the Vikings, first from the ship that sailed behind us, who had also been able to hear it, and then from our own. They were loud cheers of appreciation as the Vikings, one by one, began to understand the poem. The slaves woke up, befuddled, unable to understand the commotion, while the Vikings began to stomp their feet rhythmically and chanting Thióðolf's name in appraisal. Arnulf came up to Thióðolf and handed him a beautiful, iron arm ring wrought with threads of gold.

"That was well-composed," Arnulf said, and looked to me; "Do you approve, priestess?"

"It was beautiful," I said, which was true, but I refrained from saying that I had not understood all of it. "Thióðolf is a great poet," I added, wanting that powerful man to feel kindly towards me.

The excitation ceased, and I sat for a long time contemplating the poem. At first, I had not realized that his poem was describing *me*, but now I understood that the Fire-Hooded Dragon Rider must be me, since my hair was red like fire, and I was, after a fashion, riding a dragon. Maiden Priestess was not hard to understand either, and Thunder Goddess was my name, even if he had used other words for "thunder" and "goddess" than the ones that made up my name. The northern lights were described the way I had explained them, only more poetical, and I remembered well how lightning had in fact struck down before my feet, and thank Thor for that. After I had deciphered almost the entire poem, I was still stuck at the last two lines:

> "Spirit-mirror bathes in wing's streams
> of the eagle, gaze of Hel"

Thióðolf approached me again, asking quietly what I had thought of the poem, really. Nobody else listened, and so I confided in him that I was not familiar with this kind of poetry and that I was uncertain about the meaning of the last part. "Spirit mirror", he said, "that is your face. It can be used about anybody's face, of course. But in this case, it is your face, and it is bathing in the streams that come from the flapping of the eagle's wings."

"What kind of streams are those?" I asked.

"The winds, of course," Thióðolf said. "In poetry, the winds are the result of a great eagle flapping his wings. He sits yonder at the end of the universe, or its beginning, and creates all those invisible streams that run across every world."

"Is it true?" I asked. My father had not told me about this.

"Who can know what the truth about the beginning and the end of the universe really is?" Thióðolf said, "But it is a beautiful image, much used by poets."

"What about the gaze of Hel?" I asked. He frowned, and looked at me, inquisitively, as if he could not believe I had asked. Then he said; "That is *your* gaze, priestess. Why else do you think you are sitting here and not down there with the rest of your village?" He pointed down at the slaves, and I said nothing. He lowered his voice into a conspiratorial whisper; "You do not need to use coquetry to impress a man, little one. It is not your best asset, and these Rus-men do not appreciate that kind of behavior in women anyway. Stick to what you *are* good at, that is my advice," he said, confirming my suspicion that he could see through my act. But he did not seem to mind it.

"What *am* I good at?" I asked, sincerely wanting his advice.

"Why, you could make a grown man shit his pants," he replied and winked at me, before he went to find a place to sleep.

A Warrior's Heart

The giant chieftain with the flaming hair and his somewhat smaller protégée, Thióðolf Skald, stood quietly at the prow, facing southeast and the growing dawn. But they were not admiring the early morning light just then. They were looking at the girl. She was sleeping soundly on her place on the prow seat, having snuggled into her white wolf fur and curled up in there, on her side, what made her look like a furry ball. The kitten that Njál had brought aboard had found its place and was sleeping almost just as heavily on the girl's thigh, and did not mind the two men's presence at all. Her face was so peaceful now that she was sleeping, and as it turned out, she was a very pretty little maiden.

"Look at her," Arnulf whispered, astonished, "she is just a small girl!"

"Whoever said that she was not?" Thióðolf whispered back, smiling a little at how they were both whispering lest they wake the child. Arnulf looked embarrassed only for a few moments before he opted for an overbearing shrug towards the rest of the ship, indicating the other men.

"They think she is a Hel-maiden, you know," Arnulf whispered, "They have been whispering about it all the while, spreading the message. Nobody seems to remember what she actually said during that introduction of hers. I cannot blame them."

"It was rather spectacular," Thióðolf agreed.

"It was, was it not? Even I could have been fooled, if I had been, of course," Arnulf said and smacked his lips approvingly. The memory of the wolf-girl stepping out of that lightning and coming to walk through their crowd to look at the burning bodies had made a lasting impression on all the men, these two included. Thióðolf agreed that even a leader of men could have been fooled, although this particular leader of men had of course not been fooled for a moment. But clearly the girl had been aided by some divine intervention from the Thunderer, her lord.

"Do you think it is true, then? That she is the last Thunder priestess?" Arnulf asked.

"Yes, Arnulf," the skald said earnestly, "I do not doubt that at all. She carries all the typical features of that tribe. The color of her hair, her fierce eyes and her bearing is one thing, the other is the fact that lightning aided her path before us and last but not least there is the pendant. Her Thunderbolt pendant is Magni's hammer, Heri. It is the closest thing you can get to the real Miöllnir. She is carrying the men's hammer, Arnulf, the Hammer of Greatness. It is a very sacred legacy that may only be passed over to the worthy. And she is the only one who will ever know when a man is worthy of that charge. The hammer itself will speak to her and let her know. *Nobody* should try and take it from her." The skald looked intently at his chieftain.

"Of course not," Arnulf said, sounding only a little disappointed. It was a nice pendant and it was obviously made to honor a big man's chest. "I am a pious man, Thióðolf. We are all pious men here, as you could see only from how we respected her yesterday."

"Uhm. Yes. When she was a Hel maiden," Thióðolf said and shifted the weight on his feet a little, trying to wrap his mind around the notion of a pious Rus Viking without laughing out loud.

"I have not the heart to tell the men otherwise," Arnulf said and sent a compassionate glance down the ship, at the rowing and sleeping men, "They think that they are being blessed."

"They think they are *blessed* if they have a Hel-maiden aboard their ship?" Thióðolf looked a little surprised, and Arnulf snorted; "We are Vikings, Thióðolf. Death is our most trustworthy companion. We men who dwell in the bays; we like to have Hel on our side."

"Oh, naturally," Thióðolf said and nodded thoughtfully.

"But the thing is, Thióðolf," Arnulf said, "Now *I know* that she is just a little girl. Not any little girl, of course. She is a noble warrior's daughter of great lineage, and is somehow in charge of a great and very sacred legacy. But she is also orphaned and without any kinsmen, and she holds promise of great beauty, like that of her sister for sure. And she is, what, seven years of age? What am I going to do with her? She is already running about pretending to be a creature out of Hel. She cannot possibly keep up that act for long. How am I going to save face when it turns out that she is just a little maiden after all? It would not sit well with the men. Or with the city council for that matter."

"But Heri, she has not pretended to be a creature out of Hel. Not even once. She spoke her name and lineage loudly and clearly and asked for your protection in the manner of a noble maiden, and you responded, and gave her that promise," Thióðolf said, a little too heatedly, clearly protective about the girl already.

Arnulf liked to see the other man just a little worried. He liked it when other folks had to acknowledge that *he* had all the power when everything came down to the core of all issues.

"Yes, I suppose I did," Arnulf graciously acknowledged, "But then there was the witchcraft what made her seem like a Hel-maiden, and then there was the glaring, Thióðolf. Even *I* was, I have to admit, a *little* dazzled. I have to admit that I actually lowered my eyes to her once or twice. Now, there is one thing with the men. They will not mind having been dazzled a while if they can only get a good replacement that entertains them just as well. Surely we could arrange for a smooth and interesting transformation, all in its own time."

"That sounds like a very good plan," Thióðolf said, and wanted to continue, but was interrupted by the Heri; "Yes, a very good plan. But I cannot be seen to have let myself be fooled by a little girl even for a moment, and made to humble myself before her. Yet that has already transpired. Now what am I going to do with her? I do not even *know* how to educate little girls. Look at her. She is soft! I could possibly break her apart if I even tried to speak harshly to such a little thing." He looked fondly at the girl for a moment before he remembered himself and set up a grim face again.

"Arnulf, the girl is very clever," Thióðolf said, "and she is a lot tougher than she looks just now while she sleeps, you know that. You saw that, Heri. She has the warrior's blood and the thunder in her veins. Give the girl a chance. There are great powers at work around that child, and you may find that you will benefit greatly from her company. And I think she will catch on very quick as to the courtesies. She does not glare out of disrespect for you."

"Are you sure about that?" Arnulf asked. He really did not like the fact that he had lowered his eyes to the little girl and that she had kept glaring at him as if she was above him.

"Of course, Heri. She is terrified. How could she not be terrified?"

"She did not look terrified at all, to me, and I have seen a lot of terror in my life," Arnulf grunted.

"No, perhaps she did not *look* terrified," the skald argued; "But do you think Bera was not terrified when the Vikings took her? Did she not tell you that she was, but that she knew how to hide it?"

"I suppose she did," Arnulf said, "although she used a rather more humble approach than this rudely glaring girl." Now that he had started to think about it, he was getting rather upset; "Even fierce Bera who had ruled whole bands of Vikings with her iron hands had known how to rule them *politely*. She had never made a warrior feel like less than a man. She voiced her orders in riddle speech into the open air and knew that her men would jump to attention the moment she turned her back, which she always did in respect for them. That is how a woman can rule men, the only way. And yet, this little girl presumes…"

Arnulf Heri looked at the maiden again. She was so little and so soft and vulnerable.

“Yes, but Bera was also a woman grown,” the bard said, “Some women know how to shield themselves from terror just as surely as warriors do, and they know how by nature, and they know when to do it how. Heri, that glare was her shield yesterday; the shield what kept her safe. And it worked well. We must commend her for that. It was a real shield, it came from a real place, and it is not her fault if anyone had particular ideas about what place that really was. I would like to remind you of that legacy of hers, Arnulf. No man can take that hammer away from her, to claim such a holy thing unlawfully will only be his destruction. It has to be passed on to the worthy, but also to one who is able to wield it, and the only sort of people what can wield that sort of hammer are the ones with the thunder in their veins. If her lineage really has been exterminated, there is only one place where we can start to look for the next man who is to carry the Hammer of Greatness.”

“And that is?” Arnulf asked curiously when Thióðolf paused politely in wait of his question.

“Her womb, Heri,” the skald said reluctantly. He had not wanted to reveal it, but he had to make Arnulf realize how valuable that maiden really was. He would just have to worry about the outcome of that realization later. “Only a son born from her womb will be able to actually use that hammer for what it was meant to be used for,” he said, and spoke the truth for his only true blade.

“What is it meant to be used for?” Arnulf whispered, and looked around to make sure nobody heard them still. The girl still slept soundly, as did the kitten on her thigh.

“Greatness. Power and Greatness,” Thióðolf said enigmatically, lowering his voice into an intense whisper that caught the Heri’s most ardent attention; “When the men’s hammer is once more united with the women’s hammer, held by a man and a woman who carry the thunder in their veins, their union will generate great power and the revelation of many divine insights, and it will lead the ones who carry them onto greatness. Not only to those two, though. Even if the women’s hammer is never retrieved, fortune *will* befall on all those who are loved by the rightful hammer-wielders. Arnulf Heri, believe me when I say that it will be a man’s greatest fortune to simply earn the love of this little girl.”

“Hmm,” Arnulf said, clearly impressed but also a very practical tradesman at all times; “Then both her affection and the womb she carries in Freyia’s hall are very precious indeed. I assume it will be the son and not the husband what gets to inherit the hammer?”

"Yes, Arnulf," Thióðolf said, trying to hide his exasperation, "Even if you married her you could not take her hammer. You would have to let that over to the son born to her."

"Oh I was not necessarily thinking of marrying her *myself*," Arnulf said, but now that he had been presented with the thought he frowned thoughtfully, "why, she is too young to even think of such things, although we can of course dally with certain notions for the future. So if we are ever to benefit from the hammer we must control both her and the father of the child she will bear."

"Notwithstanding the benefits you will enjoy when you only get her to love you," the bard reminded him again, "for the power of the men's hammer is channeled through the wielder's affections."

Arnulf raised an eyebrow, and clenched his jaws together. How on holy Earth was he going to make a little maiden whose tribe he had destroyed, *love* him? And how was he going to raise a girl of such great importance and value without humbling himself? He did not like the fact that she was noble and he was not, actually. Arnulf always preferred to have the upper hand in all ways.

"Indeed. And now I fear that she will have too much power after all," he growled, "I thought it almost better when she was a Hel-maiden. A man can *deal* with a Hel-maiden, if he knows the Contrary ways, what I actually do, even if you may think I am a simple sort of man."

"Not at all, Heri," Thióðolf said politely, "But if I may counsel you. She is still a child and it would not serve her or anybody else if she is not properly educated. You worry about her rudeness and possible disrespect, and we agreed that all that was a shield to protect her from terror. That shield is, as you so wisely have pointed out, no longer appropriate, but we still have time. The men are still in the Hel-song. Before they even wake up to another song, we can teach her other shields. She needs to learn the ways of respect and all the courtesies. And if you wonder where to begin, let me help you. You have seen how clever she is. I might just have to give her a few nudges in the right direction, with your permission, Heri. I happen to be very good at speaking to the soft."

"That was well-spoken, even to a hard man like myself," Arnulf said gruffly and cast one anxious glance at the girl again.

"Arnulf," Thióðolf said mildly, "I think you must be worrying about how to be with her. Let me assure you that the best way to be with the soft is to be true to them. You can just be yourself, and let the teachings unfold in their own time. They always do. She may have to learn how to respect you before she can love you, but that is not the worst path you can take with a girl. We Norsemen have raised children forever. It is in your blood, Arnulf. You are already doing such a good job with Ivarr."

"Yes, I know that. Yet young Ivarr can tolerate a kick in the butt and a thunderous rebuke every now and then. He is a boy. But a *girl*? Imagine all the things we have to shield her from… what is more or less… impossible, when I come to think of it. I cannot change my whole court because of her. She will be a noble maiden come to live among Vikings and their slaves. I worry."

"There is very little we can shield this girl-child from now," Thióðolf argued, "she has already seen most of what we are, and most of what we have left to show her will be a lot more pleasing to her than what she has seen so far. You know how it works when you pull them from bad to better. At least, from now on, it is going to be better for the most part."

"For the most part," the chieftain agreed, and by the pondering expression in his weathered face, he was obviously thinking about a thing or two they still might want to shield her from.

"You may want to hold the thunderous rebukes and the butt-kicks, though. She *is* a girl," Thióðolf suggested hopefully. The North Way man did not know how the Rus raised their maidens, having so far not met any Rus maiden at all. Arnulf nodded gravely and looked like he had gotten a terribly heavy responsibility on his shoulders.

"Slaves cannot raise a free, noble maiden. And I have no wife and no other Síf to charge the girl with. What leaves *me* to the task. I am a warrior. How do I raise a girl?" he asked, voice lowered again, leaning conspiratorially towards the bard; "I was honed most viciously by my father, and quite harshly by my mother also, although she was a good woman, bless her. And my little sister honed me so fiercely I never really paid attention to how she was raised at all, although a good job was made of it, all things considered. But she had our mother and our grandmother to teach her, and I grew up in the warriors' Hall. There are very few things I would admit to not knowing my way around, but I shall have to admit that I do not know how to raise a soft child what will only stay soft even when she grows, on account of being woman-kind. And now you say I even have to make her *love* me, at that."

"Then, uhm, then you may want to seek the help and aid of those who may know how to relate to a soft child of woman-kind and know how to earn her love at that," Thióðolf said modestly, and Arnulf's face brightened up.

"I shall ask for the counsel of Hallgrim Hidden Spear!" the Heri exclaimed eagerly, and Thióðolf sighed in secret. Rather than presenting himself now, he graciously agreed that a council with the shadow walker could be a wise way of dealing with this most unexpected and novel prospect of a free noble maiden, one of great and ancient lineage no less, to be raised by a band of rogue Vikings and slavers, lawless men forced into exile.

Yet as Thióðolf had suspected, it was the very prospect of raising a *girl* in itself that the Viking lord worried most about. They were Rus, and Rus were Vikings, and they descended from the landless men of bays and ocean steeds. They were not exactly the most homebound family-men that anyone had ever encountered. So far, from what Thióðolf had seen of these people, they were like the war bands of old, men without family or tribe, organized in warrior bands rather than in clans, most of them living in groups of six who shared just about everything except their weapons and the wealth that they could carry on their bodies at all times, which was why they always wore so much jewelry and looked like a band of particularly vicious peacocks as far as Thióðolf was concerned.

These Sixers, as they called them, would cluster together in larger bands of men that also lived together, and often traveled and fought together. They would live communally in a hall led by a warrior of the first rank elected from their own midst, and they would be sworn to a Heri and House-Bond who owned their hall and the ship they were a crew on. The Heri always had the decisive word in every venture they made together, but apart from that, they decided all matters in common council and shared just about everything. They even shared their women, who were always slaves.

Only a man who could afford his own halls and ships could afford concubines, wives and lawfully free-born children, and only such a man could afford to take care of other family members, such as Sífs of the blood and Sífs of the oath, or even possess a Hold to keep them safe within. As Arnulf was living proof of, not even these powerful men could always be bothered to marry unless they felt an obligation to do so. The great Heri had admitted, during a drunken brawl, that he had lived for so long as a Viking of the Hall before he became the Heri of a Hold and Court and as many as three Halls that he was shocked when he suddenly found himself with a wife and a concubine what did not like each other, and the wife had the concubine murdered in the most gruesome way. After the deaths of his last wife and child, Arnulf said that he could not but admit that he much preferred to keep himself with slave concubines, who were a lot easier to deal with on account of not having any say in any matter anyway, and on account of being humble women who knew better than catering to lowly jealousy.

As for children, Arnulf had claimed to be content with raising his nephew, seeing as the son of a full blood sister is as much of a direct descent as a son of one's own. The Viking Rus did not increase their numbers through the birthing of descendants as much as they increased whenever young and landless men without other options sought their halls and offered their services to the lords of those halls. In Aldeigjuborg, that sort of increase in the population happened a lot more often than the rather novel births of free-born children with known fathers. What also meant that most of the free population consisted of grown men who had little experience with freeborn children, and especially not with maidens. But being this sort of men, the Rus had never minded a challenge either, especially not if there was a reward in the other end. Thióðolf observed the subtle change in Arnulf's doubtful attitude towards the sleeping girl. The maiden owned the Hammer of Greatness, after all, and carried a name that even legends spoke of.

They both looked tenderly at the outstanding little girl, who was beginning to move as if she was just about to wake up. Both men swiftly and quietly withdrew from the prow, so as not to have her wake up with two old warriors looming above her.

"You know, Thióðolf," the old Viking lord said cheerfully as they turned to take their place at the oars for a while, letting two brothers have a well-earned rest in their stead; "I think that the challenges proposed by this little she-scoundrel may provide a quest what makes a warrior's heart sing."

Lowering the Eyes

Rather early the next day, I noticed a small change in Arnulf 's attitude towards me. The day before, he had been utterly awed by me and kept averting or lowering his eyes before me. All the other men either averted their eyes before I could meet their gazes, and if I happened to meet their gazes, they immediately lowered theirs. I had understood that this was significant, and that it was a way of respecting me, and so I stared directly at them all, knowing that they saw my wolf eyes, or what they for some reason called the gaze of Hel, and nobody had seemed to think twice about the fact that I stared them down, as if it was expected that I should. Father had told me that what the villagers may find strange about me would easily be better appreciated among the Norsemen, and so I glared to my heart's content. Today it seemed to me that Arnulf maintained eye contact with me longer than he had the day before, and that he appeared uncomfortable when he finally averted his eyes, without having lowered them even once, after which he suddenly shrugged and walked away from me without saying a word. I knew that he had thought to speak with me, but then changed his mind, and his dismissive behavior made me sense that something was wrong. I felt a little chill crawl up my spine.

Suddenly, Thióðolf stood next to me at the prow and asked me if I would come down and sit with him on the deck close to the side board. I did, and settled next to him. He was not as big as my father had been, but still, seated like that, I felt very small and childish next to him.

"Voices carry far above water, and with the wind," he began, "better we speak here, shielded, and in voices low. You find yourself in a very dangerous position, girl."

Girl. That sounded bad.

"Your father was a Norseman, and you speak our language well. But I am not sure how much you understand about us, girl" he said, "The men are still high after the raid and so there is yet time for you to get your act together. But you must listen to me carefully, now." He looked at me, and I nodded attentively.

"You made a great spectacle yesterday, you and the powers that guide you. It was very impressive. No matter who and what you are, and no matter whether we see through your act or not, we honor you for that. Such spectacles are sacred to us. There is hardly anything in the world we Norsemen appreciate better than a good act, and the Rus are no different from the rest of us that way."

He paused a little and looked around to make sure that nobody was listening. The rest of us, he had said. His accent was certainly different from the rest of them, who all seemed to share my father's accent. Clearly, Thióðolf Skald was not from the same part of North Path Island as the rest of them. The men were all busy working, rowing or talking to each other, and he continued, speaking to me in a low voice.

"Now, we are, apparently, pious men, Thordís. Ah, may I call you that?"

"Better than calling me *girl*," I said, feeling rather worried about the fact that he did not address me as priestess anymore, and all the things he said about seeing through my act.

“Good. Thordís. We are pious men, but we are not stupid. We are all impressed by your act and there are clearly higher powers that guide you, but you are balancing on a very sharp and narrow edge here. It would take very little to make you fall. It would only take the realization of one warrior aboard this ship that you are in fact just a little orphan girl and that you rank lower than us all. And Norsemen are very concerned about rank, Thordís, the Rus even more so than most. These men are Rus, and they are not used to lowering their eyes before little girls. Nor are they used to averting their eyes to maidens, or being glared at by their inferiors.”

He looked intently at me again to make sure I was following him, and I made it clear that I was with another quiet nod. He had an authority about him that was hard not to respect.

“We have a very complicated ranking system, Thordís, but the show of it is subtle. I have been to lands were free men will fall down on their knees to kiss the feet of their superiors. We never require such demonstrations. It disgusts us to see free people kneel. But that does not mean we are not concerned with rank. The thing is, we do not like bowing, and we do not even bow to the gods. We do not think the gods expect us to act like less than men.”

I stared dumbly at him, feeling a sense of dread.

“We are every bit as concerned with rank as most other people. How we signal respect, authority or submission is all in the movement of the eyes. Look there,” he said, and nodded towards Arnulf, who was being approached by a crew member.

“Look at their eyes when they speak. Arnulf is the captain, and a very powerful man. The other one is just a warrior. Look now. Watch the language of the eyes.” I looked. The warrior approached the captain, and I saw how their eyes met just long enough to establish contact, before the warrior lowered his eyes briefly, while Arnulf maintained a direct gaze. Then the warrior met his eyes again, and they both made a very subtle nod before they both averted their eyes a little. They started to talk, and while they talked, I noticed that while they were keeping regular eye contact, the warrior kept averting his first, and Arnulf then respectfully averted his a few moments after, before their eyes met again. This happened throughout the whole conversation, and I watched in fascination while I remembered the things Father has told me. I understood that the warrior lowered his eyes to Arnulf to signal that he acknowledged the superiority of the Heri and that he was willing to obey him. When they had agreed upon that arrangement, Arnulf signaled respect for the fact that the other was a free man and a warrior by averting his eyes a little after the other had averted his.

"The lowering of the eyes is submission. Averting the eyes is respect. But there are many small and subtle details to be observed about exactly when to do what. Submission is not only paid to superiors. You should lower your eyes to anyone who teaches you, or offers you a verdict on your behavior that you accept," Father had told me after I had asked him about why he had lowered his eyes to Zivah that night when she had confronted him with his past. He had lowered them to signal that he accepted her verdict on him and in that way submitted to her opinion.

I let my gaze wander and saw two warriors about to engage in conversation. I saw that the two men established eye contact before they both averted their eyes at the same time. Then their eyes met with that same small hint of mutual understanding before they kept talking. Whenever one averted his eyes, the other immediately did the same. And more of my father's words seemed to sing themselves once more from within my mind: *"When you speak to a person who you regard as your equal, you will show respect by always averting your eyes if he or she does, so as to not imply that you are above him or her. You can also show the courtesy of averting your eyes first, what is very appropriate for a woman if she is greeting a man of the same rank as her, or above. A woman should always yield first unless she wants to indicate that the man is not worthy of her respect, which is very insulting if that is not actually the case. In any case, for a woman, refusing to yield first when greeting a man of similar ranking is the same as a challenge against him on behalf of the men who protect her. So, unless you want to instigate a war, your will pay respect to men. But when you show your respect in this way, you will expect that he follows you immediately. These are ways of knowing how much the other respects you, Thordís, or who thinks himself overly superior."*

I looked at two other men and saw how their eyes met, establishing the contact, before the one averted his eyes. The other waited a few moments before he averted his, signaling that he regarded himself as higher than the other, but still respected him as a fellow warrior of the same rank. They followed that pattern throughout the whole conversation. The younger man did not seem offended when the elder took his time averting his, and it seemed to me that they were both showing each other respect while still acknowledging rank.

"Do you recognize the language of the eyes, Thordís?" Thióðolf Skald said in a low voice. I nodded. Now Thióðolf gazed over at the slaves, and I saw that a warrior was standing, facing the slaves and staring intently at them.

"Slaves," Thióðolf said, "must always lower their eyes immediately before a free person. They do not even meet the eye. They always lower them, signaling submission. A free man will acknowledge that the slave is behaving correctly by averting his eyes eventually, but if he feels provoked, he will stare the slave down, like that man, Hialti, is doing now. He is teaching them their place."

He looks cruel, this Hialti, I thought, and as if Thióðolf could hear my thoughts he replied; "Yes, he is. There is no need to do this here and now, but he takes a liking to that sort of thing. For us, it serves to illustrate a point. Staring."

He turned to me and stared directly into my eyes, and I had to struggle to be able to stare back.

"Staring, Thordís," Thióðolf said, locking my eyes in a silent battle, "staring is very, very threatening and very rude. You do it to people you want to challenge, or force into submission. And *you*, little girl, you stare all the time. In fact, little girl, you *glare*. You *glare at free men*."

I gulped nervously and felt my gaze waver all by itself, losing the battle of rank just like that. To complete my humiliation, the man kept staring at me until I lowered my eyes in submission. Thióðolf smiled and made a show out of averting his eyes a little while after I had lowered mine.

"You see?" he said, "I can respect you now, better than I could respect you when you kept challenging me as if you thought yourself above me."

"I see," I whispered. He smiled and patted my back.

"Now, these men appreciate your act, Thordís, as I just told you. They believe you are sacred and special. Even if they don't believe it, they still honor your act, because that act in itself is sacred. They want to believe you are a creature come out of Hel, which is a very fortunate mascot for a Viking crew. They adore you, and so they do not mind lowering or averting their eyes before you, as long as you maintain that act."

"Why do they believe I am a creature out of Hel?" I asked, utterly astonished, "I told them that I was a Thunder priestess. I think I was very clear about that."

"Few of these men even know what a Thunder priestess is, Thordís. They are Rus. They are exiles. Many of them have hardly even been to the homelands since they were barely more than boys of no lineage. They do not know your noble lineage, and they do not know the order of the Thunder priests. They just saw the powers that came from you, they think you came out of a flash of lightening, and that you were sent from Hel to be their mascot. You see, they are very fond of Hel-maids. And if they want to honor you as such, you better play up to it and quit the Thunder priestess act, swiftly."

"Why?" I whispered, feeling utterly confused.

"They are high after the raid, little one. Their minds are swimming. No man is cold after the slaying of a village, after the taking of crying women and frightened children. Their minds are swimming in water and seeking the sky. They see an image of a Hel-maid come to honor them, and that image will stick with them if you play up to it. But if you fail to do that, if you begin talking and asking childish questions and insisting that you are a Thunder priestess, the sacred spectacle will be forgotten and they will see you for who you are, a little girl who could not possibly be a priestess, and yet she tries to stare down warriors. And that is dangerous for you. Very dangerous."

"Would they hurt me?"

"Not directly, seeing as you are a child. Our people do not approve of child molesting. Had you been a woman grown, they would have humiliated you. But it could occur to them that a pretty little thing like you would fetch a very high price from some old creep who *does* like to rape and torment little girls." I felt my heartbeat almost like a drum inside my head.

"I… I *am* a priestess, you know," I said to him in a timid whisper. My father had said that a priestess ranked as high as any warrior, but I was not sure if this was still the case now.

"No, you are not," he said.

"I was born as one," I said.

"You were born to a heritage that you have not yet claimed," he corrected me, "but you cannot be a priestess until you have bled. That is, until you have become a woman. And even then, you would have to be ordained first. Then you would be a priestess, and men would avert their eyes before you, even lower them if the situation craved it. But as yet, you are but a novice, and you are in want of a mentor, which makes you even less than a novice. By law, you are just a girl. Nobody here knows about the nobility of your lineage. When they start to think things through, they will realize that you are but a warrior's daughter, and in no way higher than they."

"Is it not a high ranking thing, to be a warrior's daughter then?"

"It is a high rank, to be a warrior's daughter, but a warrior ranks higher. And we are your elders. And we are men."

"Oh," I said. I remembered father had told me that men and women related differently towards each other among his people. He had explained the issue of rank to me which had seemed awfully complicated. People's rank depended mostly on what family they had been born into, what clan, what tribe, and what fathers they had. A mother's rank was an important addition if she was related to some important man, but on a general basis all rank was inherited through the father line. And when a man and a woman was of equal birth and title, born to equal rank, like brother and sister, then the brother would rank a little higher than the sister, just as all clansmen would rank above their Sífs. Only a priestess, a holy woman or a queen should ever expect to be respected as equal or even above free men and warriors.

I had stuck to that notion when I approached the Vikings, demanding respect as a priestess of ancient and noble lineage, and they had been so awed by my miraculous entrance, my bearing and the signs of our Thunder lord that they had played along. But it had only taken one night to have them wake up and realize that I was just a little girl. And I had been disrespecting them.

"Even if she ranks above some men, it is very important for women and girls to always show respect for free men," Father had said, *"because if she does not, she is implying that she has good reasons not to respect him, on account of him being either dishonorable or a coward. And that is an implication that is taken very seriously among our folks."* I felt a surge of fear run through my whole self. I was so very much at loss as to how to proceed.

"Thordís," Thióðolf said, "Do not worry. There are those among us who see more than others, that is all, and there is still time to get your act together." He paused, and suddenly I recognized my father in him, the way he always taught me by implying something and then wait for me to ask a question in return before he continued.

"How can I proceed, Thióðolf?" I asked meekly.

"It is very simple. These men will believe in you or pretend that they believe in you for as long as they find it in them to respect you. And you must realize that if the men are to continue respecting you, you must also respect them. You must stop provoking them by staring them down and glaring at them."

"Shall I lower my eyes to them also?" I still felt a little humiliated.

"No way! You must *not* do that! At least, not now. Not yet. For the time being, you must play up to your act. Look as scary and mad as you possibly can, you are good at that. Think of yourself as a Hel-maiden, and you will continue to be one for them. And do not talk to them, because when you talk, men realize more swiftly that you are but a maiden after all. Talk to me and to Arnulf, but maintain your distance to the rest. Glare and stare all you like, the more the better, and never lower your eyes. But do not stare them down. Avert your eyes in time to let them know that you respect them as free men and as warriors. This is my counsel, and I also counsel you to heed it."

"I will," I said timidly. I felt as if he had pulled away all my shields and left me naked, and thought of the crying girl my father had told me about, the one who had been tormented before the whole crew. I was painfully aware that this man could destroy me within moments, if he wanted to, but somehow he seemed more interested in advising me.

"Now as to Arnulf," Thióðolf said, "he believes in you, that you are a Thunder priestess, but he also knows that the men believe you are a Hel-maiden, and he is letting them think you are, because he sees they prefer that story, and he likes you well. He wants to help you, and if it will help *you* that the men see you as a Hel-maiden, then he will not press the issue. Yet, he is starting to realize the things I have just told you about, that even if you are noble born and priestess born, you are still an orphaned little girl with no mentor and no position. Arnulf, on the other hand, is a man, a warrior, a captain, and a leader of men. He is a very powerful and rich man, and he is utterly ruthless, Thordís, even if he is kind to those he likes and respects. He has shown you great honor. He has offered you his protection and his hospitality, and it will simply not do for you to keep challenging him. A Síf who disrespects her warrior without good reason may find that he dissolves his oaths to her and removes his protection. Nobody would blame her if she has good reason to disrespect him. But Arnulf has in no way given you good reason, on the contrary he is not even your own blood, and still he has agreed to protect you and house you. And yet, you are disrespecting him."

"I will avert my eyes to him then," I said.

"No, Thordís, you will *lower* them, like we all do. We do it because he is our Heri. You will do it because he is both your Heri *and* a man who has offered you his protection. For as long as he protects you, feeds you and houses you, he is in every way your superior. You must lower your eyes to Arnulf, to show him that you accept his protection and that you, in turn, are willing to obey him. And that you respect his superiority and his status." I nodded, and Thióðolf continued; "The first time you lower your eyes to him, you will also bow your head to apologize for having disrespected him before. Bowing the head is the same as apologizing, unless you are a slave who will bow her head anyway. And you must return the favor he shows you when he calls you "priestess". You must call him "Heri", like the rest of us do. That will please him, and because he likes you and believes in you, he will protect you and house you for as long as you need it. But if you do not submit to his authority, he will begin to feel dishonored."

"What about the men? What will they feel when their Hel-maiden lowers her eyes to Arnulf?" I was getting a bit confused. I had already lowered my eyes to Thióðolf before the whole crew. I noticed how the men were casting careful and discreet glances at us. They had all seen the skald display openly his power over me. My act already seemed utterly fragile.

"They will think him a very great man, respected even by Hel-maidens," Thióðolf said and winked at me. I gasped. What a cunning man he was. And I could not even glare at him to show my dismay.

"Is that so," I said finally, feeling truly outwitted and somewhat grim of mood, yet I kept my eyes appropriately lowered to acknowledge that I had been taught and that he was my better. The cunning man chuckled.

"Do not think it a defeat, that you submitted to me," he said, "the men already know me for a clever sort of fellow and would expect no less of me. And you should certainly not think of it as a defeat when you apologize and submit to Arnulf Heri. He is a great man. Everybody will be happy, and they will be particularly happy because many of them already know that you are but a girl, yet they *like* you, Thordís, you have made this venture special for them. They will not think less of you for submitting to him. Maidens are supposed to submit anyway, and your submission to him means that there will be no need to expose you for being nothing but a maiden. They do not have to disregard their story about you as a magical creature for the sake of honor. And that will please them, because they *like* the story of the Hel-maiden. "

I soaked up the skald's counsel with all of my being and almost shivered with the realization that I might yet have been brought down by my ignorance. When Arnulf approached me again somewhat later, I met his eyes at first, the way I had seen, and then I quickly lowered my own, bowing my head just long enough for it to be noticed by anyone who watched. And I greeted him by saying *Arnulf Heri*. When I met his eyes again, he looked relieved and happy. His shoulders seemed to relax, and I knew that the skald had come to my aid just in time, since the matter of my total failure to submit had clearly begun to disturb the captain. Now that rank had been established and I had learned some manners, he seemed to be extremely proud of me, and the men also seemed to relax.

Seldom again have I ever glared directly at a man's eyes, unless it was in fact intended to destroy him. As long as I was on that ship, I glared through the men, or through air and open space, just to let them enjoy my Hel-gaze. I was no longer doing it to impress them. I did it knowing fully well that I was *entertaining* them, and I think perhaps they all knew it, even those who were fully entertained. My act was to be the Hel-maiden. And they liked my act so well that all of them continued to treat me with great reverence, and kept their distance, as I kept mine. It was as the poet had told me, I realized. They wanted my act, and they would do just about anything to help me maintain it, and so they did not even speak to me out of fear that I would break the spell.

I knew now that I really had a friend aboard this ship, and so I went over to Thióðolf again after he had taken his turn at the oars, and lowered my eyes again. It was pleasing, the way he immediately averted his own to signal his respect for me in return.

"You are a fast learner," he commented while he dried the perspiration from his face with a towel.

"You are helping me," I said quietly, "why are you helping me?"

"Firstly, because the norns led me to your aid, and you clearly have the favor of high powers. Secondly, because even if you are just a little girl, you have created a marvelous act, and I honor you for that. I appreciate a sacred spectacle as much as any other Norseman, even more so because I am a skald, and acting is my art also. Thirdly, because I know of your lineage and its greatness, and can see no other reason for our meeting than it is a sign that I should help you retrieve your legacy."

"My legacy?"

"The women's hammer," he glanced at my pendant, averting his eyes before it; "The one you are wearing is the men's hammer, is it not? That is Magni's hammer. You are carrying it for someone else. Perhaps you are carrying it for a son to come. This is the Hammer of Greatness and can only be wielded by a man who is also a Thunder

Warrior. You are a daughter of your clan, and you should have the women's hammer. Your rightful heritage is the hammer of Thrúð. Yours is the Hammer of Power." I thought the world trembled.

"How do you know about our hammers?" I whispered.

"I am a skald. We tend to know about sacred lore. I know well the story of the hammers, passed down through the generations of the ancient Thunder priest lineage. We who deal with sacred lore must help each other. I am not a Viking, Thordís; I am just a poet from Hálógaland, which lies far away in the northernmost parts of North Way. My fate has brought me here among the Viking Rus, and then you turned up. My heart tells me that greater powers have sent me to your aid."

I was speechless. And Thióðolf went silent, looking thoughtful, before he finally turned to me and regarded me for a moment. Then he said; "Even though I see through your acting, Thordís, I know that your act is born from truth. I know that your act was guided by your lord and by your ancestors. There is not a doubt in my mind that you, little Thunder Goddess, you *are* a creature out of a sacred story. We shall speak more when the appropriate time for that council reveals itself. I do not know when that will be, but it will happen, and then we shall return to this subject. For now, suffice it to say that a Viking ship is hardly the place for this sort of lore-wording." I stood and gaped while the dark-haired wise man went to find himself a place to sleep.

Rape Island

On the second day of our journey upriver, a while after I had spoken with Thióðolf, a woman from the ship behind us suddenly broke free, managed to climb the side board and dived into the river. The Vikings tried to keep her from diving, but once she had dived, they just stood there and looked after her as she swam away in the opposite direction, back towards the village. Then Arnulf shrugged and said; "That was a good dive. Her freedom is well earned." The other men agreed with head-nods and approving little snorts and turned back to whatever chore they were doing. It was the first time that I observed this odd combination of ruthlessness and fairness that was so endemic to my father's people. Even if she had been but a captive slave, she had impressed them by her courage and by her skill at diving, and for that reason only they let her go. A couple of the men made sure to secure the ropes and chains of the other captives.

Their dragon ships moved so much faster than our rafts. It was only afternoon on the second day before we had already reached the river junction where I had gone to the market with my family two years earlier. We must have already passed the place where Father once slayed six soul-eaters during the night. When we reached the junction I spotted two more dragon ships there and discovered more Vikings, more men hanging from trees, and a crowd of frightened captives. These were now herded fast aboard the five ships along with other goods before we moved on. I stood and watched the dangling men at the shore and was joined by Arnulf Heri and Thióðolf.

"Why do you hang the men, Heri?" I asked, hoping that I was not being rude.

"To honor them, priestess," Arnulf said, and when I still looked rather confused he added; "they are the men who fought well against us but who were nevertheless defeated while still alive. We took from them the chance of dying in battle, but in recognition of their courage we give them the honor of dying like gods. Carrying the mark of the hanged god they come to the shores of Hel and the great verdict, so that the Ladies may recognize their virtue at once. Surely they will pass the judgment and dwell among gods after."

"I see," I said uncertainly, "Thank you for the explanation, Heri."

"You must learn to think of life as a story, as a drama unfolding before you," Thióðolf said, "If you cannot perceive life like that, the story unseen will engulf you and overwhelm you. Life, little priestess, is the great tapestry of Fate, the great Saga, mother of all creation, in which human beings live and fight, hate and love, die and move on. Yet life is nothing more than that, a drama, a story played out to entertain the gods."

"Is that all," I said and felt a little sad.

"All? Thordís, the stories are sacred, and characters that make great stories are, in many ways, also sacred. Good entertainment needs good entertainers, characters that stand out and make a difference – such characters are pleasing to the gods, who are the greatest song-smiths of all. Anything that may stir the imagination and inspire great poetry must be honored, for it is, ultimately, sacred."

Arnulf and I were impressed, and the Heri nodded gratefully. "Wise words, Skald," he said, "You have honored us." I had already lived through verses that were the stuff of our most sacred songs, stories to be told by the campfire and sung by the hearth during long winter nights, stories to entertain the gods themselves. And something stirred in my soul then, a sense of gratitude and excitation, as if I had been given the seat of honor before a sacred spectacle called life.

Understandably, my sister Zivah and the other slaves failed to see their situation in such a light. Theirs was the act of despairing and fearing. I did not approach them again after that first day, when I tried to speak to Zivah and my presence among them produced glares so hateful I could feel them like arrows piercing through my body. And so I kept my distance, learning by the whispers I heard that they thought I was an evil sorceress, demonic of nature, who had called this misery upon them, that I was in league with the Vikings, a traitor to my mother's people. It was unfair, I thought, for I had called no such thing, and had been as powerless to stop the raid as they had been, but it was among the Vikings that I now found my place. The great ladies who carve the runes of fate into the trunk of the world tree had decreed it so. And so the tapestry of life was woven with new colors. The journey continued downriver, towards the east. I had not yet spoken to Zivah on account of the hateful glares that she and all the others sent in my direction. I wished it was different, but I did not wish to take my place among them either. My fate was my own.

When we had traveled for another day and night, the Vikings finally made camp for the night on a little island at a lake that they had obviously already marked out for the purpose. They were all tired, and not one of them had cleaned up after all the slaughter. Now they hid their ships in a small bay and disembarked, taking the slaves with them. The Vikings took turns undressing and bathing in the river. I noticed that all of them were good swimmers, as my mother's people had been. They used soap bars made out of animal fat to clean up properly, even their hair and their beards were carefully rinsed. When they had all bathed, they ordered the slaves to undress and herded them into the water, giving them soap and making them clean up as well. The men pretended not to be interested in the naked women, but I saw that they cast some leering glances whenever they thought themselves undetected.

I got into the river last, when most of the men were busy herding the slaves back to their chains, and only Thióðolf remained in the water with me, for my protection or for company, or both. As the dust and sweat from the last days on the river vanished, I felt reborn. When we got out of the water, the Vikings were already making the camp ready. Daylight would last a few more hours, and so a few men went hunting, and soon returned with two deer, which they butchered and began roasting over the fire. Meanwhile, the rest of the men had made sure to comb and braid their hairs and beards again, or straightening their spikes, or making up their dreadlocks, ever concerned with their appearance.

Vessels of beer were brought about, and the evening turned into a veritable feast, the men in good spirits as they ate and drank, chattered and sung. Their singing was a bit like those of our Spirit Callers, a deep rumble from the throat. To the surprise of the slaves they had been loosened from their bonds and sat around the fire in between their captors, who shared their food and drink with them. At first, the new slaves seemed utterly miserable. Even without shackles or ropes around their limbs they seemed to have settled for the obvious; that there was little point in trying to escape or attempt anything at all. But when they had stuffed themselves with meat and beer and gotten a little more used to the present situation many of them actually loosened up a little and began drinking heavily. The children ran around playing before the fire while the adult captives drank and even sang and brawled along with the Vikings. As the children began to fall asleep, the Vikings turned their attentions more particularly towards the captured women.

Zivah always referred to that place as Rape Island ever after. At some point, Arnulf gave a nod, and a few of the men gently gathered the youngest girls, the children and the male captives, herding them back to the ships where they were shackled up again. When the men returned, I was the only child present to watch the party unfold. Some of the women were weeping now, because all of them understood what was about to happen. But most of them seemed to have given up and thought that nothing mattered anymore, and that they might as well party for as long as they could. In fact, it looked like they were grasping at whatever comfort and friendliness that they could find. Relieved to be treated almost like human beings again, some even laughed and flirted with whatever men provided them with more drink. As they were all getting terribly drunk, most of the captives began to cheer up a little, and some were senseless, abandoning themselves to stupor. But I doubt if all of the women appreciated it as most of them, one after the other, was led away from the fireplace by a Viking or three to be on their own with them. Some went along with it, others went passively, and a few went weeping, some even begging. But as the night proceeded, all the women but one were taken.

Thióðolf sat with me the whole evening and tried to talk about other things, but I was too observant to not notice what was going on, and too curious to not ask questions. And so I asked him if he was not going to take a woman like most of the other men did, and he said glumly, but in a rather low voice, considering the other men; "No, Thordís, I do not rape women. I never have, and pray that I never will. I think it is dishonorable of a man to abuse his power thus against defenseless folks. And even if there was not my honor to think of, I am convinced that rapists are so hateful to the norns that such men what did such, and what never atoned for it, will after death find themselves doomed to wade forever in the icy, blade-sharp streams of Hel without ever getting across to new life."

Thióðolf was not the only man who was not going to abuse his power, at least not on that night, but the men who stayed behind to guard the ships and the shores or sit by the campfire were not the majority either. It was quite late when the only people left by the fireplace were some ten Vikings apart from Thióðolf, Arnulf, Zivah and I. The last man had left with the last girl and Arnulf was starting to cast some very meaningful glances at his new concubine. All evening she had been seated next to him, and all evening she had been staring relentlessly into the fire and only sparingly sipped at the beer he had tried to give her. I dared to look at her then, looking so tiny next to Arnulf, who was in good spirits while she was looking fearfully around, the only one among the captives who was still completely sober. Although she stood out as the most beautiful among all the women and caught many lustful and admiring glances, nobody had approached my sister, since mighty Arnulf Heri had publicly claimed her for his own.

"Thióðolf," I whispered, leaning over to him, "a concubine, is that like a wife?"

"Where I am from that is so," Thióðolf whispered, "concubines are usually just a little lower ranking, but they are free women. Not so with the Rus. Among them, a concubine is always a slave."

"Oh," I said, starting to feel that I had not fought hard enough for my sister's sake.

Now that he had eaten and drunk with her, and tried to cheer her up without any success whatsoever, Arnulf was getting impatient. He started to look at me as if he was curious about when I was going to pass out from exhaustion, and then he started to look at Thióðolf as if he wanted him to take me away somewhere to sleep. Thióðolf cast one glance at Zivah and then one at me before he looked back at his Heri and shook his head slowly. I could not help but shake my head also. Arnulf looked a little upset and suddenly he glared at us both. We returned his gaze brightly, then quickly lowered our eyes in a humble display of obeisance, before we completely failed to oblige. I was not going anywhere for as long as my presence might save Zivah, and Thióðolf seemed to agree with me.

Arnulf snorted and settled back in his place, ignoring us all. The other men exchanged nervous glances, and an awkward silence descended around the campfire. From the night's silence erupted the muffled sounds of crying women all over the little island, women who were whimpering and sobbing and sometimes even screaming. Zivah looked nauseous and the men looked somewhat embarrassed.

"So tell me, Njál," a man called Sígtrygg said, to break the uncomfortable silence, "How come you aren't running after girls anymore? You started taking after your friend Runarr there or what?" All the men started to laugh softly, and Runarr went a little red, but laughed with them. He reminded me conspicuously of how my father had used to look when the villagers laughed and he had to laugh with them at his own expense in order to save face. Njál with the spiky hair was playing with Mother's kitten and now looked up with a grin, displaying his sharp filed teeth.

"Naaw, Sígtrygg," he said, "Cannot say I am. It is just that ever since I had them teeth filed all the girls start screaming when I try to be friendly with them, like. The last time I tried to take a girl she never stopped screaming, even if I tried to reassure her and all."

"By *smiling* to her?" Sígtrygg and all the others were snorting with laughter.

"Well, I am not a very bright man, Sígtrygg," Njál said, "and I just kept forgetting about them teeth. In any case she screamed and screamed, so I just gave up. Since then I stick to them girls what already know what a kindly fellow I really am."

"A wise choice, regardless, Njál the Foolish and Sharp-Toothed," Sígtrygg remarked, the men almost rolling over with laughter by now.

"You owe me a name-gift now," Njál said, and Sígtrygg took off a golden finger-ring and tossed it across the fire. Njál caught the ring with a hand and held it up proudly for all to see.

"Why did you get them teeth filed, though, Njál the Foolish and All That?" one of the other men said, who went by the name Agnarr, causing another round of laughing sobs.

"It was the Kindly One who inspired me, to tell you the whole truth," Njál said, and added proudly; "She cannot abide me at all." The men exchanged some mysterious glances, and I could see that they were trying to not show how impressed they were. I dared not display my ignorance and just strained my ears to listen and understand what they were talking about. After a few moments of awkwardness,

Sígtrygg resumed his teasing role. "What, you thought she was going to marry you if you had matching teeth?" he asked.

"Naaw, Sígtrygg, we all marry that one at some point or other, fangs or no fangs. It is just that I saw what she did and then I thought it would be nice to know what it felt like to actually tear open an enemy's throat with my own teeth and drink his blood, like," Njál explained patiently, not at all baffled by the laughter of his friends, what quickly subsided anyway.

"So how is that working for you, then?" Agnarr inquired, looking curious.

"It is working real well," Njál the Foolish replied and grinned charmingly, displaying his rows of sharp fangs; "You could say I have developed a taste for it."

Mother's kitten suddenly jumped into his lap, and the fanged warrior cooed fondly at it and took it up into his hands to cuddle it, muffling his face into its soft fur. When he looked up, he had all our attention.

"This cat's name is Hel-Hound," said Njál.

Not a Fool

After our night on the island we soon reached a very large river running westwards, although we were going eastwards on that same river, which meant that the men had to row a lot. Two days had passed since that night on the island, and Zivah still sat with the other slaves and looked as miserable as ever. Arnulf had not been very happy about the fact that Thióðolf and I had stopped him from taking Zivah away from the camp fire that night, I had gathered that much. He was still kindly to me, but after having tried to approach Zivah with smiles and offerings of food and drink several times, only to see her cringe away from him and look as if she was going to be sick, he had stopped looking at her altogether and if she passed by his vision at some point he would frown and then cast a doubtful glance at me. She made no secret out of how much she resented and detested him. And after Thióðolf and I had stopped him from claiming her it seemed to Arnulf that no matter how pretty the girl was, she was not exactly concubine material for him. Thióðolf, on a short break from all that rowing, suddenly took me a little aside.

"Thordís," he said, "I think you need to speak to your sister, to Zivah."

"She is not very well disposed towards me, Thióðolf," I said. He nodded, having noticed that.

"Well, it is probably hard on her to see how revered you are while she is a slave and... you still want to protect her, don't you?"

"I always protect Zivah if I can, Thióðolf. I always have." Thióðolf regarded me curiously for a moment, but left the matter alone, urging me instead; "Tell her to not show just how much she dislikes Arnulf. Tell her to try to smile at him and be a little friendly, and, and with the head bowed, of course. It is the better path for her, even if it is not exactly what she wants there are far worse options to replace it. Trust me in this."

"I could try and talk to her," I said, feeling a by now well-known chill up my spine.

"I know she does not want him but he is her master and I do not know how long Arnulf will accept her behavior, Thordís. I am not so sure now that we acted wisely when we stopped him from taking her back at the island. It is her fate to be his slave and his concubine, and she has to submit to him and at least put up a friendly face. Now, she is offending him. He could just decide to get rid of her at the next slave market, when he has the chance, even just for the sake of showing us all who is in charge. She has to... she has to hide her feelings and remember her position. You need to make her understand."

There was such urgency in his voice, and such sadness in his eyes when he spoke those words to me. He really cared. I nodded gravely. I knew that I had to do something.

The first thing I did was to go to Zivah. It was hard, because the people hissed at me when I approached, and I heard their whispered curses. *Demon child. Sorceress. Traitor*. They seemed to think that I at seven years of age could somehow have changed this course of fate. I closed my ears and eyes and sat down next to my sister. "Zivah," I said, "I know you do not want to be with Arnulf, but he is the only one who can protect us both. If you do not like him he will not like you either and then he will sell you off to other men who are much worse than him." Zivah regarded me resentfully.

"How can you tell me to like this man and give myself to him in exchange for protection? What sort of protection is it for me if I am raped? I think you have sold me to this brute so that he can protect *you!*"

She wheezed those words to me.

"I could not have sold you, Zivah, you were not mine to sell," I tried to explain, "He had already seized you. I just thought that it would be better to belong to just him than to… to all the others."

"I do not see any difference between these rapists and killers, Thunder Goddess. Leave me alone, I have no need to see you triumph over me. You have won. Are you happy now?" She turned away from me, clearly unwilling to speak more to me.

I withdrew feeling confused because I did not understand what she meant with triumphs and winning, but what I did understand was that she was too burdened by grief and fear to be able to see the one escape which I had seen, and that it went through Arnulf Heri. I looked thoughtfully at Arnulf and wished I had been a little older. If I had only been a woman grown I could have taken Zivah's place so she would not have to, but I was just a small child.

On the other hand, Arnulf *did* seem to mind how she felt about him. He could have just taken her, if putting his Freystone inside of her was the one thing that he really, really wanted. But he had not, and he was obviously considering letting her go because she was failing to give him something that was not just her body. There was something else that he wanted, and maybe I could provide it. I studied him cautiously and tried to sum up what I knew about him so far. After some pondering I was quite certain that he wanted to be respected, admired, needed, and trusted almost as much as he was feared. Almost. I had a feeling he was quite partial to the sort of trust that comes from not having any other choice but to trust him and that he liked well to live up to that sort of trust.

He had taken a break from the rowing himself – for even the Viking captain joined in the rowing as often as not. Now he was standing up by the prow where I used to sit, by the dragon's neck, and I had gotten used to this being his time to speak with me or just stand next to me, something he seemed to enjoy for reasons I did not know. I suspected that he just liked me, which was an encouraging thought. So I went up to him and stood there for a while, just stood there right next to him and looked at the flowing water of the river like we had often done already. After a while of silence I peered up at him and said; "Heri, are all the men of your lineage of great stature and bearing such as yourself?" Arnulf frowned and looked down at me.

"I mean, you are very, you are so very big and tall and strong," I said, "and you look really powerful and I thought perhaps, perhaps there was something that runs in your family."

"Do you, now," he said drily. I wondered what I was doing wrong.

"Uhm. It was just that I started to think of it. You remind me of my father. He was also a very strong and fearless warrior and he had red hair just like you. He could also be a little scary, but he was really very kind and took care of us all very well."

"Are you scared of me, priestess?" Arnulf asked. He was indeed starting to scare me a little.

"I may be, a little," I said uncertainly, hoping that would be the right answer.

"You should be *very* scared of me," he said and locked my eyes with his. Now that he glared at me I saw how piercingly blue his gaze was, like sharp edges of blue steel boring into my soul. I wanted to avert and lower my eyes from those sharp steel edges, but he seemed to be holding my gaze locked. While he kept my eyes locked with his, he slowly moved to squat down so that we were of a height.

"Now tell me this, Thordís Thorbjörnsdaughter, seeing as your father was a warrior. Would you have gone out to meet me in combat, wielding a rotten twig in my face?"

"No," I said and shook my head gravely. I would probably not have tried to wield anything in his face at all, but I was pretty certain that he meant this figuratively.

"No. You would not. Nobody would be that foolish. The only thing you ought to wield against me is a real blade. Because that is the only thing that just might work, if you are fortunate," he said. I shifted the weight on my feet and felt very uneasy, but he still maintained the eye-lock. "You are a child, Thordís, and you are of woman-kind. So I do not blame you for trying to combat me in the way of a girl or a woman. You have already seen enough of this world to know that the only arms you are ever going to be able to wield with the remote possibility of success are your affections," he said, "and it is possible that you can wield false affections against fools and win. But do not ever, Thordís, do not ever try that with a proper warrior. I may not be a particularly wise or clever man, I may be simple, but I am no fool. Do not ever disrespect me like this again."

I felt my jaws drop. Arnulf studied me curiously, as if he wanted to see if I was going to cry like any ordinary child would have cried at such a frightening rebuke, but I had no memory of what it was like to cry and could not even play the frightened girl-child convincingly. As soon as he left me off the eye-lock, I bowed my whole head.

"I am so sorry, Arnulf Heri. I meant no disrespect. I am not sure if I understand," I whispered.

"You were wielding false affections against me, Thordís. Though I shall commend you for knowing exactly what I want. You have seen that I want you to admire me and need me, trust me and respect me, and fear me, just a little. It is true. You are a very perceptive little maiden. But you have disrespected me by underestimating me. You have taken me for a conceited fool who is so hungry for compliments he will let himself be swayed by false affection. You are like an inexperienced warrior wielding an imaginary stick, or perhaps a rotten twig, in the face of an angry boar. You just cannot do that with the likes of me. If you are going to wield weapons of affection against a man, especially if that man has actual power over you and is a warrior, then you better start wielding true affections. Because if it is not true; I am not having it. It is not going to work. It will only serve to provoke."

"Oh," I said and tried to gather my thoughts. I did not know what to say now, and I had angered the only person who could possibly provide us with a life. I felt so desolate and more terrified than I had ever since the raid. It was as if all my resources and all my weapons and shields had been taken away from me. I was utterly defenseless and unfit to protect my sister. A darkness of heart descended upon me and I turned to Arnulf and heard the despair in my own voice as I spoke quietly to him.

"Arnulf Heri, I am very young and have very little experience with men such as yourself. I wish there was anything I could do. I wish I could put myself in her place. I would. I mean, I will, if you want to, or whenever you think I am big enough. I will not cringe from you or flinch or resent you or anything. I will… I would give you my whole self. Gladly," I said, locking my gaze with his again.

We looked at each other for a long time, while he searched my soul to see if I really meant that. I did not fear that scrutiny now because I had meant every word with all my heart. He saw that.

"Yes," he said eventually, and his eyes were so hard, "yes, you would. Maybe you will, too."

That was all he said. I drew my breath and gave myself over to my fate. "Then, whenever you want…" I began, and thought my trembling voice sounded like a squeaking mouse's, but he placed his finger over my lips.

"Do not offer that which only a woman grown can give a man," he said, "and thank your lord that I am not the sort of man who would have taken you up on that offer. You are a child of seven summers, Thordís, however did you even think of this?"

"I was hoping you would say we could wait a little," I said, "I will grow, Heri."

"Yes you will grow, and I am not saying that I could not imagine how that would work, Thordís. You could even have become my wife, seeing as you have that name of yours. But there will be at least another seven years before you are ripe to be plucked, and in seven years I may be dead." He paused for a moment, and I just stood there and bit my lower lip. I had nothing to offer him.

"There is another issue also," Arnulf said, "one that you may just want to acknowledge. What if I said that yes, I would take you and use you when you were older, but still did not want to take on your sister. What if I just took you, and not her? What would you do then?"

That moment I thought that all hope was lost. It was true what he said. I could not bargain even with myself. It was as I said to Zivah. How could I sell to him what he had already seized? I had lost the battle, and there was only one honorable way of losing a battle, my father had always said, and that was with grace. I drew my breath again, and myself up to full height.

"Arnulf Heri," I began, lowering my eyes as submissively as I could, "my father taught me that recognition of rank and power is best shown through courtesies and deeds, and not through direct description. But if it is so that I have failed you and you wish to hear the words, then I will speak them; You have all the power here, and I have none. I am powerless against you, and so is my sister and all those you have taken from their lands. Our fate is in your hands. We are yours to do with as you please. I can only hope that you will honor those words you spoke to me on the first day that we met, words that were surely witnessed by my lord, who is also your lord, Heri. I am so sorry if I offended you by thinking those words meant more to you than they actually did."

I kept my gaze down while he seemed to be absorbing or considering my speech. To my surprise, Arnulf's arm suddenly reached around me, and he scooped me up to sit inside of his great elbow, where I had just enough room. My hair flowed in the wind and when I met the warlord's gaze I saw lights of amusement and something that could be affection, glittering in his blue eyes. "See there, Thordís. Now you are fighting with real blades. You have given me all that I really want now. You have given me your fear, your need, and your wish to please me, and your total recognition of my power over you. You have made me your lord, and you have done it all for real, and you have appealed to my sense of honor. And do you know what, Thordís?" He peered humorously at me. I shook my head. "This time it is working," he said and smiled, holding me closer. "If I ever doubted that I wished to have you for my Síf, then I no longer doubt it," he whispered into my ear, "You are a warrior's daughter, Thordís, and your courage is about to become legendary."

"Courage?" I asked. I thought I had just been quite utterly defeated.

"Yes. Courage. My gods, child, you just used you own helplessness as your most effective weapon, and you used your real feelings of powerlessness to wield it. And you wielded it with precision and like the sharpest blade. That takes great courage and I am proud of you."

Then he looked doubtfully over at Zivah and added; "At least it is working for you, Thordís. That is the problem with these sorts of blades. They are fought by solitary warriors. You cannot substitute your sister, little one, but I do commend you for trying. I do commend you for wielding your actual feelings for the purpose of a greater cause. I commend you for using your own bodily self to bargain with for the sake of protecting another, although I think you may want to postpone that sort of bargaining until you are somewhat older. Your fight here speaks of your noble character and we Norsemen admire that sort of women, child. But falseness will never do with the likes of us. Even the silliest men among us have been trained to look through that sort of thing."

He sighed, and I thought perhaps his features softened just a little; "I shall have to think about it, priestess. Now hop along and… be a child or something. Tomorrow we reach Khazaria."

Be a child, he said. I did not know what that meant anymore. All I knew was that I had to thread carefully and pay attention to many things if this was ever going to work, and if he wanted me to be a child from now on I would try as well as I could. I knew I had, miraculously, won a round here, and that there was only a small part missing. If I had not fully grasped it before I grasped it now. That man was my lord and could not be disturbed now that he had dismissed me, but my father's example had taught me a lot about how to appeal to the men who rule you. I looked at the water and away from him, and touched the men's hammer lightly.

"Oh lord Thor," I said, not directing myself to Arnulf at all, "I pray you will protect me and my sister and not ever let anyone separate us, for she is all that I have left in this world." I sighed and turned to spy a place to sit awhile, and let out my breath with release when I saw

Arnulf shrug and grunt in the manner of a free man who will consider something he is most likely to also grant, in his own time.

Khazaria

We were considerably far to the south of our home village, but apart from that I had no idea where in the world we were until, after three more days rowing upriver and eastwards, we came to a great river junction harbor. There was a settlement there, what I thought was a veritable town, because it was a lot bigger than the village. I had never seen so many people and such a big settlement before, but learned soon that many of the buildings were hardly more than tents. It was really just a permanent market, a typical trading harbor of sorts. When we moved slowly in towards the harbor, Arnulf pointed to the southeastern steppes and distant mountains.

"That there, priestess, is Khazaria. Beyond their lands to the south is a large sea, one called the Black Sea. And beyond that sea are the great kingdoms what buy our slaves and our other goods. On the southeastern side of that sea lays Big Tunic land, where them eastern Tunic men live, and their main city is called Baghdad. And to the southwest of the Black Sea lies the land of the East Romans, who are Greek, don't ask me how that works. These folks have cities so large and so splendid it cannot be imagined until you have been there, and their demand for slaves is never ending. But we Rus have to go through Khazaria to trade with them, and more often than not it makes a lot more sense to trade with the Khazars right here."

We disembarked in the Khazar trading town's harbor and were met by the shore by a group of some fifteen warriors and a very small, middle aged man whose skin was darker than any human skin I had ever seen before. I stared at the little man, and when he discovered me his jaws dropped and his eyes seemed to widen with fear. Arnulf noticed and made a small gesture for the man to approach. The little man hurried towards us with his whole head bowed, what made me understand that he was a slave. Now that I saw him closer, I noticed that he was wearing a sort of thin iron collar and that his face was shaven and his black hair cut quite short, as opposed to the Vikings who obviously were his masters. I looked curiously at him while he maintained his gaze on the ground, looking quite uncomfortable.

"House-Bond," he said to Arnulf, who just grunted in return.

“Greet my new guest, Shumayl,” Arnulf said, “This is Thordís the Thunder priestess, although some call her a Hel-maid. Priestess, this is my personal slave, Shumayl. He takes care of my finances, the health of my men and my household and my slaves, and provides many other services on account of being a very clever little man.”

I was pleased to be acquainted with the odd little man, but he was clearly not as pleased with me, for his eyes widened and despite the darkness of his skin, I could see that it paled, what made me so impressed that I began to lean forward to look closer. I had put on my white wolf coat, and the wolf-headed hood was pulled backward atop my head, causing me to feel the sharp fangs of the wolf mouth on my forehead, and a small tear of blood trickled down to my eyebrow. The slave looked utterly frightened, as if he had to struggle not to turn and run away, and whispered a strange word, “*djinn*!” and retreated a few steps away from me. He looked anxiously at Arnulf, who began to laugh, but gave the slave a nod.

“And you think us superstitious, Shumayl,” he said, grinning, “well run along now and check on the slaves. The men are well cared for, you can look to them later. We want to finish this business swiftly.”

“At your service, Maiden,” Shumayl mumbled while he cast an embarrassed look at me before scurrying along to fulfill his master’s orders.

“That was cruel, Arnulf,” said a very tall man from the party of warriors who had met us at the shore with Shumayl, “you know how skittish he is.”

“I could not resist, Hallgrim,” Arnulf chuckled, “it was the face what he put up when he saw her.”

“A Thunder priestess, no less,” Hallgrim said and looked curiously at me.

“Yes. I shall tell you the whole tale later. For now, Hallgrim, I introduce you to Thordís my ward and my Síf. Thordís, this is Hallgrim Hidden Spear, the foremost among my warriors and leader of my men, and besides a very skillful fellow in many ways.”

“I greet you, Hallgrim Hidden Spear,” I said and lowered my eyes politely to the third Viking, gathering that this one was on par with Thióðolf and Arnulf and would not appreciate my glaring Hel maid act, what the rest of the men still seemed to find very entertaining. He studied me thoughtfully for a moment, and only averted his eyes when I looked back up at him. His eyes were deep and dark. I thought they could be naturally a deep blue, but it was as if the black in his eyes had expanded so that his eyes seemed like dark wells. I felt a chill in my spine and knew that here was another cunning man who could see right through my soul's core. To my relief, I seemed to pass his piercing gaze.

"I greet you, Thunder priestess," Hallgrim said politely and averted his eyes.

I stood for a while and watched all the commotion when goods from the ships as well as slaves were disembarked, checked, counted and lined up in a system that seemed to be devised and discreetly also led by Shumayl. He had the oddest way of making the Vikings follow his orders. The little Tunic Man slave would just stand there looking submissively down at the ground while seemingly talking to himself about all that needed to be done. The Vikings pretended not to listen at all, but as soon as he had made a statement or other, the men immediately followed the suggestion and made it seem like they had thought of that all by themselves. In that way Shumayl ruled without ruling a most effective organization of all the goods, while steadily making little signs on a wax tablet. I studied the slave carefully now, seeing as the skittish little man was rather clever at ruling a whole band of fierce Vikings without ever letting them know that they were being ruled at all, a skill that occurred to me as being very useful, seeing as I was not that much higher ranking than a slave myself.

Just as I had gotten used to the darkness of Shumayl's skin, five huge men in the strangest looking clothes came marching by carrying foreign-looking arms and more importantly had the darkest skin I had ever seen and had never imagined ever seeing. They looked almost black. All the slaves stood staring with jaws dropped at the black men as they marched by, and the Vikings glared at the slaves to make them lower their eyes. The black men, apparently, were high ranking warriors, and it would not do to have slaves staring at them like that.

"Who are they?" I asked when Thióðolf came up to stand by my side.

"They are Blue Men," he said.

"Blue men?" I asked.

"Yes. Blue Men."

"But they are brown. Or black, almost. Like dark soil."

"Yes, which is why they are called Blue Men."

"Oh," I said and frowned.

"They come from a place far south in the world with blazing heat all day long, so their skin has been burnt dark from the Sun," Thióðolf explained, "and that place is called Blue Land."

"What are they doing here then?"

"They are fierce warriors who have been hired by the Tunic Men of Big Tunic Land, and then they are sent up here to escort the Tunic men traders."

Just as Thióðolf was talking of Tunic Men traders, some of them showed up. They were dark of hair and dark of eyes, and a lot smaller than the Vikings, and their skins quite tanned, although only one of them was as dark as Shumayl, and none as dark as the Blue Men. They wore colorful clothes of fabrics yet unknown to me, and some had only very large shirts on. There were also some Khazars there, people who looked a little like the Tunic Men only they tended to be taller and more light-skinned, and they were wearing more fur and leather. The Khazars and the Tunic Men had apparently agreed more or less on what they were going to buy beforehand, and after checking the goods and going through things with Shumayl, Arnulf and Hallgrim, there was an exchange of gold and silver and other metals, some of which were coins, what I had never seen before, and then the Tunic Men and the Khazars called out for some strong man slaves with bowed heads who began carrying the things that the Vikings had stolen and place them onto charts pulled by some strange large beasts what turned out to be mules and horses.

"Why are they called Tunic Men?" I asked when the foreign traders began to disperse.

"Because they hardly ever wear anything but their tunics," Thióðolf said and gestured towards their long wide shirts that reached all the way down to their ankles.

"What do they wear in winter then?" I asked.

"There is always summer down in their lands, Thordís, it is almost as hot there as in Blue Land. But the Tunic Men from Big Tunic Land call themselves things such as Persians or Arabs, while down in the western smaller Tunic Land, what they call Al-Andaluz, they are called Moors, and all of them are, uhm, Moosol…Moosoleems. That is a sort of ritual custom."

"A ritual custom?"

"Yes. Did your father tell you about a Full Troth?"

"Yes. Lord Thor was his Full Troth, and is mine," I said.

"Good. And your mother, did she have a Full Troth?" Thióðolf asked.

"Yes," I said, "Her Full Troth was the Freyia Medeiné."

"Meh-day-neh?"

"Yes."

"What sort of goddess is Meh-day-neh?"

"She is the soul of the forest," I explained, wondering if he did not know her also.

"Oh, I see. We know her also, and we have many other names for her," the skald said thoughtfully, "I suppose as many names as there are forests. But like your father, she believed in many different goddesses and gods, is that not so?"

"Of course," I said.

"Well, as it is among our people and that of your mother's people, everybody have different Full Troths and some have more than one also, and everybody honor all the gods they are aware of besides. But the Tunic Men, that is, the Moosoleems, they all share one Full Troth and they believe that he is the only Full Troth anybody should have. They think that the other gods are evil demons or false."

"Oh," I said, completely at loss for words. It was the strangest notion I had ever heard. Thióðolf waited patiently until I remembered that it was my turn to ask. "What do they call their Full Troth then?"

"They call him *Al-Laah*."

"What spheres does he rule then?"

"Everything. They think he rules everything."

"Like Dievs," I mused.

"Who?"

"He is the father of all the world," I said, "only I never heard of anyone who had him as their Full Troth. He has too much on his mind to bother with mortal folks. At least that is what my mother said."

"Huh," said Thióðolf, "it seems to me that many people believe the same things but call them by different names. Even among Norsemen we have many different names and masks for him."

"What would you call him, Thióðolf?"

"Óðinn," said Thióðolf, "although many believe the true face of the all-encompassing one is Heimdall. Often we just refer to him by some of the old words for lord. Like Freyr or Rig or Dan or Drott… even Heri, sometimes. Or simply by one of our words for "god", like Týr, or Fimbultýr, the Great God. Or we call him Father of Men or Father of All, or by countless other cover-words, like the Great Speaker or the Great Veil or Tree… What would you call him?"

"Great Thor," I said determinedly, and he raised an eyebrow but said nothing.

When the slaves had been lined up, Zivah amidst them, I looked quizzically at Arnulf and suddenly felt a grave dread. Now I watched the Heri, who met my eyes. Just before the men approached the slaves, Arnulf swiftly interfered and had Zivah taken out of their ranks. He held her by the ropes around her wrists, still without looking at her, while we all watched the men cutting off the slaves' clothes. It was unbearable to watch after a little while, so I walked a little away from the spectacle, only noting that the slaves were herded into the river naked to wash, and came out of it, and were brought naked to the market, herded by several Vikings.

When the slaves were herded off Arnulf looked at me and then called to Thióðolf; "My friend, why don't you take the little priestess for a look around town, at the other markets? You can have Njál and Runarr and whoever wants to go with you; and Shumayl for translations."

Thióðolf nodded, looking thankful about it, and Arnulf peered down at Zivah, who was just standing there with an expression of horror, watching the line of naked slaves being herded like cattle towards the market.

"Maybe you should take Zivah with you," Arnulf began, but Hallgrim, who had been watching Zivah with those deep well eyes for a while already, suddenly interfered.

"No, Heri. That girl needs to see what fate could have befallen her," he said gravely. Arnulf took another look at Zivah, who noticed and flinched. A look of severe displeasure passed across his face.

"I hear you, Hallgrim. Let us go," Arnulf said, and pulled roughly at Zivah's rope. She turned her face around to look at me once, just before she followed her master to the slave market, there to watch how her friends were sold, one after the other. Her eyes were already so empty. I thought she was saying goodbye in her own way.

I could only place my trust in Arnulf Heri.

Our little party led by Shumayl strolled into the market town where I saw so many foreign sights, I almost swooned from trying to register each sound and each sight and each smell. Thióðolf looked carefully at me and suggested that I try to concentrate on a few things at the time, which seemed like an impossible task. I always took in everything that transpired around me. Then he suddenly said "concentrate," in such a commanding tone that I concentrated anyway. I peered up at him sideways and wondered what had just happened. He just smiled at me and winked.

There were the strangest animals there, some in cages, a little human-looking fellow clad in fur that made me think of the little forest people that Mother had sometimes talked about, they who once had ruled the forests all alone. But Thióðolf assured me that it was a beast, much like a cat. There were cats there too, and some really colorful birds what seemed to be talking in a foreign language. And the people were all sorts of sizes and colors and looks, and clad in so many different sorts of clothes I thought it must be one of those huge tribal gatherings that Mother said had used to happen in the past, before the age of wars. People seemed to be shouting and screaming all the time, and all in so many different tongues.

There were stalls with precious fabrics that made me think of Zivah and wish that someone would at least give her a new dress, but nobody seemed to be thinking of that. Every time I saw the huge dark stain in her leather dress I thought of how she had been rocking Mother in her arms after she was killed.

Then I saw some very large animals, larger than elks, and Thióðolf told me that they were horses. I had heard of horses from so many stories and knew that one was supposed to ride seated astride them, what shocked me now that I saw how enormous they were. But then I saw some smaller ones and started to imagine what it would be like to sit so high and move so fast. And then another sort of beast showed up, which turned out to be cows. I saw domestic pigs for the first time, and even something they called camels.

We reached the end of the market and started walking amidst tents where the dirtiest looking children I had ever seen seemed to be running around on their own, although I saw some women working at the hearths. Then I began to see large wooden pens filled with both animals and people. I saw naked slaves being pushed into the pens.

The men quickly led me away from there and ended up by a large almost empty field by a stream. There were some poles out there on the field, poles upon which some small and colorful flags had been tied, now blowing in the wind, and a few men were standing out there in a circle, praying.

"They are Khazars," Njál said, peering at them.

"They are, Heri," Shumayl agreed.

"I thought the Khazars worshipped inside temples," Runarr mused.

"Yes, that is so, Heri," Shumayl explained, "but some of the Khazars are still Heathens, and so they worship out here on the heath just like your people do."

"What gods are they praying to then, these Heathen Khazars?" Thióðolf asked.

"His name is Tengri, Heri. He is the lord of the sky," Shumayl said, "He is married to the Earth."

"Like Thor!" I said and looked curiously at the Khazars, "What is a Heathen, Shumayl?" I asked. The little slave looked fearfully at me and lowered his eyes quickly.

"That is a word I learned from the Rus, Maiden," Shumayl said, "I know that is not what you call yourselves but I was trying to explain our… our concept of pah-gah-noos, and then I was told that Heathen was a good word for that."

"Pah-gah-noos?" I asked.

"Yes, it is a Roman word," Shumayl explained. And then he told me that a Heathen or a Pah-gah-noos was a person who worshipped many gods and goddesses and believed in the sanctity of Earth and also knew of many spirits. When he had finished explaining, I was more confused than ever. As far as I was concerned he had just described the actual world.

"What he means is that a Heathen is someone who believes like we do in the customs of our ancestors and pay heed to all the great and holy powers of above and below," Thióðolf explained, "and because of that we are also Heathens just like these Khazars, even if our customs are different. But Moosoleems and most Khazars apart from these ones, they have taken a new faith where only their Full Troth is thought to be good and holy and all other powers as well as the Earth herself are, uhm, neither good nor holy. They say that we Heathens believe in false idols and demons."

"So most of the Khazars believe in Al-Laah?" I asked.

"No, no they are not Moosoleems. They are Jews. They believe in…" Thióðolf frowned; "what is his name again, Shumayl?"

"Jehovah," said Shumayl, "or Jahveh, as some say. Forgive me, Heri, but the Khazars are not Jews. They are of a different stock altogether, but they converted to Judaism more than a hundred years ago. They say that they are the thirteenth tribe."

"Thirteenth tribe of what?" Agnarr asked.

"Well there are thirteen tribes of Jews. They believe they are the chosen tribes, the chosen people, Heri," said Shumayl.

"Chosen for what?" Agnarr looked intrigued.

"I am not sure, Heri," said Shumayl, befuddled, "but they are the chosen by god."

"What god?"

"Uhm. God. Al-Laah. Jehovah. Deus."

"All of them?"

"They are names for the same god, Heri," said Shumayl, "He is just called different things by different peoples. The Jews and the Moslems and the Christians, they all believe in the same god," The men frowned and nodded as if they understood, although I am not sure if they all did. I for one wondered what the difference between those Jews and those Moosoleems and those Krees-tianees was if they all believed in the same god, but it was already so complicated that I decided to just listen in.

"But are not all people chosen by their gods?" asked Runarr, scratching his head.

"Uhm, well, Heri, the case is that, uhm, both Jews and Moslems, and Christians for that matter, they all believe that there is only the one god. They believe that he, whatever name they call him by, is the only true god," Shumayl said nervously. The men looked incredulously at each other and broke out in roars of laughter.

"That is like saying that out of all the stars in heaven only one is true!" Agnarr barked, causing another round of laughter, while Shumayl was looking deeply uncomfortable.

"One can only start counting the visible gods to grasp that the notion is ridiculous," said Runarr and shook his head in disbelief, grinning.

"So if this is true," Njál said humorously, "does that mean that them people are the only people chosen by the only god there is then? Leaving the rest of us as, sort of, *not* chosen?"

"That… that would sum it up, Heri," Shumayl whispered.

"Well they got some nerve, I will give them that," said Njál, and all the men guffawed with laughter again, even Thióðolf, who so far had only listened to the conversation that had followed.

"So what did he choose them for then?" Agnarr pursued.

"It is very difficult, please excuse me Heri, my best explanation is to say that he chose them for a special destiny."

"Are not all people chosen for their special destiny?" asked Njál, and all the men looked quizzically at Shumayl, who had gone a little pale.

"Uhm, the Jews, and the Khazars, well, as I said, they believe that they are the only chosen ones," he said meekly. Agnarr leaned over towards him and glared a little. "Is that what you believe also, Shumayl?"

"No, Heri."

"But you said them Jews and them Khazars and them Krees-tianees believed in the same god what does you Moosoleems," Agnarr objected, and I pricked my ears for the explanation.

"Yes, but, uhm, Heri, Moslems, on a general basis, believe that, uhm, that we Moslems are the only real chosen ones now. Not the Jews."

"Is that so," said Njál and grinned at Shumayl, who flinched at the sight of his fanged teeth.

"While the Christians believe that they are the chosen ones. Although I have heard that even within these three large tribes there are countless fractions, all arguing about which of them is chosen by the only god that can choose anyone anyhow," said Thióðolf, finally intervening again.

We all stared at him for a moment before the men burst out laughing again.

"They do sound a lot like little children," Njál said, pondering, "arguing about which of them are best loved by their father. Even I could not nurture notions as foolish as all this."

"They even wage wars about this issue of who the chosen ones really are," Thióðolf continued, and the men were now rolling over with laughter.

Eventually they calmed down and looked quizzically at Shumayl.

"Honestly, Shumayl, I know you for a very clever little man. Do you really believe in being chosen above all other folks on account of having a particular sort of Full Troth what is the only real one in the whole wide world?" It was Agnarr who asked.

Shumayl drew his breath and spoke bravely and truthfully; "Heri, I may be a Moslem, as you say, but I would not have been standing here if it was not for the fact that I also believe in the sanctity of all existence and the divine immanence in all things. I do not think your gods are false or demonic. I think your gods are different masks of the one true divinity."

"Huh?" said Njál and Agnarr together.

"You two are too foolish to understand that sort of talk," said Runarr patiently, and Njál nodded in enthusiastic agreement while Agnarr frowned. Then all three of them looked to Thióðolf for clues. Thióðolf was gazing at Shumayl with an expression of keen interest.

"What Shumayl speaks of is from the lore of the Red Gold," Thióðolf said, "so there is nobody expecting you to grasp it, but I can assure you that his words stem from a wisdom that is known to many cunning folks." The men nodded thoughtfully and cast some admiring glances at a beaming Shumayl who had enough wits to keep his head down regardless.

"But what good is that wisdom if it was the sort of ken what made him stand a slave here today?" asked Runarr, and everybody looked brightly at Shumayl, who seemed to be blushing, going even darker.

"I was… I was persecuted for my faith by the great Caliph Al-Mahdi. That is our king in Baghdad. His line of Full Troth is very strict and he does not allow people to believe and worship in the way I did, and my fellow brothers did. We were threatened with slavery or death. I tried to flee, but I was abducted by Khazar slavers and sold right here on this market, several years past. That was how I ended up as a slave and was sold to Arnulf Heri," Shumayl said.

"You were persecuted for your beliefs and worship?" Agnarr asked, incredulous.

"Yes," said Shumayl.

"It is like with them Christians down in Frankland," Njál said, "I heard they slay people and torture them if they don't believe in some particular words. It is on account of not being chosen, although nobody has really agreed on who was chosen, so they kill away all those they are certain of, I think. Maybe it gives them a better overview so it will get easier to determine which of the survivors have been chosen."

We went quiet for a while, all pondering the strange customs that seemed to be astonishingly common in other places despite their obvious foolishness.

We began to walk back towards the harbor, and we went quiet. I was wondering how Zivah fared now. I kept experiencing little surges of panic that I fought hard to suppress, imagining seeing Zivah being pushed into a slave pen. I suddenly clenched my fist and drew my breath.

If she ended up in a slave pen, then so would I. I would just go in there right with her. I could not leave her. I would have given them anything they wanted from me if only they kept my sister with me and as unharmed as possible. But I could never submit to these Vikings if they sold my Zivah to other men. I would go with whatever men wanted her and offer myself to them too. And if anyone tried to force me away from her I would make a spectacle that would end up having both me and my sister killed for sure, but that would be better than this, better than leaving my sister to the soul-eaters all on her own. All fate is sacred, all songs are great, and if Shumayl and Thióðolf had any truth in their souls then our gods reside within each one of us, and in each and every fate, no matter how miserable that fate may appear. I knew no fear of death, and as to life, I had never been so very concerned with anything but the present moment at all times, so I had never even considered worrying about my own future. I had only ever really feared for my sister, and what I feared the most for her was that she would be alone in the world. I was not going to let that happen if I could stop it. I would rather share her slavery. I had decided.

But as we rounded the corner we spotted Arnulf standing outside the market with Zivah in tow, talking to Hallgrim. Then he turned for a moment and looked fondly at Zivah, who looked up at him with a small, endearing smile before she humbly bowed her head, which he patted as if he was rewarding an obedient dog.

*

Aaahrn-oolf. She tested out the name in her mind, tried to pronounce it correctly with her mouth even as she stayed quiet. Arnulf. With the passing days he had seemed less and less like her stepfather than he had when she saw him first, but somehow that had not been reassuring in any way whatsoever. The less she saw him as a twisted version of Thunder Bear, the more she saw the giant-sized and ruthless pirate captain all covered in horrible scars and demonic tattoos, so very ugly and cruel looking, his red hair and very pale skin only serving to make him look ever more terrible.

He wanted to have her as a… a *freeh-leh.* That was what they called it, but she remembered Thunder Bear speaking of his *freeh-leh* and said she had been a sort of wife to him. She saw how the man ruled all those other beastly men with the glance of an eye or the nod of his head, and knew that if she thought *they* were scary, and they thought *he* was scary, then the man who wanted to have her for his wife of sorts was a very frightening man indeed. Sometimes she had laughed bitterly to herself, what irony of fate, that she had wanted to be whisked away into the great world by a prince, a leader of men, only to find herself the unwilling woman of an ugly, old, murderous and cruel pirate warlord.

She wished she had asked her stepfather more about the customs of his people. When Aaahrn-oolf had pointed at her and shouted those words, and she recognized the word *freeh-leh*, she had been terrified, but after a little while she had had the practical sense to wonder why she was still wearing slave-chains and seated among the other slaves if she was supposed to be a kind of wife to him. He had not in any way approached her after that, there had been no sweet-talk and no gifts or any other implication of him wanting her until they reached Rape Island. On the island, when she had noticed how much he desired her right then and there, he had still not done anything about it. She was starting to suspect that she had misunderstood the word and that she was not going to be any sort of wife to him at all. He had not even given her a new dress, letting her walk around in her bloodstained long leather tunic.

Now her master was pulling her by the ropes around her wrists as he walked after the line of naked and broken people, and right next to her walked that tall Rus they had met at the harbor who had been looking at her with those strange dark eyes. He reminded her of the

Spirit Caller who had lived in the village before, and oddly enough his presence made her feel strangely calm about everything.

Then she forgot all her ponderings as they came into a large square crammed with all sorts of strange-looking foreign peoples, all so different and all so very loud. In the village people had always talked in calm voices. Even the Rus tended to be remarkably silent most of the time. But here people seemed to be screaming at each other all the time. There were so many new sounds and smells and sights that she began to feel dizzy, and noticed the tall man with the dark eyes put out a hand to support her. Arnulf had suddenly left them, and her lease had been given over to the very tall man.

"You must watch, Zivah," the tall man said quietly, his voice deep. She did not understand the words but for some reason she knew what he was saying to her. Zivah regained her balance, closed her eyes for a moment and drew her breath. Then she watched. She saw the people of her tribe being paraded around, naked and paralyzed with fear, while all sorts of strange-looking men walked around them, touched them, made them open their mouths, checked out every inch of them, and began to bargain in loud barking voices. Arnulf and a few other men were there bargaining right back, looking quite large and frightful compared to most of the other foreigners, and then deal after deal was being made for a whole eternity as one after the other of her people were being sold away like goats.

Zivah saw her doting friends stand there, trembling from terror, while men pinched at their bellies and their breasts and most parts of their bodies, and then they were sold off too and they were led away in shackles or ropes. Tears began to stream down her face. Princes and heroes and dresses made of silk; that was what they had talked about. She felt as if she had lied to them for years. She could not watch anymore and tried to look in another direction, only to see a woman being bent over a table surrounded by several men, and then the first one started to rape her. Zivah turned around again and wished she could just run and run and run forever. The tall man pulled gently at her rope.

"You must watch," he repeated, "You need to know this."

How she understood what he was saying was a mystery to her, but she did. And he was the first Rus-man who had actually spoken to her apart from giving orders. She dared to peer up at him sideways. She had begun to notice their language of the eyes and knew enough by now to understand that she was supposed to keep her eyes lowered and her head bent most of the time, so she had begun to explore new ways of looking at the men that did not cause them to glare at her with those murderous eyes. A sideway upwards glance seemed to be acceptable to them.

"I am Hallgrim," he said, and she thought she detected some amusement in his eyes.

"*Hah-ahl-greem*?" she tried.

"Yes. Hallgrim. Like hall," he gestured up to the ceiling of the large hall, "and mask," he made a sign that surely meant mask. He was the Hall Mask. Hallgrim.

The Mask of the Hall suddenly pointed at the woman who was being gang raped right next to them. "Slave," he said, and then he turned and pointed at the people who were being sold in the square and repeated the word "slave". She understood. Slave was the word they had for the people they owned and sold like goats. Then Hallgrim pointed right at her and said the same word. She was a slave. Zivah bowed her head and nodded to signal that she had understood. Then by way of words and gesticulation he let her know a second time that the woman next to them was a slave also. Zivah was not certain, but she thought he was trying to explain to her that the slave woman had displeased her master and had been given to many men to be taught a lesson. If a slave rejects a master, there is no saying what sort of masters she will be given to instead. Better stick to that which is known.

"Zivah," he said and made her look up at him again, "Zivah is a slave. And Arnulf is Zivah's Heri."

"*Heh-reeh*?" she tried. She thought she had heard people call Arnulf that word quite often.

"Yes, Arnulf is Heri. Zivah slave, Arnulf Heri. Understand?" She nodded uncertainly, and he began to point at other men to illustrate that they were *Heh-reehs* to the slaves they were pulling away in chains from the slave market. A Heri was a master and a lord and the owner of slaves. She nodded again to signal understanding. Hallgrim caught her eyes again and pointed at Zivah and then at the slave market, looking quizzically at her as if he wanted to know what she would prefer.

"If you want a new Heri, Zivah, you can go out there and see who buys you. Do you prefer that to being Arnulf's slave?" He repeated and gesticulated until Zivah had gotten the message.

She cast another brief glance at the market and the leering cruel eyes of men everywhere she looked. Men who wanted to devour her and kill the lights of her soul. Somehow, Arnulf had never looked at her exactly that way. She did not know for certain what the difference could really be, but it was there and there was a choice between something that was at least partly known and something that was not but seemed to hold few if any promises. She was a slave and she had to have a master. Like a master-less dog, she felt now, those strays which sometimes had passed through the village, hoping for someone to take care of them no matter what. She could no longer afford to be picky.

Pale-faced, Zivah whispered; "Zivah slave, Arnulf Heri."

"Then you must smile at Arnulf and call him Heri before he sells you off, girl," Hallgrim said gravely, and Zivah seemed to understand at once.

*

Arnulf braced himself and returned to Hallgrim and the girl. He had begun to seriously regret his promise to the little priestess. The slave looked like she wanted to vomit whenever he drew near. And the way they had stopped him from breaking her in when there had still been time to… He stopped his musings. To his surprise, young Zivah blushed charmingly and smiled cautiously up at him.

"*Aaahrn-oolf Heh-reeh*," the slave girl said, still smiling, and bowed her head gracefully. "Hmm," Arnulf said and raised an eyebrow at Hallgrim Hidden Spear. It was perhaps not his charms that had turned the girl's mind, but that did not matter. She had acknowledged him at last, and if her smile was still forced, her submission was real. Affection could come later.

*

When we walked back to the ship and I saw my sister tag along after her master with her head bowed, attempting to please him like a despairing stray dog, I found myself trying hard to think of just about anything other than this. I turned to Thióðolf again because something had occurred to me, so I tugged gently at his sleeve; "Thióðolf?"

"Yes, Thordís," he said, absent-mindedly. He had gotten this sad look about him after we saw Zivah and Arnulf together, even though it was supposed to be a good thing.

"You did not tell me who your Full-Troth is. Will you tell me?" I asked.

"Of course, Thordís. My Full-Troth is the heavenly Freyia." He pulled out a pendant that I had tried not to look at before, seeing as it was rude to stare at other people's sacred things. Now that he showed me I glanced respectfully at it from various angles and made out a beautiful woman figure holding a drinking horn. Father had made those drinking horns out of cow horns that he had bought from traders, so I recognized it.

"Is she like the Sun Maiden?" I asked. For all I knew, Freyia was just the title of a noble lady and could be used for any of the goddesses.

"You could say that," Thióðolf said, "although you could also say that she is the Sun of our hearts and our souls. She is the light and the all-knowing one. And I believe she resides in all living existence, spinning our fates from within each one of us who are alive. And…" he paused, and suddenly he seemed to be shining with a light that grew from within. I felt myself gasp. "She is love," he said and looked at me with those deep blue eyes, so full of that love he spoke of. It was as if I saw that love in him for the first time. I looked solemnly at him and reached out my hand.

"You offered me your friendship earlier. Please forgive if I am late in responding, Thióðolf, but I have never had friends before, apart from my family. I would very much like to be your friend," I said. He took my hand gently and tugged it. I thought I saw a few tears around the corners of his eyes, and that he was actually too moved to even speak that moment. I felt a little embarrassed. Father always said that I should look another way if men were weeping, out of respect for them. But Thióðolf was not actually weeping beyond that moistness, and I just changed the subject instead.

"Do you know what Zivah's Full Troth is?" I asked, although of course he would not know.

"No, Thordís. I did not even think to ask. What is Zivah's Full Troth?"

"Danu," I said.

"*Daah-nooh*?"

"Yes. Danu. She is the great river goddess, the mother of all rivers."

"That is very great tidings, Thordís. Your people believe in old Danu?" he looked genuinely surprised.

"Yes," I said, "do your people not?"

"Well there we have many names as well, Thordís, but Danu is certainly one of them. The Danes are said to have stemmed from her, although they too have given her new names. Not long ago the name of the ancient goddess gave title to their kings, who were all called Dan. I find it very curious to hear that your mother's people also know that goddess."

"They said all the rivers were born from her. They said that our ancestors were born from Danu, but then they spread out in to all the daughter rivers and ended up in… in the village," I explained.

"Those are our legends too," said Thióðolf thoughtfully, "although your village may not take such a central place in our songs. But Danu is an ancient and distant name for the goddess of our people. In fact the name means just the same as the name we use for the goddess now."

"What name is that?" I asked.

"Freyia," he said, "although we no longer think of her as the river. She is just the lady of all that flows with life. But it is the same name and the same meaning."

I could understand that. Father said that even if all the tribes spoke a similar language there were also lots of words used by one tribe and not so commonly by another tribe. And with time there had come to exist many names for the same power, and often the names meant just the same thing but sounded different. Like Danu and Freyia, the great Lady of flowing life. And suddenly I realized something interesting.

"But Thióðolf , Freyia is your Full Troth also," I exclaimed, "You have the same goddess as my sister does!"

"Yes," Thióðolf said and frowned; "She is hardly a goddess for slave girls, though. Where I come from she is worshipped by kings, by great warriors and by sages and poets. She is a goddess of mysteries that hardly any woman will ever dare to seek."

"Zivah was not born a slave, Thióðolf," I reminded him, "and where I come from Danu belongs to everybody." He stopped to scratch his head.

"Yes, yes. The Lady has created new paths wherever she has been. But I cannot help wondering. Why did Zivah choose the goddess for Full Troth?"

"Because she wanted the mother river to send her a prince," I said, "a prince from faraway."

"Did she, now," Thióðolf said and looked really, really stunned. But he spoke nothing of it.

*

That evening, Thióðolf sat out in the night by the river when Hallgrim Hidden Spear suddenly appeared next to him, and Thióðolf startled. The skald smiled and shook his head approvingly, seeing as being able to startle the Tribeswolf was rather impressive, all things considered. It took a great cunning man to sneak up on another cunning man like that, but then, Hallgrim was a seasoned shadow walker.

"You have the appearance of a sad man, poet," Hallgrim said.

"Sadness is a feeling what must be enjoyed in quiet," Thióðolf replied dismissively.

"You feel for the young woman," the shadow walker stated, "You pity her." Thióðolf shrugged and grunted.

"I cannot help but pity her, Hidden Spear," he said, "I have seen her a while. She is a very special sort of woman, and she has the misfortune of being rather delicate. A bit too delicate for her master, I fear. And she is grieving. That is her mother's blood on her dress."

"I know," Hallgrim said, and waited as if he was expecting Thióðolf to say something. But the bard had little more to say.

"I feel for her too, in case you wondered," Hallgrim said eventually, "but I am curious as to what you are thinking about it."

Thióðolf frowned. Hallgrim was Arnulf's man. He chose his words carefully. "It is just that she is… That place what she was taken from was very sacred, Hallgrim. I told Arnulf and the men it would be sacrilege to attack those people, but they had come thus far… and now I fear she might be somewhat too delicate for Arnulf's embraces. I fear she might break from them."

"Yes," Hallgrim mused. They watched the darkness before them, quietly.

"Do you know that she has prayed all her life to the river mother for a prince?" Thióðolf did not know why he said that. The thought just came out, as if it needed to be heard.

"Has she, now," Hallgrim chuckled. Then he was gone. Thióðolf thought he saw that mischievous grin of the cunning man reflected like light in the darkness for a long time after.

In a Tent on the River Islet

We left Khazaria the very same evening. Arnulf said something about one Gunnarr Beak-Nose having already passed by and turned homewards, and that he did not want that one to reign alone in Aldeigjuborg, so he set after him, so to speak. The river we took now was running north, and the men could relax the oars most of the time, letting the northern-going flow take us gently downriver. We did not stop for some days, and Arnulf still did not touch Zivah on the ship, but he kept casting anticipating glances at her, and she always made sure to smile in return. She was not good at hiding her true feelings, but at least she made an effort and also did whatever she was told, and ate and drank what she was given. She was the only woman on the ship now, and a very beautiful one. There was no way the men were able to not look in her direction some times, and there were a lot of them while she was all alone. She seemed so deeply shamed by her situation now compared to mine that she hardly looked in my direction at all, and if I approached her she almost flinched as much as she did when any of the men came too close, so I left her alone.

After three days and nights voyage downriver and to the north, we made camp at another islet in a small lake. There was a deal of merriment, but without any women except the quiet Zivah, it was a lot mellower than last time we had spent the night in a similar place. As soon as we disembarked, Arnulf had some men set up a tent for him, and then he led Zivah over to me, led her in a tow as before, her wrists still tied up, and told me to help his slave bathe. I had a feeling that he was testing me, so I took the lease without complaint and tried to make eye contact with my sister. But she was oblivious. The shame and embarrassment seemed to be covering us both like a cloud of poison as I led my own sister the slave in a tow to bathe her in the river so that her master could ride her after.

With some warriors positioned around but politely turned to look another way, Zivah and I bathed in the river, and I combed her hair.

"Zivah," I said, "I am sorry that you have to do this, but I see no other way. I am too little. I asked him and he said that he would not have touched me in another seven years and then he might be dead. I am so sorry, Zivah, but you are the only one who can do this. At least you are a woman grown, so it should not hurt you. Father was almost as much bigger than Mother as Arnulf is bigger than you."

Zivah looked strangely at me, as if nothing I said made any sense to her. I swallowed my despair, understanding that she could not possibly deal with my needs now. It just hurt a little when I had struggled so hard for so long while she did not cooperate at all. Ever since the raid she had let me make all the decisions myself, even though I was the child. I knew that Father had told her to do that, but sometimes I still wished that she could just start helping out more. I could only assume that it was a part of the plan. I had to do everything myself, and I did it gladly, but nothing seemed to be good enough. She seemed to expect much better results.

"I am doing the best I can," I whispered, "but I am not… I am not grown, Zivah."

She just looked at me with that strange expression again, as if she had no idea what I was talking of, and there was a moment there when I suspected that she did not even know how hard I was fighting for our case. This was the first time she had to do her part in this battle, but she seemed to think I ought to have done that for her also. The unfairness of it hurt a little, but I shook that hurt off at once, sensing that my sister was in deeper despair than I could even imagine. Now that I stood there and washed my sister's indifferent body I wished that she could just understand that I was trying my best and that the other options seemed worse. I stopped trying to talk and remained silent while I combed and braided Zivah's hair.

When we got up, I realized that we had no clothes to change into, but I had seen the men often wash their bodies and then get into the same now rather stained clothes, so we put on what we had worn before. Zivah's dress was still stained by old blood smear. The blood of our mother.

I led Zivah back to our camp and let go of her ropes just before we got there. But not before Shumayl had seen us. He was standing a bit outside of camp, studying some herbs that he had found there, and when we came he turned to us and frowned. Then he remembered his manners, lowered his eyes to me and said; "Maiden." But he looked at Zivah and then at me and seemed to be making up his mind about something. I had a feeling he might share Zivah's conviction that I had done a terribly bad job at protecting her, and that feeling made me maintain a distance from Shumayl for a long time.

We sat around the campfire where we ate with the others and spoke little. Zivah spoke not at all, but did start to look pale again. Arnulf had not yet taken Zivah, but there was no way that my mere presence was going to stop him this time. She was his slave, after all, supposed to be his concubine, even, and this was the price for not being sold at the Khazar slave market. It was obvious that Zivah had understood that part also. Arnulf paced back and forth for a while, casting leering glances at her, and a few apologetic glances at me. Finally he went over to her and tapped her shoulder. She got up from where she had been seated on the ground and followed her giant master up the trail to the tent he had made ready for them. Her shoulders were slumping as she walked, and I thought of the girl whose soul had died when my father took her. When I almost got up to follow them, because I had always followed to protect my sister, Thióðolf took a firm grip around my arm and made me sit down again. "It is her fate," he said, "Both you and she must accept that."

*

Arnulf knew that Zivah still feared him and that she was a far way from finding him attractive, even after days of trying to show her that he was not going to eat her alive. She was still skittish, though. But the girl had not been broken in and it was beginning to show. The uncertainty of what is going to happen is always the worst for new slaves, he knew, and it was better to get it over with. She had to come to terms with her new situation and that had to happen before he brought her home. Arnulf could not have a weeping girl in his hall among his women. She had to get used to it before they got that far. He regarded her when she got into the tent. There had been a considerable improvement in the way she tried to please him with smiles and she did not look like he made her nauseous anymore, at least not quite as much as before and she tried hard to hide it.

Her smiles were forced, he knew, but he knew slaves enough to not bother trying to force her to feel anything genuinely. The point was that she acknowledged him in the proper ways. Affection could develop later, with little attentions and gifts to her over time, things that she would not have expected and therefore could appreciate like no wooed wife could. He liked having happy women around him, but he had been a slaver so long that he knew how it worked regardless. The first time with a newly made slave would always have to be a demonstration of who was in charge.

He placed the lit oil lamp on the small table his men had placed in one corner of the tent and untied her wrists. The moment he no longer held her in tow she moved backwards and away from him until she stood in the furthermost end of the tent, looking as terrified as ever, even after a whole evening of what he, at least, considered sweet-talk. Arnulf sighed and decided to just get started. Sometimes a firm hand could be more reassuring than the soft, just as it could with a skittish horse.

"Clothes," he said, and gestured for her to take off her clothes while he settled in. Slowly, with trembling movements, the girl began to take her clothes off and then held them in front of her while staring into the ground. He approached her and gently removed the clothes and then her arms and made her stay up so he could look at her. What a lovely shape she had, and it was sweet the way she at least tried to smile shyly at him now, so vulnerable yet ready to please him. He made her lay down on the bed that had been prepared for them. He stood tall, hovering, looking down at her naked body and beheld how beautiful she was. Zivah opened her golden eyes and looked at him, met his gaze, tried to force another smile and suddenly burst out in tears.

Arnulf closed his heart and concentrated on her body instead, expecting to be aroused by that sight alone, but found himself somewhat lacking in enthusiasm. He sat down next to her, still dressed, and when the sobbing stopped, he reached out and touched her breast gently and attempted a smile. She dried her tears and tried so hard and so hopelessly to smile back at him that he suddenly resorted to turning her around so that he would not have to see those eyes. She crouched obediently where he had positioned her and Arnulf began to feel his lord stone stir after all. He began opening his breeches. Then the girl began crying violently again, though she did not even move from the spot. The Heri got up and scratched his head.

He could just take her. He knew by experience that if he just showed a new slave who the master was, she would become more docile later and not mind it anymore, and often enough she would end up enjoying it. If only she grew accustomed to it, she would learn to be eager for the kindly attention he bestowed on any girl who pleased him. That was a trick what often worked. But not always. He took one more look at the girl's beautiful young body and met her weeping eyes as she turned her face to look at him, again trying to force forth a smile that seemed more like a grimace of terror.

The captain sighed. It was one of those times.

Arnulf found Hallgrim seated outside not far from the tent, but on his own. Hallgrim often enjoyed the night better than the campfire. The Heri sat down next to his first man.

"Hallgrim my friend, I could need some counsel," he said after watching the darkness for a while in silence.

"I should think so, old man," Hallgrim said, grinning knowingly.

"It is the slave girl. Zivah. She was going to be my concubine."

"So I heard."

"But she does not like me, Hallgrim. I cannot have a concubine what doesn't like me at all. I think she thinks me a troll."

"Most likely she just thinks you are too big, and too scary, and too ugly and besides, too old," Hallgrim said casually. Arnulf frowned, and Hallgrim bowed his head apologetically for speaking so bluntly.

"Is that what you think is the matter," Arnulf finally replied, "or is it perhaps that I was the one who abducted her and almost raped her when I found her weeping by her mother's corpse, her mother being killed before her eyes by one of my men, and besides, because I led the attack that destroyed her village, and because I sold all her friends into slavery?"

"I should think those issues also matter," said Hallgrim, "and have the effect of making you ever the more old and scary and ugly in her eyes."

"And big," Arnulf added sourly, thinking that obvious quality about himself the most redeeming cause for that pretty young woman's disgust with him.

"And big," Hallgrim confirmed, trying hard not to show his enjoyment too much.

"She is not going to change her opinions about me," Arnulf said, "and I cannot take her as a concubine. But I promised the little priestess that I honor that slave more than others. They had the same mother."

"Did they," said Hallgrim, and it looked like his mind wandered for a moment, "well that is a bond what many would deem a strong one." Arnulf just grunted in response.

"So, Hallgrim," said Arnulf after a short silence, eyeing an opportunity to get back at Hallgrim, "You are in all ways a deal smaller than me, are you not?"

"In many respects, Heri," Hallgrim gracefully admitted, "I am the smaller man." Arnulf snorted contentedly and proceeded; "So maybe, since you were not a part of the raid and all, and you are not too big nor too scary, although I am not sure about the handsomeness, but all in all: Do you want her?"

"Me? Heri, that would be cruel. I must share."

"I was thinking that you could be granted dispensation in this case, seeing as you are now a senior and my first ranking warrior. You could move into the Hold, even. If you want her, she is yours." Hallgrim turned to look searchingly at him before he shook his head determinedly.

"That is very generous, but I am sorry, Heri, that girl is… she is not my type," he said.

"I should think that girl is just about anybody's type," Arnulf objected, but Hallgrim shook his head and the Heri did not pursue the issue. "But I promised the little priestess," he said uncomfortably, "I cannot give her to either of the men because the others are going to be jealous and wonder why I favor one before the others, and I cannot give her to any of the Sixers because the other Sixers will be jealous, and I cannot give her to all of them because, well, you know. I am not a cruel man. What do you think I should do?"

"Have you thought of what you can give to the girl?" Hallgrim asked.

"What to give to the *girl*? To Zivah?"

"Yes, to Zivah. I see you, Heri. I will not speak the words loud but I know why you cannot find it in you to take that girl. There is no blaming you. So grasp this opportunity to become a better man. Instead of thinking of who to give her to, think of what you can give to her, something to atone for what you took from her."

"You cannot be serious," Arnulf objected, "she is a slave. It is against all laws and customs."

"Apart from the laws of the Contrary," Hallgrim said, and proceeded when Arnulf just stared at him in surprise; "I am serious, Heri. Obviously you cannot let her or anybody else know that you are making amends to her on account of her being a slave and all. But you can still give to her what she has probably yearned for all her life."

Arnulf raised both his eyebrows incredulously, clearly impressed at Hallgrim's words. The shadow walker knew all sorts of weird things.

"How can you know what she has yearned for all her life?" He asked curiously.

"Oh come on, Heri, look at the girl," Hallgrim grinned, and Arnulf turned to look at the quiet tent where he had left Zivah weeping. "I meant that figuratively," Hallgrim said patiently, "What I mean is that she is a very young and very beautiful woman who was free until the moment you took her away. She has not nurtured slave dreams. You know what all young girls like that dream of unless they grow up as slaves. You took away all her dreams. So give her dream back to her in a way that she never expected."

Arnulf still looked dumbfounded.

"A prince, Heri. Give her a prince," said Hallgrim Hidden Spear.

*

Arnulf returned to the campfire looking very bright and contented, and I noticed the men exchanging meaningful glances and little smiles. My poor sister. I wondered when I could go to her. But Arnulf sat down next to Thióðolf, patted his back and spoke loud enough for all to hear.

"Now, you all know me. I have never been the sort of man what runs after the youngest women," he began, and everybody nodded uncertainly. Njál looked like he was going to comment on that but quickly shut his mouth.

"And when I went up there to get… acquainted with my new woman, it started to dawn on me that although she is pretty as a sunray, she is very young, and she is a fragile sort of thing, and I have come to a stage in my life when I actually appreciate more what I have got at home and is well-known to me, than all sorts of new influx."

We all nodded obediently again.

"So then I started to think, and then it occurred to me that Thióðolf Skald here is the sort of man what never seems to want to share women with other men, and yet he has no woman with him, and is bound to me for three years. And then I thought how good a friend he has been to me so far and how much I am looking forward to have him stay at our court, just as I have enjoyed his company so far, and then I decided to give the girl to you, Thióðolf, as a token of my esteem of you."

Arnulf smiled encouragingly to Thióðolf, whose jaws had dropped. I was quite amazed myself, but said nothing while we all waited for the skald to reply. A gift offered in private could be rejected without shaming anyone, but a gift offered in public could not. There was nothing else that Thióðolf could do than thank his Heri for his gift, and I saw how countless thoughts and concerns suddenly ran through Thióðolf's mind just then. Finally he opened his mouth.

"I thank you, Arnulf Heri. I am very honored. Of course I accept your gift. I shall make you a great poem."

All the men cheered and drank, and Thióðolf sat there looking absolutely stunned.

"What are you sitting there for, man, go! She is in my tent. You two can use it for the night," Arnulf said to his skald, and Thióðolf looked like he was panicking. He met my eyes.

"I shall take Thordís with me," Thióðolf said and we both started to get up.

"What are you taking Thordís for? She stays here," said Arnulf.

"I thought she could translate," Thióðolf said pleadingly, but Arnulf shook his head.

"There is nothing you two are going to do what needs translation," the Heri said, and it was said in a way that made me sit down and leave my sister's fate up to her new master.

*

Thióðolf went up to the tent and saw that it was lit within. He strained his ears to listen and thought he heard some anxious breathing. He squatted down and tried to gather his mind around this new situation. All the other men were dazzled by her beauty, but all he had ever seen in her was a terrified young girl who had suffered a loss the scope of which he could hardly imagine and who now found herself in what must seem to her a nightmare there was no waking up from. And she was Thordís' sister.

He had seen how she flinched and cowered whenever a man looked at her, and men were looking at her all the time, what left the girl in a perpetual state of terror.

There was nothing he could do about it, except making sure that he, at least, was not contributing to her discomfort, and so he had refrained from looking at her at all. What dark humor the Ladies have sometimes, he thought. It was impossible for him to just go in there and take her the way Arnulf thought he ought to. Now he looked at the tent and then back at the campfire and knew that he had no choice but to go in there after all, if for nothing else so to let her know about the new arrangement, and hopefully to get a place to sleep. He did not want to scare her more than necessary, so before he opened the tent entrance he called her name softly.

*

Zivah had not dared put on her clothes again. She did not know why the Heri had suddenly left the tent, but he could surely return any moment. Yet after a little while in that humiliating position she turned around to sit, and after waiting a little more, and since she was feeling naked and a little chilled, she deemed it safe to hide beneath the blankets of the bed. The villagers had accused her of being false, she mused, and she had worried about it herself, that maybe they were right. She had taught herself how to charm a man witless just for the fun of it, but her play went no further than that.

Zivah knew now that she had no talent for acting at all. She was unable to hide what she really felt, and even when she had tried to hide her disgust with that terrible Rus-man who owned her she had just not been able to. What people had mistaken for falseness in her was rather the fact that she was always in tune with her feelings, and yet her feelings simply changed sometimes, or else people did not like to know the truth of what she really felt, because they wanted her to feel other than she actually did. She dried her tears and wondered if she would ever be able to just submit to the Heri without weeping. She knew that she ought to. He had made that clear to her when he let her see how her friends were being sold to men that seemed even worse than him. But it was impossible. And now he had just left her without finishing what he had so obviously planned well. She wondered where he had gone. A surge of fear seized her again. What if he had gone tired of her wailing and had decided to punish her in some way or other? She remembered the woman in the market and Thunder Bear's story of the wailing girl, and began to fear that she had made her fate even worse than it already was with her childish tears.

Her heart almost stopped when she heard someone outside the tent. But Zivah braced herself. She was going to smile to him now, she had decided, she was going to smile and not cry and let him do what he wanted and be over with it.

"Zivah," another voice said. She pricked her ears and tried to recognize the voice that surely did not belong to her master.

Oh sweet river mother have mercy on me, she thought, *this is his punishment. He is going to let the others use me instead.* The tent entrance came open and surely enough another man slipped in. She cowered beneath the blanket and stared at him. It was that dark-haired fellow who often talked to Thordís. All the Rus were the same to her, big brutes, terrifying and beastly, but this one whom they called *Tschooh-dolf* was actually the last man she had expected to see now. He was the only one among them who never looked at her at all. He seemed altogether too dazzled by her little sister to even notice that she existed.

Now Tschooh-dolf approached carefully and without looking directly at her. When he sat down next to her she flinched, and she saw that he noticed and quickly sat down on the bed without facing her, and kept his eyes diverted from her. It actually seemed like he wanted to show her that he was harmless. She held her breath, but when he did not attempt to uncover the blanket that protected her and still kept facing unthreateningly another way, she began to feel that there was something relaxing about him, and let out her breath at last. He sighed and said something. She frowned.

"Not understand," she said in Norse, having started to catch up on some words.

"Arnulf. Your Heri," Tschooh-dolf said, followed by some words that, when repeated accompanied by obvious gestures, she realized was a question about whether Arnulf had taken her. She shook her head slowly and felt her face burn.

"No, Arnulf not touch Zivah," she whispered, although he had touched her breast once, and then touched her to turn her around, but that was not what she wanted to convey. She noticed that Tschooh-dolf let out his own breath in relief, as if it had concerned him whether Arnulf had raped her or not. That was unexpected. Zivah peered at the man, alerted.

*

When he had entered the tent and saw how she cowered in terror, naked beneath the blanket, he had felt a sense of dread. Only then did it occur to Thióðolf that Arnulf had probably already used her before he decided to give her over to someone else. He was a Rus, after all, and a Viking. They always bragged about having the right to take whatever they wanted and were strong enough to take, and they rarely minded sharing their women - or their victims - with good friends. Somehow he had not counted on that when Arnulf told him to go and take the girl he now owned. And now he had to deal not only with the unexpected possession of a freeborn slave but also with a raped woman.

His kinsmen had taught him how to approach a newly raped woman, and it was much the same way a man would approach a maltreated animal. He made sure to direct his front and face away from her and kept looking another way when he sat down, signaling in every way he knew that he would not hurt her. Her nervous whimpering regardless only seemed to confirm to him that she had been raped, but he had to ask. When he was certain that she said that Arnulf had not touched her, he felt a surge of relief. She was just frightened. He had already decided to just go and sleep on the outside, but he needed to inform her of their new arrangement.

"Zivah," he said, feeling a little embarrassed, "Arnulf…he gave you to me. Gift. Understand? You are a gift from Arnulf to me. Arnulf. Give. Zivah to Thióðolf." She stared at him.

"It means that I am, uhm, I am your Heri. You are my slave. You understand? Zivah belongs to Thióðolf. Zivah is slave to me."

She shook her head slowly. He sighed and started over again as patiently as he could.

*

Zivah thought that the world was going to fall down on her head all over again when she began to understand what had happened. She had been given away like a goat to another man who now wanted to do to her what Arnulf for some reason had lost interest in, or perhaps as a way of punishing her. She shook her head as if she did not understand, because she did not want to. But Tschooh-dolf pointed amiably at her again and said "*slave*", and then to himself, and said "*Heri*". Then he looked expectantly at her, clearly hoping that she had understood at last.

Zivah broke out in fresh tears.

*

When all the men had fallen asleep around the campfire, I snuck out of camp and went quietly to the tent. I found Thióðolf sleeping on the ground outside and Zivah within. I tiptoed inside and lay down next to my sister. She turned to me and opened her eyes. There was no hatred in her gaze now, only confusion, and her soul had not died yet. I had a feeling she almost felt happy that I was there.

"Did they hurt you," I whispered, because I was not at all sure that they had not.

"No," she said, and looked like she could hardly believe it, "Arn-oolf was going to… to… but then he changed his mind and then I thought that Tschooh-dolf was going to… to… he said so many times that he was the master and I was the… the slave… so I thought he wanted me to… but then he said that I should sleep and turned off the light and went outside."

She spoke in whispers, but so quickly, completely forgetting that I was usually so hateful to her.

"Thióðolf is nice, Zivah. I think you are going to like him," I said, liking the skald better than ever, now that I knew he would not hurt my sister.

"Maybe," she said thoughtfully and peered searchingly at me for a while until she fell asleep. My sister put her arms around me during the night and held me there until dawn, for the first time since I could remember.

The Hidden and the Known

Thióðolf woke up at the first signs of dawn and to the sounds of men approaching quietly. All the Rus walked as softly as the best of Sámi hunters. He sat up groaning and tried to stretch his neck back into place. Five men came into the clearing before the tent and all started grinning when they found him there. There was Hallgrim and Sígtrygg, Njál and Runarr, and finally Agnarr, Arnulf's berserker champions all.

"Did you sleep rough this night, skald?" Sígtrygg asked gleefully, in a hushed voice. Thióðolf peered at the men and shrugged. Fortunately these fellows were among the ones who could understand. So far he had never seen any of them take a woman who seemed less than willing.

"The girl was crying," he whispered, "I thought to give her more time."

The men grinned again and squatted down around him, exchanging glances. "So let us count events already," Sígtrygg whispered, "firstly we have a very pretty slave girl what has been left completely un-taken by any man ever since she was stolen, which is now mounting up to more than half a Moon-circle."

All the men nodded thoughtfully and grunted in agreement.

"And then we see said slave girl reject both her masters – first a mighty Heri, and after that a great and noble skald," Sígtrygg proceeded.

The men nodded again.

“Upon which,” said Sígtrygg, “the slave girl is rewarded with a tent of her own, fully furnished, while her masters are sleeping outside on the ground.”

The men nodded a third time.

“Which about counts up the whole thing,” Sígtrygg concluded, grinning broadly.

“Don’t forget the whispering,” Agnarr volunteered, whispering.

They all looked at each other as if they had not realized before now that they were also whispering lest they wake the slave girl in the tent. There was a surge of amusement going through the circle of warriors, whose shoulders were shaking softly from silent laughter before they calmed down and looked expectantly at Thióðolf.

Thióðolf drew his breath, but then Njál spoke, still in whispers; “So, is she one of them blade honers?” he asked. Four pairs of eyes looked curiously at Hallgrim Hidden Spear and then at Thióðolf Skald, and the gaze of both men met each other and averted at exactly the same time in mutual understanding. The two cunning men nodded in unison. There was no other way to explain this mystery. The young slave was the sort of woman that made men want to become their best so much they actually did something about it.

“It is Bera all over again,” Sígtrygg whispered, and the men smacked their lips approvingly.

“I thought Bera was had by the whole crew before she…” Njál began, but stopped quickly when the others glared at him. He grinned foolishly to appease them, thus reminding them of his proper part in things, which was to be the fool, and they averted their eyes after a short while in respect for that. Everybody has a part to play in the great songs of fate.

“There are those events of the past that are better not spoken of at all times. The core issue here is that Bera moved from slavery to the ruling seat of a Sea King’s fleet. On account of being a great and cunning as well as an already trained blade honer,” Hallgrim whispered and looked around. He had all their attention. “They are all different, these spear enticing shield brides,” he continued mutedly, “it is their unpredictability what makes them special. Bera had her own ways of reaching into the hearts of men. This Zivah is… she is something else.”

All the men including Thióðolf grunted again in their way of agreement.

“But she is also a slave, unfortunately,” Hallgrim continued, “and a slave cannot hone free men. It would be a terrible risk for her and besides unlawful and dishonorable to us. We are Rus.”

"Bera was a slave too," Njál whispered, somewhat confused.

"No, Bera was born free," Hallgrim replied, "she was abducted by Vikings."

"So was this girl," Njál objected, on account of being foolish.

"Yes, but Bera was a Norsewoman. She was taken off the shores of Svíthióð back when we still raided the homelands, and so she was one of us. She spoke our tongue and knew our ways, and she was also a trained honer before she was taken. That was how she could rise from the well-used beds of an entire crew and rule them all. Zivah, however, is not of our people," Hallgrim explained, "and there are laws in Aldeigjuborg what forbid her to use this power and forbid us to train her."

He suddenly turned to Thióðolf and locked his dark eyes with the skald's.

"You have a great charge there, young Skald," the older man said gravely.

Thióðolf was surprised at the subtly spoken comment and the eye-council of Hallgrim Hidden Spear because he had no clue as to what the shadow walker meant or expected of him. It was as if being the owner of this slave meant something more than just that. But before he could reply or ask, there was a movement behind the tent entrance and all the men hushed down and stared expectantly as the cover was flipped aside carefully. To their surprise, the little Thunder priestess was looking out all of a sudden. Must have snuck out of camp and past him in the night, unseen, which was just like her. A little wolfling, she was. Now she peered curiously at them all with her piercing wolf eyes before she noticed that they were all staring back at her. Then, surprisingly, she lowered her eyes politely to all of them for the first time. *What a timing*, he thought, amazed.

"Greetings, warriors," she whispered and kept her eyes lowered long enough for all of them to take full notice. The warriors immediately averted their eyes politely and replied, still whispering; "Greetings, Maiden." Dazzled by her sweetness and flattered by her unexpected recognition of their rank, he saw how the men's faces softened, and he half expected them to begin cooing at her the way they cooed at Njál's little cat. They clearly thought she was adorable and seemed to have completely forgotten about the ferocious little Hel-maiden who had awed them for days on end until they started to get used to her and had begun thinking that she was cute. They kept up the reverent act because it kept entertaining them, on account of the little one being so good at it. There was no doubt that she was special, even if she was but a little maiden. And she had that legendary name and lineage attached to her.

If there was any little orphan girl who could do well among the Væringja Rus, it would be this one, although he had some thoughts of his own as to her future. He had been told to find the missing piece, and it seemed that he had found it and that Thordís was its keeper.

"Thordís," he said gently, "maybe you could get yourself and Zivah ready? We are going to leave at first sunlight."

"Yes, Thióðolf," she said obediently and withdrew into the tent.

The men got to their feet and exchanged humorous glances again as they began walking down to the ship.

"I think we got ourselves two of them honers," Sígtrygg mused.

"And there is at least one of them what is both free and one of us," said Agnarr. The men exchanged glances, eyes lit, and they stopped to hold council halfway down to the shore.

"Does that mean we are supposed to train the little one?" Njál asked, and they all looked at Hallgrim.

"I should think so," the shadow walker said, "For she has been given to us at an age when she still needs training, and to fail to train a blade honer properly can be the doom of men."

"How is that done, then?" Runarr asked.

"She has no father and no brothers," Hallgrim said, "And so we will be her new fathers and her new brothers. We cannot tell her this directly, and we must never give her reason to think that she is above us. A blade honer rules best when she is ruled well. She must know the way of men and the ways of respect. We must simply teach her like we would teach any young maiden."

"I don't think we ever trained a maiden," Njál pointed out.

"Men have always trained maidens," Hallgrim said.

"Well I was not thinking of that sort of training, she is a tad bit young," Njál objected.

"I was not thinking of that sort of training either," Hallgrim said, "I was thinking more in terms of the warriors' court." They were all stunned.

"I am not sure, Hallgrim," Sígtrygg spoke slowly, "I thought the girl fierce at first but she does appear to be very… maidenly."

"That is true and is only fitting, seeing as she is a maiden," Hallgrim said, and the men looked a little uncomfortable.

"Yes, Hallgrim, but if she is soft, then how are we going to deal with that?"

"In the homelands we still train girls from the age of seven if they show a keenness of interest in the warrior's arts," Thióðolf inferred. The Rus regarded him doubtfully for a moment.

"They learn to fight properly, then?" Runarr asked.

"There are those girls with a warrior's chant in their souls, Runarr. You of all people should be able to understand that," Agnarr chuckled.

"For the most part the girls cannot be honed like boys," Thióðolf said, "they break too easily, as if they just collapse from within and succumb if the situation is too threatening." The men nodded. They all knew that well.

"But we teach them regardless, adapting to how they respond. That is how you teach the soft."

"What is the point, then?" Runarr asked. It was the warrior what had to adapt, not the foe.

"It can make a remarkable difference to have a woman around who knows how to cleave and strike," Thióðolf said, "even if she is no warrior there are times when even a little skill is better than no skill, and besides women do not have to worry about the honor. They can fight as dirty as they like and nobody would ever blame them. But of course most of the girls who continue their training already have the warrior's chant in their soul songs. I have seen shield maidens who could match even you men in combat."

"Shield maidens," Njál said dreamily.

"They are not exactly the maidenly sort," Thióðolf smiled, "they are often more fond of other maidens than they are of men."

"That is understandable," Runarr said, "how can you submit to the lord stone if you are a warrior, even if you happen to like men?"

"You tell us, Runarr," Njál said and accepted a kick to the leg without complaint. "Is it true that they will only lie with the men who can defeat them in combat?" Njál asked instead.

"I think they lie down with exactly the men they like," Thióðolf said, "or the women."

"But I have heard a man has got to fight and defeat them shield maidens before they let themselves be taken," Njál insisted.

"That is called rape, Njál, and often happens when a woman is defeated by a man," Thióðolf said.

"Oh," Njál pondered, "well if they are fighting properly and he wins he cannot just kill her, she being a woman and all. It would be dishonorable and cowardly, really. Nobody cheers a man what comes home with a woman's head either. A man must sort of demonstrate his victory differently when it is a woman." The others nodded thoughtfully.

"You Rus have some strange honor codes," Thióðolf muttered, mostly to himself.

"It occurs to me that you men have forgotten our subject matter in light of the thrilling tales of warrior women," Hallgrim said, and they stopped to brood for a while again.

"I am not sure, brothers," Sígtrygg finally said, "Despite her indubitable courage little Thordís sings deep a very maidenly soul song. She is soft."

"That she does, and that she is, which is why this is already a great challenge to us," Hallgrim said, "which is good, seeing as the whole point of having a blade honer is to become better men and raise to them challenges. And one of the most important things we must remember is that the little priestess cannot be honed like we hone boys. We cannot even make her fight, although we can encourage her if she wants to. The power she carries within will emerge in its own time, and meanwhile we must think of her as we think of all soft folks, and treat her accordingly. We must regard her as we would regard any Síf, always protect her and make her feel safe and act politely around her. And teach her anything she wants to learn, and encourage all her talents. And she must know the manners and the courtesies. She is already there. You saw how she lowered her eyes to you men now, after all this time. She already knows her place."

"But she is a sort of goddess," Agnarr said uncertainly. He had rather liked the glaring girl, and so had the other men, who nodded fondly at the memory. Such fierce eyes she had, it was adorable.

"I would rather say she carries a goddess power within – and something else besides that I have yet to see the full scope of," Hallgrim said, "But she is also a little girl who needs to know her way around the world of warriors. And a blade honer is dangerous if she gets to be in direct control. She cannot handle it. She is not a man."

"I have known some women who handle control very well," Sígtrygg said.

"Yes, there are those women who carry the ruling chant strongly in their soul songs, but it is not so with the blade honer. The blade honer's true power is born from the humility of woman," Hallgrim explained, "We must teach her the codes and the rules and never let her think that she is above us, and yet we must always respect her divinity. The blade honer must be ruled well or else she cannot be ruled at all. If we fail to rule her, and if we fail to rule her with care, the twisted mirror will appear. If we rule her well, the teachings will unfold of their own accord. That is all we need to know for the moment."

"Then we have got ourselves a charge too," Agnarr said, and there was a round of grunting agreements. There was another pause while the men let the very notion of having a blade honer on their hands sink in. Most of them had never even known one.

"It is as I said," Hallgrim concluded, "We must speak to Arnulf Heri and the men about this, but it is good that we here are already aware of our charge. We shall be her fathers and her brothers and we shall love her yet also teach her the ways of men, and then we shall see the blessings of the divinity she carries bestowed on us from day to day in ever increasing flow."

The men smacked their lips approvingly.

"There are lots of us, though," said Agnarr, "I worry about how to proceed."

"She will have fathers and brothers from the whole court," Hallgrim continued, "but we will not tell her most of what we do. We are men. For the most part we will show it through our actions. But we need a spokesman. Thióðolf, you are the sort of man what knows how to speak to the soft. And you are a wise man, even as you are still young, and you have been taught by blade honers. If you have been taught by one, then you can also teach one. And she is a priestess born. A skald has much to teach a young priestess. You never tire of her company either. I say it is only fitting that you be our spokesman with the Maiden." Hallgrim said and winked at Thióðolf, who nodded solemnly.

"I will be your spokesman with the priestess," he said, because it was the appropriate response to such a charge made before men, and because it had been the role of bards to be the war band's spokesman when dealing with holy folks since time immemorial.

He felt the burden of responsibility weigh him down for a moment when he walked down to the ship with the other men. Nobody had spoken of Zivah's training, seeing as she was a slave, but it appeared he had subtly been given the charge of training both a hidden and a known blade honer, and even if he had been taught by blade honers he had never known how *they* were taught. That part had always been a mystery to him and never explained, and he had thought they were women's mysteries only. Thióðolf stood there by the river shore and found himself lacking. But there he was, receiving a new charge from the fates. And it seemed to him that the charge of the fates coincided with the charge of the holy women that had made him travel to Garðaríki in the first place.

Humility can make great the man. If he knew nothing there was only so much more to learn. He drew a deep breath. It was as Hallgrim had said, the teachings would unfold of their own accord if the two sisters were just taught how to live with these men. It was decided. The young bard submitted to the charge and decided to let Knowledge unfold herself in her own time, as she always did.

Zivah´s New Master

Zivah sat aboard the ship and peered cautiously about her that whole morning. Everything seemed so different all of a sudden, as if an iron hard and cold grasp had released itself from her neck, and only now did she notice that it had ever been there. She was breathing more deeply than she had managed ever since the raid, and felt as if she was gasping for air to fill her lungs with life once more. Nobody had tied her wrists and led her in tow that morning, and she tried not to show too much how she enjoyed having her arms free after so long. She remembered the kinswoman who had escaped by diving that first day on the pirate ship, but Zivah was not going anywhere. The slave man called Shumayl, the one man aboard who did not frighten her and who seemed to take an interest in her out of compassion, had managed to communicate to her that the area swarmed with slave hunters and brutal men.

She realized with some pain that she had never paid enough attention to all the forest survival skills known by most of her people on account of having been ever so concerned with making pretty clothes and jewelry while waiting for her stupid prince. Now she regretted her shallow choices before. And she had never ever slept alone out in the open except for that first Moon blood ritual, when she had sworn that she would never do that again. There had been a giant hog snorting around her campfire all night. If she was to brave the forests on her own, relying on those skills she had not paid enough attention to but must surely remember deep down, there would still be those men who hunted women like they were animals. So did the men who had captured her, but at least among these men here she was beginning to feel a little familiar despite her resentment of them, and somehow, familiar was better than totally alien even if they were also exactly the same sort of men.

The Rus-men seemed to look at her a little differently this day, and when she had been climbing aboard one of the men had taken her gently by the hand and helped her over the sideboard. It was the first time anyone ever helped her except as an excuse to take a firm grasp on her buttocks and push ever so slowly. She looked briefly up at him, sideways. His name was *Nyaaahl*, if she remembered correctly, the one with the fangs who was surprisingly kind to her mother's kitten. When he let go of her he had smiled briefly only to close his mouth real swift, and she realized that he was trying not to scare her with his teeth. She rewarded him with a very small but genuine smile and went to sit where she did not seem to be in anybody's way, which she had learned was very important.

To her surprise, Tschooh-dolf approached her, squatted down next to her while she kept her gaze to the floor, feeling embarrassed about the night before all of a sudden, wondering what he thought about her. It was hard to put her mind around the fact that he owned her life and body, but it was a great deal less horrifying than the idea of being owned by Arnulf. She had never really been able to grasp the reality of slavery until he had turned her around on the bed and made her crouch there on her knees while waiting for the rape. She had started crying again and at the same time she had remembered that she needed to smile to him as well lest he sell her off to even worse men. So she had turned her head to smile at the would-be rapist and then he had gotten such a strange look in his eyes and just left her, and, as it turned out, given her away to someone else.

She decided that she would not try too hard next time even if she had to hide her disgust. For there was no doubt that the next time would come. She almost just wished that it did so she could be over the dreadful waiting and know more about what sort of treatment she could expect. It was the uncertainty that was the worst, really, not knowing what they were going to do to her. She remembered the screams of the women on Rape Island and thought she would almost wish he had taken her then because then she would already know what it was and not had to go through all that terror of not knowing what to expect. She recalled a time when she had seen a patient suffering terribly and she had begun crying from compassion, feeling so very sorry for that person, imagining his pain. But Mother had turned to her and said that many painful experiences seem a lot worse to the outsider than it feels to the insider. Because when it happens to you, you own it. If it happens to another, it is beyond your ken, and your imagination will be worse than the experience.

If there was any good thing to have come of this it was the certainty that she was not such a false woman as the villagers had accused her of. And maybe another good thing came from it too, she mused, and peered cautiously up at her new master. Sideways. If it was to be Tschooh-dolf then maybe it would not have to be so terrible.

He had called for Thordís to come and translate, and the girl had said that he wanted her to know that she was allowed to move freely around the ship and that he recommended that she did not try and escape because these lands were crammed with slave hunters and that she should not worry about anything, he would take care of her and protect her for as long as she was his slave. There had been some other words but all she had really heard well was the part where he would take care of her and protect her, and it made her feel a little like she had been rescued by a man who loved her, like in the stories. She had already discarded those stories as foolish illusions, but now they came to her again. Her heart seemed to jump out and grasp at that promise, that small hope. She had smiled brightly then, and all those men who had seen it exchanged meaningful glances. It was the first time any of them saw her smile, and they clearly noticed it for some reason or other. The thought that anybody would even notice what she felt about anything at all had suddenly seemed so novel to her, which was almost amusing since that was something she had always taken for granted before. For the first time since she was abducted she felt she had the grace to look beyond the hateful image of simple brutes who all wanted to rape her, and wondered what else they perceived.

From a distance she watched her new master while she pretended to be absorbed with the wooden floor. She had been so certain that he was just the first of many men who had been given the right to use her and that this was why he was trying to establish his superiority over her. He had been very friendly and almost shy, but she had seen enough of these men to know that most of them would always try to be friendly with a woman they wanted, but that this did not mean they would not take the desired woman regardless of her response.

She would never forget what she saw around the campfire on Rape Island. There had been a man there who had actually seemed very charming for a while. He had been talking to her childhood friend, Neilé, and he had smiled so sweetly and made her laugh, even, after a few drinks. He had only touched her very gently. And then he had suddenly pulled her up and led her into the shadows. She had heard Neilé weep when he took her, and he had not been the first to do so either. The day after, Neilé had looked different. She had been raped during the raid too, but then they had all been so stunned it was as if the women hardly even remembered it, being too soaked up in every frightful moment after. But after that night on the island, Neilé and the other women had looked like tamed and frightened dogs. They just sat there, no longer harboring any hope of ever being more than empty shells with holes that could be used by men. The lights of their souls had gone out in their eyes. And then there had been the market.

So when Thióðolf was being friendly with her, she had known that her nightmare would begin. But then he had sighed so heavily, gotten up, turned off the lamp and said, "Sleep, Zivah. Nobody is going to disturb you. I will not touch you. I will be outside. Just sleep."

She had understood the message if not all the words, but for a long time she had stayed there, listening, waiting anxiously, until suddenly Thordís had crawled into her bed and looked at her with such an unexpected expression of genuine concern, and asked her if they had hurt her. And apart from the humiliation Arnulf had put her through, she could honestly reply that they had not. It still surprised her. And there had been something else that surprised her too.

When she had looked into the little girl's worried gaze that night – that was the first time she realized that her sister had been concerned about her well-being, and that she had not been in power to stop any of the men from doing whatever they wanted with her, not even her friend Tschooh-dolf. All this while Zivah had thought that the little monster was having the time of her life getting back at her older sister by letting the men keep her in tows, living through all this misery and terror from day to day. She had been wrong. And Zivah watched her little sister up by the prow, always talking to some of the men, but mostly to Tschooh-dolf. She recalled one time when she had complained to Mother about the little girl, how she often followed her about like a shadow, sneaking up on her and spying on her, and acting like a half-wit, some of the many things she had always detested about Thunder Goddess.

And then Mother had looked thoughtfully at her and said, *«But Zivah, have you not yet grasped that your sister is looking out for you? Do you not remember the men from the market? It was your sister who followed you and alerted us. You think she is witless to love you when you reject her? Ah, Zivah, It does not matter what you think you feel about Thunder Goddess, because she sees deeper than that. She is you sister and she will always protect you."*

Zivah was suddenly about to realize just how true her mother's words had been. The little one had known how to escape slavery by speaking their language and knowing their customs and by some miracle of Pērkons her true lord, and also by using those wolf eyes that had always been somewhat disturbing to the villagers but appeared to be highly regarded by these Rus-men. But she had not been able to prevent Zivah from being taken as a slave, and for a long time Zivah had thought that it was because she could not be bothered, and thought that she was laughing at her in secret. She had never been a good older sister to the little one. And yet she was here and still not raped or really harmed, and suddenly fortune had provided her with a new master who was, when truth was to be told, a lot less ugly, scary and old than Arnulf Heri, and even somewhat smaller even if he was also large.

Most importantly, he even seemed to care about her feelings. In all this time, he was the first Rus-man after Hallgrim who actually spoke to her, and he had even asked her about… about what had happened to her. As if it mattered to him.

They had all looked much the same to her for a long time. They were all big, they were all imposing, and they were all terrifying and fierce and beastly and unpredictable. She could not imagine how they all had gotten those scars all over their bodies. She had had nightmares about the one who lacked a nose, that he was trying to kiss her and suck her soul out with his gaping nose wound. Fortunately he seemed to have transferred to another ship. But now that she had gotten more used to them she began to see that they were all very different. And the more she looked at Tschooh-dolf the more she began to see that behind that imposing warrior ferocity he was a truly handsome man in all respects. He was fully grown but still quite young, perhaps no more than some ten years older than herself, not twenty or thirty like Arnulf. For a moment he had turned and met her gaze and smiled encouragingly at her. He had such blue, blue eyes, like deep crystal waters. His dark hair and beard framed his face so well. And he moved, he moved so graciously and looked so centered and calm, and he was so well groomed and well dressed and clean and so gentle mannered compared to the other men. His largeness and ferocity suddenly felt more protective than threatening.

She had begun to figure out what his name meant. The last part, the –olf, that was the same as the –olf in her departed brother Thorolf's name, and it meant wolf. They liked wolves, apparently, because they used them a lot in their names, it seemed. She had gathered that Arnulf's name meant Eagle Wolf, but that did not interest her quite as much as trying to figure out what *Tschoohd* meant. Going through her memories it seemed to mean "people", but then someone had used to word to describe something really great and awesome. Thióðolf meant the Great Wolf, or the Tribeswolf.

Zivah gazed at her master again, absorbed in conversation with the child. How good he was at treating children, she thought, so attentive, so kind, and so very much in charge without ever letting the child feel less than free and safe. The girl was orphaned and but seven years old, and she needed parents. What better parent than her older sister and… and this man who knew how to be with those who are vulnerable … Her heart jumped a little again at the moving thought of how he had taken care not to frighten her the night before. A kind man. The fates had given her a kind man. Or more precisely, they had given her *to* a kind man, but now that she had seen him better that did not seem so bad. She had never imagined how much she would appreciate simple kindness in a man. There had been more than enough excitement for the time being. She took another glance at the dark-haired Norseman. Come to think of it, he looked like a *prince*. Zivah smiled to herself.

Now that she knew better how this world of theirs worked she knew that she had to make sure that her master liked her well, and she must take care to not displease him like she had displeased Arnulf, which was surely going to be a lot easier than it had been not to displease Arnulf. Zivah stretched a little, feeling a surge of excited anticipation. She knew well the game of love, she thought, and had been able to render men helplessly in love with her for as long as she had been a woman grown, which was now four years. She knew especially how to appeal to the kindly and well-meaning ones. If she had thought that worth her while just for the fun of it before, then that could only have served to make her more capable of this far more pressingly important conquest.

Her life depended on this now, and if it was so that she had to be some man's legal property then she could at least make sure that she held his head in her hands as surely as she had held the head of that man who had once tried to trick her. *You can always change your fate, Zivah*, her mother had once said, or perhaps it had been Thunder Bear, or perhaps it was just one of those many things they both had agreed upon. And it is not the fate that befalls you which constitutes the verdict of your life. The verdict will come at the end of your life when the fates sum up what you did with that fate which was allotted to you, and then they will consider how you dealt with the challenges. Zivah liked a challenge when she thought she had the resources to face it, and her beauty and her charm had always been her greatest weapons. She might as well work out how she could, ever so subtly, make her master into her slave and not the other way around.

*

Thióðolf was pleased with the change in his slave girl that first day. She had smiled shyly at him and acted a lot more calm and in acceptance of the whole situation. And then he could not help but notice just how beautiful she was. Her hair was a bit messy and her leather tunic dress was dirty and torn and had that large and by now rather old blood smear all over the front, but like any other Norseman Thióðolf could well appreciate the harassed combination of beauty and gore, and he started to think about what she would be like in his arms and then he tried not to think about that anymore lest it showed and the men started teasing him, or worse, little Thordís began to ask questions as to why he was looking at her half-sister that way. Or even worse questions. The child had a talent for curiosity. So he looked another way and pretended not to be affected by Zivah's presence at all, even though his head sometimes began to swim a little with the possibilities that now had opened up.

He had still not quite gotten used to the idea of owning a girl in this way. There had never been a short supply of pretty women who would gladly play Freyia's games with him, and he had always thought the very notion of buying a pleasure slave or making use of one was far beneath him. The men of his clan prided themselves in being honorable. And yet if the girl actually started to like him the way she seemed to do, then it could not be so very dishonorable after all. Even his most honorable kinsmen dallied with slaves if the slaves were obviously willing, and as part of their honor code they also gave them a treatment which that sort of girls rarely expected, in a good sort of way. They knew the runes of the goddess, the people of his tribe.

Then in the evening she had started to act out of turn. The next day she was even worse. He was a bit confused, wondering what he had done to make her lose respect for him. It took several instances before he realized that she was trying to charm him, seeing as she was failing miserably. That day they had finally reached lake Ilmen and made their final trading outside of Aldeigjuborg for that year, trading foreign goods from the south to the Finnish and Slavic tribes that lived in this area. When they had walked about the market stalls the slave girl had looked curiously at all the things and even started to touch them as if she was considering making a purchase, and when he had met her eyes as she was holding up a bracelet and a green linen dress, she had smiled at him and blushed in a manner that made him think she had that sort of blushing smile well-rehearsed for a long time. He had thought to buy her something, a new dress to start with, but the shame of her all too direct behavior in his presence made him change his mind, and he saw the surprise in her eyes when he shook his head brusquely. She was obviously not used to being denied anything. In fact, he had a feeling that she was underestimating him for some reason, as if she thought he was a fool that she could easily control. He scratched his head and tried to remember if he had done anything to give her that impression, but for his bare life he could not think of anything.

Later, she had stood at the harbor with her sister, whom she had suddenly taken an unexpected liking to, even holding her little hand while they looked out at the great lake and the sunset. When he came to them she had completely failed to bow her head and call him Heri, but had instead flashed a sweet smile before she had spoken to Thordís, who explained that they had never seen the ocean before. That comment made him smile and forget her impertinence for a moment, and he had explained to them that this was just a lake and that the ocean was infinitely much bigger, upon which the girl had gasped and put a hand over her mouth while peering at him with eyes searching for his admiration. Again, it had seemed so well rehearsed. He had turned around and walked away, but that had not stopped her. She seemed to think of it as a sort of game or a conquest, and the less he responded the more she tried, and there was surely a sort of despair that had given rise to it, so he had tried to be patient and hoped that she would catch up on the fact that her little charm wiles just did not work on him and would not work on any Norseman, and even less likely here among the Rus.

But she was a bit slow on that matter. Now the men were beginning to notice, and there were some raised eyebrows that night around the campfire, when the girl continued to show him attention in the most outrageous ways. And each time he rejected her little giggling blushes and lingering gazes and other utterly foreign methods of courtship she looked so confused that he finally understood that this was exactly what it was; foreign methods of courtship. From the confident way she used those methods he guessed that she was used to making those puny men of her tribe follow her around like obedient dogs, the way he had seen men sometimes behave in foreign countries when a woman had them dazzled and their minds in tow. He felt a little worried. A natural blade honer who had no respect for men was dangerous, and the fact that she was a slave made it all the more dangerous to herself.

Zivah had begun to actively try to understand their language, which was commendable, but now she suddenly asked random men what this or that thing was called, and forgot to mind her manners when she so did. Not only did she just ask them directly, without saying "Heri" or bowing her head, without asking permission to ask a question, acting as if she took for granted that they would pay attention to her, rewarding their replies with coquettish smiles. Fortunately the man next to her at the campfire, apart from Thióðolf, had been Njál who was among the more relaxed members of the crew and who obviously liked Zivah. He had been playing with the kitten and patiently replied to her questions about the meanings of words even when the other men had looked strangely at them. But then she had suddenly taken the kitten from him and interrupted him even as he was talking to Thióðolf, and she did not even notice that she had interrupted free men. Then even Njál went quiet, ignoring both her and the cat while looking into the fire, embarrassed. A terrible silence suddenly descended on all of them. The men peered cautiously at Thióðolf, waiting for him to do something.

He got up and signaled for Zivah and Thordís that they should follow, and then he took them down to the ship where several men were standing guard, and made them lay down beneath a simple tent cover and told them to go to sleep. He nodded at the men, who nodded back and kept watching out as they always did. Then he returned to camp. They were some thirty men around that fire, and they were still quiet and watching him when he sat down among them.

"I heard you did not take the girl on that night I gave her to you, and I have not seen you do it since," Arnulf said bluntly, "and I did not give her to you for show."

"I appreciate your gift, Arnulf Heri, but that night did not seem right, and I am not used to play these games in public."

"Indeed. And look at where we stand now. She has no respect for you, man. Her disrespect is beginning to spread towards the rest of us. She is playing little tricks intended to make us into something less than men. She seems to think we have potential for being tail-waving dogs with nothing better to do than running after her skirts and attending to her every whim."

All the men nodded gravely at the Heri's words. Thióðolf wished that he had talked to Zivah earlier. He was more lenient than the Rus, but they took such matters very seriously. They were slavers, after all.

"What if it is on account on her being a blade honer? Last I heard, their ways are special," Njál said, feeling sorry for Zivah, "I heard they are the sort of women what transgress rank all the time."

"That must be your famed foolishness speaking, Njál," said Hialti, a man Thióðolf always thought of as Hialti the Detestable even if he did not say that out loud. The rat-like man looked around, pleased to have their undivided attention for a change, seeing as most of his talk was largely ignored.

"The girl is a slave and there are no special ways for slaves and there is no honorable way for a slave to hone a man," said Hialti.

"Says a man what cannot be honed," Runarr growled, and there was a tense silence before Hialti decided that it was better not to take a man like Runarr up on a challenge and pretended that the comment had not been heard. The other men relaxed and pretended that they had not heard it either.

"Well even if some here think she is a blade honer born, the fact is that she is firstly a slave and she is acting in a way that not even a free born woman of noble blood would ever dream of acting in the presence of warriors," Hialti said, "and even as she offends one of us she offends all. But if you men do not think that is a serious matter you should consider how this is going to look when we return to Aldeigjuborg. There are laws against such behavior in slaves. You all know that. What she just did could have earned her a treatment from the City Council."

Everybody turned to look at Hallgrim Hidden Spear. The shadow walker always had the answers.

"It is true that there are laws, and that the laws will be ruthlessly followed, no matter how well most of us actually like the girl and no matter her inborn nature," Hallgrim said slowly and met Thióðolf's eyes, "You are her master, so it is up to you, my friend, to take action before your slave does something that will serve to not only hurt your honor and ours, but herself the worse. You do not want the town council to fall down upon her, do you?"

Thióðolf paled and shook his head. "No, Hallgrim, I do not wish that."

"Then you must discipline the girl before we get there. It is very important," Hallgrim said, still locking his eyes with the younger man. It was not a challenging lock, but a private conversation in the midst of many people.

"The skald is too soft-hearted to do the deed," Hialti snorted and grinned, "but I will gladly do it for you, Thióðolf."

He laughed but stopped short when nobody else laughed with him. Thióðolf glared at him until he lowered his rat eyes and bowed his rat head.

"My apologies, Thióðolf Skald," he said, "I may have had a little too much to drink."

Thióðolf cast a glance at Arnulf who was staring at him and who now gave him a nod. When he got to his feet, so did Arnulf, and they both returned to the ship together. "I can take the little priestess to sleep with me," Arnulf said, "she has taken to sleeping next to me when she is not sleeping next to you, and it seems to calm her. She is probably already asleep anyway and will not notice if we carry her off. And then you can take Zivah at last."

"I thought I was supposed to discipline her."

"That is how you discipline her, man, unless you want to beat her."

"But Arnulf, I cannot do that, I do not even know how."

"I find that somewhat hard to believe, pretty-face," Arnulf snorted.

"What I meant, Arnulf Heri, is that I am well used to playing those games with women who actually want me. It is a different matter with a weeping girl who just lost all her friends and family."

"She wants you fine, Thióðolf. Remember how miserable she was for as long as she thought she was mine, and how outrageously happy she went when she knew she was yours? She was so happy she went and offended all the men because she forgot all the courtesies that she ought to have learned already now. You have the looks and the charms that I lacked. And Aziza told me that you know the runes of the goddess."

Thióðolf blushed a little at the memory of Arnulf sending his dark-skinned concubine to his bed. The Rus were not shy.

"So how is that going to work in the sense of discipline?" the skald smirked, "Your woman has not exactly been trembling at the sight of me after that. It is rather more as if she thinks of me a friend." They both laughed, and Arnulf shook his head in fond memories of his woman.

"And yet she observes the courtesies," he pointed out.

"Oh yes, she behaves, but there is familiarity and genuine friendliness, and she likes talking to me, and it is obvious to all that she loves you, Arnulf. She is like a wife to you in many ways. I find it hard to see how your relationship could ever have become so blessed if you started out by raping her," Thióðolf said.

"Believe me, Thióðolf, this is different," Arnulf said, "Firstly, Aziza was already a slave when I got her, and she lived in one of them rental slave places, so she has always considered me to be the man who rescued her. And as to lending her out to you, Aziza was rather happy with her charge, when truth shall be told. I saw the way she looked at you and decided to give her a treat through the laws of the Contrary. It is how you give gifts to good slaves, by way of giving them pleasant commands every once in a while."

“You seem to be giving them quite often, seeing from the way she moans in the night,” Thióðolf giggled. Arnulf grunted fondly.

“Indeed. She is a good woman and she deserves it. Says I am the first man who ever even bothered to please her. She deserved to have a Freyia’s man with her if only once. And now I know all about your skills on Freyia’s path and will probably never hear the end of it. Ha!”’

They stopped before the ship, and the giant captain turned to look at Thióðolf. “Zivah is another thing. She is a slave that has not been broken in yet. You have the skill it takes to please women, but you are used to wooing them first. Now, as to slaves, you do not woo, you just take, especially when they need to be disciplined. But do not think that you have to be beastly and cruel about it. That is not the point. Maybe you have to be rough when you punish a male slave, but most women are so easy to break that you can even do it quite gently. You do not have to act so very differently than with a free woman. The only real difference lies in the fact that she must know at all times that you are in charge and that she has no choice, while you would often have to do the very opposite with a free woman, at least until she trusts you.”

“Arnulf, I cannot…”

“When you go in there, just imagine that you have already gotten to that state of trust, because the slave has no choice but to trust you anyway. So you just have to be masterly about it all the while, even from the start, which I can attest will come easily to you, as can my concubine, it seems. You are the ruling sort of man, Skald, you just need to rule the situation like you would in one of them word duels that you cunning folks keep engaging in. There is always a winner and always a loser but both parts enjoy that game mutually. You see? Nobody here likes to beat women, except perhaps Hialti. But the lord stone can rule without hurting. It can be a most pleasing way of establishing such matters, even to the girl. And she will respect you afterwards. She may even like you better.”

“Arnulf Heri, I respect you deeply and you are my friend. But I have sworn oaths to holy women and this is a matter of honor as well as character for me. I have to do this my own way.”

“I honor that, Thióðolf, but what way is yours?”

“I thought I would speak to her. With words. The girl needs to understand our customs and courtesies before she can be punished for breaking them, do you not think? Little Thordís can translate.”

“Oh, Thióðolf,” Arnulf laughed, “You have a soft heart and I do not blame you. The men say I am soft-hearted myself.”

“Do they,” said the skald, not knowing exactly how to respond to such a statement from such a man as Arnulf Heri.

"Yes, and it is true also. Ask my women when we come home. But a man has got to do what a man has got to do sometimes, especially in this sort of business. You are still young and you have much to learn. But she is *your* slave. As long as she behaves come morning I shall not press the matter any further. At least there is nothing lacking when it comes to your eloquence."

*

I had been so pleased those days because Zivah seemed to be growing happier and was now talking to me again, asking questions about the Norsemen and trying to learn their language and their customs. And she seemed to like Thióðolf, although I had a feeling that she had finally met someone who could stand up to her charms. I had started to worry a little because he seemed to like her less and less the more time he spent with her, and Zivah intensified her efforts and seemed oblivious to the fact that they did not actually yield any pleasant results. When Thióðolf told us to go to sleep, I tried to tell her that she had acted rudely towards some of the men when she forgot very important details regarding manners, and that even I who had a place among them would never act before them the way she did, but she would not listen to me, laughed it away and said they had just been a little confused and perhaps shy, and when I asked her how she knew that she said that it always happened with men when she charmed them. I was not so sure this was the case here and almost said that these men were not the sort of men she had known before, but she looked so excited and happy. I had no heart to tear Zivah out of her newfound happiness after all that she had been through.

Then there was a sound outside the cover and when we peered out Thióðolf was squatting there, and seeing as we had not slept yet he asked us to come outside and sit down, because he had something to say to Zivah and needed me to translate. When we came outside, Arnulf was there, nodded to me and ignored Zivah before he went to sleep at his place close to the prow. Zivah sent her new master a carefully designed smile and stopped smiling when he glared at her with obvious anger. Then he had me translate for him.

"Zivah, I do not know where you were taught the sort of behavior that you have been employing for these last two days, but I have to tell you that it is not acceptable among our kind. Such behavior is not acceptable in free women and it is even less acceptable in slaves. Your ways are offensive to free men and warriors, and not the least to the Rus. We are going to live in a town called Aldeigjuborg, and I can tell you right now that if there ever was a slavers' town, then Aldeigjuborg is it. There are laws made for slaves especially, and they are very strict and offenses are mercilessly punished. So I am going to tell you how you must behave, Zivah, if you are to even survive there. Because if you shame me in public, or if you shame any free man or woman, there will be nothing I can do to prevent them from punishing you. They can even kill you, and all I can do then is accept a small payment for your set price. And if you have offended a free and high-ranking man in public, including myself, then the city council will fall down upon you and make a public statement of you to show all the other slaves what fate they can expect if they fail to follow the rules and mind their manners. It is very important that you pay attention to this. I do not want anything bad to happen to you, and so you have to know how to act."

Zivah was staring at him, dumbfounded, and he sighed.

"First of all, we can start with that sort of staring. Stop that immediately," he said, and as I translated, Zivah's gaze began to waver uncertainly.

"Lower your eyes and bow your head," he commanded, and suddenly there was no gentleness to have from him. He glared at her until she had bowed her head, but even in the pale half-moon light it was clear that she had gone a deep red, and she looked more angry than sorry.

"I can see that you are angry," he continued, his voice hard, "but the feelings of a slave are of no importance in the place we are going to. You must hide your anger." Zivah struggled to compose herself, but it was hard for her to not show how she felt, and right then she looked like she hated him.

"If you ever act this way before me in front of other men, I must strike you," he said gravely, "and I will if I must, so I ask you to consider that before you display your anger or any other hateful feeling towards me or any other free man. And you must always – always, Zivah – lower your eyes and bow your head before free folks, and never talk unless spoken to, and if you do have to talk anyway you must approach with bowed head and greet that person as Heri if he is a man or a boy, and as Freyia if she is a woman, and to little girls like Thordís here, you must say Maiden. This means that you will bow your head to me and call me Heri if I speak to you or any other man speaks to you. And that is also how you must approach me if you need to speak to me, or any other free person."

She looked as if she had a question, but Thióðolf continued: "You must also realize that your thoughts and questions are of no importance either. You cannot ask free folks about things just to satisfy your curiosity about something. You must consider carefully whether it will be worth the while of your superiors to have you speak to them at all. And then, if you think it very important, you may approach with bowed head, remember the titles and ask permission to even ask the question or tell the tale." He paused again and cast a glance at me.

"You can begin right here on the ship. The only person you do not have to bow to is Shumayl because he is a slave like you. Everybody else is free here. So you will bow your head to Thordís and call her Maiden. And you will bow your head to all the men and if they address you or you them, you must call them Heri. And if you need to refer to me when I am not around, you must refer to me as your House-Bond and not by my name. To you, I am Heri and House-Bond."

I repeated his words and Zivah looked like she wanted to sink through the ship. She had no problem keeping her face down now, having no wish to let us see her spirit mirror anyway. I felt rather embarrassed about the whole thing, but I sensed the urgency that Thióðolf felt and knew that these were important counsels, not meant to offend her.

"Do you understand, Zivah?" Thióðolf said. Zivah nodded vaguely. "What?" he said.

"Yes, I understand," she wheezed, still angry.

"Apparently not. The next time you snarl at me like that I will strike you. What are you supposed to say when I ask if you understand?"

"I understand, Heri," she whispered and bowed low her head.

"Good. And apart from the courtesies you also have to obey free folks. Always. That means that you must obey all the men here, and your sister too."

"All the men?" she whispered, eyes widening.

"What did I say to you about courtesies?"

"I am sorry, Heri, I just… may I ask?" Her voice sounded a bit muffled.

"Yes, you may ask. And you already did, so the answer is that yes, you must always obey the men in everything. If they tell you to do something, you do. Understand?"

"Yes, Heri," she mumbled and sounded like she was close to tears again.

"The only thing you do not have to obey is another man's order what turns out to be contrary to my orders. It means that nobody can tell you to do something I have told you not to do, because I own your life and your body, Zivah, you are my slave and I am the one who gives the orders in your life. So if a man asks you to do something I have told you not to do, then you will refer to your House-Bond's orders and refuse while you make sure to apologize profoundly and keep your head bowed. Understood?"

"Yes, Heri."

"Good." He regarded her a little and saw how crushed she was.

"I am not going to give you to other men, Zivah, at least not if you behave. I do not want to have you worrying about having to obey that sort of orders. If a man tells you to spread your legs you apologize and tell him to ask me first." Zivah looked terrified, completely failing to understand that he was trying to comfort her after a fashion, and more pressingly help her survive. I had a feeling Thióðolf put that "if" in because he thought it necessary for her to understand how serious all this was, but all Zivah seemed to hear was that he *would* give her to other men if she did not behave.

"I am saying this for your own sake, Zivah, it is a harsh world out there and you do not know our customs. I hope you understand that," he said finally. Zivah looked up at him and it looked very much as if she wanted to ask him something, but she had the wits to finally understand that she had no right to ask him anything, and bowed her head again. There was a silence before she remembered to whisper another "Yes, Heri." Thióðolf offered a grunt for approval.

"Thordís," he said to me, "thank you for the translation. Thank the Maiden for translating this for you, Zivah." Zivah's lips were trembling and her eyes filled with water when she looked meekly at me and whispered; "Thank you, Maiden."

I did not know what to say. It was as if I had not quite realized before that day that my sister was really a slave to my own people. Like a speaking goat. Thióðolf nodded at me, and there was an apologetic look to him when he said goodnight to me. Then he just turned without saying goodnight to Zivah and left us there. And Zivah stumbled back to her bed and started sobbing. I heard a muffled snort of laughter from where Arnulf was sleeping before I went into the cover with her.

"I think he was just trying to help you, Zivah," I said quietly.

"Help me? Oh you know nothing of men, Thordís. He was playing nice, probably on account of liking you so much. But all he really wants is for me to bow and scrape and call him master when I spread my legs for him."

I did not know what to reply to that. I recognized that I probably did not know that much about men as such, but suspected that Zivah knew a great deal. My sister looked at me for a moment, and suddenly her gaze turned cold.

"How you must be laughing behind those stone cold eyes of yours," she snarled at me.

"I never laugh," I objected.

"No, that is true. You never laugh and you never weep. Sometimes I think the villagers were right when they said you were of demon-kind. How I must have offended you before, that you will let me suffer this now."

"But Zivah, I have no power over this," I whispered, and she regarded me doubtfully.

"Maybe you do not, Thunder Goddess, but when all is said and done you are the one they are treating like a princess while I am less human to these people than a dog. Let us not make pretense," she said before she lowered her eyes to me, bowed her head and spoke in the Norse language; "Good night, Maiden."

"Good night, Zivah," I whispered and saw my sister turn her back to me again. I lay watching that back a little, and thought about how much I missed to be held by loving arms in the night. I had always slept next to my whole family, snuggling in between my parents and Zivah, who sometimes in her sleep had even embraced me back. I felt really lonely.

Then Njál's kitten suddenly appeared in front of my face. It looked at me strangely and yawned, showing its sharp teeth. It made me think of Njál's fangs. The little beast looked closely at me and I thought I saw other eyes in its face. The loving amber eyes of my mother, first, what made me reach out and touch it gently, feeling another sting of sadness. Before I could drift into the grief of Mother's death, however, the kitten's eyes changed.

Then I saw the eyes of Njál the Foolish, as he was now often called. He really seemed to like us sisters, and now it felt as if he had come to watch over us by way of his cat, which had once belonged to our mother.

And then the kitten's eyes changed again, and the dark pool eyes of Hallgrim Hidden Spear turned up, what made me stop caressing it and just look back. It was as if they had all taken turns looking out through that cat's yellow eyes, watching out for these two daughters of the river lands. I felt as if Mother's voice suddenly whispered through my mind that even if I was the child and not the other way around, Zivah needed comfort more than I did.

The kitten suddenly crawled up over Zivah's back and snuggled in between her arms. I saw her back stop shaking from sobs and knew that she was embracing the little fur clad one. I could somehow feel her arms around me too, as if the kitten was me. It slept there with her the whole night.

The World According to Arnulf

We rowed across the great lake Ilmen at dawn the next morning, going ever further north. There were seagulls there, shrieking, birds that I had never seen before. They said these birds were common to all coasts and shores of the great world circle, and when I pointed out that this was a lake and not the ocean, at least if I was to believe what Thióðolf had told me, they pointed to the northwest and said that the ocean was over there somewhere, and then they pointed directly north and said that there was another great lake, much bigger than this one, and that it was so closely connected to the ocean that seagulls found there ways into the large inland waters. The great lake to the north was the Aldeigja. We were drawing close to our destination, and for the first time since the raid it occurred to me that I was following my father's route back to the slavers' town. At what seemed to be the northernmost end of the lake there was a great river running north, and there was also a warm southern wind blowing through, so the men raised the sails when we had entered the river and finally relaxed their oars.

"This river running north is the Volkhov," Arnulf had called to me when they raised the sails, and I remembered that name from my father's account. We would soon be in Aldeigjuborg, the slavers' town. The men seemed more relaxed all over, and there was a lingering sense of anticipation and talk about the girls back home. Zivah sat rolled up in the shade of the sail with her face down, resting on her knees, and had not spoken any other words than "Yes, Heri," and "Yes, Maiden," all morning. At least she behaved, but her resentment was still visible and sometimes the men exchanged glances. Thióðolf looked a little worried, but seemed to think it was better if she got time to let it all sink in, for he did not rebuke her.

It felt so nice to move downriver with wind in our sails, and the landscape was changing little by little. Surrounding the river on both sides were smooth rolling hills and large fields mostly clad in forest rolling into the endless and almost flat lands to the east and west. I thought I could see mountains to the northeast. There was more pine here than I was used to, and less oaks. In many places, the riverbanks were sand beaches, and I suddenly remembered the pleasurable sensations of rolling in the sand before and after a river bath, and felt a sting that seemed to emerge from a locked chamber within my chest.

After that night on the islet when Arnulf had given Zivah up, I had understood that he had only taken her aboard after Khazaria because of me. I had already sensed the importance of catering to his pride, and after Zivah had miraculously rejected him and lived I devoted myself to the one role she had refused him – the part of the role that had to do with flattering and pleasing our lord. I had to do that for Zivah and for myself. His favor was our only hope in this world. If Zivah failed to please him, then I would have to please him instead. I would not try to offer myself up in any way again, but now I knew what he wanted and had no problem giving it to him either, because it was the actual truth that I feared him, needed him, and hoped that he would be good to us, and even though I knew him for a rather nasty sort of man, I could not help but respect him deeply.

He had a power about him that had not so much to do with his strength and the fact that he owned a lot of things and ships and people, as it had to do with his character and the great and turbulent story which he had emerged from. Sometimes when I looked at him I thought I could see generations of fighting pirates trying to survive and grab hold of something to call their own. And then they had found a place, and fought to hold it even though they were surrounded by enemy tribes. I looked at him and got this image in my head of him, the image of a warrior born out of suffering and battle and carnage and who had had only two options apart from death, namely to become a ruthless warrior or to become a helpless slave, and he had fought all his life to secure his place in the world.

I looked at my Heri and thought about these things, and about how very much I needed him to like me, and every time that he looked back at me he could see the awe I felt for him, and he was pleased. I did it consciously to please him, but I wielded true blades, and that was all that mattered. It was simply a fact of life that to have a protector such as Arnulf Heri could make a very serious difference to me and Zivah. It could be a matter of life or death, freedom or slavery, wealth or poverty. And the more I pleased him the more seriously did he take that fatherly role, which prompted me on to find ever new ways of pleasing him. That day I stood beside him, and when he acknowledged me, I asked him what land we were in now.

"This is the land of the Rus, priestess," Arnulf said, and made a sweeping gesture to cover the surrounding forests; "Although of course, right now all you can see is wood. But this land belongs to us, to the Rus, the people of Aldeigjuborg. It was once just a small settlement where our ancestors used to come to spend the winters. We came from the homelands, clan-less Norsemen from Gotland and Gautland and Svíthióð. In my grandmother Bera's time we made a new land here and created our own rules. We are Vikings, priestess, born of the bays, grown up with battle, the sons of Sea Kings. We had no place in the old lands, where people feared and hated us, and so we made a new place for ourselves. We have become a tribe in our own right. We are the Rus. That name was given to us by the Finnish people who lived here before we came, and it just means that we are often very light-haired. In the homeland, they call it Garðaríki, and they call us Væringjar, since we have stayed here, but there are many other names for us, given to us by different people. Rus is the most common term for us."

Arnulf smiled and got a dreamy look to him; "One day, I think they will know this country as Rusland. Or Rusiyah, perhaps. That is what the Big Tunic Men call us and our land, anyway, Rusiyah. We have been joined here by other people, by those tribes that were too strong and warlike for us to take down, and nowadays, we are often called Rus, the lot of us, even if there are those among us who are not Norsemen. Most of the others are Finnish folks, such as the Ests and the Tschudes and the Merian folks, but there are also those of Slavic stock, like the Krivich. And there are some Khazars among us as well, and traders from all over the world."

I pricked my ears, always curious to know everything.

"You know this river as the Volkhov already," Arnulf continued, "From this river we can reach the other end of the world. This river will take us on to new rivers that lead all the way to rich and distant lands in the southern and eastern regions of this great World Circle."

"Is that the land called Big Tunic Land, Heri?" I asked, curious. I remembered Father had said these lands were situated in the south, stretching both eastwards and westwards.

"Some of it is the Big Tunic Land, but there are many others as well, lands that we must pass through to get to Baghdad. You have already seen the outskirts of Khazaria. We deal with the Khazars and Avars and Magyars, and we even have some dealings with a great city that we call Miklagard. She is a marvelous city, but her glories fade compared to Baghdad," Arnulf said, clearly eager to convey his geographical knowledge to me. I was equally eager to hear more, so I asked where Baghdad was and what kind of city it was.

"Baghdad – she is the greatest city in Big Tunic Land. It is where the caliphs live now, but when I lived there they were still moving to make the city worthy of their rulers. But it was an astounding place even then. They build their houses out of rocks and make them tall as mountains! Sometimes the rock they use for building is so precious that the whole house shines, and they decorate them most exquisitely, and there are lots of quarters in each house! They hardly even share their beds if they can afford the space, as if they don't like to sleep next to each other like we do, and women have their own quarters and keep to themselves as if they don't like the company of men. And they don't, if I am any judge of the matter."

"Don't they ever wear breeches, the Tunic Men?" I asked.

"Yes, they sometimes do, especially their warriors. They actually have some great warriors among them even if you wouldn't think it from the soft ways they like to live. But even if they wear breeches, these are enormous. They like to wear really wide clothing because of the heat and because they don't like to think about the fact that they have legs for some reason."

"Why are they so important for you, Heri?"

"That city, Baghdad, is a very important trading partner for us because those Big Tunic Men are very rich and love many of the things we can offer them what is not found in the southern lands, and most importantly they never cease their hunger for new slaves – especially slaves with light skin and lightly colored eyes and a variety of hair colors."

"Why?" I asked, "Is that not the most common kind?"

"No, priestess, oh, people come in all sorts of colors and sizes and strange features and even stranger clothing. We are like flowers, people, we are all sorts. See Shumayl there. Most Tunic Men have black hair and brown eyes like he does, and they are often darker of skin than we are, sometimes very dark. Although there are those with green eyes, like my Aziza… ah, Aziza! Now, she is from Baghdad, well, at least that is where I bought her. She is my first concubine."

Arnulf got another kind of dreamy look in his face, and I gathered that he was very fond of this Aziza; "But they have a different kind of hue to their skin than we do, even if they can be very light in the color, they are more blue than light red like us if you understand. Aziza has the color of cinnamon," Arnulf concluded.

"Who are the caliphs?" I asked, and Arnulf said they were a kind of kings who lived in huge palaces and had more slaves and concubines than it was even possible to imagine. Apparently they liked to cut off the balls of male slaves so as to make them capable of dealing with women, what had confused Arnulf no end. There had used to be a caliph called Al-Mahdi, who was the one who had made Shumayl into a slave, but now his son ruled, and his name was Harun-al-Rashid. Apparently, ever since he was but a young prince, Harun liked to walk through Baghdad disguised as an ordinary fellow, and he had with him a very big slave man who raped tradesmen in the market if they tried to cheat Harun. There was a joke about a tradesman who always made sure to cheat the caliph when he came to the market that made Arnulf laugh, while I frowned uncertainly, and Arnulf quickly changed the subject, addressing one of my earlier questions. A palace, he told me, was a very large building made out of a rock and cased with great plates of marble and small painted ceramic squares fastened to the walls for decoration. I made another image inside my head to fit the description, which I have sadly never had the opportunity to revise in face of reality. Satisfied with his answer about the caliphs and their palaces, I asked when he had lived there.

"I was a very young man then, and I came to Baghdad seeking adventure and a future. The place dazzled me with its beauty and many marvels, as well as its many opportunities for building up a trade. And so I dwelled there for many years and learned the language and their customs. They have many very strange customs, some that are very sensible and even pleasurable, and others that are nothing but madness and folly, but they have many very wise men among them who know things far beyond my ken, and live in houses made out of stone, and they bathe and scrub themselves every day! But one does perspire a great deal down there and I have to say I appreciated the baths, and I did not want them to think I stank. I heard them speak of Christians and how they stank, and I wanted nothing to do with that, and so I washed every day. It is hot there, and dry most of the time, and their beliefs are incredible. I was not allowed to speak of the gods there or even make sacrifice! I had to pretend I was a Christian and walk around with a cross around my neck, because even though they do not like Christians very much either, they truly hate Heathens."

"Where do the Christians live?" I asked, "and do you know their customs also?"

"Well," Arnulf said, "Christians are people who live to the south and the west of here and they also have many very strange customs and beliefs, even if many of them look and speak more like we do. There are two kinds of Christians, the eastern ones, who hold Miklagard, and the western ones, who live in Frankland and England and Italy, whatever is left of the old Roman Empire. The eastern ones have the sense to buy slaves from us although they do not like to have Christian slaves. They have all sorts of rules protecting Christian slaves, like one what says a man cannot use his Christian women-slaves for pleasure, what is rather odd, all things considered."

Arnulf frowned and shook his head dismissively; "The western Christians also have slaves, and they do not mind having Christian slaves at all, but for a while now they have refused to buy anything from Heathens and have all sorts of rules about trading with Heathens, making it impossible to deal with them. I have heard that Norse traders in the west, those who live in the western homelands, North Way and Denmark, have become so exasperated about these idiotic Christian rules that they are beginning to cultivate Vikings among themselves, which is a laugh, seeing as these western folks of the homelands have always despised us Vikings before. But need makes changes, and the northern lands have always depended on trade seeing as we have not the soil and the fields it takes to make a good living at home. Now these North Way men and Danes and Svear get to know what it feels like, to see no other way of living well than taking what they want." Arnulf chuckled triumphantly.

"But I feel for them. As trading partners, those Christians are a far worse lot to deal with than the Tunic Men. Ha! Even if the Tunic Men despise us Heathens they still have the sense to trade with us. Those Danes and North-Way men are presented with quite a handful! You cannot even talk with them Christians for more than a little while before they keep trying to make you into a Christian as well. But I suspect there will be less talk and more pillaging if they continue to act as if they know better than us even as it is clear to everybody else that they are crazy! At least they are not much of a match for the likes of us. Most of their men are not even warriors! They live like slaves and even kneel to their masters."

"What do the Christians look like then?" I asked, wondering if they had some unusual colors to them also. Arnulf shook his head.

"The eastern ones are punier and often somewhat darker than we are, and they speak a language they call Greek, which is very different from our language. The western ones are more like us, even if you would not believe it by hearing what they talk about and seeing how they live. Despite being Christian, the Franks and the Anglo-Saxons are the people who are most like us on the outside, having similar looks about them, and clothes, although they are generally punier than us, but that has more to do with how they live than with how they are built from nature. You see, we grow very big and strong because we train at all sorts of heavy arts from the day we start to walk. I was trained for combat and rowing and swimming and climbing and carrying and everything you can imagine from the time I was three years old and still a toddler! Most Norsemen are trained that way, and we do eat a lot of meat and grain and dairy things what make the body swell. But the Christians, even if they are of the same stock, are punier than us because they do not cultivate and hone their men the way we do. They think that people ought to live in fear. I am not sure why, but they keep saying they are god-fearing people. Can you imagine that?"

Arnulf mused, having his own opinions as to why the Christian were so fearful; "I think they are more fearful than we are because they make their women weak and unable to bear so many strong sons. A child in the womb lives by the blood of its mother, you know, and if the mother is fearful and weak, so the children will be born with those traits. We know this because we see well how boys born from slave women turn out compared to those what are born from free Norsewomen. Those Christians treat even free women as if they were slaves, and so their men are not warriors except a few of them, only they are not warriors either, but something they call soldiers. But the men who lead these soldiers can be quite good at planning battles, it is something they call strategy, and so they have won some battles against our kind even so, by applying cunning and treachery as if they were women."

"What do they look like, then, Heri, apart from being puny?" I asked. I thought it sounded like they looked like us, but not like us anyway.

"They don't have tattoos and wear their hair in very boring fashions, they have hardly any style to them at all, except for some of the richest ones, and they don't ever wash themselves it seems, so they stink, believing that bathing once a week and washing every day like we do is bad for you. Yet it is clear to see that we are related, and they descend from Norse folks. It is true. Their ancestors were people who came out of the homelands many hundreds of years ago, speaking the Norse language. They mingled with other great folks down south, Britons and Gauls, Iberians and Greeks and Romans, even Slavs, and so they changed over time. But even now they speak a language it is possible to grasp quite easily. But after they became Christians they went all nuts. You will know what I talk about if you ever meet them. Their minds are far removed. In fact, they are the craziest people I have ever encountered."

Arnulf paused a little, lost in memories, before it occurred to him that he had still not explained what a Christian was. Until then, I had assumed that they were just another tribe. But it had to do with beliefs, it seemed. Arnulf summed it up in his own particular way; "Now, all the Christians, whether they are western Franks and Englanders, or else eastern folks like the Miklagard-people, believe in a priest who was the son of a god who is supposed to be the only god in the whole wide world. They think that the other gods are false. And so they fight everybody else all the time because they want them to quit honoring their false gods. But do you know what is more funny still?"

I shook my head, hardly able to imagine anything weirder than that.

"They also fight each other," Arnulf laughed, "These one-god people are the craziest lot I have every dealt with. They fight about the strangest things – not for power or land or honor or lootings, but for their beliefs. At least that is what they say, as if they need beliefs to make their fights legitimate. They have all kinds of little fractions who are willing to wage war on account of disagreements about the true nature of this one single god of theirs and what he wants from them. I have heard of wars where the warring sides were really just arguing about whether the son of their god is the same as the god or just the son. Well if anybody said to me that a son is identical to his father I would probably want to slap them a little too, but waging a war over those kinds of matters? Over in Miklagard they are presently waging wars and killing each other over an argument as to whether they ought to have images of their holy people or not. It is as if we were going to wage war about whether Óðinn has one or two eyes or which one of his sons is the best. Whoever cares? It is beyond my ken, priestess, and it all seems like folly to me, like children arguing over whose father is the strongest warrior."

"When the Christians are not busy hating each other, they hate the Tunic Men, especially after the Tunic Men conquered Iberia and made another Tunic Land down there. Came a little too close, there, for their comfort," Arnulf chuckled, "It is called Al-Andaluz, I have heard, and it is a sort of Caliphate as well, only they call it an Emirate, and it is ruled by an Emir, which is pretty much the same as a Caliph, which is to say a sort of king. As to the Christians, they hate these Tunic Men. But the Christians also hate Heathens even more than they hate the Tunic men. Now, if you wonder what a Heathen is, that would be people like you and me, people who still sacrifice to the old gods and believe in the wisdom of the ancestors. Christians do not do that anymore, and neither do the Tunic men. The Tunic Men also believe in only one god, but instead of a priestly son, that one has a priest servant whom they call a prophet, which is a bit like a Thúl, that is, a cunning man who knows what the gods want and speaks with their voice. Only this one was only saying what that one god wanted, and that other gods were either false or monstrous. They call that belief Islam and those who believe in Islam are Muslims. If you are going to pass for a Muslim, you have to be able declare a particular kind of spell saying that you believe that this priest-man was a prophet and that there is only one god. If you do not believe that and are unable to recite the spell correctly in their language, and unwilling to go through all the rituals they are doing each and every day, why then you have to say you are a Christian or a Jew and then they will let you pass even if they think you are thick in the head."

"Why do you have to say you are either of those things?" I asked incredulously.

"Because," Arnulf said, "in Baghdad, as in all the Tunic lands, and just like in the Christian lands, anybody can kill a Heathen or enslave a Heathen if they want to. And believe me, there are many enough who would grasp that opportunity! You see, these one god people will be reluctant to buy people who share their belief in the one god and his prophet or his son, so I could not raid for slaves down there, and besides they are too well protected. The Tunic Men are also reluctant to take Christian or Jewish slaves, for they can convert to Islam even if they are slaves, and if they convert, even if it is of their own accord and not with the permission of their Heri, why then they must be freed. But a Heathen is powerless there; if you were a Heathen when you were enslaved, you cannot even convert. Rather than giving myself away as a Heathen, I deal with the Tunic Men by pretending I am a Christian and sell only Heathen slaves to them, and I wear a Christian symbol when I am there, a cross pendant. If I was ever caught and made a slave, I could just recite the spell and be freed. Clever, huh?"

I nodded in agreement, since it sounded very clever to my ears, even if I wondered how he could think it was fine to sell Heathens to these strangers if Heathens were people like himself, but Arnulf did not appear to possess any such inhibitions. I admitted to myself that there were many things here that I did not yet understand, but which would be revealed to me little by little. I got the impression that the world was a lot larger and filled with a lot more people who were all very much more different from each other than I had previously imagined.

"Heri, the men told me that the Khazars are Jews. Can you tell me more about them?"

"The tribe of the Jews come from a place that we know as Jórsalaborg, and before that they came from Egypt, and it is said they used to be slaves there, but that they escaped into the land where Jórsalaborg lies, and that land is called Canaan. They attacked and slaughtered all the people who lived there before them except from some of the youngest women what they took as slaves, and then they lived there a long time and became a great nation. Sounds a lot like us Rus, does it not?"

He seemed proud of that, so I nodded politely and said "Yes, Heri."

"Although we tend to let live all those who cannot fight, of course. Them Jews slaughtered *everyone* as a sacrifice to their god. Even the livestock, they slaughtered. Said it was pleasing to their lord, they said. Oh, yes, Thordís, they also believe in just the one god, but I do not think there is a son involved," Arnulf proceeded, "and it so happened that a far more powerful nation came out of Italy and crushed them, and filled their land with lots of other people. The Tunic Men invaded that land more than a hundred years ago, and now most of the folks what live down in Jórsalaborg are Moslems and Tunic Men. The tribe of the Jews has long since been dissolved and they are without a land now, and they have spread out into the world and find themselves living among other people. Some of them are slaves to Christians and to Tunic Men, or else they live among them."

"Are the Khazars descended from these Jews what had to flee, then?" I asked.

"A sound deduction on your part, little priestess, but it is not so, actually. Many hundreds of years ago, the Khazars of the east, who I think are descended from the Huns who were Heathens just like us, and great warriors also, actually joined the Jewish tribe because they wanted to, and now they call themselves Jews even if they look rather different from other Jews. We have to go through their land to get to Big Tunic Land, and the Khazars are a fierce lot, and much more like us than any other people. Many of them even worship their old gods despite being Jews also, and they still have Spirit Callers among them. Yes, they are a little like us, the Khazars. They are flexible folks."

He grinned a little deviously, and I thought about the way he had worn a Christian symbol among the Big Tunic Men; "Living so close to the Big Tunic Land, they are rather clever, actually, seeing as they are less likely to be taken as slaves when they are Jews," Arnulf said, confirming my ponderings.

"I often trade with those Khazars, and so I know that the Jews have a law against making slaves out of other Jews if they are men, but it is written carefully down in very holy runes that it is perfectly permissible to sell their own daughters as slaves to others, can you imagine? Selling a Síf as a slave! Ha!" Arnulf shook his head in disbelief; "But even if the Khazars are more like us they don't regard their Sífs as highly as we do. They are afraid of their own women's verdicts on their conducts, so they make sure to scare them off from speaking out, which is about the most foolish thing a man can do, seeing as a woman's verdict on her kinsman will work in hidden ways if it is not let out in the open. Oh, well. They are still very clever, the Khazars. You see, those holy runes also say that those Jews can enslave anyone of their neighbors who is not of the chosen, and their neighbors cannot even convert that easily, since it is a tribal thing, at least if I have understood it right. The Khazars enslave their neighbors as often as they can, regardless of their beliefs. That was how Shumayl came to be among us. He had thought he had come among other people of the… the book, as they say, that would be the one god folks, and he had heard that the Khazars had large communities of Moslems and Christians as well as Heathens, and that they allow for all sorts of beliefs in their country. But it turned out that this particular brand of one-god-folks has no qualms about enslaving just about all the neighbors they can conquer, and Shumayl had nobody to protect him, and as you can see the fellow can hardly fight for himself."

"What sort of pendant do you wear when you are among them Khazars, Heri?" I asked, and Arnulf laughed; "Among the Khazars we do not have to pretend we are anything but Heathen, seeing as they will enslave anybody who *can* be enslaved, quite like we will. In Khazaria we just have to show ourselves as menacing as possible, even as we deal with them regularly. Fortunately we are able to understand each other well, and they are practical enough to understand that we Rus are valuable partners in trade." Arnulf frowned and scratched his head a little.

"These rules about slavery among the people who believe in only one god are very odd, priestess, do you not think? What god would care what thoughts and beliefs stir in the hearts of slaves? I would enslave *anybody* whom Fate carves into my path and who is too weak to stand against me," Arnulf concluded, not without a certain pride regarding his own far more pragmatic and rational sense for good business. Then he frowned, trying to think of more things to say about the matter. The old Viking shook his head as if to release himself from some incomprehensible matters of the mind.

“I know the things I know, priestess,” he said, “I honor the gods and trust in them, yet I trust even more in my own strength and cunning. I perform the proper rituals and the sacrifices and fulfill my oaths, but beyond that I have little knowledge about these things. I am a warrior, not a thinker.”

Arnulf went quiet and stood guard at the prow, watching, ever the alert warrior, ready for anything. I looked at him and at the men, and began to understand something about them. None of these men could take anything for granted, and their lives and well-being depended on their perpetual readiness to respond swiftly to whatever turned up on their path. Having lived all my life in a peaceful and protected village, I had never seen anyone so much like wild animals as the Vikings, even if they possessed a far greater range of tools and things and methods for constructing all kinds of vessels and abodes than we had owned. The look of the men, now that they were gliding downriver without having to use the oars on account of going with the stream, reminded me of the wolf-pack that my parents had once let me observe one day as we were practicing our shooting skills and we managed to sneak up on a hill to watch a pack of wolves, alert for the hunt.

The sudden stillness and the way their minds appeared to extend silently outwards, as if trying to see and hear in all directions at once, picking up every little detail of the landscape, was the same, in wolf and Viking. They were wild, somehow.

I can do what they do, I thought, and felt somewhat at ease. *They are survivors just as I am,* I thought*, they will do anything to survive.* If you have to put on a cross and pretend to believe in the most outrageously absurd things in order to survive for a while, then you do that, and then you move on. That is the Viking way.

Kinsmen

Late in the eve of our second day of our voyage on the river Volkhov, the landscape changed and began to reveal large fields of grain and flax and other culture, as well as fields for milking cows and horses, in between all that forest land.

“Who own these lands, Hallgrim?” I asked the man next to me.

“The House-Bonds of Aldeigjuborg own these fields and farms,” Hallgrim replied; “They are run by slaves and guarded by warriors sworn to the House-Bonds.”

"Hallgrim," I said, "I am a little confused as to what a House-Bond really is. Shumayl addresses Arnulf as House-Bond while the rest of you address him as Heri. My father always told me that a House-Bond is simply the master of a Hold and basically I thought his wife would call him that."

"Well, in the homelands a House-Bond is simply a land-owner, however big or small. But we hardly have land-owners here in Rusiyah. Here, a House-Bond is a man who owns sufficient land and riches that he can afford keeping a court of his own."

"What is a court then?"

"A court is the place where the Bond lives. That is, the House-Bond. As you will soon discover the court consists of both a warrior´s Hall for his blood-sworn warriors, and a Hold for the House-Bond´s family and friends and household slaves. The members of the Hold call him House-Bond, whether they are free or slaves, male or female, grown or small. That is why Shumayl addresses Arnulf Heri as House-Bond."

"Is Thióðolf a visiting friend?" I asked.

"Yes, that he is. He lives in the Hold with Arnulf, just as you and Zivah will."

"So then we must call him House-Bond?"

"No, Thióðolf is not a member of Arnulf´s Hold, he has his own Hold back home in his country, Hálógaland, and is a House-Bond in his own right. And Zivah belongs to Thióðolf, so she will address Arnulf as Heri just as he does."

"And I?"

"You… hmmm," Hallgrim mused and peered carefully at me and then at Arnulf, who was standing too far away to overhear us. He still lowered his voice; "Thordís, I recommend that you regard yourself as a visiting friend until you are told otherwise. Better not give the old man any ideas, yes? Call him Heri like the rest of us, like you are one of his sworn warriors, even if you are his Síf."

"Thank you for the advice, Hidden Spear," I said gratefully. Then another question formed itself in my ever expanding mind; "Are the household slaves the people you take on the raids?"

"No, most of the household slaves are taken from the estates where they were born. You see, the farm slaves who run these farms, they have often been slaves for generations and they are allowed to marry after a fashion, and they are hardly ever sold unless they misbehave. Although as you will see there are many pretty young she-slaves at court who work as household slaves but who are also pleasure slaves for the men, and most of these have been bought from slave markets like the one you saw down in Khazaria."

"Oh, why is that? Would it not be cheaper to just take some of the raided folks home with you?"

"Of course not. Taking home a slave who sees you as the enemy is never a good idea. We want our slaves to feel that they have come to a better place than they ever knew before. Happy slaves are the best slaves, always, they will be loyal and they will…" He paused a little and squinted into the horizon before he continued; "I suppose we like to return to a home where people are happy to see us there and are prone to welcome us. We have no families like other men, we have only our slaves and each other and we must share everything..."

He looked a little sad.

"But Zivah has been brought home from a raid," I said quietly.

"Yes. Zivah is an exception, Thordís, and it is only thanks to you that she is still here with us. I thank you for your efforts to save your sister. But it will be hard on her to live with the men that she saw slaying and raping and enslaving and selling her people… Hard on her and hard on us."

"Hard on *you*?"

"Harder than you can ever know, little priestess, and thank your lord for that," he said.

We stood quietly for a while before he started talking again.

"In Aldeigjuborg there are only twelve House-Bonds with a court each altogether, and only six of them are very powerful and besides of Norse stock. The other six men who rule a court and a Hold are relatives of the Norsemen´s native wives and ambassadors of their tribes. They keep courts of their own but they are relatively poor compared to the great lords."

"Is Arnulf one of the great lords?"

"Yes, he is one of the six warlords who rule Aldeigjuborg together. And like the other five lords he not only owns a court, but also great estates and several ships. The six Heris each have the sworn allegiance of several independent warrior´s Halls including the one they keep in their own court. I am the leader of Arnulf´s court Hall, elected from our own midst, and our Hall consists of five Sixers."

"What are Sixers?"

"A Sixer is a group of six men representing each of the six ranks. They call each other brothers and share everything with each other, even our slave. We can only have the one, lest we burden the Hall and the Heri too much."

"Oh," I said, "so there are five Sixer groups and, uhm, one slave for each group in a Hall?"

"In our Hall, that is how it is, yes. But the number of Sixers vary, of course, depending on the Hall. A Hall will consist of any number of Sixers coming together to swear allegiance to the one and the same lord."

"And do the Sixers rank differently?"

"Each Sixer consists of one member of each rank, and so, all the Sixers of a Hall are equal to each other. I was elected leader of the court Hall some years ago, but that does not mean that my Sixer group is higher ranking than any of the other. I represent the Hall to our Heri, Arnulf. Most of the crew on this ship come from our court Hall, although we have taken aboard two Sixers from another Hall to replace the ones we left behind to guard the court. The other ships are manned by members of other, independent Halls, sworn to Arnulf Heri."

It was a lot to take in, and I stood watching the estates for a while, sleepy summer farms where slaves walked merrily about looking almost like free folks, while warriors seemed to be keeping watch, not so much over the slaves as to whatever moved in the forests and the rivers.

"Are these estates the ones that Arnulf Heri owns?" I asked.

"No, our Heri's estates are situated further to the north of Aldeigjuborg. But the warriors who guard the fields also guard the land of the Rus," he said, and pointed.

As we glided upriver in the Sunset, we saw men on the hills who raised large horns called lurs, and through them they blew a haunting tune that seemed to fill the whole world with a strange sadness, and I heard the call echoed over and over until I realized that it was not an echo but the sound of other lurs responding. They were warning the city of our arrival even days before we reached it.

Hallgrim left me to speak with Arnulf and several other men for a while, and I stood alone by the sideboard listening to the tunes that steadily repeated themselves. The sound of the lurs stirred sadness in my heart. I gazed at my sister who looked so empty and lost, and who refused to talk to me unless I ordered her to. She was still too weighed down by fear and grief to understand anything at all, I thought sadly, and I wondered how I was going to manage this all on my own. I was doing my best but sometimes the burden seemed too heavy for my narrow shoulders. I was just a little girl. And yet I was the only one of us who could get us through this, exactly because I was a child and she was not.

It was almost dark when I felt a large hand close gently on my shoulders and looked up at Arnulf Heri.

"Heri," I said and lowered my eyes. Then more men came up to us and I lowered my eyes to them too. I was supposed to do that to all of them now, so much I had figured out by myself, but it still flattered them when I did it. And when I acknowledged their rank that way I saw those lights being lit in their eyes, followed by affectionate gazes and little treats such as a swirl through the air or ten, what made me feel like I was flying free and being held by strong and trustworthy hands at the same time.

And even without twirls in the air I had suddenly discovered that I enjoyed it when men responded fondly to some gesture of mine, such as the lowering of the eyes. The softening effect I had on a man when I acknowledged what he was to me always made me feel as if I had made myself yet another big and strong protector. As I saw it, a girl could not have too many of those. The more their affection for me grew the more I felt as if I was growing a shield wall around me of warriors willing to die to defend me, and the more protected I was the more would I be able to protect Zivah. As the world had begun to reveal itself to me, a seven year old orphan girl, it was a matter of fact for me that there was nothing more rewarding than the fondness and affection of strong and fearless men. I was in no place to pass judgment on their conducts.

"Priestess," Arnulf said after they had greeted me, "We shall soon be in Aldeigjuborg where I keep my court and my household. And there you will live in my house as my Síf and ward."

"Thank you, Arnulf Heri," I said. He grunted and drew a deep breath. It was almost as if he was nervous. The other men also looked a little tense.

"I would like to ask you something," Arnulf said. I lowered my eyes again to signal that I was willing to obey.

"Did your father ever tell you of blade honers?" he asked. I peered around and saw the curiosity in the eyes of all the men.

"Are they the sort of women what hone men's blades and entice their spears?" I asked, trying to remember the stories. The men went very red, and after a little confusion I thought I had got what they thought was so embarrassing and funny.

"I know those are words to cover other words," I explained, "it is not that the women actually sit there and hone the edges of weapons or, or, uhm, I am not sure how spears are enticed but at least that is not what is meant. I know that. My father told me the blade honers hone sharp the souls of men."

“Oh, good,” said Arnulf with a strangely strained voice and there was a round of coughing all of a sudden. All the men seemed to have gotten an urge to pull at their beards while they snorted and coughed uncomfortably. I regarded them curiously for a moment until I shrugged and decided that there were some men’s matters going on that I would probably never grasp anyway. I wondered if they knew that father had told me that Zivah was a blade honer born, but I did not dare to ask because I was still very uncertain about what slavery among the Rus really meant apart from being abducted and raped and sold and how that connected to the dallying farm slaves I had seen recently.

The men looked meaningfully at each other.

“Little Thordís of the Serious Face,” Hallgrim said fondly, for they were beginning to give me nicknames already, “You are Arnulf Heri’s ward and his Síf, and we men gathered here from Arnulf’s court want you to know that we regard you as our Síf and as such we will protect you with our lives and honor you in all ways appropriate for a little maiden of noble birth, for as long as you stay with us. In return we ask that you obey us and honor us in all ways appropriate for warriors.”

I was a bit stunned. I let my gaze wander towards all of them and noticed that all the other men aboard were looking also. And then I lowered my eyes to the whole crew. “I will obey you and honor you as warriors for as long as I stay with you and for as long as you honor and protect me,” I said gravely and looked up at them again. There were those melting features again, the softening of their hearts. I was beginning to grow quite certain that most of them liked me a great deal. I lowered my eyes a little again just to reward them for liking me and could have sworn that somebody was cooing.

“You honor us. You are our ward too, and it is our duty to train and raise you, Thordís. We have assigned Thióðolf to care for you as if he was your mother’s brother, while Arnulf stands in your father’s stead. You may consider the rest of us your kinsmen and elder brothers,” Hallgrim said.

“Warriors, you honor me,” I whispered, and felt something stir within my long closed heart.

I stood and watched their faces and wondered what sort of feeling it was that now made itself known from within the depths of me. And then I felt something wet run down my cheek, just as a sob escaped me, something I had not known since my brother Thorolf died four years past. I touched the wetness on my cheek with a finger and looked at it, surprised.

It was a very large, singular tear.

*

That night Njál came over to Zivah and squatted down next to her where she lay with his kitten in her arms once more. Her heart beat so hard from fear she thought it would burst.

"Zivah," Njál said.

"Yes, Heri," she whispered anxiously.

"I have your House-Bond's permission to command you," he said. Zivah just looked at him, wide-eyed. It was happening at last. She was too numb to even move or speak. Surprisingly enough, she thought she saw a light in his eyes, a glimpse that spoke of compassion, not of lust. She would know the difference by now, but she could not allow herself to believe it.

"My command is that you keep that kitten," he said.

"Keep… keep the kitten?"

"Yes. I called it Hel-Hound. I think it is a she. She likes you, Zivah. No wonder. She is a holy sort of beast and she has chosen you, and even a foolish man like me knows better than to object to holy choices, especially when even he can see the wisdom in it. She is yours to keep."

The Viking with fangs for teeth winked at her and left.

The Humbled Warrior

The day we reached Aldeigjuborg I was riding the dragon's neck as usual when Thióðolf came up to me and greeted me, saying that he wished to speak to me.

"Thordís, there are many things in our world that must be unknown to you. To tell you the truth there are things in this world of the Viking Rus that were unknown to me also. But as I told you before, Aldeigjuborg is a slavers' town. It is ruled by Viking slavers and run by their slaves. And there are many laws regarding slaves here that we must all pay heed to whether we like it or not. Now, do you see Shumayl over there?"

I turned and looked at the dark skinned little man. He was standing at the other end of the ship and seemed to be enjoying the landscape. Even though he was a slave, and Zivah too, neither of them had been put to work on the ship. The men said they had no use for the efforts of land crabs on their ships and claimed those things were a man's work, which somehow did not include Shumayl, who they seemed to regard as something else than a man. They were fond of Shumayl, I saw that, but they regarded him as a weakling.

But there was something else about him that seemed to induce respect even if he was a slave and something less than a man in their eyes. He had that calm about him and those wakeful eyes, and seemed to have accepted his place in the world with grace - a combination of qualities that I had understood the Vikings held in high esteem. While Zivah sat sulkily in her space and stared at her feet or played with Hel-Hound, Shumayl used to stand or sit in a place where he could watch the running water and the ever changing surroundings. But Shumayl was not the one who could expect to be raped at any time either. He sometimes sat down with her and just sat there, and when there had been a lot going on aboard and it was not so silent, I had noticed that they talked a little and that he was teaching her more of the Norse language. She was catching on really quick, and I think it might have been because she had heard that language spoken ever since I was born and probably before that too, seeing as there had been more of our siblings once.

Now I looked at Shumayl, and Thióðolf said; "Do you see the thin iron necklace around his neck?"

"Yes, Thióðolf. Is that a slave thing?"

"Yes, my little Síf. It is a slave thing. It is a bit like a collar. It is inscribed with the name of his House-Bond. He has to wear that necklace at all times. You see, everybody in Aldeigjuborg and Rus-land generally must be spoken for. They must have a name and lineage of consequence or else a bond to some of the men who are citizens here, or both. Now, you have both a name and a lineage of great and ancient fame, and you are bound to Arnulf and his men."

"And to you?"

"Yes, me too, but my bond to you is personal. I am not one of Arnulf's life sworn men. I am just his guest and sworn to him for a period of time in order to have his protection. If I did not have the protection of powerful friends here in a place where I have no blood kinsmen, anybody could challenge me just to take my goods, and nobody would consider it murder if I could not protect myself. I would have had no rights. So you see, we both depend on Arnulf's protection here, which is why we call him Heri."

"The men call him Heri as well."

"Yes, because the men also depend on his protection, and the protection of his band of warriors. It is up to Arnulf to include or exclude them, because they live in his halls and fight from his ships."

"Now, when we get to town, you will be spoken for and introduced, but you are a new and rather special face so it is of vital importance, Thordís, that you stick to us men at all times and never leave our sides or our midst. Honorable men would never try to seize a girl who stands among men, but we have enemies in this town and they are not honorable at all, men who will stretch the laws as far as they can. If they see an opportunity to spite us by taking a maiden we all love, then they will, and if they do that lawfully there is nothing we can do about it unless we want a war with their house."

"But how can that be lawful?"

"As said, for as long as you have not been spoken for and introduced to the city council, you have no rights here. We have asked to be your brothers and you have accepted, but it is still not formalized and by law anybody could seize you."

"But would you not stop them?"

"We cannot stop them if they claimed you by noosing you."

"Noosing?"

"It means that they put a rope around your neck in a public place. Then they have claimed you for their own, and only a trial where you proved your lineage and name and where men were willing to speak for you, could free you."

"Oh," I said, feeling a little anxious.

"Thordís, know this. If anybody tried to do that with you we would fight them. You are our sister now and we would go to war for your sake. And even if they did catch you we would stand up for you and vouch for your name at trial, and we would go to war if we lost the trial. You are not in danger, but we would not really want to have to go to war and trial and see you abducted in the first place, now, would we?"

"I suppose we would not," I said uncertainly. He smiled a little.

"Exactly. Which means that you need to comb your hair and put on that fierce looking wolf coat of yours and make sure that you stay between us men at all times, and make sure you walk like a queen. Attitude shows bearing. Well, you have no trouble with that, just do not forget yourself and run off as if you were any other child."

"I am not like any other child," I remarked. I had not run off anywhere since my brother died, unless it was to look after Zivah.

"No, you are not, which is why I do not worry so much about you. I just want you to know for your own safety. But now I have another thing to tell you."

He paused to wait for the question.

"What is that, Thióðolf?" I asked.

"Nobody would fight for Zivah," he sighed, "Nobody would stand up for her if someone noosed her. And she is far more vulnerable than you are, firstly because it is obvious to everyone that she is no

Norsewoman, secondly because she is extremely beautiful, and thirdly because she is a new face that nobody knows and nobody has spoken for, so she will attract attention."

"Would… would not even you protect her?"

"Thordís, if this had been out in the wild… but here in Aldeigjuborg there are laws, as I told you. If a man nooses a stranger who has not been spoken for, then he is acting within the law. He has the right to claim her, and I would be ridiculed if I tried to speak up for her, because unlike you she has no case. It is not because I would be afraid to fight for her but the case is that I would have no right to challenge a man for that reason, seeing as he made a legal claim in public. If I fought him, nobody would support me, not even Arnulf and his men, because I would be acting unlawfully and by that I would have dishonored them. And then I would lose their protection, and believe me, Thordís, without their protection I could not protect neither you nor Zivah for very long. And if I killed the man for making a lawful claim I would be condemned as a murderer and then I could be lawfully killed or even lawfully claimed as a slave by anyone."

"So… when we go into town, anybody could just put a rope around Zivah's neck and tow her away to be their slave instead of yours?" I asked, soaking it all up with dread.

"Yes. And whereas our enemies will recognize that you are big trouble for them and probably never attempt anything with you, they are almost certain to try and take a beautiful young woman like Zivah, for just as it is obvious to all who see you that you have a bearing that means something to our people, so it is equally obvious to everyone that Zivah is defenseless and will fetch a really good price at any slave market. And even if she was not this pretty they would do it just to spite us, because that is the sort of thing these lowlife rogues do."

"Thióðolf, is there no way that we can protect her?" I asked, growing rather frightened now.

"There is but one thing that I can do, Thordís," he said and suddenly looked terribly embarrassed.

"What is that, then, Thióðolf?"

"I have to noose her myself, Thordís. I have to lead her in tow by the rope to show the whole town that I have claimed her lawfully. She has to wear the noose until it is exchanged by a lawfully approved slave collar with my name on it."

"Oh," I said. I had already seen Zivah and so many other slaves being pulled around by ropes to their wrists, but those ropes had a certain practical feel to them, they were simply there to make sure the captives stayed captives. The thought of Zivah being noosed and led in a tow that way seemed to me so humiliating that I almost wanted to say that I was willing to take the risk he talked about earlier, but he had not asked me what I thought; he had just told me. I was the one who was supposed to obey. I had not thought about what that really meant before, and now I found myself regretting my oath of submission to the men in return for their protection and care. And yet there was sincerity in Thióðolf as he spoke so well, and tried so eagerly to make me understand why it had to be done, so I lowered my eyes to signal that I had heard him and submitted to his decision. There was not much else I could do anyway.

"Thióðolf," I said, feeling sad.

"Yes, little Thordís?" He sounded sad too.

"Maybe we could explain it to Zivah. So she understands too."

"No, Thordís. We cannot do that."

"Why?"

"Because she is a slave, and as I said there are rules about slavery and how you deal with slaves by words and deeds, and these rules of conduct must be observed, at least when we are among men. How we deal with slaves in private is up to us, but how we deal with them in public is a matter of formal procedure and failure to follow the rules may have dire consequences. It is hard to explain this to you when you have not experienced it yourself, but I am doing my best. The thing is that I cannot go and explain to my slave why I am doing anything. I cannot let her expect me to explain my commands or intentions to her." He looked around and suddenly lowered his voice.

"At least not here before everybody else," he whispered, and I suddenly understood a great deal more about Norsemen and their contrary natures.

"I see, Thióðolf," I said sulkily.

"I should not really have to explain myself to a little maiden either, Thordís, but… you are special. Everybody knows that. We want you to understand us well. I am honored to stand in your mother's brother's stead and be your mentor. And when I approached you that first night and offered my friendship, I meant it, Thordís. You honored me when you accepted that offer later. So I tell you this because I think you need to know and because I do not want you to think ill of me when I… when I noose your sister."

It was so very hard to imagine him doing that. It was only a little later that we turned another bend in the river and saw the town of Aldeigjuborg, and then Thióðolf produced a rope and stood there with it in his hands while closing his eyes and drawing his breath for a moment. Then he went over to Zivah, who was seated as usual, and told her to stand up. She stood, head bowed, and I saw the startled reaction in her body when she had to force herself to stand still and accept the rope that was laid around her neck and tied like a noose. He gathered his composure as he stood there with the lease that held his slave and pretended like nothing had happened as he began to watch the shore. Zivah seemed to have gone all paralyzed and just stood there, and her skin seemed to alternate between red and white. There were tears that she was trying to hold back. It was so painful to watch that I had to turn away.

I turned and looked right into the face of Hallgrim Hidden Spear. He was the only man among them who always knew how to appear right next to me without me ever noticing how he got there. But they said he was a shadow walker who knew the art of silent and unseen stalking like nobody else. He had squatted down next to me and was observing Zivah's reaction just as I did, and now he turned to me, and there was this peculiar light in his eyes, so peculiar that I forgot to lower mine, but he did not seem to mind.

"Thordís, there are things that happen in this world that are hard to accept. Sometimes it seems impossible to see anything but misery, loss and humiliation. But sometimes, and more often than people know, great and fortunate things are born out of misery and loss and humiliation," he said quietly, "and humility can sometimes be the only way for a great and holy power to release itself from the slavery of petty thoughts."

"You men could learn something from those words," I whispered, and bowed my head immediately to apologize for my disrespect.

Hallgrim chuckled. "It is an art women are often far better capable of, all things considered," he admitted gracefully, "and I submit to your verdict, Maiden, you have honored me and taught me," and then he surprised me by lowering his eyes to me in recognition of my verdict. And he did that before all the men to see. I actually gasped.

"Don't gasp like a slave girl," Hallgrim said, resuming his superior role as my elder and my teacher and besides a man, "you are a warrior's daughter and a Síf to warriors, and as such you cannot ever be neither skittish nor squeamish," he said, and proceeded; "You may think yourself quite powerless in our world, and for good reason, but never forget this, Serious Face, that even as you must observe the ranks and the courtesies and obey us in all things, it is also a fact that a maiden's verdict on our conduct is holy to us, and something we consider as a channel for great powers, because the fates speak their verdicts and the gods speak their commands through the songs of women's hearts and the many open gates of their souls, and so even as you are more humble and more easily humbled on account of those gates, you women often know the greater scopes of fate."

He paused and glanced at Zivah again. "Your sister has her fate to fulfil, and you have yours. She will be humbled, and in many ways, so will you, because we are your lords just as we are hers. But I think you will find, Thordís, that even if we cannot obey you and you must not command us, your counsel will always be heard and always taken seriously, and we will always respect your verdicts on us even if we do not always follow up for various reasons."

He smiled at me. "You have a she-wolf's soul. Sometimes it will be hard for you to rank beneath so many men, but you are not our slave even if you rank lower than us. You may be surprised at how easy it will be to follow our commands every day when you still feel and know for certain that you are always heard and seen and taken seriously."

He leaned over towards me to come closer to my ears; "The relation between a kinsman and a Síf is a very holy and ancient trust that was established by our ancestors and serves to balance the weight of power between us, and even we who are the most rogue Vikings in the world respect that bond. You are our sister and through you the Ladies of the Loom and the gods themselves speak to your kinsmen, so do not think we would ever take lightly on your words or your verdicts."

I felt like a sponge as I listened to his every word.

"And although I cannot say we have proven ourselves to you yet," he concluded, "the truth is that we would die to protect you and that we consider your happiness to be the most holy and important witness to our worthiness as men. This is my counsel to you, my Síf, that you keep that in mind and use your goddess power wisely and only as you grow into better understanding of the ways of men. I think you have seen for yourself how that power can turn on a woman if she lacks the wisdom and the understanding it actually takes to wield such immense and fate altering power successfully, to wield it with the precision of a warrior destined for victory."

We both looked at Zivah, who had been forced to stand by the sideboard to watch as we entered the river harbor of Aldeigjuborg. She had lost this battle, it seemed, succumbed to the trial of slavery. Memories of her from the village blew briefly through my mind and I could see, now that Hallgrim had spoken the words, how there might have been a fate altering power within her that had turned on her and created a twisted version of all her dreams and fears, because she had surely been wielding that power unconsciously and conceitedly, playing with men's affections because it made her feel wanted and needed by many. And then she had been utterly disarmed by these men.

They would never respond to the only arts she had ever bothered to really learn well. She had always used her charms as weapons, and found them quite useless when she met the Vikings. For the first time in her life she was completely powerless, and her beauty had become her own worst enemy.

And now that she had lost and all she wanted was to disappear, what she had showed by sitting for days with her face into her lap as much as she could, she was suddenly forced to get to her feet and face another trial: That of coming to a new place and being led through a new town by a noose around her neck.

She stood tall though. It would take more than this to crush my sister. There was a moment when all the men went quiet, watching the slave girl as she seemed to suddenly accept her humiliating situation and relaxed into it. There was that grace to her then. They saw how she suddenly calmed down, they saw her eyes light up in survival mode, lit with a certainty that she could go through this and maintain her self-respect all the way. Her stubborn inborn pride caused her spine to rise tall into her full height. Her neck straightened even as her face looked down. This was not *her* shame.

Zivah of the river lands was ready for her greatest challenge.

Lights were lit in the men's eyes, and where their gazes had often been lustful before, I saw well that these were lights of admiration. I looked at her and saw what my brothers saw, as the humiliated slave girl transformed into a woman warrior; standing up to face her destiny of impossible odds; standing up despite everything, even if all seemed to be lost, facing her new challenge with eyes wide open. And while she looked straight ahead, as if Aldeigjuborg was the next enemy she had to face now, the men looked at her with awe in their eyes.

"Can you see it, Wolfling?" Hallgrim whispered, looking at Zivah with the same expression of awe, "can you see how greatness may be born out of humiliation?"

"I can see it, Hallgrim," I whispered.

"Good. Because it is not what fate befalls you that constitutes the verdict of a man's or woman's worthiness. It is how you deal with that fate. Look at your brothers, little priestess. They have put your sister through a nightmare few would come out of without being broken, and yet she stands tall. She is terrified and she is all alone in the world now, and yet she faces her fear head on. She has become a warrior. Can you see how we respect her?"

I nodded slowly. I could see how they respected her now. I respected her too. "She is the bravest of all here," I said quietly.

"Yes, she is that. But Thordís," Hallgrim whispered conspiratorially, "if she is to learn from this we cannot let her know that we think so for a moment."

Masters and Slaves

We disembarked in the river harbor of Aldeigjuborg, and my job, as well as that of Shumayl and Zivah, was to stay out of the way while the men expertly emptied the ships and moved them about. The men from the other ships greeted us and then left. I was told that they lived in their own halls and ruled their own courts, but that their halls were sworn to Arnulf, whose ships they used. Njál picked up Hel-Hound the cat when they were all finished, because Zivah seemed to have forgotten all about her little charge just then, and looked almost ill from exhaustion, even if she managed to maintain her dignified pose. It was a rather frightening place for us that first day.

Then we began to walk into the town, Arnulf, Thióðolf, Zivah and me, accompanied by a procession of some twenty of the Vikings who had been part of the crew on Arnulf's own ship, the ones who had become my sworn kinsmen.

The town was much larger than our village had been, and far more dirty. I saw children in tattered clothes running around, others better dressed, but all boys, playing at some strange games I had never seen before. The streets were muddy but in some places covered with wooden planks that made it easier to stay out of the dirt. Like at home, there were many domestic animals, many of which walked about freely. Everywhere people gathered to look at us, and the men were greeted by other free men, most of whom looked like Norsemen yet some others who looked different. There were lots of people around who wore the slaves' necklace, and the difference between them and the free people was considerable. They even walked differently, I noticed. I thought about what Thióðolf had said about the rules and how slaves had to act, and glanced up at Zivah, who looked like she was sleepwalking.

We passed through what I thought must be a market, with stalls everywhere and people haggling and discussing various items and their prices. There was a stall where textiles and even ready-made clothes were being sold, and Thióðolf suddenly stopped, looking at Zivah 's dress. It was torn and stained all over with old crusted blood and dirt.

"I need to get a new dress for my woman," he said to Arnulf, who nodded, and the whole party stopped and began looking at the things that were for sale while Thióðolf led Zivah into the stall where the clothes were being sold. The salesman picked up a grey, woolen dress, very plain, the same kind I had seen worn by many slave women that we had passed. Thióðolf agreed that it was just the thing his slave needed and paid a coin for the garment. The salesman folded the dress and wrapped it in another piece of cloth and gave the parcel to Thióðolf. Since the skald had several things to carry, he gave the parcel to Zivah, smiled and said, "Take it, it is my gift to you."

Zivah looked at the parcel he was holding out to her and shook her head, refusing to take it. Thióðolf looked distressed, and tried to push the parcel in to her hands.

"Take it," he demanded, but Zivah shook her head again.

"Thordís," Thióðolf called to me, his voice strained and anxious, trying to keep it low: "Can you please tell Zivah to take the parcel? *Now*!"

I told her, but Zivah replied icily, "I will not have that dress. It is *ugly*."

I knew too little or was too young to understand the seriousness of the situation, and so I promptly translated what she had said with a voice loud enough for everybody around to hear it, and suddenly all eyes were directed at us, and more importantly, at the young slave girl and her House-Bond. Some were already beginning to grin and nudge each other, and Thióðolf looked desperate. He tried to give her the parcel again, but this time, Zivah took it only to throw it at his feet, shouting: "I don't want your gift!"

She managed to say the words in heavily accented Norse, having picked up quite a bit of the language already, and besides her disrespectful gesture, her words only made everything worse. The whole market went deadly quiet, and there must have been some hundred faces or more looking at the scene. I saw Njál turn around with his back to the spectacle in the market, burrowing his face into Hel-Hound's fur. I saw Hallgrim Hidden Spear turn white as snow. And I felt Arnulf 's hand close around my shoulder and then hold me in a tight grip, forcing me to stay put.

"He must beat her now," the Heri said quietly, "He has no other option. Do not interfere, priestess. It is the law."

I tried to speak, but Arnulf stopped me by squeezing my shoulder so tightly it hurt. "Do *not* interfere, priestess," he repeated gravely, his jaws clenched.

Thióðolf looked at me then, his eyes hollow and blank. Then, before I could even react, he struck Zivah across the face so hard that she fell backwards and tumbled into the mud. Some of the people began to laugh as Zivah tried to get up, still too angry to understand what was really happening, but before she could make matters even worse, Thióðolf held her by her hair and forced her back down into the mud before his feet, so that she was made to kneel, what I knew was a terrible humiliation to the Norse. His grip held her head down.

Fortunately, Zivah seemed to suddenly realize that she was being humiliated before the entire town as a result of her actions, and rather than continue provoking even worse punishments, she stopped struggling and remained seated on her knees with her face down even as Thióðolf released his grip. Somehow she managed to look dignified despite everything. He looked relieved when he saw that she was pacified, but the throng that had gathered was still staring expectantly at them.

"It is not enough," Arnulf said to me, still with a very low voice, "he has to punish her more." He still held my shoulder, but like Zivah, I was not going to move until I was permitted to do so, realizing that we were now amidst laws unknown to us and certainly not created for our benefit. I waited for another blow then, but it did not happen. Instead, Thióðolf looked at me sideways and seemed to try and convey something to me. Arnulf understood what he was trying to make me do before I did, and whispered between clenched teeth: "Tell her to apologize to her Heri. Loudly."

I told Zivah, who had gone a deathly white. She was bleeding from the nose, I saw. A single tear ran down her cheek as she spoke, her voice thin but loud enough to be heard; "I am sorry, Heri."

Thióðolf relaxed his shoulders a little and told her to pick up the parcel. She began to move to get up, but he held her down again, and so she had to crawl on the ground to get the parcel she had thrown, and people were giggling and whispering among themselves. She took the parcel and looked up at Thióðolf, who nodded that she could stand up. She got up and stood with her head bowed, and I saw how blood from her nose was dripping down upon the dreaded parcel.

"Now she must thank him for the dress," Arnulf whispered, and I told Zivah. Still with her head bowed she said, "thank you for the dress, Heri."

Thióðolf looked around, and a buzzing sound grew as people were discussing, exchanging glances and frowning. They were not satisfied, I realized, they wanted to see more humiliation, perhaps more violence. Some of the words spoken reached my ears, speaking of how a slave should not be suffered to even live after such an outrageous display of disrespect towards a Heri who had only tried to offer her a gift. It would not do to let other slaves see one get away from a crime as grave as that.

I had never felt anything like it. It was as if the crowd had become one single beast with many heads all of a sudden, one single violent beast that wanted, inexplicably, to make my defenseless sister suffer. The situation had swiftly turned more terrifying than any other I had so far experienced - even the Viking raid had been less tense than this; when a whole town singularly turned against my sister and seemed to demand that she be beaten to a pulp and left for the dogs. Zivah had begun to realize her predicament as well, and to my surprise she did not wail or sob at all. Instead, she seemed to grow taller, even as she kept her head low, as if she suddenly found new strength from within, and a reason to relax and let go of everything. She looked strangely dignified and calm, even as she awaited her punishment.

She is looking forward to her death. I felt something break within me, and the second teardrop shed rolled down my cheek.

Thióðolf noticed the change in Zivah's attitude, and perhaps it was her regal pose combined with her surrender that gave him the idea. Whatever it was, he suddenly turned towards the throng and applied his poet's voice, that deep voice which ranged so widely and could be heard by anyone.

"This woman is new to slavery," he said, "and she was a princess in her own land, far to the east, before she was captured less than a Moon`s cycle ago. She has not yet learned her place, but how can you expect her to? How can a woman be a princess the one day, and then wake up the next day a slave, without making some mistakes?"

The crowd listened, and a new ambience seemed to spread, as people whispered to each other, and I saw some nods and even expressions of sympathy. Arnulf looked around and whispered between clenched teeth: "Great. Now we have to invent a whole new eastern kingdom for her benefit."

But Thióðolf saw the opportunity of such a fiction as the crowd mind was turning, and continued: "This woman, who was a princess only few days ago; she does not speak our language well, and does not know our rules or our laws. She hardly knows what it means to be a slave. I ask you, people of Aldeigjuborg, should I not show clemency just this once? Could I not be merciful, and let this pass? Had she been any other slave, I would have punished her more, but she is special. She is beautiful and dignified, can you not see? Can you not see that she is royalty? Can you not see her regal stature? I would not want to ruin her."

The crowd murmured sympathetically, and the bard raised his voice; "It is her first day here, and she knows not what misery she has woken up to. She will learn our laws and bend to our rules, but she has not been taught yet. Do you not think that it is enough punishment for a newly captured princess to be slapped and forced to kneel before the town? Can you not see that this is to her as great a punishment as any that your council could devise for her? Can you not see that she has already understood her mistake? Let me have my slave princess, not ruined, but whole, and I will teach her how to behave, as I have already started in view of you all."

He looked around at the expectant faces and added slyly; "This very night, I will train her more. How, you can all well imagine."

The spectators grinned and chuckled, knowing that sort of training well.

"I would not want her ruined for that purpose," Thióðolf called out, feigning exasperation, and made the crowd laugh out loud at last. He finished his masterful speech when the laughing subsided.

"She is being duly punished, for one of her origins. Are you really craving more than that, people of Aldeigjuborg? Are you not men of honor? I think you are!"

His eloquence, his voice, his words and his flattery - and the little lie about my sister being a foreign princess - all of it seemed to affect the crowd and change its mind as swiftly as it had been turned against her. The tension had dissolved, the crowd slowly dispersed itself, and nobody craved more punishment. I heard the ongoing discussions all around me, but now there were words of sympathy for Zivah. They were looking at her posture, the way she moved and walked and looked, for even as she was still wearing the bloodstained, tattered dress, now even more dirty from the mud, even as she was bleeding from the nose and holding the parcel to her chest with lowered eyes, she managed to look every bit the princess.

"A pity," I heard someone say behind me, "a woman like that will never be able to accept the slave 's fate. Look at her, she walks like a queen. She should be seated high and use her hands for spinning precious linen and threads of gold, not crawl around in the mud for the sake of a grey woolen dress."

"Bah," another voice replied, "a woman like that will get out of slavery more swiftly than you and I can empty a drinking horn. If she is clever, that is."

The crowd parted respectfully as we continued our walk, and Zivah had that look about her what always made me keep my distance, even though I wanted to go to her and comfort her. I knew she would not appreciate it if I did. Despite his obvious relief, Thióðolf looked so sad that I went over to his side.

As soon as we got more space around us, I said; "My father told me that a man should not beat a woman. He said it was as dishonorable to the man himself as it was to the woman."

"She is a *slave*, Thordís. It doesn't count the same. But I did not want to do that," he said, "I abhorred doing that. But I *had* to. You heard the crowd. I already told you two about the laws. If I had not done that they would have made a case out of it, they would have wanted to make an example out of her, to scare the other slaves. I hope you understand, Thordís."

"I do," I said, and looked at Zivah walking, majestically, even as she appeared defeated and humble.

"But *she* doesn't," I pointed out, and felt Thióðolf sigh heavily beside me. He had managed to save the situation before it got out of hand, but it was still a disaster. Zivah seemed to have a natural talent for acting correctly yet clearly showing her displeasure at the same time, and now her hostility seemed to be reeking from her even as she had surrendered in all other ways.

"I am a monster in her eyes now," he said.

"Yes," I confirmed, and Thióðolf grumbled, "I hope she will understand later."

"She will probably hate you forever and ever," I volunteered, thinking that he would be pleased to know what he could expect, and wondered why he rolled his eyes to heaven.

Arnulf's Household

Arnulf's court was situated in the rich end of the town, at the end of a street and close to the surrounding hills, and looked more like a fortress than an actual house. It consisted for the most part of two very large and long buildings joined by a common courtyard, within which there was a stable and a washing area with a well behind, and the entire court with the two halls was enclosed by high wooden walls. There were four watchtowers at either corner of the court. There were no entrances to the halls from the street, only one to the courtyard, which was guarded by two warriors who greeted their master with smiles and a swift lowering of the eyes. We entered the courtyard and found that Arnulf's household had set itself up to greet us. There were some warriors who stood by the wall of one of the buildings, and they greeted us first with half an arm raised and with lowered eyes to Arnulf, whom they called Heri.

While Arnulf talked to the warriors, I noticed a strong-looking young boy about my own age, with hair so light it was almost white, and very light blue eyes. He came up to Hallgrim, who greeted him by throwing an arm around him, and then the boy turned to Arnulf, who lifted him up and gave him a hug. Njál whispered to me that the boy was called Ivarr and that he was Hallgrim's son and Arnulf's sister's son, but that his mother was long dead. I turned my attention to five pretty women standing behind the warriors, women who wore the slave collars as well as necklaces made out of lilac-colored stones. Njál told me that the necklaces indicated that they were the Sheaths of the Hall, what meant they were slaves who served the men in the Hall. The Hall, he said, meant the house where most of the warriors lived, and it was referred to either as the men's hall or the warriors' hall, or just the Hall.

The other long house was the Hold, where Arnulf lived with his household, and both the house and the people of the household could be referred to as the Hold. The House-Bond and Heri swiftly greeted all the warriors and ignored their slaves before he turned his attention to the Hold. The entire household consisted of slaves, which I gathered from the iron necklaces that they all wore. A group of mostly quite young and pretty women as well as a few young men with shaved faces and short-cut hair all stood with their heads bowed, fronted by two very beautiful women who, in addition to the iron necklaces also wore another kind of necklace, one of green stone beads. Njál said that the bead necklaces signaled that they had special status as concubines, and that they belonged to Arnulf.

The one who stood in the very front was so beautiful I thought she must be a goddess or a forest sprite, slender, yet with all the desirable, generous curves, and her skin had a dark, golden-red hue which I assumed must be the color that Arnulf had described as cinnamon. Her long hair was thick, wavy, shiny and completely black. I could not see her eyes yet because she kept them lowered and her head was bowed, but I remembered how Arnulf had told me that Aziza from Baghdad had green eyes. The second concubine was not as ethereally beautiful as the first, and far plumper, but she had a very sweet face and even more generous curves than Aziza. She looked like she was about to giggle, even as she kept her head bowed like the other slaves. Her hair was light in color, as her skin was, and she had a Finnish look to her, with broad cheekbones and a rounded face. Both concubines wore quite practical yet elegant and pretty dresses. The other slave girls looked almost plain next to the concubines and the Sheaths, even if they were pretty too.

Arnulf marched up to the one called Aziza. Still with her head bowed, she said; "On behalf of your household I greet you, House-Bond. Welcome home. We trust you are well and that your journey was prosperous." To that formal speech, Arnulf just cried, "Aziza, my dove!" and lifted her by that narrow waist and twirled her around in the air while they both laughed. They hugged, and the way she hugged him made me think she might really love him, despite being his slave, and the kiss that followed before he set her down again seemed to confirm my notion. When Arnulf had greeted his first concubine, he moved on to the second, and they went through the same ritual of her formal submission, rewarded with a flight, a hug and a kiss. The second concubine was called Laimi, and she was not a dove, but a honey-jar, and she giggled loudly when he swung her through the air. She was a youngish and giggly kind of woman, where Aziza was dignified and mature. Arnulf now turned to the rest of his household and regarded them with interest, yet with far more emotional distance.

"I trust I find you all well, my Hold," he said, and they all replied at once, "We are well and we thank you, House-Bond." Arnulf just grunted in reply, but then turned to Aziza. "Where is Skeggi?" he asked.

"Skeggi is dead, House-Bond," Aziza replied. I heard that she spoke the Norse language well, but she had a special accent that I thought was similar to that of Shumayl. Theirs was a Baghdad accent.

"Dead?" Arnulf looked surprised, "What happened?"

"Gunnarr Beak-Nose killed him, House-Bond."

"Gunnarr *killed* my slave? Why?"

"I don't know, House-Bond. We were told that Skeggi had behaved insolently towards Gunnarr, and so he cut him down. We were paid the set price for him, House-Bond. Unless you wish to settle the matter yourself, I have the money."

"No…" Arnulf pondered. He actually looked a bit sad, and to my surprise, a tear suddenly fell down his cheek, and he wiped it off with an angry sweep of his hand. "I *liked* Skeggi," he declared, "I had gotten *used* to him. He has been a part of my household since I was a boy. We used to play together as boys sometimes. And I cannot think that he would *ever* have dared to be insolent towards Gunnarr Beak-Nose."

"House-Bond," Aziza said, just to agree with him without actually voicing an opinion.

"This is an insult to me," Arnulf continued, "To take down my slave without consulting me first, and surely for no reason whatsoever. But the deed is done and the price has been paid, so what can I do?"

Aziza just nodded to that and looked quite sad as well, as did the whole household, I noticed. But no one was supposed to grieve overmuch for a dead slave, so the sadness was soon wiped off their faces and buried somewhere in their secret hearts. Arnulf shook his shoulders as if to shake off the matter of the killed slave and then turned to us, making a sweeping gesture towards me, Zivah and Thióðolf.

"Household, you already know Thióðolf Skald." The slaves nodded, bowed their heads again and said, "Greetings, Thióðolf Heri."

Thióðolf just nodded to the slaves. He still looked very serious after all that had happened and appeared distant, lost in his own thoughts.

"Thióðolf will continue to stay in my house as my honored guest," Arnulf proceeded, "He will have the guest bed, and with him his new household slave, Zivah."

All the slaves now looked directly at Zivah, openly curious and with no averting of the eyes. Zivah was standing a little behind Thióðolf to his left, holding on to her bloodied parcel as if it was the only thing that currently kept her alive. Her head was bowed, but the blood that had run from her nose after Thióðolf hit her was still there, as she had made no attempt to dry it off, and her torn dress was rather outstanding with its large and dark bloodstains. I could see that Aziza and Laimi looked concerned, pitying the new young slave woman who looked so utterly miserable. Thióðolf looked ashamed.

"Now, Zivah here is new to slavery," Arnulf said, and then looked sideways at Thióðolf with a mocking grin, "Apparently, she was the princess of a completely unknown eastern kingdom, who was taken as a slave. As you can see, she had not yet quite understood her position, so she had to be punished. But *you* will go easy on her, at least to begin with."

All the slaves nodded sincerely, and I saw glimpses of pity in all their eyes now. Arnulf looked at Thióðolf as if he expected him to say something, and Thióðolf suddenly broke free from his private musings and looked around, saying; "Yes, of course, my slave will help you with all your chores. Just tell her what to do."

"Thank you, my friend," Arnulf said, as if Thióðolf had offered the help of his own accord, which he obviously should have done. Thióðolf bowed his head apologetically to his captain, but only briefly, seeing as it was in the sight of the slaves.

"But not tonight," Arnulf continued, directed against the slaves, "The new slave is exhausted from the journey and will not begin to do her chores until tomorrow. Now, I have one more guest, and she is new to you all." Arnulf now gestured towards me, and I walked forth, looking curiously at the slaves, who were now bowing their heads again. I had gotten used to understanding a bow of the head as an apology, and now it looked to me as if the slaves were constantly apologizing for their very existence.

Arnulf spoke loudly, so that not only the slaves, but also the warriors could hear him, "This maiden is noble born and a warrior's daughter, and she is of the Gaut tribe. She is born a priestess of the great Thor, and even though she had not been ordained yet, she has great powers. She has walked through Hel and been reborn in lightning. She is not only my guest: She is my Síf, as she is Síf to all my men and Thióðolf too, and you will treat her with all due honors. You will take care of the feeding and the dressing, but no more. Free folks should be raised by free folks, even if we are men and she is a girl. I will be fostering her. Thióðolf will be in charge of her education. She is not to do any chores at all, except those fitting for her noble birth, which is none of your business unless I tell you it is. Her name is Thordís Thorbjörn's daughter, of the Thunder priest lineage in Gautland. You will address her and refer to her as Maiden, until she comes of an age to be your Freyia, which she is rather likely to become."

I looked at Arnulf and wondered what he meant, and noticed that the boy, Ivarr, was looking rather curiously at me. I thought I would burn up.

"Arnulf's household greets you, Maiden," the slaves spoke as one, still with their heads bowed.

I said nothing to the slaves, since neither of the men had spoken to them, but cast a swift glance at Thióðolf to see if I was behaving correctly, and he nodded towards the warriors, who had now all gathered before the warriors' hall, some thirty in number altogether. I turned towards the men, twenty of whom had already been with the crew. I let my eyes sweep over them briefly to take all of them in without staring directly at any of them, and then made a very noble little nod with my head, lowering my eyes like a maiden must, and said; "Greetings, warriors."

The men all nodded back to me, averted their eyes respectfully and said; "Greetings, Maiden." They seemed to have completely forgotten about the Hel-maiden from the ship and now all of them cast polite glances at me as if for the first time, and seeing no longer a magical creature, but a noble born maiden with a holy association. I thought it odd then, but now I know that whereas a Hel-maiden is a welcome and appropriate mascot for a Viking crew, the most hardened of men are always far more comfortable with a noble maiden when it comes to bringing one to the place where they actually live.

And so the men pretended that I had never been their Hel-maiden at all. When I glanced at Thióðolf again, he nodded appreciatively, and I knew that I had mastered the subtle art of showing respect to men in the manner of noble ladies, generating respect in return.

Hamam

The strangest thing awaited us when we entered Arnulf's hall. Never in my life had I seen a bath before, having always bathed in the river during summer, and rolled in the snow after sauna during winter. In the end of Arnulf's hall there was a private quarter, divided from the rest of the hall. At the very end of the quarter there was indeed a sauna, but it was not in use since it was still summer. Before the sauna, however, the floor was made out of polished and beautiful rock bricks which they called marble, and in the middle of the room there was a large tub built from the same rock bricks, and the tub was filled with water. Round stones were being heated in a fire and brought into the tub to heat the water by the slaves as we stood and admired the unimaginable.

"This is my very own *hamam*!" Arnulf proudly exclaimed.

"What is a *hamam*, Heri?" I asked.

"It is a bath! The best invention those Big Tunic Men ever made," he replied, and winked at Aziza, who beamed with pride when he revealed that she had revised the building of the *hamam* and ordered the marble bricks for it. He ordered her to tell me why she did it.

"When I came to Aldeigjuborg, Maiden, I was quite shocked at the fact that your people did not have any baths. I know you are cleanly after your fashion, but to me…" Aziza looked anxiously up at her House-Bond, who laughed; "She thought us disgusting, that's what. She thought us dirty and stinky! I know your people, Aziza, I have lived among them. I know exactly how your lot thinks. But I don't mind. In any case, she came at me with those beautiful green eyes and flashed her lashes and spoke sweetly to me until I had given her permission to buy the most expensive bunch of rock I have ever heard of. But I thank her for it today, and so will you all when you have felt what a *hamam* is like! Now, the first thing we have to do is take our clothes off."

Neither nudity nor pleasure games were unknown to me. The River People had been relaxed about both things, but always made sure to be a discreet about it. As I was to learn, the Norsemen, especially the Rus, were even less concerned about nudity than the people I was born among, and never thought twice about being naked among friends. They were also a lot less discreet when they were playing Freyia's games than I was used to. In fact, the Rus, at least, were not discreet about it at all. It was not the people engaging in these games of pleasure that were obliged to find a private spot. On the contrary, it was the people around who were obliged to look another way unless they wanted to be deemed rude.

Being a child, this did not concern me much, since these games were clearly the business of adults, but Zivah was not a child, and not accustomed to such openness. Thióðolf and Arnulf began to undress, and I could not get undressed fast enough, excited about the idea of doing something utterly foreign. But Zivah stood as paralyzed and just stared blankly into the air.

Suddenly she was approached by Aziza, who was holding a pair of iron scissors, with which she simply cut off Zivah 's dress, deeming it fit for the pyre. Zivah stood suddenly naked, exposed, and began to shiver with terror as the two men that she abhorred were now naked in the same room. The men exchanged glances when they saw her horror, and then simply turned around, standing with their backs to us, and Zivah 's shoulders relaxed a little. They did it for *her*, I sensed, having no wish to make her more scared than she already was. But to Zivah, they were still just rapist brutes, temporarily in check.

Aziza and Laimi now assisted Arnulf while other slave-girls helped the rest of us. We were first swiped all over with moist towels, before they began to massage our bodies with scented oil. There was not a part of our bodies they did not reach, and Zivah winced a little when they became very intimate, but accepted the treatment seeing as it came from other women. Arnulf complained a little about the flower scent, but Aziza just murmured to him that people would only think he had been with a very interesting Freyia, an argument he seemed rather content about, and complained no more, especially not as Laimi squatted before him and did something I could not see but which seemed to make him very happy.

When we had been thoroughly oiled, the slaves began to scrape off the oil with wooden devices made for the purpose. Then they poured water over us, scrubbed us with sponges from the ocean, and poured more water. Just when one would have thought oneself cleaner than ever before, we were to enter the bath. Having two assistants, Arnulf was ready first, and now he turned around to face the bath, which in effect meant that he was facing me and Zivah directly, and we both gasped at the sight that faced us. I had seen many naked men in passing, seeing as it was perfectly common to bathe or take sauna together, but they had never stood there before me like that. Even my Norseman father had not been that direct, and had always been rather swift to cover himself in my presence. Now Arnulf stood there before us in all his glory and stretched absent-mindedly.

Never in my seven year old life had I beheld such a Freystone up close. Not only was it unusually large, but it also seemed to rise up on its own accord, as if it was trying to reach the heavens. The sight was utterly novel to me, and I could not help myself, but stood and gaped at it, wondering how he had managed to keep such an impressive marvel hidden under his clothes.

Zivah, on the other hand, began to cry again.

Thióðolf turned around and swiftly grasped the situation, and had to struggle hard to keep his face straight, while Arnulf kept making sounds of oppressed laughter. Not wanting to torment his slave anymore, Thióðolf made a silent signal to Aziza, who went over to Zivah and put a large towel around her, marching her out of the room while holding her trembling shoulders for comfort. I was too curious about the bath and Arnulf's amazing Freystone to run after her, knowing that she was in good hands already and sensing that she did not want me there anyway, and so I followed the men and slipped into the bath with them, enjoying the awesome sensation of hot water closing around my body and causing my muscles to relax for the first time since the raid.

It was the most wonderful sensation I had ever experienced then, and I lay soaking a long time before I opened my eyes and found that both men were studying my chest with great fascination. Being seven, I had nothing very interesting on my chest then, except my birthmark, which had been shaped as Thor's hammer. I met both their gazes and lowered mine respectfully.

"You have Miöllnir on your heart, priestess," Arnulf said quietly, "If I ever doubted you, I never shall again. You have truly been chosen. I am honored to have Thor's Síf as my guest."

Thióðolf nodded when I looked at him for counsel, and to my astonishment, both men suddenly lowered their eyes to me. When they looked at me again, Arnulf gave me a wink.

"Don't tell," he said, and they both smiled at me.

River Child

"The men call it Hel-Hound," Suri whispered to the other slave girls as they watched the little cat-child play around the hearth of the Hold. Fanged Njál had given the cat over to one of the girls, who had brought it into the Hold. The sweet beast was now on its back throwing a small ball of linen thread repeatedly up in the air while the slaves stared fascinatedly at it.

"*Hel-Hound*?" another girl asked, and they all began giggling hysterically.

"They are crazy," Suri explained calmly, feigning patience with those who had not yet realized that obvious fact. Her little show was followed by another round of muffled laughing snorts. They went silent when Aziza suddenly came out from the Hamam with the new girl, who was naked and crying. Aziza led the weeping girl into the Hold and had her sit down on a chest in the far end while she helped her dry herself with a towel. What a beautiful girl, she thought, poor thing. She handed her the formless grey dress and saw the new slave girl put it on so quickly it was clear to all that she did not wish to be seen naked. The slaves exchanged glances and some bit their lower lips. Oh dear.

Zee-vah, they said her name was. Aziza shook her head and smiled to herself. How odd. The girl reminded her of herself, Aziza thought, wondering if the awe she felt when looking at the younger woman was similar to what others felt when they saw her. Just like Aziza, Zivah had such special colors and such a delicate yet voluptuous frame, and even now when she was so very frightened she had this gentle gracefulness about her, a witness to some powerful nobility within. And she had those large yellow amber eyes so full of life and soul even as her gaze darted fearfully around. The other slave girls started to gather round, pretending to be doing their chores and doing them also, even though their attention was directed towards the pretty new girl. The first concubine heard their whispers. She is so, so pretty, they whispered, almost prettier than Aziza.

"Do you think?"

"No, not prettier. Maybe almost as pretty."

"I think they are just as pretty, both of them, but this one is younger, and new."

"Is she going to be his concubine?"

"Let us hope so for her sake."

"Oh gods, poor thing. Too pretty for her own good." The girls nodded thoughtfully. Being very pretty usually just meant a lot more work and less sleep from their point of view. "Shhh, there is nothing poor about her. She belongs to Thióðolf Heri. I would give anything to belong to that one. They say he does not even like to share his girls."

"But what if..?"

"Bah! Thióðolf Heri is… He is one of them honorable ones. She is fortunate."

"What is she so frightened of? Look at her. She is trembling."

"She started to cry when she saw the House-Bond's lord stone!"

The girls burst out in giggles.

"Probably never saw one that size before." The giggling continued.

"I would be frightened too if I had not. My gods."

The giggling reached new heights.

"Maybe she is ill. She looks nauseous," one spoke, sounding concerned, and the giggling stopped.

"They are in the bath now," Laimi said as she and the last slave girls came out of the Hamam, "The little maiden is with them and they seem to be having fun talking to her. I expect they want a talk a little before… he said he wanted you first, Aziza."

"Good. And our guest?" she asked.

"He is not having, so I think it is better to wait until he is ready to leave the bath," Laimi said and looked meaningfully at Zivah, then frowned, and asked, "What is wrong with her?"

Aziza looked thoughtfully at the young woman who looked as if she could faint at any time. She sat down next to her and patted her cautiously on the back. The girl was shivering, but when the kitten came to her and jumped up into her lap, she held her hands around it and seemed to be breathing a little.

"Zivah," Aziza said gently, "Do you speak Norse at all?"

"Words," Zivah whispered, "Zivah not speak good. But understand. If slow. If easy."

"Good, Zivah. Little one, I can see you are afraid. Frightened. Are you frightened, dear?"

The girl nodded. Aziza felt how the heart was hammering violently in the girl's chest, and felt a continuous tremble that seemed to have festered in her entire body. So very frightened. Poor thing.

"You do not have to be frightened here, Zivah. We are not frightened. See? We are all slaves. Like you. And we are not frightened. We are happy here. We are good. Our masters are kind to us, see?" She made Zivah look up and around, and all the slave girls who had gathered nodded and smiled encouragingly at the new girl.

"It is not dangerous here, Zivah. We are fine. You have come to a good place," Laimi said and sat down on the other side of Zivah. The girl tried to draw her breath and they heard the fear she felt.

"You came from bad place, Zivah?" Laimi asked, "Bad men? They hurt you? Hurt?"

Zivah looked like she was struggling to understand their words.

"Bad men make Zivah go ow, ow, ow? Hurt? Pain?" Aziza tried, using her face and body to illustrate her meaning.

"Men hurt," the girl whispered, and new tears ran down her cheeks. Both of Arnulf's concubines put their arms around her. "Yes. Some men hurt. But Zivah, these men here, our masters, they do not hurt. They will not hurt you. Arnulf Heri, Thióðolf Heri, other men in Arnulf's court, they do not hurt. They do not like hurting women. They want you to be happy. Is that not so, girls?" Aziza looked around.

"It is true," the slave girls agreed, and Suri volunteered, having caught up on the easy word trick; "They not want Zivah ow, ow, ow, they want Zivah go mmmmmmm."

The women nodded reassuringly at Zivah, and Laimi contributed to make the message clear; "The men here not hurt, no want hurt. They want girls to go mmmmmmm."

Zivah looked doubtfully at them all, and seemed somewhat confused, caressing Fanged Njál's kitten. They said he had ordered the new girl to keep it and look after it.

"How mmmmmmm?" she asked nervously.

"Like in pleasure," Laimi said and smiled, "Pleasure when fuck."

Zivah frowned.

"Fuck…?" she asked, obviously searching her memory for the meaning of the world, and Aziza guessed that the men stuck to the word "take" when it came to their captives from their raids, a term that was more suitable all things considered, just as they would use very poetical terms when it came to free women. But "fuck" was an old and well-used slave word.

"Yes, fuck," Laimi said and illustrated with her hands to the great merriment of the Hold, but stopped and frowned when the girl looked like she was panicking. Oh, she has been hurt, poor girl.

"It is true, Zivah," Aziza said and patted her back reassuringly, "The men here don't want to hurt. They just want to fuck."

But the girl's eyes flashed up in fear again.

"You do not want to fuck?" Aziza asked. Zivah shook her head fearfully.

"No…" she whispered, "Zivah no want… no want fuck."

The tears streamed. Oh dear.

"I think she came to the wrong place," Suri whispered, and some of the girls began giggling.

"Hush with you," Laimi wheezed angrily, "Can you not see that this girl has been through something bad? Maybe she really has not even been a slave before."

The women went quiet and studied the new girl curiously. All they knew was that she had been brought here from Khazaria, where slaves had all sorts of backgrounds. But it was obvious that she had been frightened almost to death by men. Aziza sighed and maintained her calming hand on the younger woman's back.

"Little one, Zivah, dear Zivah," Aziza spoke soothingly, "We are slaves, Zivah. Zivah slave. Aziza slave. Laimi slave. Suri slave. All women here, slaves. We have no power, no choice, and no decision. What we feel and want matters not, Zivah, not to our masters. We are bound, like animals, like horse, like pig, like dog, like cow. Like… kitten. We obey. Slaves must obey. If we not obey we get bad treatment. Pain. Or sold and sent away to where we do not know what awaits us. Better to be somewhere we know. And this is a good place compared to most. Very important you obey to stay here. Understand?"

Zivah listened and looked so terribly sad when she nodded that she understood.

"When Heri commands, slaves obey," Aziza explained, "When Heri says do, slaves do. We do not cry. We just do. We obey. And when Heri says fuck, we fuck. Not cry."

Zivah cried.

"Oh Zivah, do not cry," Laimi said, "Please do not cry. If you cry, if you sad all the time, if you frightened, they will sell you. They will give you away. They don't like if you cry. And then maybe you will come to *very* bad men." Tears were streaming down Laimi's own face. She knew what she was talking of.

"They… bad men," Zivah whispered.

"Who? Who are bad men?" Aziza asked.

"Tschooh-dolf. Aaahrn-oolf. Men. Rus. All bad. Heri bad," she said. The women exchanged glances and frowned. They had all known far worse men than those who now owned them.

"She came as the only slave girl on their ships since Khazaria," one of the girls suggested.

"Rat-Hialti was on that ship too," another said, and a collective shudder went through them all.

"We do not really know what they are like out there, do we?" They looked at each other.

"They are a scary lot if you are not used to them anyway," one girl volunteered, "I took a long time getting used to them myself. I thought Fanged Njál was going to drink my blood."

"Seeing as he gave her his Hel-Hound, Fanged Njál probably has something to make up to her for in that regard," Suri chuckled, but the Hold had gone somewhat less merry as they pondered why Zivah was so very fearful of her new masters, and nobody broke out into laughs as before.

"Oh, Zivah, poor Zivah," Laimi said, "They must have frightened you so. But they are at home now. It is different at home. They will not hurt you here. They will be kind."

"There are much worse men in this world, Zivah," Aziza said, "You are fortunate to be here. They are good men. They do not hurt you. Look at us. We are all fine. Look. We all know bad, bad men before. All of us. Very bad. They hurt us. We go ow, ow, ow. We cry. But not here. The men here are good to us. They like it when we are happy. They want women to smile and laugh." She nodded to her own words and continued, "And when they fuck us, they like it when we go mmmmmmm. Good fuck."

She smiled, and the women laughed and looked hopefully at the new girl, wanting her to understand. But she looked as terrified as ever.

"It looks like she does not even know what a good fuck is, poor thing," Suri said, and the bondswomen looked at the new slave with tender compassion and exchanged little smiles. New girl was in for a treat.

"Zivah," Aziza said, "I am concubine to Arnulf Heri. He is my House-Bond. I am going to go into him very soon now. Arnulf will fuck Aziza. He is going to put Freystone inside Aziza." She illustrated with her whole body, pointing out at the bath while she spoke her master's name and then at herself. Zivah looked like she was pitying her with her whole heart. Aziza smiled. "Zivah don't have to pity Aziza. When Arnulf fucks Aziza it will not hurt Aziza. No hurt, no ow. It will be *good*. Aziza will go mmmmmmm. Aziza happy. Pleasure. Arnulf Heri is a good fuck."

The women giggled and sent some cautious glances towards the Hamam, where the free folks were now laughing at something. That strange Gaut maiden seemed to entertain them a great deal.

"And Zivah, your House-Bond is Thióðolf Heri," Aziza continued, "And believe me, I know. Thióðolf fucked Aziza before. Aziza likes a lot. Mmmmmmm. Thióðolf Heri is a very good fuck. Very good. He will make Zivah happy. Zivah will go mmmmmmm. Pleasure."

"Nooo," the girl wept, "No good fuck. Hurts. Bad. Kills." She looked like she really meant that.

"Kills?" Suri asked, and made a gesture to illustrate the lord stone, "Do you think the Freystone will kill you?" Some of them giggled.

"Is weapon," Zivah whispered, "Freystone… is weapon. Kills." The giggling stopped.

"What does the lord stone kill, Zivah?" Aziza asked gently.

"Kills… light… light of eyes," Zivah whispered.

The room went utterly quiet.

Shumayl entered the Hold just then and came up to the women. He cast a glance at Zivah and then looked quizzically around the Hold for explanations.

"She does not want to fuck," one of the girls whispered to him, "she thinks the lord stone is a weapon. Says it kills the light of the eyes."

There was some nervous giggling before Shumayl spoke. He looked gravely at the women.

"Until less than a Moon cycle ago, young Zivah lived free in the great river land forests," he said; "She had never known bondage before, and never been treated with anything but respect and care. Her people had no slaves and no lords, and knew nothing of war and violence. They lived in peace and happiness. Zivah roamed free in the forests and swam in the flowing river and had a family that loved her. Then the Vikings came. Their village was destroyed. Their menfolk were killed. Zivah saw her mother killed, and her sweetheart was hanged from a tree. The women were raped. They and their children were taken and stolen. Young Zivah saw her friends and relatives sold as slaves in the Khazarian market, and then she was brought here as the only woman and she-slave amidst a fleet of five Rus Viking ships. And if any of you girls think it is funny when she speaks of the lord stone as a weapon, then, then… then I suppose you have been a deal more fortunate than she has, and rather than joking you should thank whatever gods you worship for your fortune."

Shumayl stopped talking, his eyes moist with tears, and looked around. There was no need for more words. Nobody was laughing now. The second concubine had gone white as a sheet and suddenly got up from the bed.

"I have to…I have to go outside a little," Laimi whispered, "Aziza, you know how to speak to her. I cannot do this."

And then the second concubine went outside for some air. Aziza turned to the lost child from the river lands.

"Zivah, oh Zivah, poor child, poor darling. Zivah, you are not alone anymore. You are not alone. We are here for you, Zivah. We are your family now. We understand," she whispered, and repeated the words until she knew that the girl understood. The women gathered round, eyes wet, and even Suri had stopped joking. Their compassion showed, and was genuine. They nodded and repeated the words spoken. *We understand. You are not alone. We are here and we see you.*

"We will take care of you, Zivah," Aziza said, "We are your friends. You can come to us and cry, and we will hold you. When the Rus do not see us. When we are alone, you cry. With them, you just obey. Not cry. You cry after, with us. We are together. And Zivah…" she placed her hand gently against the young woman's chest, right above her heart. Aziza had a very soothing touch. Her hands listened and never judged.

"Feel, Zivah, feel my hand. Beneath my hand there is a place, a place within you. A place where you can go. It is peaceful there," Aziza said, "you find a good place there. Can you feel?"

Zivah closed her eyes and breathed deeply, feeling, feeling. Then she nodded slowly.

"*Danu…*" The girl whispered, a word in her unknown foreign language, and yet again, so familiar.

"*Dah-nooh*?" Aziza asked.

"River," Zivah said in Norse. Her face seemed more relaxed now.

"Yes, river," Aziza confirmed, grasping at the great image; "think of river, Zivah, go to river. Zivah my child, my poor darling, when they take you, when the Heri commands, you just do. You open legs for Heri and then you go inside. To river. Not cry. Not feel. Just do, obey, and go to river inside. In peace. Can you do that?" Aziza held her hand against the river daughter's chest and felt the pulse slow down and the trembling stop. Zivah looked as if she was almost falling asleep. A final tear rolled gently down her left cheek. She suddenly took Aziza's hand and held it firmly.

"*Mātė*," Zivah whispered, her voice trembling. There was a yearning in that voice. *Mah-teh*? Aziza frowned, and then knew.

Oh, child, child.

"Mother?" Aziza asked, and felt an old heartache to match that of this lost river child.

"Mother," Zivah whispered again, with her eyes closed, "Mother…"

"She wants her mother," Suri whispered and began weeping, as did several of the others.

"The large bloodstain on her dress, did you all see that before you burned it?" Shumayl asked, his voice hoarse and tense. The women nodded, speechless.

"That was her mother's blood. She has worn it all the way since the raid," he said quietly.

"Oh sweet fates have mercy," one of the girls muttered.

And Aziza felt her own tears flow in violent streams down her face as she turned and spoke to the other slaves; "I, Aziza, first concubine and housekeeper, command all the slaves of the Hold and the Hall, and you can bring this message on to all the others, that you all be at your very best with young Zivah from the river lands. I command you to be gentle with her and kind to her and help her in every way you can, and this is not because she is above you or better than you, but because she has lived through a terror the like of which few of you have the misfortune to even be able to imagine."

Aziza's voice almost broke as she proceeded; "And she is new to slavery, and she is still a child at heart who wants her mother, and she does not want to *fuck*."

*

Zivah could hardly believe the sudden gentleness with which she was met. How these stranger women gathered round her and caressed her hair so gently, speaking words of comfort. She had so long been terrorized by the constant threat of violence and brutality that she had not realized before now that the greatest pain she felt was the growing conviction that nobody would ever care for her again, that nobody would ever want anything else from her than her bodily shell. She had been so alone.

And now they came to her one by one, they looked her in the eyes and she did not have to bow, they touched her to give comfort and she did not flinch, and they made her see that they meant what they said, that they were genuine and sincere.

We are your friends, they said, we are your sisters. All the slaves here. We are sisters. Brothers. Family. We take care of you. We will love you. We see you. We hear you. We will hold you. No matter what they do to you, you will always have someone here who will comfort you. You are not alone anymore. You are not alone. We understand you. We see you. You are one of us.

Not alone.

"*O Danu Mātē*," Zivah whispered, and prayed humbly in her mother's language; "Oh great River Mother; my heart sings in grateful praise for this mercy."

Men's Talk

"Arnulf Heri," I said after a little while, when the hot bath had almost caused me to doze off, and the image of one of the more impressionable sights of late drifted past my inner eyes, "How come you managed to hide your Freystone when it is so large and, and, and outstanding?"

The men stared incredulously at me before they both broke out in loud guffaws of laughter, what confused me since I thought I had asked a very reasonable question. Before I could press the matter further, Aziza came into the room and smiled at the laughing men. Now that there were no other people present than us, she did not act as submissively as she had before, but got herself undressed and swiftly washed before she entered the bath with us. She was even more beautiful naked than dressed and I kept gaping at her until her body was hidden in the water, but before I could make any more sensible comments, the concubine had somehow flowed through the water where she was received in Arnulf's arms, who began to kiss her.

I wanted to stay and watch, since they were obviously about Freyia's pleasures, but Thióðolf rose and took me by the hand, leading me out of the tub.

"I just want to see how Arnulf uses his Freystone," I explained, reluctant to leave them, but my comment caused only further incomprehensible roars of laughter. Still laughing, Thióðolf told me that it would be impolite to watch, and content with that explanation, I went with him to dry myself with a towel and slipped into a new, woolen nightgown that the slave-girls had left out for me. Thióðolf likewise found new clothes, but they seemed to be his own.

Well out of the bath we entered the rest of the Hold. It was the first time I was actually inside a Norse long-house, but my father had described them well for me, exempting the bath, which was a Tunic Man invention. Along the walls there were beds large enough to hold at least four adult people in each. They were made in a fashion that allowed for some privacy, like small rooms of their own with walls and curtains. The most splendid looking and closest to the door and the bath belonged to Arnulf, who shared it with his two concubines. Then was another, which was the guest bed, in which Thióðolf would sleep, and with him his household, which in his case meant Zivah. The other beds were shared by the slaves. Three beds belonged to the serving maids, and two beds belonged to the male slaves, except Búi the stable boy, who always slept in the stables. There was a deal of extra space in those beds, and they were sometimes used in the day just to get some privacy.

Where there were no beds, there were chests and other arrangements for storing things, and a lot of things hung from the roofs as well. In the middle of the room there was a long and narrow hearth on the hard dirt floor, where food was cooked. A beautiful tapestry was hung on the short end wall where there were no beds, and by the other short side, close to the door and bath-room, there was a great long table with equally long benches on both sides, around which everybody in the household sat together and ate, slaves and free together, although rank was established by the choice of seats. There was a High Seat at the end of the table where the Heri sat, and the highest ranking people would be seated closest to him, and the lowest ranking would be seated furthest away. In our case, Thióðolf and I were the only free people in the house, since the warriors lived in the other hall, the one at the other side of the courtyard, which apparently was forbidden to me. So we would sit on either side of the top end of the table closest to Arnulf while the slaves would sit further down the table according to a ranking system of their own, where the concubines were obviously the ones who ranked highest, followed by Shumayl and then the other slaves. All this was explained to me by Thióðolf, and most of it fit with what my father had told me about Gaut customs as well.

When Arnulf and Aziza after some length of time had finished their somewhat noisy business in the bath, we were all served food by the long table. It was a nice gathering, with the slaves sitting down to eat and talking almost as freely as we did. They just took turns helping out with the serving, so all of them got to sit down and enjoy the long lasting meal. Arnulf look happy and content where he sat in the High Seat, with Thióðolf and me on either side at the top end of the table, his concubines next to us again, and then the rest of the slaves seated further down, and Zivah among them.Zivah was now wearing the grey woolen dress that Thióðolf had bought for her in the market, and she looked calm, but exceedingly tired. She seemed to feel comfortable with the other slave girls.

The other slave girls. It was so strange for me still.

After having eaten, I was starting to feel the spell of sleep descend on me also. Thióðolf realized how tired we were and said to Aziza that Zivah could go to bed, and that I could sleep there with her. Arnulf frowned and looked at Thióðolf, who shrugged, and the Heri did not overrule the skald's decision. I was happy to stay close to Zivah and not have to sleep with lots of people I had never known before. The slaves had not addressed me or tried to talk to me at all, but treated me with formal submissiveness. It was all very new to me.

As soon as we had gotten into bed, Zivah turned away from me, with her face against the wall, and pretended to fall asleep at once. For all my sleepiness I could not sleep, so I moved to a position from which I could spy on the others as they still sat around the table. The slaves were either retiring or went silent when they sensed that the free men were about to have a serious conversation. They were quiet for a while, and I could see Thióðolf looking thoughtful. They cast some glances towards our bed and finally decided that my sister and I must surely have fainted with exhaustion by now.

Arnulf grinned teasingly at his skald and said; "Well for all your fancy words and charms and good looks, you didn't fare much better with that one than I did, huh?"

Thióðolf sighed and shook his head, "I wish I had not given her that dress. I should have waited. I should have known she would not respond well."

"No," Arnulf said, "what you should have done was take her. You should have taken her down there on the island when I gave her to you. If you had done that she would have known her place already and you would not have had to beat her."

"No," said Thióðolf ironically, "I would only have raped her."

"Believe me my friend, it is better that way," Arnulf said, "I know you for a great warrior, a great sage, and for a man with a very strong sense of honor, but you have never been a Viking. You may have been around us sometimes, you may have joined us on this summer's raids, but you are no Viking. You do not know the Viking way, and that is why you make mistakes such as this. We Vikings have had long experience with such matters. We do not like beating women either. But listen to me." He leaned forward across the table and looked intently at Thióðolf. "First of all, these women here are not like our women. They do not have the wolf spirit or the serpent venom that they hone at home. They have no shield maidens, no brides in armor. You will not find a valkyria soul among them. It never even *occurs* to them to plot vengeance. There is not a woman among them who would serve your own children to you for breakfast just because you had your way with them. Even their men are useless, they will just stand there and gape when their women are taken. These people fear punishment and death more than they fear for their honor. It is just the way it is. They yield at the sight of us. They are born to be taken."

I heard those words of the Viking chieftain echo through my mind over and over and over.

"Honestly I do not think I care to learn the Viking way, Arnulf. With all due respect, Heri, these… these things I saw you do… they weigh too heavy on my heart," Thióðolf muttered..

"No? Well," Arnulf said, "well I am not surprised, although it grieves me since it was a great delight to have a skald aboard, and it cheered the men. But truly, Thióðolf, you are a man of many words, and I heard how you tried to instruct your little slave girl on that other occasion where you ought to have just shown her. How on holy Earth did you expect her to understand a word of it?"

"I thought I made myself very clear. The priestess translated," Thióðolf replied.

"Now what you need to understand about people who have been raided, my friend, is that there is no point trying to tell them anything whatsoever. They will not understand anything you say. It is the truth," Arnulf said, and emptied his horn, holding it out for another draught. Aziza filled it for him, and he turned back to Thióðolf. "When they have been raided and stolen, their minds are in all places at once. Their souls run away in all directions. They lose count of time and place. They become mindless. You cannot make them understand your instructions. The only part of them that understands is their bodies and so you must speak to the body. That is why we took the women down at the island. Once she has been taken, or perhaps some times more than once, a captured woman from these tribes will know where she stands."

Thióðolf just look incredulously at his host.

"Believe me, I have seen this many times," Arnulf proceeded, "There is no need to beat her or instruct her. Just take her, and suddenly she knows everything. You don't have to be violent about it, they are too weak and too frightened to fight you anyway. You can be as gentle about it as you like, she will always yield and no bruise will be brought upon her. Just take her. That is enough. Then she will walk the slave walk and talk the slave talk. And you will never have to beat her. And the boys, why, once they have seen what happens to their women, they become docile too."

"Is that so," Thióðolf said, clearly unimpressed.

"Yes, Thióðolf, it is so," Arnulf said, "Making a woman bleed and crawl in the mud before a laughing crowd is no better than a nice and gentle easing her into her new role, when you are alone together. In fact I think the latter is preferable, because you actually have a chance of giving her a good time, if you are clever about it, and you do not have to hurt her. It is as I said, they yield at the sight of us. There is no need to be violent. It is amazing how far you can get with charm even if the girl is frightened and unwilling. She will still understand that you are the master, but it will make it easier for her to accept it. Take her to the waves, and she will not even mind it much. You have that ability in you, I know. You will see that she will submit willingly the next time, and she will behave. You should heed my council, brother, for I have much experience in these matters."

Thióðolf looked utterly uncomfortable.

"You think me dishonorable now, I can see that," Arnulf said, "But there is no more honor in beating a woman, my friend, or to make her into a laughing stock. Then you have a slave what must recognize your authority but will always secretly despise you for it."

"Thank you very much for reminding me," Thióðolf said, hiding his face in his hands for a moment to signal his shame.

"But it must be done, if she is a slave and misbehaves," Arnulf said, "Now come on, poet, don't look so grim. It is not the end of the world, and you served them a great story that will be sung for centuries to come. Your slave will forever be remembered as the Eastern Princess. But you should have had the sense to take her when she was still formable. Instead you gave her time to regain her spirits and her hope and *then* you crushed her. Now *that* is cruel. See?"

Thióðolf looked pale, and now he glared sideways at his Heri, in the way an inferior may let a superior know that he feels dismayed without challenging his authority. "You could not bear her tears either," he said after a while of silence.

"Well I don't want them to cry," Arnulf said, "I am a Viking but I am not made out of stone despite everything. I was trying to give her time. I thought I could make her feel better, maybe get her to laugh with me and drink a little. She was going to be my concubine, and I would have done it eventually, had I not gotten the bright idea of giving her to you instead, seeing as you are my friend and in lack of a woman, and besides I think she suits you a deal better than she suits me, seeing as I like them somewhat less delicate. I suggest you do what I did not, as soon as possible. Even tonight, before she gets more rebellious ideas in her pretty head. We can find another place for the little priestess to sleep. She is probably passed out by now, and you can just carry her over to the maidservants' bed. And then you can do your thing. You even said as much in the marketplace, that you would teach her more this night."

"I just said that to calm down those bloodthirsty men what seemed to want her dead or beaten to a pulp," Thióðolf said, looking glum.

"Really," Arnulf said drily, "As if the thought of her thighs around you has not struck you. She is your *slave*, Thióðolf, and you are going to share a bed. It is not rape, it is your *right*."

Thióðolf said nothing to that, and Arnulf turned to his second concubine, Laimi, and said, "Is that no so, my sweet? Come, sit on my lap." Laimi giggled and sat down on his lap, and he caressed her back gently and smiled, "Now Laimi here, she cried at first. But I made her laugh, didn't I?"

"You did, House-Bond," Laimi smiled, and giggled even more.

"I played with her, entertained her, fed her, drank with her, toyed with her, and tickled her, until she laughed. And after that she was like butter in my hands. As she has been ever since. And she is happy, are you not, sweetheart?"

"I am very happy, House-Bond," she agreed and kissed him on the cheek. The two of them began to kiss and touch, making it clear that the serious conversation between the men was over, and Aziza began clearing the table, immediately followed by the other slave-girls.

Thióðolf went outside and was away for so long that I almost slept when he finally returned. I pretended to be fully asleep like he expected me to and felt how he leaned over me and lifted me up, carrying me away from the bed. I opened one eye slightly and peered up at him but briefly.

His eyes shone like a wolf's in the darkness.

I swiftly closed my own eyes and felt how he placed me gently into another bed next to a sleeping slave girl, tucked me in beneath the blankets and touched my head softly.

"Sleep little Thunder priestess," he whispered before he turned away and went back to Zivah. I heard him as he took off his clothes and knew that my most respected new friend was going to rape my sister after all, and forever lose his place in my heart. And there was nothing I could do without breaking all the rules and disregard his rank above me, at the risk of calling down the wrath of all these powerful and ruthless men whose concern with rank was rather serious, and whose protection I depended upon.

But what sort of protection was this? How could I feel safe if my sister was not? A strange song seemed to rise within me then. The words of Hallgrim Hidden Spear that same morning, those words now blended in with the more recent words of Arnulf's. The men's words created a strange song that seemed to knock on the door of my soul. As if their words were messages, secret messages meant for me on this very night.

And then a third man's voice seemed to join the chorus: *Now you must be the she-wolf of your secret heart.*

I remembered my father's deep voice, his words that had worked like a spell. I remembered the kicking of dead and mutilated corpses, the taste of blood. And then, just like that, I suddenly knew who and what I am.

Sharp-Spoken Blade Honer of the Fearless Heart

When Arnulf left their council to proceed onto his second concubine, Thióðolf went out to relieve himself, and when finished he leaned against the stable pillar, sighing. His heart was so crammed with contrary paths and on one of those paths he hated his new slave girl.

He had never, ever beaten a woman and never thought he would ever have to. He hated her for making him do something as dishonorable as that. Not even slave women got that sort of treatment from him. When that was said, he had never owned a slave personally before. He tried to remember the slaves of his home, people he knew and who he had grown up with, and sometimes played with as a child. Few people owned slaves of their own for personal use where he came from. Those slaves they had, they had all belonged to the clan, and they were in many ways a part of the family. They had been with them for generations and it was thought shameful of a man to use a slave girl against her will. Those few times when punishment on slaves had been meted out it had not been him who did the deed.

Now he stood here in a foreign country that seemed like a twisted mirror of his own, and was the owner of a personal slave who happened to be a young and unusually beautiful woman. Who had also been abducted from the wild forest lands just a few weeks before.

How he pitied her, even as he hated her. He had tried to make her understand. He had warned her. And then she had gone and done something like that in public. In Aldeigjuborg. In a slavers' town. But how could she have understood? She had not even known of slavery before. His mind wandered back to the moment when he beat her. He had tried to go soft on her but he was not used to beating such weak folks. It was hardly a smack and she had gone thump to the ground. And there in the mud, poor girl, trying to get to her feet. He had seen the faces and heard the comments and known that it was not enough. He remembered the feel of her hair in his hands when he held her down. The shame of it was unbearable.

She will hate you forever and ever, the girl had said. And with good reason. Zivah was free born, even if she was a slave, and where he was from, doing something like that to a free woman was the sort of offense that could make a man end up as a silver skull cup on the offended woman's kitchen shelf. She was a slave now, but being born free, ah. There was no saying how deep this grudge could dig itself into her soul.

The story had just come to him. The story that would make them admire her and pity her just as he did when she finally stood - and how she had stood! Like a slave and a queen at once. Even with her nose bleeding and all covered in mud she had stood like a goddess, and Thióðolf had never seen a woman so beautiful.

River goddess, he thought, *I must make a poem about you.*

The sounds of Arnulf and what supposedly was still Laimi were echoing through the empty night court, and there were other muffled sounds from the warriors' Hall and from the stable too, and that beautiful woman was lying in his bed and she was his slave. Thióðolf felt his lord stone stir. Arnulf's counsel ran another round through his mind. *You can be as gentle as you like*, he had said, and he had turned to the pretty slave concubine and surely there had been lust in her eyes. Even love. Arnulf's concubines really loved him, that much was clear, and obviously also enjoyed his attentions. And Thióðolf knew far more about how to make women roar with the goddess's waves than his Rus Viking lord did. When he thought about that, the stone stirred again and it suddenly dawned on him that it would be near impossible to own that sort of woman and have her sleep in his bed every night without playing with her.

Arnulf had said that it was the way to make them come to terms with their new place in the world. If she came to terms with that, then she would not bear a grudge either. If she accepted her inferior position there would be no thoughts of vengeance, because she would know that he had the right to beat her if she broke the rules. And then perhaps she would not hate him so, but submit to him freely.

If she just replaces her free spirit with a slave's soul, then she will like me. What sort of thinking is this? Have I sunk so low that I have grown fearful of the verdicts of free women upon my conduct?

He brushed the uncomfortably sharp thought away, feeling a little dizzy from all the beer. She was a slave, and that was simply the truth of the matter. He had to help her see that. It would help her. And relieve him.

His mind moved back to that night in the tent when he had seen her cringing away in that bed and she had been so very frightened. That was the core of the issue. She was frightened, and how could she not be? He could understand that. He had always known how to calm down frightened folks and other beings too. He had always known how to make them trust him. What if he went in there and touched her gently and held her close, comforting her, and then little by little he could caress her in ways that would entice her and please her. He knew well those arts and could go on for as long as it would take for her to open up. And then he could show her ways of pleasure that she had probably never even imagined existed. And then she would not just submit to him properly but even *like* him.

It felt like such a good idea all of a sudden.

He went inside quietly and found little Thordís sleeping in his bed. He lifted her gently and felt how light she was, like a feather. He smiled as he watched that sweet face and flinched a little when one of her weird eyes suddenly opened and then closed itself. She was such a marvelous creature. He tucked her into the slave girls' bed and touched her hair softly. "Sleep, little Thunder priestess," he whispered and turned back to his own bed.

Zivah was on her side with her back to him looking like she was trying to vanish into the wall. Poor thing. But she would be surprised eventually. He climbed carefully into bed and took off all his arms, laying them strategically around the edge of the mattress, and turned to his slave. She still had that meaningful back turned towards him and obviously pretended to be asleep. He leaned over and touched her shoulder gently. She flinched.

"Zivah," he said softly. There was a moment of silent anxiety followed by the grudging acknowledgement.

"Heri," she whispered hoarsely and rolled over to lie on her back. She kept her face slightly averted, her gaze averted even more to study the wall further, and then to his horror she lifted her legs beneath the blankets and spread them.

It was not exactly what he had had in mind. His chest suddenly hurt with a sort of heartache. He looked at the young woman lying there with her legs spread like the obedient slave girl she was supposed to be and knew that this woman was no longer the frightened girl from that tent on the islet. This one did not care anymore. She had already been broken in, as Arnulf used to say. She would mind her manners and do what she was told. But it is well known in all parts of the world except perhaps to some of those chosen folks; that you can rule the body and life of another living being, but you cannot ever rule its soul.

He would never be able to reach her now, not the way he had intended. She had given up and acknowledged her defeat fully, but there was no way she was ever going to be able to pretend to feelings that she did not have, or open up to the man who had humiliated her. This amber-eyed river land girl had no slave chant in her soul song.

On one side it was almost impossible not to respect that sort of self-respect. On the other side the frustration and the helplessness that stirred in him just as the lord stone stirred made him feel like just taking her, then and there, if that was the way she wanted it, if only to get release and a feel of being in control of the situation. It did not seem to matter anymore to her anyway, which in itself was infuriating and made him wish to force her to feel something at least. He began to remove the blanket that covered her waiting body, and then hesitated.

No. No this is not me, he thought. He looked at her face. She looked peaceful, withdrawn. She had gone somewhere else inside her mind. Oh gods. This was what they told their women to do if they were raped.

As tough as they were, their Sífs, they were often little more than half the size of their menfolk and did not have the same training. It could not be considered shameful for a woman to yield.

If it happens, and you see no way out, girl, then you yield. There is no shame to it. It is natural for a woman to yield. Go to the sacred space within, and afterwards you can start plotting. Know that. The game of vengeance can be very sweet. He had heard it said by his mother to his sister, all women knew this art. His mother had owned five silver skull cups and often bragged about how they belonged to those five cowardly fellows what had ganged up and raped her when she was young. She had told her children that when she found herself alone in their presence and there was no arguing with them, and she knew she could not fight them, then she had yielded and let them do. She had withdrawn into that place within like her mother had told her to do if she was raped, and she had stayed there until it was over. Then she had gone and told the whole world about it. The shame was all on the men who committed the crime. And the skulls' former owners had not quite counted on her kinsmen.

Unlike his mother, Zivah had no kinsmen. There would be no gift to her made out of his head. But she was still doing that thing. She had gone to the within place so that his abuse would not hurt her too much.

It was surprisingly hard to admit that his little project would be meaningless, most probably harmful, and contrary to all laws of honor and all holy vows, and that the only thing which really drove him now was frustration, and drunken lust. Thióðolf was a warrior. He was no slave, not even to his lusts. And yet…he hesitated. The lust was, admittedly, a rather powerful adversary right this moment. He took a deep breath, hoping that he could conquer that lust which now seemed so urgent. He had never doubted his ability to conquer his lust for women, but the truth of the matter was that he had hardly ever had to. Women tended to throw themselves at him. He could hardly remember a time when he had needed to stop himself and where his lust had been quite this powerful at the same time. The poet touched his Freyia pendant and prayed for help. He got it immediately, and from a rather unexpected place.

He felt a piercing stare, like blades cutting deep into his side, and turned to see Thordís standing on the floor by the bed. She was glaring at him. Glaring with her wolf eyes, and they shone bright in the darkness.

"Thordís," he whispered, swiftly covering the slave up and fortunately losing his lust at once; "I thought you were asleep a long time ago."

"No, I was listening to your conversation with Arnulf Heri before," she replied, whispering also.

"I bet you were," he said, and was quite thankful for the darkness.

"May I come into the bed? It is cold out here," the little one said, sounding just like the little girl she was, and something melted within him.

"Of course," he said and watched as she climbed into the bed and then proceeded by climbing over him too as if he was a piece of furniture, before she tucked herself into the blankets between him and Zivah, where she had clearly decided to spend the night. She turned towards him and continued glaring at him. He felt like a shamed little boy beneath that fierce maiden's gaze and averted his own involuntarily. Some sisters they were.

"Thióðolf," she said, "Do you and the men think of me as a Norsewoman?"

"What? Yes of course, Thordís. You may be a tad bit young for the term but there is no mistaking you. You are one of us. You are a Norsewoman to the bone," he said, feeling a little puzzled.

"Good. Because I listened to your council…"

"You are not really supposed to do that, Thordís. Little girls should not spy on men's business."

"I see. But it so happened that I did," she continued calmly, "and I am quite convinced that I am the sort of girl what would actually cook a man's children to him for breakfast if he hurt me or my kind. Or something along those lines, all things considered."

The little scoundrel paused and maintained her rudely direct stare, "You are my friend and my mentor, Thióðolf, but I have to tell you that my sister, Zivah, she is *my* Síf, even if she is your slave. Father told me that sometimes a man has got to do a woman's job and sometimes a woman and even a child must do a man's job, and it so happens that Zivah and I are both women and there are no kinsmen around to protect any of us, but somebody has got to do that in this world ruled by big strong men. Zivah is soft, Thióðolf, she can be crushed if she is not treated with care. But I am strong. I can take anything and not be crushed. I just know it. I have to protect her. I am the Thunder priestess and a she-wolf and I am the sort of girl what gets to hold her enemy's head in her hands."

Thióðolf felt his spine chill as he watched the sincere little face of the eloquent maiden, who had just paused to ponder something that had passed her mind and suddenly added; "although I am not certain about the whole defecation issue. I think it may be a figure of speech."

"What?" He said before he remembered his words to her before, on that first night they spoke, and almost broke out in laughter at the sudden and unexpected reminder of her considerable youth.

"Never mind," Thordís said and drew her breath before she proceeded; "Perhaps it is your right to take Zivah as Arnulf said, but it will still be rape for *her*, and then you are going to see the lights of her soul go out in her eyes, Thióðolf. It is my duty to protect her. I am too small to fight you, and so I cannot really stop you, but if you rape my sister I can no longer be your friend or novice. I would have to consult my lord Thor about you."

Thióðolf was so stunned it took him some moments before he was able to reply. "Do not worry, child," he finally whispered, "You will not need to call down the wrath of the Thunder lord upon my head."

He smiled at the girl, and saw how she noticed the sadness in his smile. She noticed everything, that one.

"I was thinking to call it down upon your Freystone," she informed him, "Since that is what you use when...."

He stopped her with a finger on her mouth, choking down a little laugh before he replied, "There is no need to curse my Freystone either, Thordís. I am not going to rape your sister. I realized that just before you came, I think. I was tempted but… oh child, I do not know if I would have, but now I know, and there is no need for concern or curses. My brave little Síf, I will not touch *your* Síf unless she really wants me to. Not ever. Is that clear?"

"That is clear," the child agreed, and finally lowered her eyes to him as if nothing had ever happened, gladly minding his higher rank now that he had proven himself worthy of that sort of respect. *She is a blade honer born*, he thought, awed. How easy and how enjoyable it would be to teach her the arts. When she looked at him again, they just watched each other for a long time. She had the most intriguing gaze, as if she could see right into his secret heart.

"Thióðolf, you told me once that you do not rape women," she finally whispered.

"And thanks to you that truth still stands," he groaned, hiding his face in his hands.

"What were you thinking?" she whispered after a little while, curious now. She was not exactly the judgmental sort of person, he thought humorously. She really just wanted to know.

"I think you may be a bit too young to fully understand this, Thordís, but it can be a great and often blinding challenge to a man's integrity and honor to have such absolute power over a beautiful woman," he whispered, wondering if she could even begin to grasp what that meant.

"But you have integrity, Thióðolf. I have seen it," the child said, "You are a very honorable man."

"And yet it seems that even my integrity and my honor can be tested," he sighed.

"Oh," she replied and bit her lower lip while she thought about that.

"Thióðolf?" she said finally.

"Yes, Thordís?"

"Did I hone your blade just now?" The girl looked so innocent when she said that, he forced down another round of laughing sobs and took her little hand and squeezed it gently instead.

"Sharp spoken blade honer of the fearless heart," he whispered sincerely and lowered his eyes to the maiden who had taught him, "This night you have honored me. This night you honed my soul's edge, and I stand sharpened and in debt to you. This night you have made a man out of me."

Thordís nodded contentedly as if congratulating herself on performing her given task to satisfaction, before she turned to the slave girl and whispered something in their language. Upon which Zivah, who had stayed on her back in the same humble position for the whole time, awaiting his orders, and mostly likely straining ears and mind to understand their conversation while pretending to study the wall next to her, simply turned around to face the wall again without even speaking to the little girl who had just saved her honor, and his.

And, if the girl was right, the lights of her soul.

His heart felt as if it was breaking into pieces at the thought.

The maiden looked at the turned back of her sister for a little while with an expression of concern mingled with something else, something that had to do with the strange way the two half-sisters related to each other. It was odd, how one sister was so given over to her emotions while the other seemed to be all watchful eyes and listening ears.

Our little Serious Face, he thought fondly, knowing in his heart of hearts that the girl felt things deeply too, but was no slave to those feelings. She probably just observed her inner landscape the same way she observed everything else, with that keenness to learn and apply what she had learned to real life with a charming and very maidenly deal of practical sense.

He wondered if Zivah even knew how much the little one had been looking after her, how masterfully the girl had juggled an impossibly frightening and dangerous situation in order to protect her sister to the best of her abilities. As it turned out, she had won the battle at last, and the one who benefited the most from that victory, Zivah herself, she did not even know.

The little girl with the Thunderer's mark had awed an entire fleet of some of the most ruthless bandits in the world, secured their affection and even their sincere respect, both of which only grew from day to day. Within a few weeks she had made a whole band of rogue warriors and a pirate lord into her sworn protectors. Now that he recalled the time that had passed, he knew that she had also been working ceaselessly to protect her older sister, and that this need to protect her sister was what had driven her on, caused her to engage in such a masterful dance with the onslaughts of fate.

But Zivah could not see that. Zivah saw, as yet, only what she felt and thought. *Thordís is the old one*, he mused. *She has an old soul within that child's heart of hers.*

The little old soul suddenly rolled into his embrace with a sleepy sigh. She seemed to fill up his whole heart when she fell asleep there in his arms, so trustingly.

*
*
*
*
*
*
*
**
****
***
*****
***
**
*

To be continued in BLADE HONER Book Two: My Enemy's Head

19250726R00185

Printed in Great Britain
by Amazon